Encyclopedia of
Women in
Aviation
and **Space**

Encyclopedia of
Women in
Aviation
and Space

Rosanne Welch

ABC-CLIO

Santa Barbara, California
Denver, Colorado
Oxford, England

Library of Congress Cataloging-in-Publication Data
Welch, Rosanne.
    Encyclopedia of women in aviation and space / Rosanne Welch.
        p.   cm.
    Includes bibliographical references and index.
    ISBN 0–87436–958–4 (alk. paper)
    1. Women air pilots—Biography.   2. Women astronauts—Biography.
I. Title.
TL539.W395   1998
629.13'092'2—dc21
[B]   98-8042
                                                                          CIP

04 03 02 01 00 99 98   10 9 8 7 6 5 4 3 2 1

ABC-CLIO, Inc.
130 Cremona Drive, P.O. Box 1911
Santa Barbara, California 93116–1911

This book is printed on acid-free paper. ∞

Manufactured in the United States of America

Contents

Preface

As I researched this book I often encountered the question of whether I, myself, was an aviator. The fact that I was not seemed to shock people. Why, they asked, was I interested enough in female pilots to undertake such an extensive study of them? The answer is simple: Though I have no burning interest in flying myself, I have a great interest in people of passion, the kind of people who find a goal at an early age and leave no stone unturned in its pursuit. For me that goal was writing, so the publication of this encyclopedia to me is like being sent up for my first solo.

The idea for this book was born when I learned that the female valedictorian of my high school class had become an astronaut. I was so fascinated by her career choice that I began to wonder about all the women who had chosen aviation as a career. They all knew it was, and often still is, a world in which women are neither recruited nor wanted. What had their lives been like? What were their challenges? How did they overcome them?

Like pioneers in any field, the women in these pages all had a dream that seemed impossible to most of their families and friends. Despite the uphill battles they faced, these women were not just dreamers; they were doers. They did not let anything stand in the way of attaining their dreams. They lived in constantly changing times and helped forge new paths so that the generations after them would have an easier time. I admire them for that.

As much as I admire the most famous of these pioneers, I am pleased to show readers that the ranks of accomplished women aviators are not limited to Amelia Earhart and Sally Ride. In today's "global village" I am especially pleased to be able to incorporate the latest information about women pilots from around the world throughout history and their contributions to aviation as well.

It was wonderful to be tackling the project in the era of the Internet. Just as the new technology of the airplane opened up new opportunities for women at the turn of the century, the new technology of computers and the Internet opened up new opportunities for me in researching this book. I could question librarians at research facilities around the world and even contact current women in aviation—such as Colleen Nevius, the U.S. Navy's first female test pilot—via e-mail to verify information.

Despite the volumes of work published on aviation I found great holes in the coverage of women in the field. Many of the autobiographies were out of publication, and histories of flight often contained merely a chapter or two on women and their accomplishments, so the whole project took on the air of a mystery for me. Local librarians in the Los Angeles, Orange County, and Burbank City library systems were invaluable in helping me locate rare books on the early pioneers, and Michaella Johnson at the Sherman Oaks Branch of the Los Angeles Public Library helped me track down the most minute of details.

I would also like to thank my husband, Douglas Welch, a true computer guru and World Wide Web surfer, for unearthing on-line information about many of the lesser-known women pilots, and my mother, Mary T. Danko, for hooking me on libraries when I was still in my stroller, for operating as my number-one research assistant on this project, and for always believing I could accomplish the impossible.

In her autobiography, Grace McAdams Harris, one of the first women aircraft company executives, was proud to write: "America's history clearly establishes that women, too, are pathfinders. Your happiest moment comes as you reach yet another frontier after a long, difficult, and often discouraging journey."

Each of the women in these pages has done exactly that. I hope you enjoy meeting them and reading about them as much as I did.

Introduction

In the early 1930s, when Janet Harmon Waterford Bragg learned that flight school classes were open to African Americans at the Aeronautical University of Chicago, she quickly signed up—and found herself the only woman in the class. She survived the discrimination of her teachers and fellow students and rose to become the first African American woman to earn a commercial pilot's license by remembering her father's favorite saying: "If Jack can do it, so can Jill."

Most women who have courted careers in aviation felt the same way, from Harriet Quimby, who in 1911 became the first American woman to receive her pilot's license, to Major Eileen Collins, who in 1995 became the first woman to pilot the space shuttle.

Jumping the Early Hurdles

The goal of the women in these pages was to fly farther, faster, or better than anyone before them, male or female. In some cases the goal was merely to fly at all. Proving themselves worthy in the cockpit of an airplane was only half the battle, usually the latter half. First they had to gain permission from husbands or parents to take flying lessons, a fact that

seems unbelievable to women today. Then they had to find an instructor who would take on a female student.

Famed aviator Amelia Earhart's parents made her take one extra step: They did not like the idea of their unmarried daughter spending so much unchaperoned time alone with men, so they made her find a female instructor. In an era when there were only a few dozen women with pilot's licenses across the United States, Earhart was lucky to find Neta Snook, the first woman to operate her own aviation business.

Many other aspiring female pilots were turned away at the hangar doors. Others found their efforts sabotaged by male pilots fiercely guarding their turf. Sand was dumped in gas tanks, brake lines were cut, and other dangerous tricks were played in an effort to keep women from entering, let alone conquering, the sky.

Breaking Down Barriers

Women who chose aviation as a vocation were risk takers in both their careers and their social lives. Pancho Barnes's parents arranged her marriage to the Reverend Calvin Rankin, supposing that the duties of a minister's wife would keep her out of trouble. Barnes did not allow her marriage to get in the way of her unique ambitions, however, and went on to become a record-breaking stunt pilot and the founder and head of the Women's Air Reserve in 1931. Barnes's husband eventually divorced her because of her escapades. She went on to build a ranch and flying club. Many ace pilots of World War II received their flight training from Barnes.

Also during World War II, groups of women defied convention en masse to fly for their countries. The Women's Airforce Service Pilots (WASPS) in the United States, the Women's Section of the Air Transport Auxiliary (ATA) in England, and the 586th Bomber Regiment of the Soviet Union were composed of women who gladly utilized their skills as pilots to help the Allies win the war. Going against the wishes of their husbands and parents once again, many women enlisted. Some were estranged from their families for years after the war because of that decision. Others hid the fact that they had served to maintain their postwar standing in society.

Among modern-day women aviators, Shannon Lucid, who holds the record for the longest time spent in space, was selected for the first class of female astronaut trainees in 1978 despite being married and the mother of three. As she explained it: "Obviously, when I was raising the children in the sixties and the early part of the seventies, it was not looked on favorably for a woman to work, especially if she had children. So you had to justify in your own mind why you were going against the norm. I took all the kids flying by the time they were a week old so that they knew that they were living with me and I wasn't living with them."

To some of the women, breaking down barriers in business was already second nature. African American pilots such as Janet Harmon Waterford Bragg, Willa

Brown Chappell, and Bessie Coleman were already accustomed to fighting to get an even chance at their educations and at their own financial security. Fighting for the right to take flying lessons was just one more challenge, one that they quickly overcame. Then they made it their business to open new opportunities for other minority pilots.

Bragg and a group of other black flying students in Chicago formed the Challenger Air Pilot's Association and convinced a local mayor to set aside some land for an airport. He did so on the condition that they provide all the labor and materials themselves. When they had finished, Bragg bought a plane with her nurse's wages with which the entire school started lessons. Later Bragg helped start a similar flight school at the Harlem airport.

Some early women pilots, such as Laura Ingalls and Anne Morrow Lindbergh, used their newfound fame to advance their own strongly held political beliefs. Although this was appropriate behavior for male celebrities of the day, it was not something that "proper" women did. In the end it ruined both their aviation careers.

Ingalls and Lindbergh were pacifists at the start of World War II. They joined the America First movement, which worked to keep the United States out of the war. As a member, Ingalls, the first woman to cross the Andes Mountains, volunteered to fly over the White House and drop antiwar leaflets. But the White House was a strict no-flying zone, and her license was revoked by the Civil Aeronautics Administration (CAA) the moment she landed.

In 1942, before Ingalls could secure funding for another record-breaking flight, she was arrested on suspicion of being a paid agent of Germany and failing to register as such. Ingalls defended herself in court, saying that she was on the payroll of the German embassy but insisting that she was a double agent. She claimed that her mission was to obtain information helpful to the Allies. Despite her protests, Ingalls was convicted and sent to prison. She was released in 1943, but her flying career was ruined.

Lindbergh, the first American woman to earn a glider pilot's license and a beloved, best-selling author, flew to Russia with her famous husband in August 1938. They were assigned to study Soviet air strength and report their findings to U.S. intelligence agencies. In October the Lindberghs went to Germany on a similar mission, but to the U.S. public it looked as if they were supporting Hitler's regime. To explain their position, Lindbergh wrote *The Wave of the Future*, which attempted to persuade the United States not to enter the war in Europe. Though the Lindberghs had been America's golden couple in the 1920s and had received enormous support during the tragic kidnapping of their first child, neutrality was akin to treason in 1938. Her book caused a great backlash against the couple. It was not until Lindbergh published *Gift from the Sea* in 1955 that the U.S. public finally forgave her.

Facing Modern Problems

Despite the dedication of the early pioneers, women today are still fighting for the right to participate in aviation to the fullest. Events like the Tailhook sexual harassment scandal in 1991 cause them to choose between being honest to their careers or to their gender, and the choice itself causes women to draw lines against each other. After Tailhook, Lieutenant Paula Coughlin brought charges against the male navy aviators who had harassed her and 82 other women during the convention. Lieutenant Kara Hultgreen, the U.S. Navy's first female F-14 Tomcat pilot, chose not to bring charges.

In the face of continual harassment, Coughlin eventually resigned her commission. Hultgreen fared no better for her choice. When her plane went down during practice landings on an aircraft carrier, the navy blamed pilot error. Finally, Lieutenant Kelly Flinn, the first female B-52 bomber pilot for the U.S. Air Force, lost her career when accused of adultery, fraternization, and conduct unbecoming an officer. That same year several male military officers' sexual transgressions were overlooked.

These women also faced accusations of being promoted for public relations reasons rather than for their own talents and skills. Even in the 1990s, most were still the first female member of their military units, which left them with no support system in times of stress.

So Why Fly?

Knowing that the life of a female pilot comes with additional burdens, one wonders why so many women have worked so hard to gain the skies.

Jean Batten of New Zealand, the first woman to fly solo from England to New Zealand, summed up her life and her love of flying: "In my heart I knew only too well that I was destined to be a wanderer. I seemed born to travel, and in flying I found the combination of the two things which meant everything to me: the intoxicating drug of speed and the freedom to roam the earth."

Amy Johnson of England, the first woman to fly solo from England to Australia, wrote: "There is nothing more wonderful and thrilling than going up into the spaciousness of the skies in a tiny plane where you feel alone, at peace with everyone, and exactly free to do what you want and go where you will."

Jerrie Cobb of the United States, the first woman to qualify for space travel in 1959, described her love of flying by saying: "For everything there are beginnings and endings, tops and bottoms, sides or limits. There is an end to all things we know on earth. Only two things can we conceive of as infinite: God and the sky. I find one in the other."

Jacqueline Auriol of France, the first woman to fly at the speed of mach 2, explained her love of flying this way: "I feel so happy when I'm flying. Perhaps it is the feeling of power, the pleasure of dominating a machine as beautiful as a thorough-bred horse. Mingled with these basic joys is another less primitive feeling, that of a mission accomplished. Each time I set foot on an airfield, I sense with fresh excitement that this is where I belong."

However they chose to explain it, the need to fly boils down to a shared passion for freedom and the need to express themselves as individuals in the world—something even those of us who have never set foot in an airplane can understand.

Encyclopedia of
Women in
Aviation
and **Space**

Acosta, Aida De

The first woman to fly solo in a powered aircraft did so six months before the Wright brothers made their historic 1903 flight at Kitty Hawk with the financial backing of their sister Katherine Wright. Acosta was born in Cuba about 1886 but was a resident of New York at the time of her flight.

On June 29, 1903, as a young debutante on grand tour in Europe, Acosta piloted the Dumont dirigible, a lighter-than-air balloon with a three-horsepower engine. She flew from Paris to the nearby city of Bagatelle, France. Her instructor and the dirigible's designer, Alberto Santos-Dumont, bicycled the same path underneath her and sent Acosta hand-signal instructions as she flew. Acosta landed safely in the middle of a polo arena during a game, shocking the audience twice: first, by the arrival of the aircraft, and second, by the disembarking of a female pilot. Acosta and Santos-Dumont watched the rest of the game as guests of the teams. Then Acosta flew back to Paris alone.

Acosta's family feared that this unladylike behavior would mar her social standing and hinder her chances of marrying well. Acosta's family used its financial standing to bar newspapers from reporting the flight, thereby keeping the world from knowing her name until years later. Her family also forced Santos-Dumont to vow never to reveal her name, a vow he broke only when he wrote his book *Dans l'Air* years later.

See also
Wright, Katherine
References
Holden and Griffith, *Ladybirds II* (1993); Moolman, *Women Aloft* (1981); Smith, *Breakthrough* (1981)

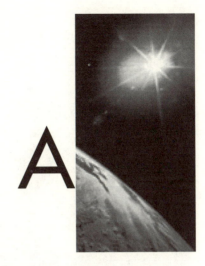

Air Transport Auxiliary (ATA)

Formed on September 1, 1939, the British Air Transport Auxiliary (ATA) recruited civilian pilots to ferry planes from manufacturers to Royal Air Force (RAF) bases to save military pilots for battle in World War II. Its motto was *Aetheeris avidi*, Latin for "Eager for the air."

The ATA excluded the many female pilots who applied until Pauline Gower, a prominent British aviator, protested this policy. In 1940 she received permission to form the Women's Section of the ATA, starting with eight pilots, who were permitted to fly only the smallest planes. These women were Winifred Crossley, Margaret Fairweather, Rosemary Rees, Marion Wilberforce, Margaret Cunnison, Gabrielle Patterson, Mona Friedlander, and Joan Hughes. They were paid 20 percent less than male ferry pilots even though they came through the first winter without losing a plane or a pilot to accidents. This first group of eight was based at the Hatfield Air Base in England.

As the war continued Gower received permission to recruit more women. Lady Mary Bailey flew with the ATA for one week in February 1940, until the negative press made her presence a detriment to the program. She was 50 at the time, and

American pilots, known as "Ladybirds," went to Britain to help the Royal Air Force ferry planes from manufacturers to air bases during World War II (ca. 1942).

the maximum age for ferry pilots was 45. Despite her previous records in aviation, the press reported that Bailey had been accepted to the ATA only because of her husband's wealth.

In May 1940 Gower recruited five new women pilots, among them record-breaking British pilot Amy Johnson, who did her best to avoid any press attention to her work after the Bailey debacle. These new recruits and those who followed were eventually allowed training on larger and more diverse planes. Soon more women were recruited, including two women pilots from the Polish Air Force who had escaped the German invasion of their country.

In 1942, while the United States debated admitting women to their ferry programs, Jacqueline Cochran recruited fellow American women pilots for the ATA. In total she brought 25 women pilots to Britain during 1942. They became part of the second unit of women in the ATA and

were housed at the home of Sir Lindsay Everhard in Ratcliffe. Eleanor Roosevelt and Oveta Culp Hobby visited the group on a tour to study the activities of women in wartime Britain. On the basis of this publicity and of the women's successful flying records, Cochran was able to create the Women's Flying Training Detachment (WFTD) in the United States.

Meanwhile the performance of the Women's Section of the ATA earned them the right to fly planes with larger engines and earned Gower the right to recruit more women. Before the war's end her roster had reached 100 women from around the world. These women ferried planes to more and more dangerous arenas of the war as the Allies advanced on Germany in 1943 and 1944.

Unlike women ferry pilots in the United States, Women's Section pilots flew to and were quartered in combat areas under constant threat of bombing from the enemy. In June 1943, because of the new realities of ferry service with the ATA, the British Parliament decreed that women ferry pilots would share equal pay for equal work with their male counterparts. The women were finally permitted to fly every piece of military aircraft except seaplanes. They were denied these planes not for technical reasons but for propriety's sake: The planes required a larger crew, which inevitably included male mechanics or navigators, and being stranded overnight with male crews would hurt the women pilots' ability to appear again in good society.

In 1944 the women pilots began ferrying planes into France to assist the Allied invasion. The ATA was dismantled in November of 1945. In total only 15 women were killed flying for the ATA, the most famous of whom was Amy Johnson, who died when her plane crashed into the Thames River.

Despite their efforts, many women pilots were treated badly throughout the existence of the ATA. At the concluding parade they were not even allowed to march along with the male pilots. There is, however, a memorial to the women of the ATA in St. Paul's Cathedral engraved "Remember then that also we, in a moon's course, are history."

Pauline Gower explained the success of the ATA by saying: "Flying is a job and like any other should be done by the people qualified to do it. Women in this service were treated exactly like the men, that's one of the things I fought for from the beginning."

See also
Bailey, Lady Mary; Cochran, Jacqueline; Gower, Pauline; Hatfield Air Base; Hobby, Oveta Culp; Johnson, Amy; Roosevelt, Eleanor; Women's Airforce Service Pilots (WASPS)

References
Curtis, *The Forgotten Pilots: A Story of the Air Transport Auxiliary, 1939–45* (1971); Lomax, *Women of the Air* (1987); Moolman, *Women Aloft* (1981)

All-Women's Transcontinental Air Race (AWTAR)

The world's oldest, longest, and largest race for women, the All-Women's Transcontinental Air Race (AWTAR) originated in 1947 when a Florida chapter of the Ninety-Nines invited the Los Angeles, California, chapter to fly to Miami for an air show. This first race was called the Amelia Earhart Memorial Race in honor of the famous aviator and charter member of the Ninety-Nines, who had disappeared ten years earlier.

From that point on, different chapters of the Ninety-Nines hosted the start and the finish of the race each year. In 1951 and 1952 the race's focus was to provide a refresher course in cross-country flying for women who might be called on to assist the military during the Korean War as they had done as Women's Airforce Service Pilots (WASPS) in World War II. During these years the race was referred to as "Operation TAR" (Transcontinental Air Race).

In 1975 the organizers were sued for discrimination by a male flyer whose application to enter the race had been denied. The organizers won, and the AWTAR remained an all-female event.

Congestion of air traffic and rising fuel costs during the gasoline shortage in the 1970s led to the decision to end the race in 1976, after 29 years. The Smithsonian National Air and Space Museum stepped in to sponsor one more race in 1977, to make an even 30. This race was named the Smithsonian Milestone of Flight, and it followed the original route of the Women's Air Derby of 1929.

Carolyn West, the race's first winner, and Jacqueline Cochran, an early supporter, met the 331 contestants in California; and Louise Thaden, Viola Gentry,

Women pilots gathered in Santa Monica, California, to compete in the 1929 Women's Air Derby, a precursor to the All Women's Transcontinental Air Race. Left to right: Louise Thaden, Bobbie Trout, Patty William, Marvel Crosson, Blanche Noyes, Vera Walker, Amelia Earhart, Marjorie Crawford, Ruth Elder, and Florence "Pancho" Barnes.

and Blanche Noyes, participants in the 1929 Women's Air Derby, met them at the finish line in Florida.

Over the 30-year history of the AWTAR there were more than 4,400 contestants and no fatalities. When asked about this exemplary record of achievement, Kay Brick said: "This is in itself a tribute to the organization's emphasis on safety, the dedication of the women racers and the diligent efforts of the FAA controllers who handled the fly-bys and supported our derby events year after year."

See also
Brick, Katherine "Kay" Adams Menges; Cochran, Jacqueline; Gentry, Viola; Ninety-Nines; Noyes, Blanche Wilcox; Thaden, Louise McPhetridge; Women's Air Derby; Women's Airforce Service Pilots (WASPS)

References
Holden and Griffith, *Ladybirds II* (1993); Lomax, *Women of the Air* (1987); Moolman, *Women Aloft* (1981)

Amelia Earhart Birthplace Museum

The birthplace of America's most famous female aviator, the Amelia Earhart Birthplace Museum first opened to the public in 1985. Operated by the International Ninety-Nines, it offers tours to between 7,000 and 9,000 guests a year.

The brick-and-timber home at 223 North Terrace Street in Atchison, Kansas, was originally built by Earhart's grandfather, Judge Alfred G. Otis, around 1862. Earhart was born there on July 24, 1897, and attended elementary school in the area. Volunteers have restored the room where she was born and collected memorabilia from her record-breaking career.

See also
Earhart, Amelia Mary; Ninety-Nines
References
Amelia Earhart Birthplace Museum

Amelia Earhart Memorial Race
See All-Women's Transcontinental Air Race (AWTAR)

Atlantis Space Shuttle
The *Atlantis* space shuttle was the fourth orbiter to become operational at the Kennedy Space Center. It was named for a research vessel that was in service from 1930 to 1966 at the Woods Hole Oceanographic Institution in Massachusetts.

Women have been actively working on board *Atlantis* almost since it arrived at the Kennedy Space Center on April 9, 1985, and flew its first mission on October 3, 1985. Astronaut Mary Cleave was a mission specialist for STS-61B, the shuttle's second mission, which launched on November 26, 1985. Her task was to deploy the heaviest payload weight carried into orbit by the space shuttle to date. From May 4 to May 8, 1989, Cleave was back on *Atlantis* as a mission specialist for STS-30 to deploy the *Magellan* Venus-exploration spacecraft, the first planetary probe to be deployed from the shuttle.

For STS-30 *Atlantis* received help from women on the ground as well. Future astronaut Yvonne Darlene Cagle volunteered as an air force medical liaison officer. Her task was to provide rescue and evacuation of the shuttle crew in

The Atlantis *(September 25, 1997)*

case of emergency at the trans-Atlantic landing site in Banjul, West Africa.

Dr. Ellen Baker made her first shuttle flight on mission STS-34 in October 1989, where her assignments included conducting a variety of medical and scientific experiments. From April 5 to April 11, 1991, Mission Specialist Linda Godwin deployed the gamma ray observatory (GRO) from *Atlantis* to study gamma ray sources in the universe. *Atlantis* also carried amateur radio equipment for voice contact, fast scan and slow scan TV, and packet radio. Several hundred contacts were made with amateur radio operators around the world.

In February 1995, Major Eileen Collins served as the first woman to pilot a shuttle on mission STS-63. This was also the first flight of the new joint Russian-American Space Program.

In June 1995 Baker was part of the first space mission to dock with the Russian space station *Mir* as part of the *Atlantis* crew of STS-71. On June 27, 1995, Mission Specialist Bonnie Dunbar helped deliver astronaut Shannon Lucid to *Mir* during STS-71, the first space shuttle mission to dock with *Mir* and exchange crews.

On March 22, 1996, with a crew of six aboard *Atlantis*, Godwin took part in STS-76, the third docking mission to *Mir*. It was on this mission that Godwin carried out the first spacewalk performed while the shuttle was docked to an orbiting space station. Godwin mounted experiment packages on the *Mir* docking module to detect and assess debris and contamination in a space-station environment.

Before being accepted into the astronaut training program in 1996, candidate Joan E. Higginbotham was an orbiter project engineer for the *Atlantis* space shuttle. She was one of the first women to hold the lead technical government engineering position in the firing room, where she supported and managed the integration of vehicle testing and troubleshooting.

In May 1997 Collins was again at the controls of the space shuttle *Atlantis*, helping deliver needed backup oxygen tanks to the *Mir* space station.

See also
Baker, Ellen; Cagle, Yvonne Darlene; Cleave, Mary L.; Collins, Eileen; Dunbar, Bonnie J.; Godwin, Linda M.; Higginbotham, Joan E.; Lucid, Shannon W.; *Mir* Space Station

References
Biographical Data Sheets, Lyndon B. Johnson Space Center (1997)

Auriol, Jacqueline

The daughter-in-law of President Vincent Auriol of France, Auriol became known as the "fastest woman in the world" in the years following World War II. She was one of the few officially qualified female test pilots of her time. In her long career in aviation Auriol was the first woman to fly at the speed of mach 2 and one of the first to fly the supersonic Concorde.

Auriol was born Jacqueline Douet on November 5, 1917, in Challans, France. Her father died of poliomyelitis in 1931, and her mother married the curator of the museum of Nantes. His influence on Auriol was evident when she began studying drawing at the Beaux-Arts and at the Sorbonne in Paris. On February 26, 1938, she married Paul Auriol after a two-year Romeo-and-Juliet-style courtship, since their families were on diametrically opposed sides in the political world of France.

Auriol and her husband continued their college careers until the Nazi invasion of France at the start of World War II. In 1942 Paul worked in the underground resistance movement, and Auriol went on the run from the Nazis with their two children. She lived under a succession of different identities to avoid capture. After the war, her father-in-law, Vincent Auriol, was elected to the presidency, which brought his family into a completely new financial class.

After being taken on their first plane ride with a French war hero, Auriol and her husband began taking flying lessons in early 1948. On March 10, 1948, Auriol qualified for her private pilot's license. She obtained permission from the government to fly military planes, which were faster and more complex than civil aviation planes, on the condition that she qualify for a military pilot's license. This required aerobatic flying, which she studied with Raymond Guillaume, one of the most famous pilots in postwar France.

On July 3, 1949, Auriol gave her first public aerobatics performance in Auxerre, France. The following week, on July 11, 1949, Auriol and Guillaume flew as passengers on a test flight of the Scan 30 plane at Toussus-le-Noble airfield. Their pilot lost control and crash-landed the craft in the Seine River. In the accident Auriol fractured her skull in three places, broke her nose, and dislodged all her teeth. It took 15 operations over two years to repair the broken bones in her face before she was able to get back into the pilot's seat. She then spent two years on and off in the United States until her cosmetic surgery was completed. During that time she studied helicopters and received her U.S. helicopter pilot's license on January 23, 1951.

Auriol took her first step into world recognition as a pilot when she borrowed a Vampire Fighter jet from the French Air Force and broke Jacqueline Cochran's women's world speed record in 1951. This began a public competition between the two female pilots that continued through the next two decades. On May 11, 1951, after 14 training flights, Auriol succeeded in reaching the speed of 510 miles per hour, making her the fastest woman in the world. She earned her military pilot's license for the effort and was also awarded the Harmon Trophy as outstanding female pilot of the year.

After gaining her glider pilot's license, Auriol was the first woman ever admitted as a pilot to the Bretigny Flight Test Center. After 16 months of training, Auriol became a test pilot at the age of 35. On August 15, 1953, she broke the sound barrier in one of her test flights.

As part of their public rivalry, Jacqueline Cochran bettered Auriol's women's speed record in 1953. Auriol took the record back on May 31, 1955, when she flew at a speed of 715 miles per hour and earned her third Harmon Trophy. In 1961 Cochran managed 784 miles per hour, which Auriol beat on June 22, 1962, by reaching 1,149 miles per hour. This pattern continued, with Cochran achieving 1,203 miles per hour in May of 1963 and Auriol beating that in June at 1,266. Each woman had held the same women's world speed record five times. When both women eventually crossed the sound barrier, the rivalry ended.

In later years, Auriol used her aviation skills for humanitarian work. For the ministère de la cooperation she tested new remote-sensing techniques to map crop species and locate water for irrigation. She was awarded the UN Food and Agricultural Organization's Ceres Medal for this work. In 1964 she was awarded the Gold Air Medal of the Fédération Aéronautique Internationale (FAI).

In her 1970 autobiography, Auriol explained her love of flying this way: "I feel so happy when I'm flying. Perhaps it is the feeling of power, the pleasure of dominating a machine as beautiful as a thoroughbred horse. Mingled with these basic joys is another less primitive feeling, that of a mission accomplished. Each time I set foot on an airfield, I sense with fresh excitement that this is where I belong. Time has in no way lessened this thrill, for I feel it just as strongly today, like a daily miracle."

See also
Cochran, Jacqueline
References
Auriol, *I Live to Fly* (1970)

Avenger Field

The only all-female air base in history, Avenger Field housed and trained the Women's Airforce Service Pilots (WASPS) of World War II. Under the direction of Jacqueline Cochran, the group moved from Howard Hughes Field in Houston, Texas, to Avenger Field in Sweetwater, Texas, in March 1943 and remained there for the duration of the war.

The base was named Avenger Field because the pilots trained there would "avenge" the Japanese attack on Pearl Harbor. At 2,350 feet above sea level, Avenger Field provided a challenging climate for training flyers. It had previously been used as a training base for British

Air Force Cadets from June 22 through August 1, 1942. U.S. Army Air Force Cadets replaced these men and remained through April 9, 1943.

The arrival of WASP trainees made Avenger Field the only military coeducational flying field in U.S. history. When the male units were reassigned to avoid problems with fraternizing between the sexes, Avenger Field became the only all-female training base in the world. It soon earned the nickname "Cochran's Convent." The women were even given a mascot, Fifinella, a female gremlin designed by Walt Disney.

Primary training at the base included flying instruction on a wide variety of military aircraft and 400 hours of ground school classes, including physics, aerodynamics, electronics and instruments, meteorology, navigation, and mathematics—the equivalent of a college aeronautics degree. In the 20 months of classes completed, none of the female trainees at Avenger Field failed ground school. The WASPS learned to pilot every model in the Air Corps inventory at that time.

In 1972 the WASPS held their thirtieth reunion at Avenger Field and there hatched the idea for the Order of Fifinella, a group dedicated to increasing public knowledge of the WASP program in U.S. history.

On May 22, 1993, a Walk of Honor listing the names of each WASP trainee, with gold stars to designate casualties, was dedicated at Avenger Field. A life-size bronze statue of a trainee was designed and sculpted by former WASP Dorothy Swain Lewis, a professional artist. It features the WASP motto "We live in the wind and the sand and our eyes are on the stars." A bronze statue of Fifinella stands in the lobby of the Nolan County Courthouse in Sweetwater, Texas.

See also
Cochran, Jacqueline; Fifinella; Order of Fifinella; Women's Airforce Service Pilots (WASPS)

References
Leuthner and Jensen, *High Honor: Recollections by Men and Women of World War II Aviation* (1989); Van Wagenen Keil, *Those Wonderful Women in Their Flying Machines: The Unknown Heroines of World War II* (1979)

Aviation Hall of Fame

The Aviation Hall of Fame in Teterboro, New Jersey, was founded in 1972 to honor local aviators. It is located at Teterboro Airport in Newark, New Jersey, the home of such aviators as Admiral Richard Byrd, who built his North Pole expedition plane there, and Clarence Chamberlin, the second man to fly the Atlantic.

Originally housed in the airport control tower, the Aviation Hall of Fame moved to the top three floors of the new control tower in 1976 and expanded its list of honorees to include women in aviation.

Each year a panel of seven selects that year's inductees, and a dinner is held in their honor. Bronze relief plaques are presented and then hung in the Aviation Hall of Fame in perpetuity. Female inductees to date include aviators Marjorie Gray, Kay Brick, and Ruth Nichols and astronaut Kathryn Sullivan.

See also
Brick, Katherine "Kay" Adams Menges; Gray, Marjorie; Nichols, Ruth Rowland; Sullivan, Kathryn

References
Aviation Hall of Fame, Publicity Department

Bailey, Lady Mary

The first woman to fly across the Irish Sea, Bailey was born into an aristocratic Irish family in 1890. The daughter of Lord Rossmore, she married Abe Bailey, a South American millionaire, and gained her title in 1911 at the age of 22. As was the custom she quickly bore heirs, having five children in all.

Bailey tested for and won her pilot's license in 1926 and celebrated by flying the Irish Sea. She then studied navigation and was the first woman to qualify for a blind-flying certificate, which meant she could fly by instruments alone. On July 5, 1927, Bailey set a new light-airplane altitude record by flying to 17,283 feet in a de Havilland D. H. 60 Moth from an airfield in Middlesex, England.

On March 9, 1928, Bailey left the Stag Lane Aerodrome in London on a solo

flight from London to Cape Town, South Africa, and back. She made refueling stops in Paris, Pisa, and Catania, Sicily, among other places. In Cairo she was delayed by a local ordinance that banned flying solo. She had to telegraph for a

Pilot Lady Mary Bailey greeted M. Renvoise, commandant of the Lebourget Airdome, during a refueling stop in Paris on her record solo flight from London, England, to Cape Town, South Africa, and back again (January 18, 1929).

male friend to accompany her in his own plane to Nimule, Sudan. From there she flew solo to Khartoum, where she visited with Lady Sophie Mary Heath, who was also flying solo across Africa that season.

At Tabora, Tanzania, Bailey had difficulty with the air pockets over the desert and broke her fuselage on landing. She had another plane sent to her and continued through Johannesburg to Cape Town, South Africa, arriving on April 30, 1928. She had made an 8,000-mile trip.

On September 21, 1929, Bailey headed back to London by way of the west coast of Africa. She chose to fly over the Belgian Congo and the Sahara to avoid a repetition of the Cairo situation. She arrived in London on January 10, 1929. For her efforts Bailey was awarded the Britannia Trophy for the most outstanding air performance in 1929.

As one of England's most formidable female pilots Bailey took it upon herself to fly to Londonderry to greet Amelia Earhart when that aviator became the first woman to fly the Atlantic solo. However, their telegrams crossed, and when Bailey arrived Earhart had already boarded a press plane for London.

In 1940 at the start of World War II Bailey offered her piloting skills to the British government, then being attacked by Germany's more powerful air force. She flew with the Air Transport Auxiliary (ATA) for one week, until the negative press made her presence a detriment to the program. She was 50 at the time, and the maximum age for ferry pilots was 45. Despite her previous records in aviation, it was widely reported that Bailey had been accepted to the ATA because of her husband's wealth.

Bailey took her flight to South Africa and back as casually as any other mode of travel of her day; she said: "Having learnt to fly and having acquired a British light aeroplane, able with reasonable luck to take its owner anywhere in the Empire, it seemed a natural thing to use it to join my husband in South Africa." And it was.

Bailey died in Europe in 1960.

See also
Air Transport Auxiliary (ATA); Earhart, Amelia Mary; Heath, Lady Sophie Mary
References
Heath and Murray, *Woman and Flying* (1929)

Baker, Ellen

A medical doctor and veteran of three space flights, Baker was born on April 27, 1953, in Fayetteville, North Carolina. Her family moved to New York City, where she graduated from high school in 1970. Then Baker attended the State University of New York, earning a bachelor of arts in geology in 1974. In 1978 Baker received her doctorate of medicine from Cornell University.

Baker interned at the University of Texas Health Science Center while simultaneously taking the Air Force Aerospace Medicine Course at Brooks Air Force Base. In 1981 she became a physician in the Flight Medicine Clinic at the Lyndon B. Johnson Space Center, where she worked with astronauts in training. In 1985 Baker became an astronaut herself.

On Baker's first shuttle flight, STS-34 in October 1989, she was a mission specialist on the *Atlantis* space shuttle. Her assignments included conducting medical and scientific experiments. In June 1992 Baker was a crewmember of STS-50 on the *Columbia* space shuttle where, over a two-week period, she helped conduct experiments in fluid physics, fluid dynamics, and biological and combustion science. In June 1995 Baker was part of the first space mission to dock with the Russian space station *Mir* as part of the crew of STS-71, once again aboard the *Atlantis* space shuttle. In all, Baker has logged over 686 hours in space.

See also
Atlantis Space Shuttle; *Columbia* Space Shuttle; *Mir* Space Station
References
Biographical Data Sheets, Lyndon B. Johnson Space Center (1997)

Barnes, Florence Lowe "Pancho"

A record-breaking stunt pilot who eventually headed the Women's Air Reserve and the first woman to fly into Mexico, Barnes was born on July 29, 1901, in Pasadena, California. Her wealthy family had been active in aviation from the time her grandfather, T. S. C. Lowe, was chief of the Aeronautic Corps during the Civil War. After the war he built the Mt. Lowe Observatory in California to study the stars.

Barnes was born on July 22, 1901, the second child of T. S. C. Lowe Jr. and his wife Caroline. At the age of nine she attended her first air show, the First American Aviation Exhibition, with her grandfather. Before entering aviation herself Barnes trained as an equestrian, winning her first trophy at the First Annual Pasadena Horse Show in 1906. She attended local public schools until her unruliness became a problem. She was then sent to the Westridge School for Girls in Pasadena and later to the Ramona Convent in Alhambra, California. At the age of 15 Barnes rode her horse to Tijuana, Mexico, to escape. She finally returned home and was enrolled in the even stricter Bishops School in La Jolla, California, from which she graduated in 1919.

Her parents arranged her first marriage on January 1, 1921, to the Reverend Calvin Rankin. She had her first and only child, William Emmett Rankin, on October 9, 1921. Despite this conventional setting, Barnes continued to come and go as she pleased, using her equestrian skills to take jobs as a horse trainer and later as one of the first stuntwomen in movie westerns.

In May 1927 Barnes and six male friends signed on to the crew of a banana boat that was running guns to Mexico during the Mexican revolution. She returned to the United States six months later with the nickname "Pancho" and the desire to learn to fly. Barnes soloed on September 6, 1928, and built a landing strip on her family's ranch in Laguna Beach for herself and her new pilot friends. In October 1928 she opened Pancho Barnes Mystery Circus of the Air, a stunt barnstorming troupe. Then she applied to the Fédération Aéronautique Internationale for a sporting license, which was signed by Wilbur Wright. On February 22, 1929, Barnes became the sixth woman in the United States to receive her commercial license, which enabled her to carry passengers.

On February 22, 1929, against contestants like Bobbi Trout, Barnes won her first competitive race at the grand opening of the Glendale Airport. This notoriety led her to obtain a position in air racing. Sponsored by the Union Oil Company, Barnes entered the 1929 Women's Air Derby competing against Louise Thaden, Phoebe Omlie, and fellow Union Oil flyer Marvel Crosson. Barnes's plane crashed into an automobile on a runway in Pecos, Texas, taking her out of competition.

On February 26, 1930, Barnes left Los Angeles to become the first woman to fly into Mexico's interior. She returned on March 9, 1930, to a hero's welcome.

On August 5, 1930, Barnes earned her first record for world speed for flying 196 miles per hour, beating Amelia Earhart's month-old record of 181 miles per hour. Barnes's record stood until Ruth Nichols reached 210 miles per hour the following year.

In 1931 Barnes and fellow California pilot Lavelle Sweeley organized a collection of female pilots and medical personnel into the Women's Air Reserve (WAR) to provide aid during national emergen-

Stunt pilot Florence Lowe "Pancho" Barnes founded the Women's Air Reserve, which provided aid during national emergencies, and the Associated Motion Picture Pilot's Union.

cies. In 1939 Barnes's friendly rival, Ruth Nichols, created a group with a similar purpose, Relief Wings.

To make money, Barnes flew for California-based aircraft companies. Then she learned about Alys McKey Bryant's stunt flying in the movies nearly 15 years earlier and decided to try that. Barnes was one of several stunt flyers on Howard Hughes's famous film *Hell's Angels*. This led her to help organize the Associated Motion Picture Pilot's Union (AMPP), which in turn led to her short-lived interest in politics. Barnes ran for county supervisor for Los Angeles's third district in 1932, a race she lost.

In 1933 the depression finally caught up with Barnes, and she went bankrupt. She sold her real estate holdings in Los Angeles and bought cheaper land in the California desert. She made money by winning the garbage-collecting rights to the local military base, feeding the garbage to her start-up hog farm, and then selling the hog meat back to the base. With this she could continue her habit of throwing raucous society parties for her decidedly nonsociety friends from the worlds of aviation and movies. Frequent guests included Amelia Earhart, Thea Rasche, and Phoebe Omlie. Young female pilots like Elinor Smith were only invited to the more sedate events.

On August 31, 1934, WAR sponsored a cross-country trip to help promote membership and to underscore Phoebe Omlie's petition for equal pilot licensing standards for men and women. Barnes and a group of WAR's charter members made stops in Kingman, Arizona; Washington, D.C.; and Philadelphia, Pennsylvania. In New York City the members were almost banned from a cocktail party in their honor. They arrived in full dress uniform, only to be told that women were not allowed to appear in public in masculine attire. Barnes argued, and they were admitted. WAR disbanded in 1941 because of financing problems and new opportunities for women pilots in the WASPS in the face of World War II.

Barnes offered her flying skills and the use of her desert ranch to the U.S. government. She started a Civilian Pilot Training Program on the ranch, teaching both male students and females, who would then join the Women's Airforce Service Pilots (WASPS). The ranch soon earned the nickname "The Happy Bottom Riding Club" since she gave the trainees free run of her stables between classes.

Barnes's second husband was one of her students, Robert Hudson Nichols, whom she married in December 1941. On July 29, 1945, she married her third husband, Joseph Don Shalita. In 1946 the 43-year-old Barnes met a 26-year-old pilot returning from the war, Eugene Mac McKendry. He became her fourth husband on June 30, 1952, in a ceremony presided over by Chief Lucky of the Blackfoot Indians. The ceremony was attended by the aviation elite of the day, with Chuck Yeager giving away the bride.

Before and after their marriage Barnes and McKendry ran the ranch, adding a dance hall and private airport, which General Jimmy Doolittle and Yeager both used on frequent visits. In 1952, however, the military wanted to expand the runways at Edwards Air Force Base to accommodate the future of space travel. Barnes would not sell her ranch. Soon rumors that the club was really a front for prostitution and that Barnes was the madam threatened to ruin her. Barnes sued the air force for defamation

of character and acted as her own attorney. When she secured an injunction against the government's taking over her ranch in 1953, an explosion demolished the dance hall, and the resulting fire destroyed her ranch house. She blamed the air force; the air force blamed her. Arson investigators found no conclusive evidence either way. In 1954 Barnes received a $414,000 settlement from the air force on her defamation lawsuit.

Barnes used her settlement to open a new club, Gypsy Springs, some 30 miles north of her old ranch. In 1964 Barnes's last marriage failed, and she was diagnosed as having breast cancer. The air force organized a First Citizen of Edwards Day in her honor on May 23, 1964. After two mastectomies Barnes recovered from the cancer and began a career lecturing about early aviation.

Barnes died of heart failure in 1975. Her eulogy was given by an old flying buddy who had become an air force five-star general, Jimmy Doolittle, and her effects were donated to the Test Flight Center Museum at Edwards Air Force Base.

About women in aviation, Barnes said: "The fact that women are women should have nothing to do with the future of flying. If a person is good, he or she can get along in any field, regardless of sex."

See also
Bryant, Alys McKey; Crosson, Marvel; Earhart, Amelia Mary; Fédération Aéronautique Internationale (FAI); Nichols, Ruth Rowland; Omlie, Phoebe Fairgrave; Relief Wings, Inc.; Smith, Elinor Patricia; Thaden, Louise McPhetridge; Trout, Evelyn "Bobbi"; Women's Airforce Service Pilots (WASPS)

References
Holden and Griffith, *Ladybirds II: The Continuing Story of American Women in Aviation* (1993); Schultz, *Pancho: The Biography of Florence Lowe Barnes* (1996); Tate, *The Lady Who Tamed Pegasus: The Story of Pancho Barnes* (1984)

Maryse Bastie (December 12, 1930)

Bastie, Marie-Louise "Maryse"

The first woman to fly from Paris to Tokyo, Bastie was born in France circa 1910. In 1929 she circled the LeBourget Airfield in Paris for 26 hours, 48 minutes to create a new women's nonstop solo flight record. In 1930 she managed 37 hours, 55 minutes nonstop and clinched the world record for male or female flyers.

On June 28, 1931, Bastie broke the nonstop straight-run (meaning no stops for fueling) record for women and the nonstop light-plane flight record, male or female, worldwide when she flew 1,849 miles from Paris, France, to Gorki, Russia. The publicity earned her a public relations job with Potez, an aircraft manufacturing firm in France. After two

years she became bored, however, and began teaching flying.

In 1934 Bastie became the first woman to fly solo from Paris to Tokyo. In 1936 she attended a dinner in honor of Jean Batten of New Zealand, who had just flown the South Atlantic solo. On December 30, 1936, Bastie borrowed a plane from the Caudron Aircraft Company to challenge Jean Batten's record-setting flight. Bastie managed the trip from Paris to Port Natal, Brazil, in 12 hours, 5 minutes, beating Batten by just over an hour. Also in 1936 Bastie became the second woman to fly the Andes Mountains, after Adrienne Bolland, who flew the Andes in 1921. For this effort, Bastie was awarded the Legion of Honor, France's highest civilian medal.

Bastie applied to the Free French Air Force during World War II and was accepted as a pilot in their ranks.

On July 6, 1952, Bastie was killed when a plane in which she was a passenger crashed.

See also
Batten, Jean; Bolland, Adrienne
References
Lomax, *Women of the Air* (1986); Moolman, *Women Aloft* (1981)

Batten, Jean

The first woman to fly solo from England to New Zealand, Batten was born in Rotorua, New Zealand, on September 15, 1909. Her father was a dental surgeon who moved his practice to Auckland when she was four years old.

Batten attended private college in New Zealand, majoring in music. Her first introduction to aviation came in 1928. Batten thrilled to the news that Charles Kingsford-Smith had flown from America to Australia. Though this feat was accomplished by a man, it still inspired her own interest in a career in aviation. She met Kingsford-Smith during his victory tour through New Zealand, and he took Batten for her first plane ride.

Both her enthusiasm for aviation and her request for flying lessons displeased her father, who feared for her safety. In order to obtain the lessons, Batten sold her piano and in 1929 accompanied her mother on a tour of England. There Batten joined the London Aeroplane Club, which had played a major role in training other famous female aviators from the British empire, including Lady Sophie Mary Heath, Amy Johnson, and Mary Petre Bruce.

After receiving her A license, Batten returned to New Zealand to look for financial backing for a flight from England to Australia. Amy Johnson had already completed that flight in 1930, but Batten hoped to make better time to help establish her name in aviation. After her first fund-raising efforts failed, she returned to England and the London Aeroplane Club to work on her B license and to study engineering, hoping these would help her obtain financial backing for her flight.

Batten made her first attempt at the flight from Australia to England in April 1933, with financing from a fellow pilot at the club. Because of engine failure, she only made it to India on the first try. This attempt bankrupted her but gave her sufficient publicity to attract the attention of Lord Wakefield, who financed the second try in April 1934. Batten only made it to Rome on this try. It was not until May 8, 1934, that she set off on what would become her successful solo flight from England to Australia, a distance of approximately 12,700 miles. In the course of this flight she became the first aviator, male or female, to complete a direct, solo flight to Cyprus, an island in the eastern Mediterranean.

After further refueling and maintenance stops in Baghdad, Basra, Calcutta, and Timor Island Batten landed successfully at Port Darwin, Australia, on May 23, 1934. The flight took 14 days, 22 hours, 30 minutes and beat Amy Johnson's record by more than four days. She flew on to Sydney for a grand reception organized by her benefactor, Lord Wakefield, and gave her first public speech. Her plane was not equipped for the nonstop flight from Australia to New Zealand, so she had to return by steamship.

Batten returned to New Zealand a hero. The government awarded her a grant of 500 pounds. She was sent on a six-week tour of the island nation that included attending banquets and making speeches at aero clubs, rotary clubs, and hospitals. The tour ended in her birthplace, Rotorua, where she was the guest of honor at a feast arranged by the local native Maori tribe.

Her newfound fame ensured her a job as a radio commentator for an air race from England to Australia organized in honor of the Melbourne centenary celebrations. Both Amy Johnson and Jacqueline Cochran participated in this race, though the final winner was the team of Charles Scott and Campbell Black. With the salary from this event and with fees for lectures, articles, and licensing her name to advertise certain products, Batten collected funds to pay off the debts of her first flight and to begin financing the next.

In April 1935, Batten flew from Australia to London to attend the Jubilee of King George V and to begin planning a flight from England to South America. Though her return flight took 17 days, 15 hours, she was now the first woman to fly from England to Australia and back, further cementing her celebrity.

On November 11, 1935, Batten began her London–to–South America flight at 6:30 A.M. The first night's scheduled stop was at Casablanca. Her flight there in 9 hours, 45 minutes set a new world record. After stops in Morocco and Thiès, Senegal, Batten headed across the Atlantic

Ocean for Brazil, a 1,900-mile solo trip which she accomplished in 13 hours, 15 minutes, the fastest Atlantic crossing to that date. Batten landed at Port Natal, Brazil, on November 13, 1935. The total time for the England–to–South America trip was 2 days, 13 hours, 15 minutes, breaking the previous record set by Jim Mollison by almost a day.

In Rio de Janeiro Batten was honored for this feat at several banquets and was even made an honorary officer in the Brazilian Naval Air Force. She was also presented with the Order of the Southern Cross by President Getúlio Dornelles Vargas. She became the first British citizen to receive this honor outside of members of the royal family.

Before she left South America, Batten flew to Buenos Aires on November 24, 1935, and received a hero's welcome as the first woman to fly from England to Argentina. There she was made an honorary officer in the Argentine Air Force as well and was granted the nickname Clavel del Aire (Flower of the Sky) by the Rotary Club of Argentina.

In February 1936 Batten was invited to visit Paris as a guest of the Aero Club of France. During yet another round of banquets and speeches she met Madame Marie-Louise Bastie, the French aviator who would challenge Batten's record for the Atlantic crossing the following September—and beat it. While in France, Batten tied with Amelia Earhart for the International League of Aviators' Harmon Trophy as best woman pilot of 1935.

In April 1936 Batten took her ever-supportive mother for her first long airplane trip, from England to North Africa via Spain and France. In France Batten received the Cross of the Legion of Honor. Back in England in May, she was made an honorary Commander of the British Empire in a ceremony at Buckingham Palace at which King Edward VIII officiated. With all these honors Batten felt ready to

attempt the one long-distance flight she had always planned on taking.

On October 5, 1936, Batten left England headed for her homeland of New Zealand, essentially flying from the heart of the English empire to its farthest holding. She followed most of her old route to Australia, arriving there in 5 days, 21 hours and breaking the previous solo record for that flight, held by H. F. Broadbent. Batten then continued across the Australian continent and over the Tasman Sea to New Zealand. She arrived in her hometown of Auckland, New Zealand, on October 16, 1936, with a flight time of 11 days, 45 minutes and a new world record.

For this flight the Royal Aero Club awarded her the Britannia Trophy for the most meritorious flight of the year by a British subject, the International League of Aviators awarded her a second Harmon Trophy, and she earned the Seagrave Trophy for the most outstanding demonstration of the possibilities of transportation on land, sea, or air.

After several months of rest in Australia Batten headed for England again on October 19, 1937. She arrived on October 24 with a flight time of 5 days, 18 hours, 15 minutes and yet another world speed record for that route. Her honors this time included becoming the first New Zealander to be represented in Madame Tussaud's world-famous wax museum in England.

In January 1938, Batten was awarded the Gold Medal of the Fédération Aéronautique Internationale. This was followed by a flying tour of Europe, including Sweden and Denmark. Her airplane was displayed, Batten gave lectures, and she even appeared on television, another technology in its infancy.

At the outbreak of World War II in Europe, Batten offered her piloting skills to the Air Transport Auxiliary, but she failed the military eye test and had to find other ways to aid the war effort. She drove an ambulance and traveled across England to raise funds for the war.

After the war Batten moved in and out of public life. She essentially retired from flying but would appear at aviation events to speak about her career on and off for the next 40 years. Batten moved to Majorca, Spain, where she lived in semiseclusion and died on November 22, 1982.

In her 1938 autobiography Batten summed up her life and her love of flying: "In my heart I knew only too well that I was destined to be a wanderer. I seemed born to travel, and in flying I found the combination of the two things which meant everything to me: the intoxicating drug of speed and the freedom to roam the earth."

See also
Air Transport Auxiliary (ATA); Bastie, Marie-Louise "Maryse"; Cochran, Jacqueline; Earhart, Amelia Mary; Fédération Aéronautique Internationale (FAI); Heath, Lady Sophie Mary; Johnson, Amy; Petre, Mary
References
Batten, *My Life* (1938); Cadogan, *Women with Wings: Female Flyers in Fact and Fiction* (1993)

Baumgartner, Ann
See Carl, Ann Baumgartner

Beall, Molly
See Reilly, Molly Beall

Beckman, Trish
Beckman, one of the first women trained to be a U.S. Navy (USN) test pilot, joined the navy right out of high school. She was trained as a flight simulator operator and also acted as a flight attendant on flights involving VIPs. In this capacity she and other enlisted women were allowed to act as crew members, but their hours were not credited toward earning flight wings. When she asked why and

was told it was because she was a woman, Beckman became one of the navy's foremost defenders of women's rights.

Beckman entered college and qualified for officer candidate school and flight training at the naval base in Pensacola, Florida. She earned her wings in 1981 as one of the first female naval flight officers in the USN. After a tour of duty in Hawaii she attained her master's degree in aeronautical engineering. With that she qualified for test pilot training.

Throughout her career Beckman has been a passionate supporter of women's achievement in the military, which led her to become vice president of the Women Military Aviators. In 1991, when the Tailhook sexual abuse scandal broke, Beckman was frequently quoted in the press. She summed up her feelings about the event by saying: "The sexual assault at Tailhook was a direct result of a small number of men feeling threatened by the repeal of aviation combat exclusion laws. Their fear was that they would have to compete with women on a level playing field. Tailhook has become the catalyst for social change in the navy. It will be the stimulus for equal treatment of all military women, because the other services are watching."

See also
Tailhook Sexual Harassment Scandal
References
Holden and Griffith, *Ladybirds II: The Continuing Story of American Women in Aviation* (1993)

Beech, Olive Ann Mellor
One of the first women to become president of an aviation company, Beech used the position to further women's opportunities in the field as well as to support charities when she could. She was born on September 25, 1903. She became a bookkeeper for Walter H. Beech's Travel Air

Manufacturing Company in 1925. In 1930 the two were married.

In 1932 they founded the Beech Aircraft Company with Walter as president and Olive as an executive officer. In 1936 the company donated a plane to the famed pilot Louise Thaden in which she and her copilot Blanche Noyes won the Bendix Transcontinental Air Races.

In 1939 Beech donated several planes to Relief Wings, a volunteer aviation organization created by Ruth Nichols to enlist pilots, their private planes, and medical personnel for emergency and disaster relief work.

In the early 1940s Walter fell ill with encephalitis, and Olive assumed all his duties as president. When he died in 1950, she carried on with the company's plans. She diversified beyond general aviation, expanding into military contracts while maintaining profits and promoting women's advancement within the company. In 1951 she was named Woman of the Year in Aviation by the Women's National Aeronautical Association. In 1968 Beech gave up everyday presidential duties but remained chairwoman of the board.

In 1973 Beech was recognized by *Fortune Magazine* as one of the Ten Highest Ranking Women in Big Business. In 1974 she received the Elder Statesman of Aviation Award from the National Aeronautic Association of the United States, and in 1978 she again appeared on the *Fortune Magazine* list.

In 1980 the National Aeronautic Association of the United States awarded Beech the Wright Brothers Memorial Trophy for five decades of outstanding leadership in the development of general aviation. That same year she sold Beech Aircraft to the Raytheon Company and remained on the board until 1982 to smooth out the transition. She died on July 6, 1993.

See also
Nichols, Ruth Rowland; Noyes, Blanche Wilcox; Thaden, Louise McPhetridge
References
Current Biography Yearbook (1996); Douglas, *United States Women in Aviation, 1940–1985* (1990)

Beese, Melli

Germany's first licensed woman flyer, Beese was born circa 1890 and passed her licensing test in 1911 despite the fact that the male flyers at her airfield tampered with her plane's steering mechanism and siphoned off some of her gas.

In 1912 Beese opened a flight school in Berlin with her husband, also a flyer. She used a plane of her own design and construction, the Melli Beese Dove, to train scores of men to fly, men who would use those skills in the German Air Force during World War I.

During the war Beese was grounded by the government because her husband was French. When she applied to the military to be a pilot she was turned away, as were Ruth Law and Katherine Stinson by the U.S. military. It was not until World War II that Germany would accept a female military pilot, and then only one, Hanna Reitsch.

See also
Law, Ruth; Reitsch, Hanna; Stinson, Katherine
References
Moolman, *Women Aloft* (1981)

Bera, Fran

The pilot with the record of most wins for the Women's Air Derby, Bera was born in Michigan in 1924 and learned to fly in 1940 at 16 years old, while in high school in Grand Rapids. She gained both her commercial license, allowing her to carry passengers, and her instructor's rating, allowing her to teach aviation, and she became a free-fall parachutist. To earn flight time Bera ferried trainers around the country after World War II ended and they were no longer necessary. Then she worked with the Federal Aviation Administration (FAA) issuing licenses to pilots.

In 1950 Bera moved to California and entered the racing circuit, competing in the Reno National Air Races and the Great Race from London to Vancouver, British Columbia. But it was in the Women's Air Derby that she gained her greatest fame. She entered each race from 1951 to 1969 and in 1976 and 1977. Bera won five second-place trophies and seven first-place ones. To earn money in aviation she became an FAA pilot examiner and licensed more than 3,000 pilots in her 25-year career.

In June 1966 Bera set a new world altitude record for flying to a height of 40,194 feet over Long Beach, California. She served on the FAA's Women's Advisory Committee and California Governor Ronald Reagan's Aviation Education Task Force.

In 1980 Bera was named Pilot of the Year by the Silver Wings Fraternity. She retired from flying in 1985.

About her Women's Air Derby record of wins, Bera said: "After a couple of wins, people began to expect it. That put a great deal of pressure on me. So nothing but first place counted. I was very competitive and winning seemed to be everything."

See also
Women's Air Derby
References
History of the Ninety-Nines, Inc. (1979); Holden and Griffith, *Ladybirds II: The Continuing Story of American Women in Aviation* (1993)

Bird, Nancy De Low

Part of the first team of women to barnstorm across Australia, Bird was born in Kew, Australia, in 1916. At 13 she fell in love with flying. Bird spent three years saving up for her first lesson, which she took on August 11, 1933. Her instructor was Charles Kingsford-Smith, a record-breaking pilot who had opened a flying school in Mascot, Australia, that would years later grow into the Sydney International Airport. Bird earned her private pilot's license on September 22, 1933, followed by her commercial license in March 1935. In working toward her commercial license, Bird became one of the first two women in New South Wales to fly at night. At that time she was the youngest woman in the British Empire to qualify for a commercial license.

On April 3, 1935, Bird teamed up with the only other female student in Kingsford-Smith's class, Peggy McKillop, on a barnstorming tour of Australia. They were sponsored by the Shell Oil Company and *Woman* magazine. They flew for three months and 22,000 miles, offering rides for pay and giving lectures at local schools and town halls.

Then Bird was hired by a landowner in New South Wales who wanted his son flown 50 miles to check out some sheep for purchase. It was a test to see if there was enough business to start an airline between New South Wales and Dubbo. Bird picked up extra money selling shares in the business.

Through this work she met the Reverend Stanley Drummond of the Far West Children's Health Scheme (FWCHS), a group dedicated to eradicating trachoma in small country towns. He asked Bird to fly Sister Webb, a nun with nursing credentials, on a round of visits to patients, a task too difficult to do by car. Bird ferried the nun in between winning a silver cup in the 1935 Narromine Air Pageant with

McKillop and starting their next barnstorming tour.

After the second tour Bird accepted a full-time position with the FWCHS for 100 pounds a year. She purchased a new plane for the job and had to build a shelter for it so that the scorching sun would not age it too fast. Shelter for the plane proved easier to achieve than a room for herself in rural Australia. Finally the owner of a hotel in nearby Bourke, Australia, heard of her work with FWCHS and offered her a room for two pounds a week. Bird took it despite the fact that it was socially unacceptable for an unmarried woman to live alone in a hotel. Bird flew for the FWCHS when she was needed and flew private charters in her spare time to help pay off the loan for the new plane.

In December 1936 Bird won the Ladies Trophy in the Brisbane to Adelaide Air Race. Soon afterward the FWCHS ran out of funds for her position, and Bird moved to Queensland to apply as an aerial ambulance pilot for the Australian Inland Mission. They turned her down, and, facing bankruptcy, Bird had to sell her airplane. Although she earned no fortune from the FWCHS, she did earn fame. Bird was invited on a world tour for her efforts and traveled the world as a guest of the Dutch, German, French, Danish, and Swedish airlines. The highlight of the tour was the chance to fly on the maiden flight of the DC-4 in the United States with Jacqueline Cochran, the woman who would someday break the sound barrier.

At the outbreak of World War II Pauline Gower asked Bird to join the Air Transport Auxiliary in Britain as a ferry pilot. Because Australia had forbidden women to leave the country during the war, Bird was unable to accept. By the time the Women's Australian Auxiliary Air Force was formed in 1939 she had married and declined to join. In 1949 Bird founded the Australian Women Pilot's Association and was elected its first president. In 1956 she renewed her pilot's license in order to participate in the Powder Puff Derby in the United States. She came in fifth and entered again in 1961.

In her 1961 autobiography *Born to Fly* Bird summed up her life by saying: "I was born ambitious, with a strong desire to put back into the kitty as much as I take out. I've struck plenty of turbulence in my time, both in the air and out of it, but I've always remembered the instructor who said, 'Don't be a fair weather pilot, Nancy. You must learn to fly in bad weather, too.' How right he was for it's true that above the clouds, the sun is always shining."

See also

Air Transport Auxiliary (ATA); All-Women's Transcontinental Air Race (AWTAR); Cochran, Jacqueline; Gower, Pauline; Johnson, Amy; McKillop, Peggy

References

Bird, *Born to Fly* (1961); Lomax, *Women of the Air* (1987).

Bjornson, Rosella

Canada's first woman to fly as captain with a major scheduled airline, Bjornson was born in Champion, Alberta, in 1947. Her family owned a plane, so she was more than comfortable with flight before her parents gave her flying lessons for her seventeenth birthday.

The next year Bjornson began attending the University of Calgary and spending her summers earning first her commercial pilot's license and then her instructor's license. She organized both a flying club at the college and an Alberta branch of the Ninety-Nines. In 1969 she took a job as an instructor at the Winnipeg Flying Club.

As she gained flying hours and qualified for larger and larger planes, Bjornson began applying to the major airlines for a pilot position. Some openly admitted they did not accept women; some simply said they were not hiring at the time.

At the Winnipeg Flying Club Bjornson met the chief pilot of Transair, who encouraged her to keep trying. In April 1973 Bjornson broke through the prejudice against hiring women to pilot jets when she accepted a job with Transair as first officer on the Fokker F-28 turbo-jet, which carried 65 passengers per trip. This made her the first female airline pilot in Canada and the first jet-qualified female first officer on the North American continent.

As the only female pilot among 2,800 male pilots for the various Canadian airlines, Bjornson saw her share of discrimination, especially when she married in 1977. Still she was promoted to the YS-11 jet in February 1979. That was also the year she became pregnant with her first child and discovered that the airlines had no policies regarding maternity.

Her struggle to achieve fair treatment created stories on the op-ed pages of many large Canadian newspapers. Should she take sick leave to retain her medical benefits and thereby allow pregnancy to be considered an illness? Should she take a leave of absence with no pay to retain her seniority and benefits or fight to have maternity leave figured into her contract?

Bjornson decided to take a leave of absence for 18 months, which allowed her, upon her return, to continue training on 737s, which she flew until 1983 when she had her second child, with much less publicity. Before the leave of absence for her second child ended, economic troubles at the airline resulted in a three-year layoff.

In 1987 Bjornson returned to work full time, and in 1990 she received her captain's stripes, the first woman in Canada to do so. She then received the National Transportation Award of Achievement and the Northern Alberta Transportation Personality of the Year Award in 1991.

Despite the accolades, Bjornson never forgot people's reactions to her desire to be a jet pilot. "When I told my high school counselor he just laughed and said it was impossible because I was a girl."

See also
Ninety-Nines
References
Render, *No Place for a Lady: The Story of Canadian Women Pilots, 1928–1992* (1992)

Blanchard, Marie Madeleine Sophie Armont

Frenchwoman Madame Marie Madeleine Sophie Armont Blanchard, born in 1778, was the first woman to make a living piloting a balloon. She was taught to handle a balloon by her husband, Jean-Pierre Blanchard, himself a successful balloonist, and she made her first ascent in France in 1805.

The couple flew together in public until her husband died in a balloon crash in 1809. In defiance of the mores of her day, Madame Blanchard continued bal-

Madeleine-Sophie Armont Blanchard (undated painting)

looning and gained such fame that Napoleon named her the official aeronaut of the French Empire. Her most noted move in that role was to convince Napoleon that a balloon invasion of England would not be feasible because of the difficulties of crossing the English Channel safely.

Blanchard's air shows involved ascending in the balloon as fireworks were set off from a small platform hanging ten feet below the gondola. During a display in Paris's Tivoli Gardens in 1817 the hydrogen that provided the lift for her balloon caught fire, causing the balloon to plummet toward the ground. When it crashed into the slanted rooftop of a nearby house, it tipped over, and Madame Blanchard was thrown into the Rue de Provence river. Despite all the risks she had taken in the air, she died on the ground of a broken neck.

References
Lomax, *Women of the Air* (1987); May, *Women in Aeronautics* (1962)

Bohn, Marta
See Meyer, Marta Bohn

Bolland, Adrienne
The first woman to fly over the Andes, Bolland was born in France in 1885 and received her pilot's license in 1920. Bolland studied flying at a school sponsored by the Caudron Aircraft Company and flew their planes in stunt shows for a few years. Her most famous stunt record was for successfully performing 212 loop-the-loops in a row.

In 1921 she decided to become the first woman to fly the Andes, the mountain range separating Argentina from Chile. Caudron sponsored the attempt by providing Bolland a plane and shipping it to South America for her. However, the plane had a ceiling of 13,000 feet—that

is, it was only guaranteed to perform safely to that height—and the lowest peak in the Andes is 14,000 feet.

On April 1, 1921, Bolland left Mendoza, Argentina, and landed on the other side of the Andes in Santiago, Chile, after a ten-hour flight. The extreme cold and altitude had almost caused Bolland to pass out during the flight several times, but she persevered. In recognition of her efforts, Bolland was made the French air attaché in Buenos Aires.

Bolland returned to France as a barnstormer, performing in air shows across the country. At one such show, on October 18, 1923, Bolland broke the record for the number of loop-the-loops by flying 98 of them in an hour. She started a joyriding company with her profits. On May 27, 1924, she completed 212 loop-the-loops in the same time.

In April 1924 the International Commission for Air Navigation decided to discontinue allowing women to hold commercial licenses, which allowed them to transport passengers. Through the efforts of female pilots of high social position like Lady Heath, this ban was overturned, but by then Bolland had lost most of her investment capital.

Bolland died in 1975 at her home in France.

See also
Heath, Lady Sophie Mary
References
Lomax, *Women of the Air* (1987); Moolman, *Women Aloft* (1981)

Bondar, Roberta
The first Canadian woman to go into space, Bondar was born in Sault Sainte Marie, Ontario, on December 4, 1945. She received bachelor's degrees in zoology and agriculture from the University of Guelph in 1968 before studying for her doctorate in neurobiology from the

University of Toronto in 1974. Bondar became a neurologist at McMaster University in 1977 and was admitted as a fellow of the Royal College of Physicians and Surgeons of Canada as a specialist in neurology in 1981.

After training as a pilot Bondar applied and was accepted as one of the six members of the original Canadian Astronaut Team selected in December 1983, and she began astronaut training in February 1984. She served as chairperson of the Canadian Life Sciences Subcommittee for the Space Station from 1985 to 1989 and as a member of the Ontario Premièr's Council on Science and Technology from 1988 to 1989.

In early 1990 Bondar was designated a prime payload specialist for the first International Microgravity Laboratory Mission (IML-1). She flew on the *Discovery* space shuttle during mission STS-42 from January 22 to January 30, 1992. Her responsibilities included performing life science and material science experiments in the Spacelab and on the middeck.

When not in space, Bondar is a distinguished professor at the Centre for Advanced Technology Education (CATE) at Ryerson Polytechnic University in Toronto, Ontario; a visiting distinguished professor in the Department of Kinesiology at the University of Western Ontario, London, Ontario; and a principal investigator studying transcranial doppler in astronauts before and after spaceflight at the Johnson Space Center at Edwards Air Force Base in California and at the Kennedy Space Center in Florida.

In 1995 Bondar wrote *Touching the Earth*. Traveling in space had always been Bondar's dream: "Even as a child I had wanted to fly into space and this was long before space travel was considered a reality. I have a picture of myself as a little child sitting on a star in space! That was my dream."

See also
Discovery Space Shuttle
References
Biographical Data Sheets; Lyndon B. Johnson Space Center (1997); Briggs, *Women in Space: Reaching the Last Frontier* (1988); Render, *No Place for a Lady: The Story of Canadian Women Pilots, 1928–1992* (1992)

Bottomley, Nora

The first woman to complete officer training as an air weapons controller in the Canadian Air Force (CAF) and the first to serve as an aircraft commander, Bottomley was born in Smithers, British Columbia, in 1951. In 1970, a year after finishing high school, she joined the military and studied to be a radar plotter, one of the few occupations open to women in the CAF at the time.

Her first assignment after training was in Shelbourne, Nova Scotia, where she flew for the first time and fell in love with it. The CAF was not yet accepting women for pilot training, so Bottomley entered officer candidate school as an air weapons controller, the first woman to do so. In 1973 she earned the rank of lieutenant.

In 1976 she earned her private pilot's license on her own time and then gained a promotion to captain. Bottomley also became the first woman to serve as senior director for North American Radar Defense (NORAD). Nevertheless, the CAF did not accept her, or any other woman, as a pilot until 1979. She, Deanna Brasseur, and Leah Mosher were the first women to pass the training.

Bottomley's first posting was on the Search and Rescue team of the 424 Squadron at the Canadian Air Force Base at Trenton in 1981. She was promoted to aircraft commander in April 1983. In 1986 at her new posting with the 440 Squadron at the base in Edmonton, Alberta, Bottomley created the Civil Air Search and

Rescue Association (CASARA), which trained civilians for emergency search-and-rescue work.

After becoming qualified for instrument flight Bottomley served as commanding officer of a recruitment center in Saint John's, Newfoundland, and then as executive assistant to the public affairs officer in Comox, British Columbia. She returned to search-and-rescue duties in 1993.

When asked how she survived being one of the only female pilots on most of her early assignments, Bottomley said: "Things were tense. I learned to let a lot of things roll off my back, to ignore the comments."

See also
Brasseur, Deanna; Mosher, Leah
References
Render, *No Place for a Lady: The Story of Canadian Women Pilots, 1928–1992* (1992)

Boucher, Helene

On November 30, 1934, Boucher was piloting her Caudron Rafale plane in rough weather and died in a crash; she was about 34 years old. She was the holder of the women's world speed record at the time of her death.

Her desire to pursue ever more difficult records was explained in an interview when she said of aviation: "It is the only profession where courage pays off and concrete results count for success."

References
Moolman, *Women Aloft* (1981)

Bragg, Janet Harmon Waterford

The first African American woman to earn a full commercial pilot's license, Bragg was born Jane Nettie Harmon in the small town of Griffin, Georgia, in 1907. The granddaughter of an emancipated slave, Bragg attended an Episco-

palian boarding school where she excelled in physics and math and then received a degree in nursing from Spelman Seminary (later renamed Spelman College). Bragg moved to Chicago and found a job as a health inspector for the Metropolitan Insurance Company. She continued her studies at night, taking graduate courses in public health administration and pediatric nursing.

While she was working and going to school, Bragg saw an ad in the *Chicago Defender*, a prominent black newspaper of the day, for ground school classes for blacks at the Aeronautical University. Recalling her childhood years of staring up at the clouds and wondering how Jesus walked among them, Bragg decided to learn to fly. She found herself the only woman in the class, and she survived the discrimination by remembering her father's favorite saying: "If Jack can do it, so can Jill."

In addition to discrimination because of her gender, Bragg faced the further problem that the class provided no flying hours because most white airports banned black flyers and the school could not afford its own planes. Bragg paid additional fees to a white pilot for instruction in his plane. Eventually she and the other black students formed the Challenger Air Pilot's Association and convinced a local mayor to set aside some land for an airport, which he did on the condition that they provide all the labor and materials. In 1934 the whole school started lessons in the one plane they owned, a plane that Bragg bought with her nurse's wages. Later she helped start a similar flight school at the Harlem Airport. Her reputation grew, and the editor of the *Chicago Defender*, Enoch P. Waters, offered Bragg a column on aviation.

In 1939 the government announced the Civilian Pilot Training Program (CPTP), offering white students the chance to obtain advanced training and flying certifications at low fees. Bragg and her colleagues countered by creating the National Airmen's Association of America (NAAA) to stimulate interest in aviation among blacks. They also wanted to protest the discriminatory practices of the CPTP. On Waters's suggestion, they flew to Washington, D.C., to lobby senators on their behalf. There they met a young senator from Missouri, Harry Truman, who was so impressed with their efforts that he brought them to the attention of President Franklin Roosevelt and Eleanor Roosevelt, and soon CPTP programs were established at many black colleges and black-owned airports.

Despite her success in enabling other pilots to fly, Bragg was twice refused admission to government programs—first to the Women's Airforce Service Pilots (WASP) program and then to the Army Military Nurses Corps—both times because of the color of her skin. After being denied a chance to serve her country in those organizations she decided to spend a month getting her commercial pilot's license from the new program at the Tuskegee Institute. She passed the written tests and the flight test, but her white instructor informed her that "I've never given a colored girl a license, and I don't intend to now." She returned to Chicago, took the flying test all over again, and this time was granted her commercial license, despite the fact that this trainer, too, was white.

By now she was working as a health inspector by day, operating a small nursing home by night, and flying in between. In 1951 she married Sumner Bragg, a supervisor at Metropolitan Insurance, and quit her job there to run the nursing home full time. In 1972 she retired to Tucson, Arizona, and began taking in foreign exchange students from Africa, which led to her meeting Ethiopian emperor Halie Selassie and touring the continent herself. She also spoke and lectured on the history of blacks in aviation, and spoke at her alma mater for the inauguration of Dr. Johnnetta Cole, Spelman's first black president.

In 1985 Bragg was awarded the Bishop Wright Air Industry Award, an annual award given for outstanding achievement in aviation. She died in 1993. "I hope that by remembering the golden rule," Bragg wrote in her autobiography, "I have done as much for others as others have done for me."

See also
Roosevelt, Eleanor; Women's Airforce Service Pilots (WASPS)
References
Bragg and Kriz, *Soaring above Setbacks: The Autobiography of Janet Harmon Bragg* (1996); Hardesty and Pisano, *Black Wings: The American Black in Aviation* (1983); Holden and Griffith, *Ladybirds II: The Continuing Story of American Women in Aviation* (1993)

Brasseur, Deanna

The first woman to fly fighter planes for the Canadian Air Force (CAF), Brasseur was born in Pembroke, Ontario, in 1952. After high school she studied to be a teacher for one year before deciding that her real desire was to have a military career, as did her father, an officer in the Royal Canadian Air Force (RCAF).

Brasseur entered the military in September 1972 as a private; her first assignment was as an administrative clerk. In 1973 she applied to and was accepted for officer training. She graduated in October as a lieutenant. She was assigned to the North Bay Air Force Base as the second female air weapons controller in the CAF. Nora Bottomley had been the first.

In 1977 Brasseur was the officer in charge of the training program for the North American Radar Defense (NORAD) unit stationed at Duluth, Minnesota. In 1978 she was promoted to the rank of captain. That year she also met Bottomley, who shared her desire to fly for the military, and Bottomley explained her plan to be prepared for that possibility when it came. Brasseur immediately began working toward her private pilot's license to be prepared as well.

In November 1979 Brasseur, along with Bottomley and Leah Mosher, became one of the first three women to train as a pilot for the CAF. The three passed training and took their assignments; Brasseur's was at the Canadian Air Force Base at Moose Jaw. There she applied to be a jet flight instructor, but that job area was not yet open to women. Brasseur argued for the position and won.

After four-and-a-half years as an instructor Brasseur took part in a task force studying whether or not women could function successfully as fighter pilots. In 1986 the study approved women for fighter-jet training, and Brasseur was posted to the Cold Lake CAF base to learn to fly the T-33 jet. She was the first woman to earn that opportunity.

In 1987 Brasseur became qualified for instrument flight, and in 1989 she was promoted to the rank of major. In 1990 she was made director of flight safety for the CAF and stationed at the National Defense Headquarters in Ottawa.

Of her early years as a pilot, during which she was often the only woman pilot on a base, Brasseur remembered: "I often got the feeling that I didn't really belong. I'd walk into a strange Mess in a flight suit; people would stare at me and I'd get that insecure feeling. I'd think, 'Do I drink my beer and run or do I pretend I belong here and stay?'" Brasseur stayed.

See also
Bottomley, Nora; Mosher, Leah
References
Render, *No Place for a Lady: The Story of Canadian Women Pilots, 1928–1992* (1992)

Brick, Katherine "Kay" Adams Menges

An officer in both the Civil Air Patrol (CAP) and the Women's Airforce Service Pilots (WASPS), Brick was born on August 8, 1910, in Dixmont, Maine. Though she took her first airplane ride at the age of 24, Brick completed her college degree in psychology and took a position teaching physical education before investigating aviation as a career.

At the onset of World War II the CAP was empowered to enlist, organize, and operate a volunteer corps of civilian airmen with their own aircraft and equipment for emergency wartime tasks. To qualify, Brick studied engineering and aerodynamics in night school and took flight lessons at Teterboro Airport; she then signed on as a lieutenant. She continued to accrue flight hours, hoping to qualify as a pilot for the British Air Transport Auxiliary (ATA). At the time the ATA was the only group accepting women recruits as full-time pilots. But Brick's timing was off: By the time she qualified, the United States was no longer allowing women to go abroad to join the ATA.

Brick joined the newly organized WASPS, which had been created by Jacqueline Cochran, and flew with them for the duration of the war. When the WASPS were deactivated in December 1944 Brick tried to return to teaching, but aviation called her. She took a job selling airplanes and flight lessons for L. Bambergers and Co. She also became an aviation writer.

In 1946 Brick was awarded the Lady Hay Drummond-Hay Award for outstanding achievement in aviation. As a former officer of the WASPS, Brick had the opportunity to join the Air Force Reserve, but she was denied entry because she had a child under the age of 18.

In 1950 Brick was elected president of the Ninety-Nines and remained on the executive board for four years after her term expired. She authored *Thirty Sky Blue Years—The History of the Ninety Nines.*

Brick was also race chairman for the All-Women's Transcontinental Air Race, sponsored by the Ninety-Nines, for 25 years of its 30-year existence.

In 1978 Brick was enrolled in the Aviation Hall of Fame in Teterboro, New Jersey. After renewing her pilot's license for 50 years running and passing the age of 80, Brick was invited to join the United Flying Octogenarians (UFOs). She died on July 30, 1995.

Regarding women's place in aviation, Brick said: "We know the future is predicated on the past, more than ever the doors for women have opened wide. Pick your goal and do it! An aviation career for a woman today presents such an exciting world, truly around the world, above and beyond."

See also
All-Women's Transcontinental Air Race (AWTAR); Civil Air Patrol (CAP); Cochran, Jacqueline; Ninety-Nines; Women's Airforce Service Pilots (WASPS)
References
Holden and Griffith, *Ladybirds II: The Continuing Story of American Women in Aviation* (1993)

British All-Women's Flying Meeting
Organized by a group of renowned British female aviators, including Mary Tribe du Caurroy, the Duchess of Bedford, this meet was staged in 1931 at the Sywell Aerodrome. Attended by the likes of Mary Petre, the event helped to boost the idea that women are capable at the controls of any new invention.

See also
du Caurroy, Mary Tribe, Duchess of Bedford; Petre, Mary
References
Lomax, *Women of the Air* (1987); Moolman, *Women Aloft* (1981)

Georgia "Tiny" Broadwick (September 17, 1920)

Broadwick, Georgia "Tiny"
The first woman to make a parachute jump from a plane, Broadwick was born in 1893. She began her career in aviation by parachuting from balloons at county fairs and carnivals. On June 21, 1912, at the age of 18, Broadwick made her first jump from a plane, which was flying 1,000 feet above Griffith Park Aviation Field in Los Angeles, California.

In 1915 Broadwick became the first person to demonstrate parachutes to the U.S. Army. Although she traded parachute jumps for flying lessons, Broadwick never applied for a pilot's license. When she retired from aviation in 1922 she had made over 900 jumps. She died in 1978.

References
Holden and Griffith, *Ladybirds II: The Continuing Story of American Women in Aviation* (1993)

Laura Bromwell (August 14, 1920)

Bromwell, Laura

Although many women earned pilot's licenses at the dawn of aviation, civilian flying was banned during World War I. Bromwell, born in 1898, was the first woman to gain a pilot's license when this ban was lifted. She had become interested in flying when Ruth Law stopped in Bromwell's hometown, Cincinnati, Ohio, on a Liberty Loan Drive during the war. She earned her license on October 22, 1919. Soon after, she joined the newly formed Women's Aviation Corps of the New York City Police Reserves, a volunteer organization created to assist with police work. She was 21 at the time.

Without financial support from the city the corps soon folded, leaving Bromwell with an unpaid commission as a police lieutenant. On February 17, 1920, she became the first woman to pilot a commercial flight over the city, dropping leaflets announcing a new movie premiere over the New York City theater district.

On August 20, 1920, Bromwell broke the then-current record for consecutive loop-the-loops by flying 87 of them at the rededication of the Curtiss Aerodrome at Mineola, New York. On May 21, 1921, she more than doubled her original record by flying 199 consecutive loop-the-loops.

Just two weeks later, on June 5, 1921, Bromwell was performing loop-the-loops in a new plane, lost control of the craft, and crashed. At the time she was not wearing a safety belt because it prevented her from reaching the rudder pedals of the plane. She died on impact.

Her devotion to aviation had been stated not long before the crash: "I am willing to give my whole life to an airplane. I don't want to marry and I do not want to devote myself to anything else in the world."

See also
Law, Ruth; Safety Belts/Safety Harnesses
References
Holden and Griffith, *Ladybirds II: The Continuing Story of American Women in Aviation* (1993); Moolman, *Women Aloft* (1981); Roseberry, *The Challenging Skies: The Colorful Story of Aviation's Most Exciting Years, 1919–1939* (1966)

Brown, Jill Elaine

The first African American woman to fly for a major passenger airline in the United States, Brown was born in Baltimore, Maryland.

At 17 she learned to fly, and for her eighteenth birthday she received a Cherokee 180D airplane. She dreamed of becoming a commercial pilot, but on her mother's advice she majored in home economics at the University of Maryland. Brown became a teacher after graduation, but she still dreamed of flying. In 1974 the U.S. Naval Air Force began accepting women for officer's training. Knowing the military would offer extensive pilot training, Brown signed up, but she found that the military was not yet ready for minorities. She took her honorable discharge six months later and decided she would have to fund her future pilot training herself.

She read about a small commuter airline in North Carolina run by a prominent African American businessman and called for a job. She sold tickets for a salary and copiloted flights to earn more hours in the air. Through this job she logged 1,200 flying hours, the requirement for most major airlines.

Brown was hired by a new start-up airline, but she soon realized she was being assigned to more publicity shots as "the first African American female airline pilot" than to planes. She resigned and took a job flying cargo for Zantop International Airlines in Detroit on October 2, 1978.

"Someone once said that to be a success you must find a need, then fill that need," Brown said when asked about her tenacity. "I felt women would someday have a chance in aviation, and I was determined to be ready for it."

References

Smith, *Breakthrough: Women in Aviation* (1981)

Brown, Willa

See Chappell, Willa Beatrice Brown

Brown, Winifred

The first woman to win the Kings Cup Air Race, the most famous cross-country event in England, Brown was a successful yachtswoman and ice hockey player before entering aviation.

She won the Kings Cup Air Race in 1930 flying her Avro Avian biplane. Then she and her plane embarked on a publicity tour that included a stop at the London Coliseum.

References

Cadogan, *Women with Wings: Female Flyers in Fact and Fiction* (1993)

Bruce, the Honorable Mrs. Victor

See Petre, Mary

Bryant, Alys McKey

The first woman to fly in Washington, Oregon, Idaho, or Canada, Bryant, who was born circa 1890, picked up where Harriet Quimby left off. Like Quimby, Bryant was a daredevil, driving cars and riding motorcycles long before it was acceptable for women to do so. Therefore she was eager to sign up when the Bennett Aero Company advertised for exhibition flyers. Bryant was offered the job and the use of an airplane if she could rebuild the recently wrecked craft herself. She did. Each time it crashed thereafter, Bryant made her own repairs.

Though she never bothered to test for her pilot's license, during her first exhibition flight, on May 3, 1913, Bryant became the first woman to fly in Washington, Oregon, or Idaho. On May 29, 1913, she married the Bennett Company's chief pilot, Johnny Bryant, in a secret ceremony. In celebration, she set out to break the women's altitude record, which she did, reaching 2,900 feet on July 17, 1913. In August of that year she became the first woman to fly in Canada at an air meet attended by the Prince of Wales and the Duke of York. Tragically, during this same meet Bryant watched as her husband crashed to his death. He was the first pilot killed in that country.

Bryant traveled the country in her grief, taking jobs as a movie stunt pilot in California and as a test pilot for the Benoist Airplane Company in St. Louis in 1915. In 1916 she took a job as an instructor for the Scientific Aeroplane Company in Stratford, Connecticut.

At the outbreak of World War I Bryant applied to the Army Air Service as a pilot, but like Katherine Stinson and other barnstormers of her day, she was rejected. She moved to Akron, Ohio, to construct balloons and dirigibles at the Goodyear Tire and Rubber Company for the war effort.

For her feats in the early days of aviation, Bryant became one of only six women invited to join an exclusive group of barnstorming pilots known as the Early Birds.

See also
Early Birds; Quimby, Harriet; Stinson, Katherine
References
Holden and Griffith, *Ladybirds II: The Continuing Story of American Women in Aviation* (1993)

Bureau of Air Commerce

The Air Marking Division of the Bureau of Air Commerce (BAC) was the first U.S. government program or department conceived and directed entirely by women. Oddly enough, it also had the distinction of being both prowomen and antiwomen throughout its history. In 1934 Phoebe Fairgrave Omlie, special assistant for air intelligence of the National Advisory Committee for Aeronautics (NACA), convinced the chief of this section of the BAC to institute a program in which each state would identify its cities from the air. Where possible, a marker with the name of the nearest town was painted on the roof of prominent buildings at 15-mile intervals.

In 1935 Omlie chose five leading women pilots as field representatives for the program: Louise Thaden, Helen Richey, Blanche Noyes, Nancy Harkness Love, and Helen McCloskey. (This was also the year the BAC proposed to ground female pilots for nine days each month during and around their menstrual periods, but the BAC backed down after a protest by the Ninety-Nines.)

By the middle of 1936, 30 states were actively involved in the air marking program, with approvals given for 16,000 markers at a cost of about $1 million. In 1939 the BAC was incorporated into the Civil Aeronautics Administration (CAA),

and the marking program was expanded. During World War II, however, the Air Marking Division markings were removed so that they could not aid enemy flyers, but they were repainted and the program expanded after the war ended.

After World War II Omlie returned to the NACA, and Blanche Noyes was promoted to head the Air Marking Division of the CAA. Noyes believed that it was critical not only to replace the airport markings that had been removed during the war but also to add even more navigational aids.

See also
Civil Aeronautics Administration; Love, Nancy Harkness; Ninety-Nines; Noyes, Blanche Wilcox; Omlie, Phoebe Fairgrave; Richey, Helen; Thaden, Louise McPhetridge
References
Oakes, *United States Women in Aviation: 1930–1939* (1985)

Butler, Ruth

The first woman to fly over both the North and South Poles, Butler began as an aviation mechanic in the 1940s. She learned mechanics in high school in Maine but did not start flying lessons until 1946. On June 13, 1952, Butler soloed and earned her first pilot's license.

In 1953 Butler signed on as the flight technician for an expedition that flew over both poles.

Her dream in flying had been "to own an airplane and to fly and service it myself and prove that there is a place for women in aviation. Nothing glamorous. Nothing sensational."

References
Douglas, *United States Women in Aviation, 1940–1985* (1990)

Cagle, Yvonne Darlene

An astronaut candidate in 1996, Cagle was born in West Point, New York, on April 24, 1959. Her family moved to California, where Cagle attended high school and college. When she decided to become a doctor she applied to the Health Professions Scholarship Program of the U.S. Air Force and studied biochemistry at San Francisco State University. Cagle received her B.A. and her officer's commission in 1981.

For her Ph.D. in medicine Cagle attended the University of Washington and interned at Highland General Hospital in Oakland, California. She received certification in aerospace medicine from the School of Aerospace Medicine at Brooks Air Force Base in Texas in 1988.

In 1989 Cagle volunteered to assist the STS-30 *Atlantis* shuttle mission as an air force medical liaison officer. The *Atlantis* crew was assigned to test the *Magellan* spacecraft. Cagle's assignment was to provide rescue and evacuation of the shuttle crew in case of emergency at the trans-Atlantic landing site in Banjul in Gambia.

On her return to the United States, Cagle worked for her certification as a senior aviation medical examiner from the Federal Aviation Administration, which she received in 1995. For this certification Cagle actively participated in medical support and rescue on a variety of aeromedical missions.

In 1994 she was named the deputy project manager for Kelsey-Seybold Clinics, where she practiced medicine at the National Aeronautics and Space Administration (NASA)–Johnson Space Center (JSC) Occupational Health Clinic. Cagle performed routine health screenings on NASA personnel and designed medical protocols and conducted screenings for NASA remote-duty operations.

In 1996 Cagle applied and was selected by NASA as an astronaut candidate.

See also
Atlantis Space Shuttle
References
Biographical Data Sheets, Lyndon B. Johnson Space Center (1997)

Carl, Ann Baumgartner

The first woman to fly a jet fighter, Carl earned this opportunity through her participation in the Women's Airforce Service Pilots (WASPS) during World War II. After graduation from the program, she was assigned to the Wright Field, Ohio. There Carl checked out on every fighter and bomber that was available between 1943 and 1944, including America's first jet fighter, the Bell YP-59.

See also
Women's Airforce Service Pilots (WASPS)
References
Douglas, *United States Women in Aviation, 1940–1985* (1990); Noggle, *For God, Country, and the Thrill of It: Women Airforce Service Pilots in World War II* (1990)

Caurroy, Mary du

See du Caurroy, Mary Tribe, Duchess of Bedford

Challenger Disaster Investigation

On January 28, 1986, the space shuttle *Challenger* exploded 72 seconds after takeoff, killing all seven crewmembers on board, including America's second woman in space, Mission Specialist Judith Resnick, and the first civilian woman in space, Sharon Christa McAuliffe. The investigation into the explosion began almost immediately.

The Presidential Commission appointed to investigate the disaster by President Ronald Reagan was chaired by former secretary of state William Rogers and was therefore referred to as the Rogers Commission. It included former astronaut Neil Armstrong, former test pilot Chuck Yeager, Pulitzer Prize–winning physicist Richard Feynman, and the first U.S. woman in space, astronaut Sally Ride, the only female shuttle astronaut on the commission.

The Rogers Commission report was released in June 1986, six months after the disaster, and it pointed to the O-rings that sealed the joints between the solid rocket boosters as the malfunction. It also announced publicly that O-rings had been damaged on 14 of the previous 24 shuttle missions, causing concern among the engineers at the National Aeronautics and Space Administration (NASA), Cape Canaveral, and Morton Thiokol, the manufacturer of the solid rocket boosters. Reports on the possible malfunction of these O-rings in cold-weather launches had been made but ignored by management and never communicated to the astronauts. More important, the commission learned that concerns over the O-rings had worried Morton Thiokol engineers the night before the launch. The O-rings had performed poorly during a launch at 53 degrees. The temperature for the January 28, 1986, launch was 29 degrees.

One of the new policies enacted after the announcement of the Rogers Com-mission report was to provide a greater role for astronauts and engineers in decisions about future launches. Another was to create and finance an escape system for astronauts in emergencies. None had been provided for the shuttles thus far because of budget constraints.

In 1988 reporter Tony Chiu interviewed Roger Boisjoly, an aerospace engineer at Morton Thiokol, about the tragedy. In regard to the lack of information sharing between departments, Boisjoly said: "If those with information don't bring it forth, how are you ever going to stop accidents from occurring again? I am not a loose cannon trying to get even with anybody. Say somebody's approaching the edge of a cliff. Would you whisper, or would you scream?"

See also
Challenger Space Shuttle; McAuliffe, Sharon Christa; Resnick, Judith Arlene; Ride, Sally Kristen
References
Anzovin, *The Reference Shelf: Our Future in Space* (1991); Bond, *Heroes in Space: From Gagarin to Challenger* (1987)

Challenger Space Shuttle

The space shuttle *Challenger* had the distinction of carrying America's first woman in space, Sally Ride, on her first mission in 1983. It also had the sad distinction of carrying America's second woman in space, Judith Resnik, and the first civilian woman in space, Sharon Christa McAuliffe, to their deaths.

Challenger was the second orbiter to become operational at Kennedy Space Center and was named after an American naval research vessel that sailed the Atlantic and Pacific Oceans during the 1870s. The *Challenger* space shuttle joined the National Aeronautics and Space Administration (NASA) fleet in July 1982 and flew nine successful space shuttle missions.

Ride became the first American woman in space on June 18, 1983. As a mission specialist on the seventh mission of the space shuttle *Challenger*, Ride and the crew launched two satellites, and she operated the shuttle's remote-control arm. In October 1984 Ride returned for a second flight on *Challenger*, joined by Kathryn Sullivan, America's third woman in space. It was the first shuttle mission to have two female astronauts.

Near the end of that mission, on October 11, 1984, Sullivan became the first American woman to perform a spacewalk. She and Mission Specialist David Leetsma tested a new satellite refueling technique outside the safety of the space shuttle.

Mission Specialist Bonnie Dunbar's first shuttle flight was on board *Challenger* from October 30 to November 6, 1985. This was the first mission to carry eight crewmembers, the largest to fly in space. It was also the first to be sponsored by a foreign country, in this case, West Germany. *Challenger* conducted 76 experiments for western European countries, including materials-processing experiments and tests on a new orbital navigation system.

On January 28, 1986, the *Challenger* and its seven-member crew, including Resnick and McAuliffe, were lost 72 seconds after launch when a booster rocket failure resulted in the breakup of the vehicle.

After canceling his State of the Union address, scheduled for that same evening, President Ronald Reagan held a press conference to praise the crew and said: "The crew of the space shuttle *Challenger* honored us by the manner in which they lived their lives. We will never forget them, nor the last time we saw them, this morning, as they prepared for their journey and waved good-bye, and 'slipped the surly bonds of Earth to touch the face of God.'"

See also
Dunbar, Bonnie J.; McAuliffe, Sharon Christa; Resnick, Judith Arlene; Ride, Sally Kristen; Sullivan, Kathryn
References
Bond, *Heroes in Space: From Gagarin to Challenger* (1987)

Chalons Airfield

Chalons airfield in France, where the first woman to receive her pilot's license, Raymonde de Laroche, studied and soloed, was owned and operated by Charles and Gabriel Voisin. There they built and tested planes of their own design and took on students.

See also
Laroche, Baroness Raymonde de
References
Moolman, *Women Aloft* (1981)

Chappell, Willa Beatrice Brown

The first African American woman to become an officer in the Civil Air Patrol (CAP), Chappell was born in Glasgow, Kentucky, on January 22, 1906. She was raised in Indiana and graduated from high school in 1923. After attending Indiana State Teacher's College she moved to Chicago in 1932 in search of work. The city was still talking about the loss of Bessie Coleman, the first African American woman aviator, nearly six years earlier.

While continuing her education at Northwestern University, where Chappell earned a master's degree in business education, she also began working for her pilot's license. In 1934 she enrolled in the Aeronautical University of Chicago's airplane mechanic class. After receiving her Master Mechanic Certificate in 1935, Chappell took flight lessons at the Harlem Airport near her home in Illinois.

After qualifying for her own license she began training other African Americans, teaching ground school at night and giving flight lessons on the weekend. Chappell taught aviation in high schools to interest young African Americans in the profession. For that she was voted vice president of the Aeronautical Association of Negro Schools in 1941.

In 1942 Chappell became the first African American female member of the CAP. She organized CAP Squadron 613 while serving as the coordinator of war training for the Civil Aeronautics Administration (CAA).

In 1942 Chappell also married Lt. Cornelius Coffee, and together they created the Coffee School of Aeronautics, the first U.S. government–approved school of aviation for African Americans. During her term as director of the Coffee School of Aeronautics, she used her connections in the CAA to have the school chosen to run the studies that led the army to admit African Americans into the Army Air Force. This was the beginning of the Tuskegee Institute.

In the late 1940s Chappell ran for Congress but lost. Her political platform included the establishment of an African American–owned airport in the Chicago area. She was 20 years too early for the civil rights movement.

Instead of a career in politics, Chappell continued to teach aeronautics. She retired from Westinghouse High School in the mid-1970s at the age of 65 and died in 1992.

See also
Civil Aeronautics Administration; Civil Air Patrol (CAP); Coleman, Bessie
References
Douglas, *United States Women in Aviation, 1940–1985* (1990); Holden and Griffith, *Ladybirds II: The Continuing Story of American Women in Aviation* (1993)

Chauvin, Marjorie
Canada's first woman demonstration pilot, Chauvin was born in Edmonton, Alberta, in 1906. When she joined the Edmonton Aero Club, however, the head instructor, a former World War I pilot, refused to teach women to fly. Chauvin did not take no for an answer. She tried to get other women to apply, but after failing to recruit more than one other woman student to the club, she turned to legal procedures. She threatened to sue for discrimination and finally won the right to take lessons.

Chauvin funded her lessons by working in banking and even took out loans when money was low. On December 27, 1929, Chauvin earned her private pilot's license. She transferred her day job to Toronto, where she hoped to find a less discriminatory climate for her aviation ambitions.

There Chauvin studied for her commercial license, attending ground school at Century Airways. She took her first test in May 1932 but did not pass. Chauvin later told friends that the examiner had made improper advances toward her and refused to pass her when she would not comply.

Chauvin joined the Toronto Flying Club to make connections in the aviation world even though she could not afford most of the social events the club sponsored. She registered for the Ladies Class of the Manning Airways Aviation College at the age of 23 and was the only woman to do so. To build up flying hours she took an unpaid job demonstrating planes to customers for the company, thereby becoming the first woman demonstration pilot in Canada. She kept her day job with the bank to support herself.

This work schedule proved too taxing, so in June 1930 Chauvin took a job as a secretary for the Aero Corporation of Canada, offering to demonstrate and ferry newly sold aircraft to customers for no extra salary.

Her husband's illness forced her to retire from flying, but she kept working in the business world to support them.

References

Render, *No Place for a Lady: The Story of Canadian Women Pilots, 1928–1992* (1992)

Chawla, Kalpana

Born in Karnal, India, circa 1960, Chawla graduated from the Tagore School in her hometown in 1976. She attended Punjab Engineering College, where she studied aeronautical engineering and earned her B.S. in 1982. She received her master's degree in the same subject from the University of Texas in 1984 and her doctorate from the University of Colorado in 1988.

After graduation Chawla worked as a research scientist for MCAT Institute, San Jose, California. Her job was to support the National Aeronautics and Space Administration (NASA) research in powered lift as well as in testing flow solvers to parallel computers.

In 1993, after completing her work for MCAT, Chawla was hired as vice president and research scientist for Overset Methods, Inc., in Los Altos, California. She in turn hired and coordinated a team of researchers to work on the problem of aerodynamic optimization. Much of this work Chawla reported at technical conferences and documented in science journals.

In 1994 Chawla applied and was accepted to NASA's astronaut program. After her first year of training she was assigned to work on technical issues for the Astronaut Office EVA/Robotics and Computer Branches. Her first shuttle flight assignment was as mission specialist on the crew of the *Columbia* space shuttle for mission STS-87 in October 1997.

The 16-day mission was fraught with problems from the start. The $10 million *Spartan* science satellite the shuttle was commissioned to release malfunctioned and gathered no scientific data. It had to

Astronaut Kalpana Chawla on the flight deck of the space shuttle Columbia *(1997)*

be retrieved from an uncontrollable spin by use of a spacewalk and returned with the crew to earth. Chawla was the mission specialist in charge of the robot arm that released the satellite. She had better success with testing the roving robotic camera.

In an article in the April 1997 issue of *Hinduism Today International*, Chawla was quoted as saying: "Do something because you really want to do it. If you're doing it just for the goal, and don't enjoy the path, then I think you're cheating yourself."

See also
Columbia Space Shuttle
References
Biographical Data Sheets, Lyndon B. Johnson Space Center (1997); Melwani, "Sky's Not the Limit" (1977); "Shuttle Returns; Inquiry Due on Errant Satellite" (1997)

Cheung, Katherine

The first Asian American woman to earn her private pilot's license, Cheung was born in China in 1904. Her parents sent her to the United States to study music at the University of Southern California when she was 17. She dropped out of college three years later, married her father's business partner, and had two daughters of her own.

In 1932 Cheung took her first plane ride as a passenger. It inspired her to take lessons as a pilot immediately. She soloed after 12 and a half hours of lessons and began appearing in air shows performing loop-to-loops and barrel rolls. In 1934 members of the Chinese community in Los Angeles pooled their money to buy Cheung her own plane. In 1935 she joined the Ninety-Nines, the first organization dedicated to female pilots. There Cheung

Katherine Cheung (second from left, back row) poses with other Ninety-Nines. She was the first Asian American woman to earn a pilot's license.

met and later flew with the likes of Amelia Earhart and Pancho Barnes.

Cheung entered several cross-country races, but having an older airplane kept her from being truly competitive. She used the accompanying publicity, however, to give speeches advocating aviation as a career for other Chinese women in the towns from which the races emanated.

In 1937 Japan invaded China, and Cheung's supporters purchased a new plane for her so that she could fly to China to teach her compatriots how to fly to help defend their homeland. However, a cousin flew the plane first as a prank during the ceremony in which she was to receive it. Tragically, he crashed just after takeoff and died, ruining the airplane as well.

Cheung's father, who had been uncharacteristically supportive of her aviation activities to this point, grew frightened. On his deathbed he made her promise never to fly again. Cheung tried to honor her promise but could not resist the urge to fly again shortly after his death. She continued flying until 1942 and then retired.

See also
Barnes, Florence Lowe "Pancho"; Earhart, Amelia Mary; Ninety-Nines
References
Rasmussen, "China's Amelia Earhart Got Her Wings Here" (1998)

Church, Ellen

Church, the first flying nurse to be awarded the Air Medal in the European war theater during World War II and the first airline stewardess in the world, was born in Iowa.

Her first dream in life was to be a nurse. As a child during World War I she knitted for the Belgian refugees and rolled bandages for soldiers at the Red Cross. The summer after her high school graduation she worked for a local doctor until she could enter the University of Minnesota Nurses' Training School.

While she was an instructor for nurses in San Francisco, Church also studied for her pilot's license. In early 1930 she suggested to United Airlines the idea of using trained nurses on flights to assuage passengers' fears about air travel. The airline experimented by hiring Church and seven other nurses. On May 15, 1930, Church became the first airline stewardess, serving sandwiches on a Boeing air transport flight from San Francisco to Cheyenne, Wyoming. Stewardess's duties also included cleaning the cabin and helping the mechanics push the aircraft back into the hangar. The starting salary was $125 a month for 100 hours of work.

The idea was so successful the other airlines began to copy it. Stewardess applicants were required to have nursing degrees until World War II escalated and nurses were far more necessary on the battlefields.

Church stayed with United Airlines until a car accident injured her foot. She returned to college, earning a B.S. in nursing education in 1936. Then she was hired as chief nurse of the Children's Department at Milwaukee County Hospital.

In 1942 Church entered the Air Evacuation Service of the Army Nurse Corps. After training she was commissioned as a captain assigned to the 802nd Medical Air Evacuation Transport Squadron and was sent to North Africa.

Prior to D-Day Church was assigned to train the nurses who would assist in that medical evacuation. She ended the war as an instructor in flight nursing at the Army Air Force School of Aviation Medicine.

In September 1944 Church was awarded the Air Medal in the European war theater for "meritorious achievement as a flight nurse while participating in a large number of difficult and dangerous air evacuation missions."

References
Knapp, *New Wings for Women* (1946)

Civil Aeronautics Administration

A government agency largely staffed by women during World War II, the Civil Aeronautics Administration (CAA) was created by the Civil Aeronautics Act, signed into law on June 23, 1938, to promote and regulate civil aviation. It directly "encouraged the development of an air transportation system properly adapted to present and future needs of foreign and domestic commerce of the United States, of the Postal Service, and of the national defense." Initially concerned with regulating air routes and passenger and cargo fares, including the U.S. mail, the agency later involved itself with safety regulation, accident investigations, and airport development.

One aspect of safety regulation involved testing and licensing pilots, mechanics, inspectors, and other aviation professionals through a string of schools authorized by the CAA to provide proper instruction in those areas. The CAA also issued airworthiness certificates to new aircraft before they could be mass produced and sold.

In 1939 the Bureau of Air Commerce, whose major function was to extend the airway system and bring it up-to-date, was incorporated into the CAA.

In 1941 under the threat of World War II the CAA's annual budget rose from $27 million to $77 million, most of which was spent on airport building and pilot training. The war had other effects on the agency. On December 8, 1941, the day after Pearl Harbor was bombed by the Japanese, the CAA revoked 100,000 pilot's licenses, recertifying only those pilots who would furnish proof of citizenship, be fingerprinted for an identification card, and take a loyalty oath. Planes were also confiscated until such measures were taken. The war years were also the period of the most employment opportunities for women in the CAA, as men were drafted into the army.

Applicants with basic secretarial skills who were between 17 and 40 years of age were actively recruited for jobs as aircraft communicators, which involved training in radio telegraph, radio telephone, and teletype equipment. Those with pilot's licenses helped fill administrative positions or were employed as ground school, flight, and maintenance supervisors at airfields across the United States.

The major contribution that women made to the CAA was as early air traffic controllers. Those women trained and hired by the CAA were also paid salaries equivalent to those of their male coworkers, a rarity at the time.

The Air Marking Division of the Bureau of Air Commerce of the CAA, headed by Blanche Noyes, was conceived and directed entirely by women.

See also
Noyes, Blanche Wilcox
References
Douglas, *United States Women in Aviation, 1940–1985* (1990); Wilson, *Turbulence Aloft: The Civil Aeronautics Administration amid Wars and Rumors of Wars, 1938–1953* (1979)

Civil Air Patrol (CAP)

One of the few government organizations to accept women pilots, the Civil Air Patrol (CAP) was created as a branch of the Office of Civilian Defense in preparation for the U.S. entry into World War II. Established on December 1, 1941, the CAP was empowered to enlist, organize, and operate a volunteer corps of civilian airmen with their own aircraft and equipment for wartime tasks associated with the outbreak of World War II. The organization of such a group helped to bolster national security, and for nonmilitary pilots it was the only way to continue flying during the war years.

The stated purpose of the CAP was to weld civil airmen and women into a force for national defense by increasing knowledge and skill in every type of aviation activity. CAP members were capable of taking over civilian aviation jobs including coast and forest patrols, ferrying operations, and radio operations in order to free military aviators for active war service. CAP pilots also flew on search missions for planes downed in training and delivered shipments from defense plants to army depots. The group came under the control of the U.S. Air Force in 1943.

The CAP helped women gain work in aviation almost accidentally: By contracting out their training to already established flight schools and instructors they were sending business to the many women in aviation who were left on the home front and offered opportunities to many other women aviators. These included such famous women as actress Mary Astor, who costarred in *The Maltese Falcon* with Humphrey Bogart and who during the war became a plotting board operator at a coastal patrol base; actress Joan Fontaine, who owned her own plane and joined the CAP branch in California; and Cornelia Fort, who had been a flight instructor in Pearl Harbor on the day of the Japanese bombing and who returned to the mainland soon after and joined the Texas branch of the CAP.

The CAP did not discriminate on the basis of gender or race. Willa Brown Chappell, an African American female pilot, was an officer of the CAP. Female interest in the group was so high even after the war years that they developed the CAP Cadets for teenage girls, a club where prominent pilots like CAP Lieutenant Colonel Ruth Nichols frequently spoke.

When the Women's Airforce Service Pilots (WASPS) were deactivated on December 20, 1944, many of their members joined their local CAP squadrons. After the war the CAP became a permanent peacetime institution on July 1, 1946.

Regarding women in the CAP, Georgette Chapelle wrote: "Women are ac-cepted in the patrols as equals with men in flying, in leadership, in the suppression of temperament. It's up to you to prove that this is the basis on which you want to remain, for every girl who accepts discipline cheerfully makes it easier for the next ten girls to follow her pioneering."

See also
Chappell, Willa Beatrice Brown; Fort, Cornelia; Nichols, Ruth Rowland; Women's Airforce Service Pilots (WASPS)
References
Boyne, *Beyond the Wild Blue: A History of the U.S. Air Force, 1947–1997* (1997); Holden and Griffith, *Ladybirds II: The Continuing Story of American Women in Aviation* (1993); Wilson, *Turbulence Aloft: The Civil Aeronautics Administration amid Wars and Rumors of Wars, 1938–1953* (1979)

Clark, Julia
The third woman to earn a pilot's license and the first American woman to die in an airplane accident, Clark was actually English by birth. Born in London circa 1890, she immigrated with her family to the United States. After obtaining her citizenship Clark married and settled in Denver, Colorado, before catching the flying bug.

Clark studied flying at the Curtiss Flying School in San Diego, California, and became the first woman to complete the class successfully. She earned her pilot's license on May 19, 1912. Like Harriet Quimby and Matilde Moisant, the first and second licensed women pilots, Clark joined an exhibition flying team to earn money from her flying.

She died on June 17, 1912, while taking a test flight at dusk near Springfield, Illinois. The wing of Clark's plane struck a tree, and the plane flipped over and crashed. She was crushed by the heavy, rear-mounted engine, which broke loose on impact and pinned Clark beneath the wreckage.

See also
Moisant, Matilde; Quimby, Harriet
References
Cadogan, *Women with Wings: Female Flyers in Fact and Fiction* (1993); Holden and Griffith, *Ladybirds: The Untold Story of Women Pilots in America* (1991)

Clark, Laurel Blair Salton

Astronaut candidate Clark was born Laurel Blair Salton in Ames, Iowa, in 1961. Her family soon moved to Racine, Wisconsin, where Clark attended high school and college. She received her B.S. in zoology from the University of Wisconsin–Madison in 1983 and her Ph.D. in medicine there in 1987.

Clark joined the navy during medical school and did active duty training with the Diving Medicine Department at the Naval Experimental Diving Unit in March 1987. Then she finished her postgraduate medical education in pediatrics at the naval hospital in Bethesda, Maryland, in 1988. In 1989 she completed training as a navy undersea medical officer and as a diving medical officer.

As both a radiation health officer and undersea medical officer, Clark was posted at Submarine Squadron 14's Medical Department in Holy Loch, Scotland. Her work there involved assisting in medical evacuations from U.S. submarines and working with navy Seals. To become a naval flight surgeon Clark attended six months of aeromedical training at the Naval Aerospace Medical Institute in Pensacola, Florida, in 1991.

Clark was then posted as flight surgeon to the Marine Corps AV-8B Night Attack Harrier Squadron, providing medical treatment in a variety of deployments around the world. That year her squadron won commendation as the Marine Attack Squadron of the Year.

In April 1996 Clark, then married to Jonathan B. Clark, a U.S. Navy captain, applied and was accepted to NASA's astronaut training program.

See also
U.S. Navy (USN)
References
Biographical Data Sheets, Lyndon B. Johnson Space Center (1997)

Clarke-Washington, Patrice

The only African American woman holding the rank of captain for a major airline, Clarke-Washington was born on September 11, 1961. She graduated from Embry-Riddle Aeronautical University and took her first job with Trans Island Airways and Bahamasair.

She left this position to become a DC-8 flight engineer for United Parcel Service, and in November 1994 Clarke-Washington was promoted to the rank of captain.

Regarding her position as one of the few women flying for a major airline, Clarke-Washington has said: "I think having grown up in a single-parent family home, where there was no male role model, it wasn't a matter of boys do certain things and girls do certain other things. I suppose, if anything, growing up, I always thought if somebody could do it, I could do it, too. I think it was to my advantage, because I didn't have the stereotypes. I've met a lot of people since I've become captain, in particular, a lot of black Americans, who have a mind-set that they can't do certain things because they're black. Fortunately, I didn't have that problem."

References
Russo, *Women and Flight: Portraits of Contemporary Women Pilots* (1997)

Cleave, Mary L.

One of the early National Aeronautics and Space Administration (NASA) female astronauts, Cleave, at 5 foot 2 inches tall, was the smallest chosen. Her height would later keep her out of flight attendant school, but it proved no problem in spaceflight. Cleave was born on February 5, 1947, in Southampton, New York, and she graduated from high school there in 1965.

Cleave attended Colorado State University and received a bachelor of science degree in biological sciences in 1969. For her master of science in microbial ecology (1975) and then her doctorate in civil and environmental engineering (1979) she attended Utah State University.

While working toward those degrees Cleave worked as a research physiologist and research engineer in the Ecology Center and the Utah Water Research Laboratory at the university. She published numerous scientific papers about that work.

In May 1980 Cleave was selected to participate in the astronaut program. While training for her first mission she served NASA in the Shuttle Avionics Integration Laboratory (SAIL) and as a CAPCOM (spaceship communicator) on five space shuttle flights and helped write the *Malfunctions Procedures* book.

On November 26, 1985, Cleave was a mission specialist on board the space shuttle *Atlantis* for STS-61B. She assisted with the deployment of the MORELOS-B, AUSSAT II, and SATCOM K-2 communications satellites. This was the heaviest payload weight carried to orbit by the space shuttle to date. Cleave's first mission ended on December 3, 1985. That same year Cleave was a recipient of the NASA Space Flight Medal. In 1988 she received the NASA Exceptional Service Medal.

On her second spaceflight, from May 4 to May 8, 1989, Cleave was back on *Atlantis* as a mission specialist on the crew of STS-30. Cleave and her fellow crew members deployed the *Magellan* Venus-exploration spacecraft, the first planetary probe to be deployed from the shuttle. They also studied indium crystal growth and electrical storms and made observations of the earth.

After that flight Cleave worked as special assistant for advanced programs in the Crew Systems and Thermal Division of the Engineering Department at the Johnson Space Center.

See also
Atlantis Space Shuttle
References
Biographical Data Sheets, Lyndon B. Johnson Space Center (1990); Bond, *Heroes in Space: From Gagarin to Challenger* (1987); O'Connor, *Sally Ride and the New Astronauts: Scientists in Space* (1983)

Cobb, Geraldyne "Jerrie"

The first woman to qualify for space travel, Cobb never had the chance to become an astronaut because of gender discrimination. She was born on March 5, 1931, near Norman, Oklahoma, and learned to fly at the age of 12 with her father as her flight instructor. Cobb soloed in March 1947 at the age of 16 and spent the next year financing her advanced lessons with a variety of odd jobs, including picking berries, waxing airplanes, and typing. Cobb received her private pilot's license on her seventeenth birthday in 1948. On her next birthday she earned her commercial pilot's license.

Cobb turned down the chance to go to college to focus her efforts on landing a job as a professional pilot. She bought her first plane with the savings from her job as a member of the Sooner Queens, a semiprofessional women's softball team, and with it obtained her first work as a pilot as a pipeline patroller. She and her colleagues were paid to fly low over the oil pipelines in Oklahoma, Missouri, and Kansas to look for leaks. Cobb received her flight instructor's certificate on her twenty-first birthday, in 1952. This en-

Geraldyne "Jerrie" Cobb (1960)

abled her to take a job as an instructor at an airport in Duncan, Oklahoma.

In 1952 Cobb placed fourth in her first national race, the Transcontinental Air Races. In June 1953 she entered her second, the International Women's Air Race, and again placed fourth. In 1953 Fleetway Ferry Service was looking for pilots to ferry planes to South America, a ten-day round-trip that involved flying over uninhabited jungles, an ocean, and the Andes Mountains. Male pilots were not answering the advertisement, so the company was forced to accept Cobb's application. When she stopped for refueling in Ecuador she was arrested as a spy, and she spent 12 days in jail before the U.S. government arranged for her release.

After two years of flying to South America, Fleetway assigned her the job of ferrying World War II surplus bombers from the United States to France. In the summer of 1955 she quit Fleetway to work as a test pilot in Burbank, California. That fall Cobb was invited by the editor of the *Daily Oklahoman and Times* to publicize the Oklahoma Semi-Centennial Exposition by breaking aviation records in an Oklahoma-built airplane. Cobb accepted.

Her first distance record was for flying from Guatemala City to Oklahoma City on May 25, 1957, in 8 hours, 5 minutes. Three weeks later Cobb broke her first altitude record by flying at 30,361 feet, but because of a broken barograph the record could not be verified. On July 5, 1957, Cobb went back up and flew to a height of 30,560 feet in an Aero Commander manufactured in her home state by Aero Design and Engineering. After she had applied many times, the company hired Cobb as a test pilot. Her first official job for them was to attend the World Congress of Flight in Las Vegas in April 1959. To show off the plane's potential, Cobb established a new world's speed record for the 2,000-kilometer closed course on April 13, 1959. She flew the course in 5 hours, 29 minutes, 27 seconds.

In September 1959 Cobb met Dr. Randolph Lovelace. As the chairman of the National Aeronautics and Space Administration (NASA) Life Sciences Committee for Project Mercury, Lovelace had tested the Mercury astronauts. He wanted to study the effects of space flight on women and asked Cobb to be his first subject. She enthusiastically agreed. Her preparation for the tests involved running 5 miles a day and riding 20 more on a stationary bike. The tests themselves were exactly the ones given to the Mercury astronauts, and Cobb matched the men's statistics on each test. For the isolation test Cobb was immersed up to her neck in an underground water tank; she stayed there for 9 hours, 40 minutes, exceeding the highest of the male astronauts' test times by just over three hours. For "her contributions to the art and science of flight" Cobb was given a special citation by the National Pilot's Association.

NASA was as yet not ready to hire female astronauts, so they thanked Cobb for her time, told her they needed to test other women as extensively as they had tested her, and asked her to keep the project a secret. Cobb returned to the offices of Aero Commander but was suddenly swamped with interviews when the news was leaked. Eventually, the commotion died down enough for Cobb to return to her management duties. She spent her free time giving speeches about the space program to civic groups around the country.

In 1961 NASA invited Cobb to join them as a consultant but did not allow her or any of the 12 other female test subjects, nicknamed the Mercury 13, to become full astronauts in the Mercury program. On July 17, 1962, Cobb testified before Congress in favor of including women in the astronaut corps. Astronaut John Glenn, the first man to orbit the earth, testified against. Cobb lost.

When it was clear that she would not be allowed in the space program as an astronaut, Cobb moved to Brazil and obtained work flying missionaries and medical personnel in and out of remote jungle villages. The first female astronauts were not hired by NASA until 1972. That first class included Shannon Lucid, Rhea Seddon, and Anna Fisher. In 1981 Cobb was nominated for the Nobel Peace Prize for her missionary work in South America.

In her 1963 autobiography Cobb described her love of flying by saying: "For everything there are beginnings and endings, tops and bottoms, sides or limits. There is an end to all things we know on earth. Only two things can we conceive of as infinite: God and the sky. I find one in the other."

See also
Fisher, Anna L.; Lucid, Shannon W.; Mercury 13; Seddon, M. Rhea
References
Briggs, *At the Controls: Women in Aviation* (1991); Cobb and Rieker, *Woman into Space: The Jerrie Cobb Story* (1963)

Cochran, Jacqueline

The first woman to break the sound barrier, Cochran was born in the vicinity of Muscogee, Florida, but no records marked her birth or her surname. She chose May 11 at random and estimated 1906 as the year she was born. She picked her own last name from a phone book when that information became necessary. Orphaned as an infant, she was raised in northern Florida by a poverty-stricken foster family of migrant sawmill workers. They put her to work in the mills early in life.

At 14 Cochran apprenticed herself to a local hairdresser to learn a trade. By the time she was 20 she had left home and was earning a living as a hairdresser and cosmetics saleswoman. Her original interest in flying came as a way to advance her profits as a traveling cosmetics saleswoman by expanding her territory.

Cochran earned her pilot's license in the summer of 1932, after taking lessons for only three weeks. By the end of 1933 she had also earned a commercial pilot's license and her instructor's rating. She divided her time between flying and cosmetics, establishing the Jacqueline Cochran Cosmetics Company in 1935. She designed many of the products herself and was able to finance her flying activities throughout her life from the continued profits of the company.

On May 11, 1936, she married Floyd Odlum, but she continued to use her maiden name in business and in flying. In 1937 she won both the women's national speed record and the women's world speed record. She did not hesitate to use her growing reputation to influence the

Collier Trophy committee. Each year they awarded a prize for a major accomplishment in aviation. Thanks to Cochran's efforts, that year's prize went to Randolph Lovelace, a surgeon with the Mayo Clinic who helped develop an oxygen tank and mask for high-altitude flying. Cochran realized that this apparatus was necessary to achieve further aviation goals.

In 1938 Cochran won the Bendix Transcontinental Air Race, an annual Labor Day event challenging the world's best flyers, male or female, to fly from Los Angeles to Cleveland in record time. Despite a malfunction in her plane's gas intake system, Cochran won the race. She continued her flight to New York City, setting a new world's record of 10 hours, 27 minutes, 55 seconds for transcontinental flight in a propeller-driven craft. She was also awarded the International League of Aviators' Harmon Trophy as best woman pilot of the year. The trophy was presented to her by First Lady Eleanor Roosevelt, who would later support Cochran's efforts to get women pilots involved in World War II.

In 1940 Cochran became president of the Ninety-Nines, a group of female aviators founded by Amelia Earhart to benefit women in aviation. Cochran held the post until 1943, using the position to publicize her views on women pilots and their potential for the military in light of the growing fear of war in the Pacific. On June 17, 1941, Cochran became the first woman to fly a warplane across the Atlantic by flying a Hudson V bomber from Canada to Britain. The flight was a stunt to publicize Britain's desperate need for pilots and equipment for their efforts against Germany in World War II. Cochran also used the stunt to highlight the fact that women could be trusted with military machinery.

The British Air Transport Auxiliary (ATA) then started recruiting women to

Jacqueline Cochran (May 18, 1953)

ferry military planes to airports where they would be readied for missions. They called on Cochran to find American women who would volunteer for the program as well. She found 25 women who signed up for 18 months of service.

The U.S. military set up a similar program, the Women's Auxiliary Ferrying Squadron (WAFS), in the United States but assigned test pilot Nancy Harkness Love to head it. Cochran was given leadership of the Women's Flying Training Detachment (WFTD), a group that recruited novice women pilots and trained them. When the WAFS and the WFTD merged to form the Women's Airforce Service Pilots (WASPS), Cochran became the new group's first director, a job she held for the duration of the war. During this time the WASPS flew more than 60 million miles and delivered over 12,000 planes.

After the war the WASPS were disbanded in December 1944. Cochran looked for work as a test pilot but was dismayed to learn that only active duty air force members were permitted to fly air force planes. Her husband, however, owned a company that provided jets to the military, and he arranged for her to become a company pilot. She was named Pilot of the Decade for the years 1940–1949.

In May 1953 Cochran broke the sound barrier flying an F-86 Saberjet side by side with her trainer, Chuck Yeager, the first man to break the sound barrier. For this feat Cochran became the first woman awarded the Gold Medal by the Fédération Aéronautique Internationale, an international air organization that defines, verifies, and compiles all world records in aviation. She was voted their president in 1958.

In 1960 Cochran's friendship with Dr. Lovelace, who had moved from the Mayo Clinic to NASA, brought her into the space age. Lovelace was operating a privately funded program to give women pilots the same tests the male astronaut candidates were receiving. Not only did Cochran participate in the tests herself, she contributed profits from her still-operating cosmetics business to cover the tests of the other 12 women who participated. Despite their high scores on these tests, NASA would not actively recruit women as astronauts for another 17 years.

In 1964 Cochran flew the Lockheed F-104 Starfighter at twice the speed of sound, her last major aviation accomplishment. In 1971, near the age of 65, Cochran was grounded by a heart attack, after which she needed a pacemaker. In the same year she became the first living woman to be inducted into the Aviation Hall of Fame.

When she died on August 9, 1980, Cochran held over 250 speed, altitude, and distance records, more than any other pilot in the world, male or female. Throughout her career, Cochran was such a visible figure in aviation that she won the Harmon Trophy for best woman pilot of the year 15 times.

"The objective in every one of my flights," she wrote, "was to go faster or farther through the atmosphere or higher into it than anyone else and to bring back some new information about plane, engine, fuel, instruments, air or pilot that would be helpful in the conquest of the atmosphere."

See also

Air Transport Auxiliary (ATA); Earhart, Amelia Mary; Love, Nancy Harkness; Ninety-Nines; Roosevelt, Eleanor; Women's Airforce Service Pilots (WASPS)

References

Cochran and Bucknum, *Jackie Cochran: An Autobiography* (1987); Cochran with Odlum, *The Stars at Noon* (1954); Smith, *Coming Out Right: The Story of Jackie Cochran, the First Woman Aviator to Break the Sound Barrier* (1991)

Coleman, Bessie

The first African American woman to earn a pilot's license, Coleman was born on January 26, 1892, in a one-room cabin in Atlanta, Texas. Before she was two her family moved to Waxahachie, Texas, and established a small cotton farm. Her one-room school closed down for the cotton-picking season so that the children could work in the fields. Despite this constant interruption of her education, Coleman excelled at math and reading. At 18 she moved to Langston, Oklahoma, to attend the Colored Agricultural and Normal University.

In 1915 Coleman moved to Chicago, where she worked as a manicurist in barbershops. Her brother, who had served in France with the all-black Eighth Army National Guard during World War I, returned from the war with stories about French women aviators. Coleman decided that she could match anything he had seen. However, no aviation school in the United States would take black students.

Bessie Coleman (1923)

On the advice of Robert Abbott, the editor of Chicago's largest black newspaper, the *Chicago Defender*, Coleman decided to move to France, where she could take lessons despite her race. It took her a year to learn French and to save the money for the trip and the tuition at a French aviation school. On November 20, 1920, Coleman sailed to France. After ten months of training at the Ecole d'Aviation des Frères Caudron at Le Crotoy, Coleman graduated and received her license from the Fédération Aéronautique Internationale in June of 1921. After further advanced lessons in Paris, Coleman returned to the United States in September 1921. As the first black woman to obtain a pilot's license, she made the front page of the country's black newspapers and the *New York Tribune*.

The publicity, however, did not help her gain employment in aviation. She realized that she would have to join an air circus for money, which would require stunt flying. Coleman returned to France for special training in 1922. On September 3, 1922, Coleman made the first public flight by a black woman in the United States in an air show in New York honoring veterans of the all-black 369th American Expeditionary Force of World War I.

Coleman followed this with a performance at the opening ceremonies of the Negro Tri-State Fair in Memphis, Tennessee, on October 12, 1922. On October 15 she performed for her hometown in a show at Chicago's Roosevelt Field. In December 1922 she contracted to appear as herself in *Shadow and Sunshine*, a film by the African American Seminole Film Producing Company. She walked off the set when she discovered that the script reinforced ugly stereotypes about her race. With her fees for these events Coleman hoped to establish an aviation school for blacks in the United States, a project that required planes, fuel, mechanics, and money. Coleman had none of those things.

She approached the Coast Tire and Rubber Company with an offer to drop advertising leaflets for a fee. When they accepted she traveled to California by train to see the plant, buy a plane, and make the drops. Although many female aviators of the day were rich women and bought the best and most modern planes, Coleman had to settle for an army surplus Curtiss JN-4; it cost $400. In California she arranged a solo show at Palomar Park in Los Angeles on February 4, 1923. Just after takeoff from Santa Monica airport en route to Palomar Coleman's engine stalled and she crashed, suffering a broken leg and fractured ribs. The show was canceled.

Her first post-crash exhibition was in Columbus, Ohio, on September 9, 1923, where she flew a borrowed plane before a crowd of 10,000 spectators. Weather and financial problems kept her from further exhibitions for almost two years until she booked a series of lectures in Texas, start-ing in May 1925. Her first flight in Texas was on June 19, 1925, commemorating Juneteenth, the anniversary of the day slaves in Texas first learned of the Eman-cipation Proclamation. At most of Cole-man's shows she knelt and shared a prayer with her audience before takeoff, flew a few stunts, frequently dropped a parachutist, and then offered rides for cash. Quite often these events were the first opportunity for blacks to take plane rides anywhere in the country.

In September 1925 Coleman performed two shows at Wharton, Texas. She capped the second one off by making a parachute jump. The woman originally hired to do it fell ill, and Coleman did not want to dis-appoint her audience. Plans for her next show for an interracial audience in her hometown of Waxahachie included sepa-rate admission gates for the two races, so Coleman threatened to cancel the show. The organizers capitulated.

Coleman's next tour covered Georgia and Florida and started in January 1926 in Savannah, Georgia. This tour included a large number of lectures because she was unable to afford a new plane and could only fly with the loan of a plane. This lack of funds held up her dream of establishing an aviation school for blacks. While in Orlando Coleman opened a beauty parlor to try to earn money. But even this pressing need for cash could not make Coleman ignore her principles. She was offered a parachute jump at the Or-lando Chamber of Commerce but threat-ened to cancel when she learned the jump would be before an all-white audi-ence. The organizers again capitulated, and blacks were allowed to attend.

Coleman was finally able to buy her own plane again with the financial backing of Edwin Beeman, heir to the Beeman Chewing Gum fortune. Like her first plane, it was an already-outdated model from a surplus sale. It was delivered to her next flying engagement in Jacksonville, Florida, in April 1926. Here Coleman was engaged to lecture around the city and to fly stunts for the Negro Welfare League's Field Day on May 1, 1926.

The day before the show Coleman went for a test flight of the new plane with William D. Wills, the white pilot who had delivered it to her. Wills flew the plane so that Coleman could study the airfield and decide on an appropriate landing site for the show. At 1,000 feet the plane went into a nosedive, and at 500 feet above ground it flipped upside down. Coleman, who wore no safety belt because it hindered her view over the edge of the cockpit, fell to her death. The plane crashed, and Wills died in the fire that followed. His death made the front pages of major newspapers across the country. Only the black-owned newspa-pers covered Coleman's death.

Coleman had frequently been asked about her fears while speaking to her many audiences. Her frequent response: "Do you know you have never lived until you have flown? Of course, it takes one with courage, nerve and ambition. If I can create the minimum of my plans and desires there shall be no regrets."

See also
Fédération Aéronautique Internationale (FAI); Safety Belts/Safety Harnesses
References
Hardesty and Pisano, *Black Wings: The American Black in Aviation* (1983); Patterson, *Memoirs of the Late Bessie Coleman, Aviatrix* (1969); Rich, *Queen Bess, Daredevil Aviator* (1993)

Coleman, Catherine G. "Cady"

Before becoming an astronaut Coleman was a chemist and engineer with the air force. Born in Charleston, South Car-olina, on December 14, 1960, Coleman was raised in Virginia, where she at-tended high school.

She received a B.S. degree in chemistry from the prestigious Massachusetts Institute of Technology (MIT) in 1983, the same year she became a second lieutenant in the U.S. Air Force. Coleman then studied for her doctorate in polymer science and engineering at the University of Massachusetts. In 1988 she was posted as a research chemist to the Materials Directorate of the Wright Laboratory at Wright-Patterson Air Force Base in Dayton, Ohio.

While at Wright-Patterson Coleman volunteered to be a test subject for the centrifuge program at the Crew Systems Directorate of the Armstrong Aeromedical Laboratory, where she set endurance and tolerance records during physiological studies and tests of new equipment.

In 1991 Coleman received her doctorate. She then applied to and was selected by the National Aeronautics and Space Administration (NASA) in March 1992. During astronaut training Coleman also worked for NASA as a flight software verifier and was the backup mission specialist for STS-83. On October 20, 1995, she went into space for the first time as a mission specialist on the *Columbia* space shuttle on STS-73, which studied Spacelab. The mission landed on November 5, 1995. While on the ground Coleman is lead astronaut for long-term spaceflight habitability issues, studying and improving living accommodations for the international space station.

See also
Columbia Space Shuttle
References
Biographical Data Sheets, Lyndon B. Johnson Space Center (1997)

Collins, Eileen
The first woman to pilot the space shuttle and the first to serve as the commander of a shuttle mission, Collins was born on November 19, 1956, in Elmira, New York. Her introduction to aviation came from her father, who took her to the local airport to watch planes take off on weekends. He also brought her to a local glider field, where she was first introduced to nonengine aircraft. Collins earned degrees in mathematics first from Corning Community College in 1976, then from Syracuse University in 1978. A series of part-time jobs, from waitressing to catalogue sales, helped Collins save up for flying lessons. After 40 hours of civilian training she qualified for pilot training in the air force.

In 1979 Collins graduated from air force undergraduate pilot training and became an aircraft commander and instructor in the U.S. Air Force Academy in Colorado for the next four years. At the same time she continued studying for her master of science degree in operations research from Stanford University, a degree that she received in 1986.

While working on her master of arts degree in space systems management from Webster University, Collins served as assistant professor of mathematics at the academy in Colorado, completing both in 1989. Then she entered the Air Force Test Pilot School at Edwards Air Force Base in California. With an accumulated 4,700 hours in 30 types of aircraft, Collins applied to and was accepted into astronaut training by the National Aeronautics and Space Administration (NASA).

In 1991 Collins qualified as a space shuttle pilot. While waiting for her first assignment she was assigned design work on the shuttle and modified its operating systems. In February 1995 she served on board the *Discovery* space shuttle as the pilot of STS-63, which made her the first woman to pilot a space shuttle. This mission was also the first flight of the new joint Russian-American space program and was the first in which a U.S. vessel docked with the *Mir* space station.

Astronaut Eileen Collins occupies the commander's seat on the Atlantis *during a rendezvous with Russia's* Mir *space station (May 1997).*

In May 1997 Collins was again at the controls of the space shuttle *Atlantis*, helping deliver needed backup oxygen tanks to the *Mir* space station.

Regarding breaking the gender barrier as a shuttle pilot, Collins has said: "I don't really think from day to day about being a woman pilot. I'm a shuttle pilot, and I don't get treated any different."

See also
Atlantis Space Shuttle; *Discovery* Space Shuttle; *Mir* Space Station
References
Biographical Data Sheets, Lyndon B. Johnson Space Center (1997); Holden and Griffith, *Ladybirds II: The Continuing Story of American Women in Aviation* (1993); Russo, *Women and Flight: Portraits of Contemporary Women Pilots* (1997)

Columbia Space Shuttle
The *Columbia* space shuttle is the oldest orbiter in the shuttle fleet. It was named after the Boston, Massachusetts–based sloop that in 1792 maneuvered past the dangerous sandbar at the mouth of the Columbia River, which extends more than 1,000 miles through what is today southeastern British Columbia, Canada, and across the Washington-Oregon border. The river was later named after the ship, as was the shuttle.

The *Columbia* space shuttle ushered in the era of reusable spacecraft on April 12, 1981, with mission STS-1. Astronaut Anna Fisher was assigned to the alternate landing site at White Sands, New Mexico, in case medical assistance was needed at an emergency landing. Fisher was also an in-orbit spacecraft communicator (CAPCOM) for the STS-9 mission.

On January 9, 1990, Bonnie Dunbar was a mission specialist aboard the *Columbia* space shuttle. Dr. Dunbar was principal investigator for the microgravity disturbance experiment (MDE) and

The Columbia *(November 19, 1996)*

See also
Baker, Ellen; Chawla, Kalpana; Dunbar, Bonnie J.; Fisher, Anna L.; Helms, Susan J.
References
Biographical Data Sheets, Lyndon B. Johnson Space Center (1997)

Cook, Edith Maud

Cook, born circa 1890, was the first British woman to make a solo flight. She entered aviation first as a professional parachutist, performing under the name Viola Spencer. In, 1910 she worked as an air show flyer for the Graham White Flying School in the Pyrenees under the name Miss Spencer Kavanagh. She continued her parachuting as well, and she died in a jump from a balloon over Coventry, England, in 1910.

References
Cadogan, *Women with Wings: Female Flyers in Fact and Fiction* (1993)

was responsible for the use of the fluids experiment apparatus (FEA) during the flight.

In June 1992 Ellen Baker was a crew member of STS-50 on the *Columbia* space shuttle. On this mission, over a two-week period, she helped conduct experiments in fluid physics, fluid dynamics, and biological and combustion science.

From June 20 to July 7, 1996, Major Susan Helms was the payload commander and flight engineer aboard *Columbia* on the longest mission to date, STS-78. The mission included studies sponsored by ten nations and five space agencies, and was the first mission to combine both a full microgravity studies agenda and a comprehensive life science investigation.

Columbia continues to be important to the history of women in space. In 1997 Mission Specialist Kalpana Chawla was assigned to mission STS-87 for her first flight.

Coughlin, Paula

The naval aviator who broke the story of the sexual harassment at the 1991 Tailhook Convention, Coughlin had an early start in an all-male world. Born in 1961, she was the first female lifeguard hired in her hometown of Virginia Beach, Virginia. She attended Old Dominion University and joined the Reserve Officers' Training Corps (ROTC) program when she was a sophomore. She graduated from college in 1984 and was able to enter the navy as a commissioned officer.

Coughlin trained as a helicopter pilot, graduating in 1987 at the top of her class. After two back-to-back six-month tours attached to a research ship in the Pacific, Coughlin became an aide to a rear admiral at the Pax River, Maryland, Naval Base. Soon another rear admiral, Jack Snyder, came to the base.

With Snyder Coughlin traveled to the annual Tailhook Convention held that year at the Hilton Hotel in Las Vegas, Nevada, in September 1991. There she was assaulted, along with 83 other women, by the so-called Gauntlet, a hallway lined with male naval aviators.

When the press broke the news of the Tailhook sexual harassment scandal of 1991 and the navy nevertheless attempted to hide the facts of the case, Coughlin stepped forward to tell her story. Her speaking out led to her being transferred from the Pax River base and being subjected to fierce attacks on her character. She was then grounded from flying for six months.

During the investigation into Coughlin's allegations in early 1992, she was reassigned to the Helicopter Support Squadron 2 at the Norfolk Naval Air Force Base in Norfolk, Virginia. On June 26, 1992, she was invited to meet President George Bush, a former naval aviator, at the White House. Even with the president pressuring the navy to handle Tailhook fairly, only three men from the Gauntlet were brought to trial for conduct unbecoming an officer, and they were found not guilty based on lack of evidence.

On February 7, 1994, Coughlin resigned from the navy. In her letter she stated that both the attack at Tailhook and the subsequent attacks on her character rendered her unable to serve effectively in the military.

On October 28, 1994, Coughlin won a civil lawsuit against the Hilton Hotel and was awarded $1.7 million in compensatory damages and $5 million in punitive damages.

Despite her treatment by the "old boys" navy and her decision to resign, Coughlin still had hopes for the future of her beloved institution. "There are guys maybe a little younger than me, their wives all work. This is a new generation, and the world is full of two-income families. And a guy starts to think, 'You know, if that happened to my wife in the workplace, I'd kill the bastard.'"

As to her decision to come forward in the Tailhook matter, Coughlin explained: "I had an obligation as an officer to stop what was going on in that hallway. I have an obligation as a human being to let everyone know you have to come forward when something bad like that happens."

See also
Tailhook Sexual Harassment Scandal
References
Vistica, *Fall from Glory: The Men Who Sank the U.S. Navy* (1995); Zimmerman, *Tailspin: Women at War in the Wake of Tailhook* (1995)

Crosson, Marvel

The first casualty of the Women's Air Derby, Crosson was a veteran commercial pilot from Alaska when she entered the race. She and her brother, Joe Crosson, had taught themselves to fly after piecing together their own plane using surplus parts from World War I planes. Born in 1904, Crosson soloed in 1923 and joined the world of stunt flyers to make a living. While at a show in California on May 28, 1929, Crosson set a new women's altitude record for monoplanes, flying at a height of 23,996 feet.

When she entered the first Women's Air Derby at the National Air Races on August 18, 1929, Crosson was favored to win. However, she experienced engine trouble over the mountains near the Gila River in Arizona. The use of parachutes was not yet perfected in 1929, so Crosson bailed out too low for her parachute to open properly. She was found with it wrapped around her near the wreckage of her plane.

Crosson was the only fatality of the race. The winner, Louise Thaden, dedicated her Symbol of Flight Trophy to Crosson and sent it to Crosson's mother. Crosson's death created a rash of editorials against women racing and even against women flying, but the races continued until 1976.

See also
National Air Races; Thaden, Louise McPhetridge; Women's Air Derby
References
Moolman, *Women Aloft* (1981); Sherrow, *The Encyclopedia of Women and Sports* (1996)

Currie, Nancy Jane Sherlock

A veteran of three space shuttle missions, Currie was born Nancy Sherlock in Wilmington, Delaware, on December 29, 1958. She was raised in Troy, Ohio, where she attended high school. She graduated from Ohio State University in 1980 with a degree in biological science. She was commissioned as a second lieutenant in the U.S. Army in 1981.

After her own flight training Currie became a helicopter instructor pilot at Fort Rucker, Alabama. Currie received her master of science degree in safety engineering from the University of Southern California in 1985. She completed aviation officer advanced training and the fixed wing multiengine qualification course before applying to the National Space and Aeronautics Administration (NASA) in 1987.

Currie's first job for NASA was as a flight simulation engineer on the Shuttle Training Aircraft simulator. In 1990 NASA accepted her into astronaut training, after which she served as flight crew representative for crew equipment, worked with the shuttle Remote Manipulator System, and worked as a spacecraft communicator.

From June 21 to July 1, 1993, Currie was a mission specialist on STS-57, which featured the first flight of the Spacelab, a middeck module for carrying out experiments.

From July 13 through July 22, 1995, Currie served on the crew of the space shuttle *Discovery* for mission STS-70. Curried helped deploy the final NASA Tracking and Data Relay Satellite and conducted several biomedical experiments.

See also
Discovery Space Shuttle
References
Biographical Data Sheets, Lyndon B. Johnson Space Center (1997)

Curtiss-Wright Cadettes

In response to World War II the Curtiss-Wright Corporation created the Curtiss-Wright Cadettes, an educational training program to teach engineering to women with math and science backgrounds.

Those chosen for the Cadettes were awarded tuition, living expenses, and a stipend to attend a participating college with an engineering program: Cornell University, Northwestern University, Purdue University, Iowa State University, or Pennsylvania State University. The first group of Cadettes included 800 women, and they chose to study either airframes or engines. Once they passed the ten-month course, Cadettes were hired by the Curtiss-Wright Corporation.

Of the Cadettes, faculty members at Rensselaer Polytechnic Institute wrote: "The Cadettes catch on in a hurry, ask more questions than do the boys, take the detail better and therefore, learn their subjects more thoroughly."

References
Douglas, *United States Women in Aviation, 1940–1985* (1990)

Daniel Guggenheim School of Aeronautics

The Daniel Guggenheim School of Aeronautics of the College of Engineering at New York University was founded by and named for the copper tycoon Daniel Guggenheim to promote the new profession of aviation. On January 16, 1926, the Daniel Guggenheim Fund for the Promotion of Aeronautics was founded when Dwight Morrow, father of Anne Morrow Lindbergh, convinced President Calvin Coolidge that it would help keep the United States ahead in airplane development. On April 20, 1927, the fund announced a Safe Aircraft Competition, with a first prize of $100,000.

On November 23, 1929, the first man to fly the Atlantic solo, Charles Lindbergh, visited Dr. Robert Goddard to ask for a donation of $50,000 from the Guggenheim Fund to further his work in aviation. He was one of the last aviators to receive assistance from the fund, as it went out of existence on December 31, 1929, but the aviation classes did not.

In 1932 women finally came to the Daniel Guggenheim School. Isabel Ebel, the first woman to earn a degree in engineering in the United States, did so as the only engineering student at the prestigious Massachusetts Institute of Technology (MIT). When she applied to further her education at the Daniel Guggenheim School, however, Ebel was denied entry because of her sex. With support from prominent aviator Amelia Earhart, she gained entry. Ebel became the first woman admitted to the Daniel Guggenheim School and she graduated in 1934.

See also
Earhart, Amelia Mary; Ebel, Isabel; Lindbergh, Anne Morrow
References
Boyne, *Beyond the Wild Blue: A History of the U.S. Air Force, 1947–1997* (1997)

Darcy, Susan

The Boeing Company's first female production test pilot, Darcy (born 1956) began with the company in 1974 as an engineer's assistant. Her desire to fly led her to take flying lessons in 1977 and study aeronautics and astronautics at the University of Washington. She received her B.S. degree in 1981.

Darcy was promoted to instructor in Boeing's training department, a position she held from 1982 to 1985. She taught airline pilots the intricacies of the various aircraft in the Boeing line and wrote chapters for the operations manuals while continuing to accrue flight hours for herself.

On October 31, 1985, Darcy was promoted to production test pilot. To fly the various aircraft Darcy had to gain ratings in each one individually; she started with the Boeing 737 rating, which she received in 1987, and she earned the Boeing 757 and 767 ratings in 1989. In May 1989, when she qualified for her rating on the Boeing 747-400, Darcy became the first woman to gain a rating as captain on that vehicle.

Besides the constant training and testing to gain ratings on each new aircraft, Darcy's job as a test pilot required her to test new airplanes and demonstrate them to their new owners at the time of purchase. Sometimes she ferried them abroad to do so.

As to how she succeeded in a largely male profession, she said: "I was accustomed to setting goals for myself and felt a need to focus in more specifically on my target. I was fortunate to have grown up in an environment that encouraged me to believe I could be anything I wanted to be, regardless of gender."

References
Holden and Griffith, *Ladybirds II: The Continuing Story of American Women in Aviation* (1993)

Davis, N. Jan

An astronaut since 1987, Davis was born in Cocoa Beach, Florida, on November 1, 1953. She was raised in Hunstville, Alabama, where she attended high school. She earned two bachelor's degrees, one in applied biology from the Georgia Institute of Technology in 1975 and the other in mechanical engineering from Auburn University in 1977.

Davis was hired as an aerospace engineer by the Marshall Space Flight Center of the National Space and Aeronautics Administration (NASA) in 1979. She received a master of science degree in 1983 and a doctorate in mechanical engineering in 1985, both from the University of Alabama. In 1986 she became a team leader in the Structural Analysis Division of the Marshall Flight Center, working on the Hubble space telescope, among other projects.

After the explosion of the *Challenger* space shuttle Davis was the lead engineer for the redesign of the solid rocket booster rings whose failure had doomed the *Challenger* crew. At the conclusion of this project Davis qualified as a mission specialist. Before being posted to a shuttle mission she worked in the Astronaut

Astronaut N. Jan Davis specialized in working with Spacelab on two space shuttle missions in the early 1990s.

Office Mission Development Branch of NASA and as a spacecraft communicator.

Davis's first shuttle mission was NASA's fiftieth, STS-47. Davis was aboard the *Endeavor* space shuttle when it launched September 12, 1992, and operated the Spacelab for the mission. Since her husband, Mark C. Lee, was the payload commander, this mission made Davis part of the first married couple to fly on the same space mission.

Back on earth, Davis became the Astronaut Office representative for the Remote Manipulator System.

From February 3 to February 11, 1994, Davis worked with the Spacelab on her second shuttle mission, STS-60, aboard the *Discovery* space shuttle. It was the first mission that had a Russian cosmonaut as a crewmember. After her experiences with the Spacelab on these flights, Davis served as the chief of the Payloads Branch of NASA before her next mission. She was also appointed chairperson of the NASA Education Working Group.

See also
Challenger Space Shuttle; *Discovery* Space Shuttle; *Endeavor* Space Shuttle
References
Biographical Data Sheets, Lyndon B. Johnson Space Center (1997)

Dawe, Anne-Marie
The first woman to qualify as a navigator for either the Royal Air Force (RAF) or the Royal Navy (RN), Dawe was educated at the Drury Falls Comprehensive School, where she was very active in sports, including swimming and hockey. She joined the St. John's Ambulance Brigade, which led her to consider a career in the service.

In December 1986 Dawe joined the Women's Royal Air Force (WRAF) but did not initially train to be either a navigator or a pilot, since women were as yet banned from those occupations. In July 1989 the ban was lifted, and Dawe applied immediately. Because she tested with a stronger aptitude for navigation than for piloting, she studied navigation, leaving Julie Ann Gibson to become the RAF's first female pilot.

Dawe took her aircrew training at the RAF base in Lyneham, England, and then at the Royal Aero-Space Establishment in Farnborough. Following graduation Dawe became the first woman to qualify as a navigator for the RAF.

See also
Gibson, Julie Ann
References
Cadogan, *Women with Wings: Female Flyers in Fact and Fiction* (1993)

Deal, Sarah
The first female aviator in the U.S. Marine Corps, Deal was born in 1969 in Pemberville, Ohio. She took her first plane ride at the age of ten on a family vacation and fell in love with flying. She attended Kent State University in Ohio as a flying major and earned tuition money by working at a local airport. Deal joined the marines but trained at the Air Traffic Control School in Millington, Tennessee, since at the time women were banned from combat flying.

In April 1993 the secretary of defense lifted that ban, and Deal immediately applied to flight school. On September 26, 1995, Sarah Deal, then a first lieutenant, completed her final flight hour at Marine Helicopter Training Squadron 302. Earning her wings gave her the distinction of becoming the Marine Corps's first female aviator.

Deal was then assigned to Marine Heavy Helicopter Squadron 466 at the Tustin Marine Corps Helicopter Air Station, where she flew the corps's premier troop carrier, the CH-53E Super Stallion helicopter.

References
Ferrante, *Chronology of the United States Marine Corps* (1995); Wride, "Right Place, Right Time" (1996)

Deaton, Leni Leoti "Dedie"

Hired by Jacqueline Cochran herself, Deaton would become the first executive of the Women's Flying Training Detachment (WFTD). A former swimming instructor, before joining the WFTD Deaton had also been a Red Cross administrator in Fort Worth, Texas.

Deaton was born Leni Leoti Clark in Hereford, Texas, on September 2, 1903. When she was 12 her family moved to Wichita Falls, Texas, where her father founded Midwestern University. When she was 19 she married Clifford Deaton. On November 8, 1942, she met with Cochran to discuss the post of administrator of the WFTD. She accepted the position immediately. She had two weeks to prepare for the first group of female pilots to attend WFTD training at the Howard Hughes Field in Fort Worth, Texas.

Deaton's duties as administrator including securing local housing for each class of new recruits, arranging for their daily transportation to and from the airport, and seeing to both their recreational and medical needs. As the classes grew larger the small Hughes airport was unable to handle their needs, so Deaton made all the arrangements for the WFTD to move to facilities at Avenger Field in Sweetwater, Texas.

In Sweetwater Deaton had to help the town accept the women at a time when self-assured, independent women were seen as socially unacceptable. She spoke on the radio and gave interviews to the local papers about the patriotic job the pilots were doing. Deaton encountered problems on the base as well. Several

male instructors were caught failing women who refused their advances, so Deaton set up and served as adviser for a review board that looked into the circumstances of women who did not pass their flight tests.

In July 1943 the Pentagon combined the Women's Auxiliary Ferrying Squadron (WAFS) and WFTDs and renamed them the Women's Airforce Service Pilots (WASPS). As the war continued, Deaton's duties expanded to include dealing with those women who washed out of the training program and handling burial and notification of next of kin when a pilot died. When the WFTD was disbanded, Deaton was in charge of closing down the base at Avenger Field. After the war she returned to work with the Red Cross in Wichita Falls, Texas, teaching swimming until 1982.

In 1972 the WASPS held a thirtieth anniversary reunion at the base, which Deaton helped arrange and which 300 women attended.

Deaton died on February 11, 1986. At the WASPS reunion that year in Sweetwater Deaton was remembered at a memorial service.

References
Letson, *Oral History of Leoti Deaton* (1995); Leuthner and Jensen, *High Honor: Recollections by Men and Women of World War II Aviation* (1989); Van Wagenen Keil, *Those Wonderful Women in Their Flying Machines: The Unknown Heroines of World War II* (1979); Verges, *On Silver Wings: The Women Airforce Service Pilots of World War II, 1942–1944* (1991)

Devine, Troy

The first female captain in the U.S. Air Force U-2 program, Devine was born on March 28, 1962. She was also among the first group of women interviewed for the program and the first accepted. The U-2 is used for reconnaissance spy missions over battle areas and for research missions to collect scientific data and flood and earthquake damage assessments for the Department of Agriculture. The U-2 is also the infamous plane flown by Gary Powers when he was shot down as a spy over Russia during the Cold War.

Regarding her position as the first woman in the group, Devine said: "The thing that stuck in my mind was, if they did have problems with it, after the interview process was over and I flew and passed and the program selected me, that was the end of it. I never felt, even once, any resistance from that point forward. The only thing that I felt from the other brothers in the community was a strong sense of support and belonging."

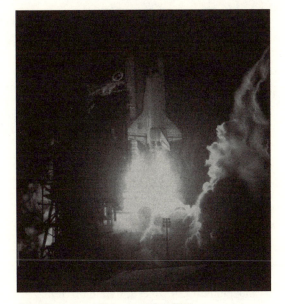

The Discovery *(February 11, 1997)*

References

Russo, *Women and Flight: Portraits of Contemporary Women Pilots* (1997)

Discovery Space Shuttle

The *Discovery* space shuttle was the third shuttle in the National Space and Aeronautics Administration (NASA) fleet. It was named after one of the two ships that the British explorer James Cook captained in the 1770s during the voyages in the South Pacific that led to the discovery of the Hawaiian Islands and on which he later explored the coasts of southern Alaska and northwestern Canada.

Discovery took its first flight into space on August 30, 1984, carrying America's second woman in space, Judith Resnik, and Steven Hawley, the husband of Sally Ride, America's first woman in space.

Discovery's first mission was plagued with technical malfunctions. Icicles formed on the exterior of the shuttle; the icicles threatened to break off and damage the heat tiles necessary for the return flight. There was also an oxygen leak that

might have ended the mission early. Both problems were solved, however, and Resnik and *Discovery* returned to earth on September 5, 1984.

On November 8, 1984, Anna Fisher was a mission specialist on STS-51A, the second flight of the *Discovery* space shuttle. This mission was the first space salvage mission in history. Fisher and the crew retrieved for return to earth the Palapa B-2 and Westar VI satellites before landing on November 16, 1984.

On April 12, 1985, Rhea Seddon was a crewmember on the *Discovery* space shuttle assigned to operate the robot arm, as Resnik had in an earlier mission. Because of more technical malfunctions, Seddon could not repeat Resnik's success, and the errant satellite that *Discovery* had been launched to repair remained out of reach.

On June 17, 1985, Shannon Lucid went into space for the first time aboard the space shuttle *Discovery* and landed on June 24, making her first foray into space her shortest.

From January 22 to January 30, 1992, Canadian Mission Specialist Roberta

Bondar flew on *Discovery* during mission STS-42. Her responsibilities included performing life science and material science experiments in the Spacelab and on the middeck.

Major Susan Helms served as the flight engineer for orbiter operations and the primary Remote Manipulator System (RMS) operator aboard the *Discovery* space shuttle for mission STS-64 from September 9 to September 20, 1994.

See also
Bondar, Roberta; Fisher, Anna L.; Helms, Susan J.; Lucid, Shannon W.; Resnick, Judith Arlene; Seddon, M. Rhea
References
Biographical Data Sheets, Lyndon B. Johnson Space Center (1997)

du Caurroy, Mary Tribe, Duchess of Bedford

One of the oldest women to receive a pilot's license in the early days of aviation, the Duchess of Bedford, born Mary du Caurroy Tribe in 1865, did so at the age of 64. Before that she was content to hire a full-time pilot to fly her to and from the art museums of Europe in the various planes she owned.

Her wealth came both from her father and from her marriage in 1888 to Lord Herbrand Russell, the second son of the ninth Duke of Bedford. In 1893 he inherited his father's title and obligations, and the couple moved to the 3,000-acre family estate, Woburn Abbey. The duchess ran the estate and founded a hospital for the town. Because she had gone deaf as a result of contracting typhoid as a teenager she had an affinity for the sick. She was also an animal trainer and ornithologist (bird specialist).

She traveled by yacht before the advent of the airplane. Then she hired a private pilot and spent weeks at a time on long-distance flights. The first, in 1928, was to Persia (now Iran). Next they succeeded in flying from England to India and back in eight days.

After that the duchess decided to try her hand at piloting and would take the controls for short periods during the flights. Finally, in 1930, she began to study seriously for her license. No more than a week after her first lesson she looped-the-loop successfully. After her first solo she copiloted a flight from London to Cape Town, South Africa, and back. The duchess passed her pilot's license exam in 1931. She celebrated later that year by arranging the first British All-Women's Flying Meeting at Sywell Aerodrome, which hosted such aristocratic pilots as Mary Petre, the Honorable Mrs. Victor Bruce.

In 1933 she and her copilot flew over Europe and the Middle East. After her copilot's death in an air race in Cairo, the duchess hired a new copilot. In 1935 they embarked on a six-week trip across the Sahara Desert, where she met the Emir of Kano and studied his culture. The duchess flew solo to London for her seventieth birthday present to herself in 1935, but her deafness caused her to cancel her next trip. Soon her vision began to fail, and it seemed unlikely that she would pass the medical test to renew her pilot's license.

On March 22, 1937, the duchess set off on her last flight. Her stated intention was to increase her solo hours, but friends and relatives later felt that she had chosen to commit suicide. When she failed to return home, her husband instigated an intensive search along her posted inland route. After over a week, her wing struts washed up on the coast of England. No other sign of her whereabouts was ever located. The Duchess of Bedford was 73 when she disappeared.

The duchess kept a diary of her travels, and she once recorded that long-distance flying was "the one perfect rest I get in the year."

Dunbar, Bonnie J.

A member of the second team of women astronauts, Dunbar was born on March 3, 1949, in Sunnyside, Washington. She received a bachelor of science degree in ceramic engineering in 1971 and worked for Boeing Computer Services for two years as a systems analyst. In 1975 Dunbar earned her master of science degree in ceramic engineering and was invited to participate in research at Harwell Laboratories in Oxford, England, as a visiting scientist.

Following her work in England Dunbar accepted a senior research engineer position with Rockwell International Space Division, developing equipment and processes for the manufacture of the space shuttle thermal protection system.

Dunbar accepted a position as a payload officer and flight controller at the Lyndon B. Johnson Space Center in 1978. She served as a guidance and navigation officer and flight controller for the Skylab reentry mission in 1979 and was then designated project officer and payload officer for the integration of several space shuttle payloads. Dunbar became a National Space and Aeronautics Administration (NASA) astronaut in August 1981 and received her doctorate in mechanical biomedical engineering from the University of Houston in 1983.

Dunbar's first shuttle flight was from October 30 to November 6, 1985, as a mission specialist on the space shuttle *Challenger*. This was the first mission to carry eight crewmembers and was therefore the largest mission in space to date. It was also the first to be sponsored by a foreign country, in this case, West Ger-

Bonnie Dunbar (1981)

many. *Challenger* was conducting 76 experiments for western European countries, including materials processing experiments and tests on a new orbital navigation system. Dunbar was responsible for operating the Spacelab and its subsystems and for performing a variety of experiments. Her mission training included six months of practicing her many experiments in Germany, France, Switzerland, and the Netherlands.

On January 9, 1990, Dunbar was a mission specialist aboard the *Columbia* space shuttle. She was principal investigator for the microgravity disturbance experiment (MDE) and was responsible for the use of the fluids experiment apparatus (FEA).

From June 25 through July 9, 1992, Dunbar flew as payload commander on STS-50, the U.S. Microgravity Lab-1 mission dedicated to microgravity fluid physics and materials science.

In 1993 Dunbar served as deputy associate administrator in the Office of Life and Microgravity Sciences at NASA headquarters in Washington, D.C. In February 1994 she traveled to Star City, Russia, where she spent 13 months training as a backup crewmember for a three-month flight on the Russian space station *Mir*, an assignment that eventually went to fellow astronaut Shannon Lucid.

From June 27 to July 7, 1995, Dunbar helped deliver Lucid to *Mir* when Dunbar served as mission specialist on the *Atlantis* space shuttle for STS-71, the first space shuttle mission to dock with *Mir* and exchange crews. From October to November 1996 Dunbar served as assistant director for NASA–Johnson Space Center (JSC) Mission Operations Directorate, where she chaired the International Space Station Training Readiness Reviews and facilitated Russian-American operations and training strategies.

Dunbar was coanchor with Dan Rather for news coverage of the second flight of the *Columbia* space shuttle, and she speaks about her experiences in space frequently. "Most astronauts will be in this business for as long as they can fly. What other job can possibly compare to this?"

See also

Atlantis Space Shuttle; *Challenger* Space Shuttle; *Columbia* Space Shuttle; Lucid, Shannon W.; *Mir* Space Station

References

Biographical Data Sheets, Lyndon B. Johnson Space Center (1997); Bond, *Heroes in Space: From Gagarin to Challenger* (1987); Oberg, *Spacefarers of the 80's and 90's: The Next Thousand People in Space* (1985)

Dusenberry, Susan

The first woman to earn an inspection authorization rating, Dusenberry learned to fly at the age of 16. She received a bachelor's degree in business administration from Francis Marion College and graduated from Darlington Tech with a degree in aeromaintenance, both schools located in Florence, South Carolina.

Dusenberry served as an associate instructor of airframe and mechanics at Florence Darlington Tech for two years after receiving her degree. Then she took a job as a pilot for a commuter airline, Air Carolina, and later transferred to Air Virginia, where she flew Metroliners for five years. The Virginia Department of Industry Development then hired Dusenberry to fly for them, which sometimes involved transporting the governor to and from events. In 1983 the state government awarded her for her outstanding achievement and dedication in aviation.

In 1985 Dusenberry joined Airborne Express and became a DC-9 captain. In 1988 she received the Oshkosh Restored Antique Airplane Award for the Culver Cadet she restored in her spare time. This led to her being chosen for a special honor on the sixtieth anniversary commemorative tour of the 1929 Women's Air Derby: She was chosen to fly the Travel Air Speedwing, with which Louise Thaden won the original race along the same course that Thaden used in 1929. She did the restoration of the plane herself.

Dusenberry left the Santa Monica airport on August 18, 1989, after visiting with a group of well-wishers including Mae Haizlip and Bobbi Trout, who had flown in the first race against Thaden. Of the race re-creation, Dusenberry said: "It was an honor to be selected to fly the route. Louise Thaden had always been the woman I admired most and I felt this was an opportunity to give her the recognition she deserves."

See also

Haizlip, Mae (Mary); Thaden, Louise McPhetridge; Trout, Evelyn "Bobbi"; Women's Air Derby

References

Holden and Griffith, *Ladybirds II: The Continuing Story of American Women in Aviation* (1993)

Belgian Helene Dutrieu, an aviation pioneer in Europe, was the second woman in the world to obtain a pilot's license and the first woman to carry a passenger in her plane (undated photo).

Dutrieu, Helene

Belgium's first licensed woman pilot and the first woman to carry an air passenger, Dutrieu (born 1877) was also the second woman in the world to gain a pilot's license. Like Marie Marvingt of France, Dutrieu's first career was as a trick bicycle rider, which helped draw her to this new form of trick transportation. She learned to fly in a Santos-Dumont Demoiselle in France.

On December 15, 1909, Dutrieu won 2,000 francs in the Coup Femina by flying 60 kilometers, 700 meters at the Aerodrome de la Beauteal Etranger, near Paris. This flight made her the first woman to spend more than one hour airborne as a pilot.

On April 20, 1910, she became the first woman to carry an air passenger in a flight at Mourmelon, France. Dutrieu set a world altitude record of 1,300 feet.

In September 1910 Dutrieu flew 28 miles nonstop from Ostend to Bruges, Belgium. Before landing she reached a height of 1,300 feet, securing the altitude record for a woman pilot carrying a passenger. Later in the year Dutrieu flew nonstop for 2 hours, 58 minutes, a new women's record. In October she entered the first international air meet held in the United States and was the only woman registered.

In 1911 Dutrieu visited the United States on a tour in which she came in second in a cross-country race against Harriet Quimby, the first American woman to earn a pilot's license. On her return to Europe, Dutrieu won the Coppa del Rey, the Italian King's Cup, in a race in Florence in May. Dutrieu was the only female participant among the 15 entrants. In December she set a nonstop flight record for women by flying 158 miles in 2 hours, 58 minutes.

In 1913 Dutrieu was awarded the Legion of Honor, France's highest honor. She was also given the nickname "Girl Hawk."

As the only female member of the Paris Air Guard in 1914, Dutrieu was one of the few women worldwide allowed to fly for her country in World War I. She also flew reconnaissance missions for the French Air Force while women like Ruth Law in the United States and Melli Beese in Germany were relegated to teaching men to fly.

Dutrieu died on June 26, 1961, at the age of 84.

See also
Beese, Melli; Law, Ruth; Marvingt, Marie; Quimby, Harriet
References
Adams and Kimball, *Heroines of the Sky* (1942); Moolman, *Women Aloft* (1981)

Earhart, Amelia Mary

The first woman to fly the Atlantic, Earhart was born in Atchison, Kansas, on July 24, 1897. Her college preparatory education was interrupted by World War I, when Earhart volunteered as a nurse for the Red Cross. On her days off she visited some of her former patients at a local airfield, and this was her introduction to aviation.

After the war, Earhart attended Columbia University in New York as a premed student, which few women did at the time. When her parents relocated to California, Earhart left college to accompany them. There she attended air shows frequently, finally taking her first ten-dollar, ten-minute flight at Rogers Field. This led to an interest in lessons, which led to a stalemate with her parents. They agreed to pay for lessons but refused to allow her to spend time alone with a man to whom she was not married. Earhart was not to be deterred. She went to Kinner Field and sought out Anita "Neta" Snook, a female instructor, who agreed to begin lessons in December 1920.

Earhart bought her first plane from Bert Kinner for her twenty-fourth birthday. She earned the $2,000 price by working in the telephone company mailroom during the week and assisting her father in his law practice on weekends. She also worked for Kinner demonstrating the plane to potential customers as partial payment. In this capacity she earned her first publicity picture in the Los Angeles *Examiner.*

In October 1922 Earhart set her first altitude record. At a fly-in at Rogers Field she reached a height of 14,000 feet. She appeared in a smattering of air shows in Los Angeles over the next year. On May 6, 1923, she received her pilot's license from the Fédération Aéronautique Internationale (FAI). But there was still not much money to be made from flying.

Her family moved to Boston in 1924, and Earhart reenrolled in college. Her lack of funds kept her from flying so she took a job as a social worker. In 1927 Bert Kinner built an airfield in Boston. Amelia invested what money she had and became a director of the company. She flew at several more air shows, and this notoriety paid off in April 1927. She was invited to join Wilmer Stultz and Louis Gordon on a flight across the Atlantic by the publicity man for this venture, George Palmer Putnam. Earhart accepted. With the successful landing of the plane on June 18, 1928, she became the first woman to fly the Atlantic. She wrote about the trip in the best-selling *20 Hrs. 40 Min.*, taking the title from the length of the flight.

After the landing she attended several celebrations in England, meeting such dignitaries as Winston Churchill and Lady Astor. Earhart also met Lady Sophie Mary Heath, the first woman to fly solo from South Africa to England. Earhart was invited to test the plane Heath used for this record-breaking flight. After the test flight Earhart bought the plane and shipped it back to the United States, where there were yet more celebrations, including a ticker tape parade in New York City. She flew the new plane cross-country to California in

Probably the most famous American woman pilot, Amelia Earhart was the first woman to fly across the Atlantic and the first woman to make a solo transcontinental flight (undated photo).

time for the National Air Derby, becoming the first woman to make a solo transcontinental flight. She became the first woman to make a solo return transcontinental flight when she flew home, returning on October 16, 1928.

To fly her new plane for profit Earhart required a transport license. On March 29, 1929, she was the fourth woman in the United States, after Phoebe Omlie, Ruth Nichols, and Elinor Smith, to receive one. In July she was hired as assistant to the general traffic manager of Transcontinental Air Transport, which provided a steady salary to be added to her lecture and writing fees.

The first Women's Air Derby in 1929 brought Earhart together with many experienced female aviators. Flying a new Lockheed Vega, Earhart came in third, but meeting so many other women pilots inspired them all to create an organization "dedicated to the improvement of women's opportunities in aviation." Ninety-nine women joined, which suggested to Earhart a name for the group. In 1930 she was elected the first president of the Ninety-Nines.

On June 25, 1930, at Grosse Isle Airport in Detroit, Earhart set a new women's speed record of 174 miles per hour on a 100-kilometer course. On July 5 she used the three-kilometer international course to set a record of 181 miles per hour, which kept her in the news as she planned her own trans-Atlantic flight as pilot.

Earhart married her publicist, George Palmer Putnam, on February 7, 1931, but never used his name formally for business purposes.

In 1931 Earhart learned to fly an auto-giro, a combination helicopter and air-plane, and set a new autogiro altitude record of 19,000 feet on April 8, 1931. With the backing of the Beech-Nut Chewing Gum Company, from May 29 to June 7, 1931, she flew an autogiro cross-country from New York to Los Angeles and back, the first woman to fly an autogiro cross-country and the first person, man or woman, to make a transcontinental return flight in one. Over the winter of 1931 Earhart wrote her second book, *The Fun of It*, but the publishers delayed releasing it until after her next flight so they could take advantage of the attending publicity.

Since her first notoriety in flying came from being merely a passenger on the Atlantic crossing in 1928, Earhart had planned to be the first woman to fly across solo. On the fifth anniversary of Charles Lindbergh's historic crossing, May 20, 1932, she left Newfoundland, Canada, at 3:00 P.M. Despite a leaky fuel tank she flew 2,026 miles and arrived in Northern Ireland on May 21, 1932. Not only was she the first woman but she was the first person to make the flight solo since Lindbergh. The flight also broke the record for the longest nonstop distance flown by a woman.

As she attended formal dinners and collected honors in England, *The Fun of It* was published in the United States with a chapter added on about the Atlantic flight. It was another best-seller. Then Earhart won the Harmon Trophy as America's Outstanding Airwoman for the Atlantic flight. She also received a special Gold Medal from the National Geographic Society for being a geographic pioneer. Earhart was the first woman to receive this honor, which was presented to her by the president of the United States.

Earhart used her fame for others. She had supported Isabel Ebel's attempt to be the first woman admitted to the Daniel Guggenheim School of Aeronautics of the College of Engineering at New York University. To repay Earhart for her assistance, Ebel plotted the maps for Earhart's record-breaking transcontinental flight from New York to San Francisco when the young engineer graduated in 1934. Earhart was also a visiting faculty member and consultant in the Women's Careers Department at Purdue University in Indiana, for an annual salary of $2,000.

After three years of lecture tours and celebrations, Earhart was ready for another challenge. On January 11 and 12, 1935, she became the first person to fly solo across the Pacific Ocean from Honolulu, Hawaii, to Oakland, California. On April 19, while on a goodwill tour for which the Mexican government issued commemorative stamps, she became the first person to fly from Los Angeles to Mexico.

In August 1935 she participated in the National Air Races again, this time with a male copilot, Paul Mantz, and they took fifth place. Mantz then came on board as adviser for Earhart's planned round-the-world flight. The trip would be funded by donations made to Purdue University and passed on to Earhart to create a "Purdue Flying Laboratory" to further the cause of women in aviation. The necessary foreign contacts and permissions to land were obtained from the State Department with help from First Lady Eleanor Roosevelt.

On March 17, 1937, Earhart took off on the first leg of the trip with 44-year-old navigator Fred Noonan. They flew from Oakland, California, to Honolulu in a record-breaking 15 hours, 47 minutes. On takeoff from Honolulu Earhart lost control and the plane went into a ground loop. Neither Earhart nor Noonan was injured, but the plane required extensive repair and the round-the-world flight was canceled.

On June 1, 1937, Earhart and Noonan tried again, this time reversing her route for weather reasons. The first leg of this route was from Miami, Florida, to San Juan, Puerto Rico. They landed safely, and their trip progressed well, as recorded by the cables and radio messages they sent home at each landing site. After completing 22,000 miles of the flight, Earhart and Noonan took off from Lae, New Guinea, on July 2, 1937.

Howland Island in the Pacific was to be their next refueling stop, at a landing strip recently completed by the U.S. Coast Guard. They never arrived. A massive search by the U.S., English, and Japanese navies found nothing. Still, it was two years before she and Noonan were declared legally dead on January 5, 1939.

Theories about their disappearance range from their being shot down by the Japanese as spies, to their being kept as prisoners of war and then executed, to their staging the disappearance so that Earhart could duck publicity and live in obscurity in Europe. Until their bodies and the plane are finally found, it is all speculation.

Regarding the risks of record-breaking aviation, Earhart had said: "The actual doing of a dangerous thing, it seems to me, may require little courage. The preparation of it—the acceptance of the inevitable risks involved—may be a far greater test of morale." She had also sent a private note to her husband, which was published posthumously in *Last Flight* and which explained her theory of failure: "Women must try to do things as men have tried. When they fail, their failure must be but a challenge to others."

See also
Ebel, Isabel; Heath, Lady Sophie Mary; Nichols, Ruth Rowland; Ninety-Nines; Omlie, Phoebe Fairgrave; Roosevelt, Eleanor; Smith, Elinor Patricia; Snook, Anita "Neta"

References
Earhart, *20 Hrs. 40 Min.* (1928); Lovell, *The Sound of Wings: The Life of Amelia Earhart* (1989)

Early Birds

Founded in the United States as a fraternity for "pilots who flew during the first decade of practical flight," the Early Birds founders included only one woman: Marjorie Stinson. Only five other women were ever accepted into the exclusive club: Alys McKey Bryant, Ruth Law, Matilde Moisant, Blanche Stuart Scott, and Katherine Stinson.

See also
Stinson, Marjorie
References
Miller, *The World in the Air: The Story of Flying in Pictures* (1930)

Ebel, Isabel

Famous not for her piloting skills but in the world of research, Ebel was one of the first female engineers in the aircraft industry. She was born in Brooklyn, New York, circa 1903, at a time when women engineers were nonexistent. Many colleges would not even allow a woman to study engineering, but Ebel persisted.

While in her third year at Adelphi College she applied to and was rejected by numerous schools. Finally, prestigious Massachusetts Institute of Technology (MIT) offered to accept her and grant her a half-scholarship based on her high grade point average. She would be their only female engineering student and one of only 30 women among the 3,000 students at the school. In 1932 she graduated with a degree in engineering, becoming the first woman to earn such a degree in the United States.

Before the onset of World War II, however, it was difficult for a woman to gain a position in the aircraft industry. Ebel opted for furthering her education at the Daniel Guggenheim School of Aeronautics of the College of Engineering at New York University. With support from prominent aviator Amelia Earhart, Ebel was the first woman admitted to the college; she graduated in 1934. To repay Earhart, Ebel plotted the maps for the famed aviator's record-breaking transcontinental flight from New York to San Francisco.

Even with this advanced degree, Ebel had trouble getting work in aviation. She supported herself as a high school teacher for a while, becoming a math teacher at Brooklyn Technical High School. The next year she became the first teacher of aviation theory in the New York City high school system. She also began flight lessons and earned her private pilot's license.

In 1939 Ebel landed her first engineering job with the Grumman Aircraft Corporation. They were one of the few companies hiring women, thanks to the efforts of Bud Gillies, a forward-thinking executive who happened to be married to Betty Gillies, president of the Ninety-Nines. Ebel was the first woman in the Grumman engineering department; she studied stress analysis on engine mounts and drafted and designed a retractable pilot tube.

After two years Ebel was hired by Brewster Aeronautical to head their development and new design department. Three months later the department was dissolved, and she moved to the aeronautical department at Snead and Company, working on a large transport glider for the navy.

In 1942 Ebel became a research engineer for United Airlines, a job she kept throughout the war. After the bombing of Pearl Harbor it was urgent to do whatever was necessary to win the war. Women were organized in the Women's Airforce Service Pilots (WASPS) to ferry planes from manufacturing plants to bases, and women with Ebel's background were finally wanted in the workplace.

Explaining her work in airplane design, Ebel said: "If variety is the spice of life we sure have plenty of spice in this department. There's no such thing as a typical day. Anytime there's an unusual scientific or technical problem to which no one else can find the answer, we're pretty certain it will end up in here for a solution."

See also
Daniel Guggenheim School of Aeronautics; Earhart, Amelia Mary; Gillies, Betty Huyler; Gillies, Brewster A. "Bud"; Ninety-Nines; Women's Airforce Service Pilots (WASPS)
References
Douglas, *United States Women in Aviation, 1940–1985* (1990); Knapp, *New Wings for Women* (1946)

Elder, Ruth

The first woman to attempt to fly the Atlantic, Elder was born in 1904. She worked as an actress and a dental hygienist before being bitten by the aviation bug.

The unprecedented publicity that Charles Lindbergh received for being the first man to cross the Atlantic attracted Elder's attention, and she decided to become the first woman to accomplish the feat. Elder took flying lessons with the money she earned as a dentist's assistant and was only a student pilot in 1927 when she announced her plans to fly the Atlantic. She would share the piloting chores with her instructor, Captain George W. Haldeman. Elder purchased a Stinson aircraft and named it *The American Girl* for the voyage.

On October 11, 1927, Elder and Haldeman started their flight from New York even though the weather was poor for flying. After 28 hours and 2,632 miles they crashed in the Atlantic Ocean 360 miles northeast of the Azores. Elder had anticipated the possibility of a water

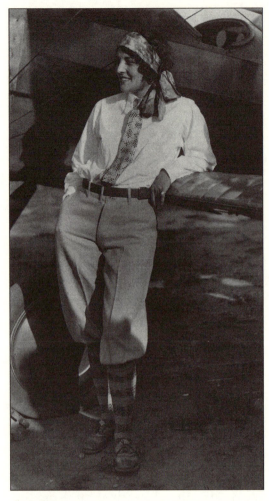

Ruth Elder (ca. 1927)

landing and had therefore charted a course over busy shipping lanes whenever possible. That foresight saved her life and the life of her copilot. A Dutch oil tanker came to their aid quickly, saving the two flyers from death by exposure, but destroyed the plane while attempting to hoist it to the deck.

To make money for her further aviation ventures, Elder went on a vaudeville tour and worked as an actress in the Florenz Ziegfeld film *Glorifying the American Girl.*

In 1929 Elder entered the first Women's Air Derby and placed fifth against such competition as Amelia Earhart, Louise Thaden, and Pancho Barnes. Elder then retired from flying to

pursue a career in films. She married six times and died in San Francisco in 1977. She was cremated, and at her husband's death both their ashes were scattered over the sea from an airplane.

Regarding her aborted attempt to be the first woman to fly across the Atlantic, Elder said: "Looking back, perhaps my drive to succeed clouded my judgment. The weather was awful. My choice of copilot was as deliberate as my choice of airplane. He was one of the best pilots of the day."

See also
Barnes, Florence Lowe "Pancho"; Earhart, Amelia Mary; Thaden, Louise McPhetridge; Women's Air Derby
References
Holden and Griffith, *Ladybirds: The Untold Story of Women Pilots in America* (1991); Lomax, *Women of the Air* (1987); Moolman, *Women Aloft* (1981)

Endeavor Space Shuttle

The *Endeavor* space shuttle was the newest addition to the four-orbiter fleet when it was delivered to Kennedy Space Center in May 1991. It was named after the first ship commanded by James Cook, the eighteenth-century British explorer, navigator, and astronomer. The name was chosen by a national competition among students in elementary and secondary schools.

The *Endeavor* space shuttle flew its first mission from May 7 to May 16, 1992, and a woman was aboard for this inaugural flight. Mission Specialist Kathryn C. Thornton performed one of the longest spacewalks to date and assisted in retrieving an errant satellite.

On September 12, 1992, two new "firsts" in space were achieved by women on *Endeavor.* Of the three mission specialists on board two were women: Mae C. Jemison and N. Jan Davis. Jemison became the first African American woman in space, and Davis, whose husband, Mark C. Lee, was the payload commander, was part of the first married couple to fly on the same space mission.

On January 13, 1993, Mission Specialist Susan J. Helms flew on the crew of the *Endeavor* space shuttle for STS-54. Among their other duties, Helms and her fellow astronauts demonstrated the physics principles of everyday toys to an interactive audience of elementary school students across the United States. They landed on January 19, 1993.

On June 21, 1993, Nancy J. Sherlock and Janice E. Voss were mission specialists aboard *Endeavor.* Sherlock helped retrieve the European Retrievable Carrier (EURECA) and performed the tools and diagnostics system experiments. Voss worked on the liquid encapsulated melt zone experiment and the neutral body position study of the human body's posture changes while in microgravity.

On December 2, 1993, Mission Specialist Thornton was back on board for STS-61, one of the most sophisticated missions in the shuttle's history. It lasted almost 11 days, and despite air pressure problems with her spacesuit Thornton made two of the record five spacewalks on this mission.

For *Endeavor*'s sixth mission, on April 9, 1994, Linda M. Godwin served as payload commander in charge of the space radar laboratory designed to help scientists distinguish human-induced environmental changes from naturally produced changes. She also spoke with elementary school students in Michigan and California by radio.

Astronaut Tamara E. Jernigan served as payload commander in charge of the second dedicated Spacelab mission to conduct astronomical observations in the ultraviolet spectral regions to fill in large gaps in astronomers' understanding of the universe. She also oversaw an experiment sponsored by the Australian Space

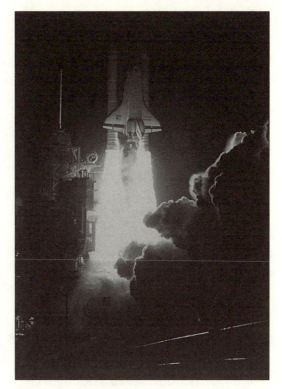

The Endeavor *(1995)*

Office to make ultraviolet observations of deep space or nearby galaxies. It was the longest mission to date, lasting from March 2 to March 18, 1995.

See also
Davis, N. Jan; Helms, Susan J.; Jemison, Mae C.; Thornton, Kathryn C.
References
Biographical Data Sheets, Lyndon B. Johnson Space Center (1997)

Engel, Connie

The first woman to earn air force wings, Engel had originally joined the U.S. Air Force (USAF) as a nurse in 1970. In 1975 the USAF announced a test program for women to be noncombat pilots and navigators. The program would be administered by Engel's husband, Rich, himself a USAF pilot.

While helping her husband organize the program Engel decided to sign up and

U.S. Air Force jet pilots Captains Susan Rogers (left) and Connie Engel (right) in 1977.

was among those selected. The group was sent to Williams Air Force Base in Texas for one year of training just as Engel's husband was reassigned to Edwards Air Force Base in California. On November 30, 1976, Engel was the first in her class to solo in a jet aircraft. In her class of 10 women and 36 men she was the class leader and won the Officer Training Award. Her husband flew back from Edwards to himself present the Commander's Trophy for overall excellence in flying, academics, and leadership.

After passing the course she became a T-38 instructor at Williams Air Force Base. She eventually attained the rank of major and then retired to raise her family.

Of her training, Engel said: "Wearing men's flight gear was difficult on the feminine identity. We weren't allowed makeup and our hair constantly looked like we'd just taken off a swimming cap. We were in a field that required physical stamina, long hours of flying and studying, and lots of running, parachute training, etc. This physical world was new to me. I was always the cheerleader, not the football player, and it hurt lots of the time. But I learned to be tough."

See also
U.S. Air Force (USAF)
References
Holden and Griffith, *Ladybirds: The Untold Story of Women Pilots in America* (1991); Holm, *Women in the Military: An Unfinished Revolution* (1982)

Evans, Sophie Mary Pierce
See Heath, Lady Sophie Mary

Fédération Aéronautique Internationale (FAI)

The international body founded to ensure that "the skill of pilots [would] always be rated by an unbiased judgment in which the whole world has faith," the Fédération Aéronautique Internationale (FAI) issued licenses to all pilots who passed the proper tests, including women, from its inception. Pioneer aeronaut Count Henri de La Vaulx petitioned for such a group to be formed, and the aims of the group were discussed and agreed upon during the Olympic Congress held in Brussels in June 1905. The founding member countries were Belgium, Britain, France, Germany, Italy, Spain, Switzerland, and the United States.

The Aero Club of France gave licenses before the FAI was created.

References
Adams and Kimball, *Heroines of the Sky* (1942)

Fifinella

Designed by the Walt Disney Company, Fifinella, a female gremlin, was the military insignia for the Women's Airforce Service Pilots (WASPS) of World War II. The company first designed an insignia for a branch of the military for the Fighting Seven Air Squadron in June 1939. Soon the company was employing five full-time artists, headed by Henry Porter, to design insignias as part of their effort to support the Allies.

Fifinella was the good sister of the mythological gremlins that first appeared in *Gremlin Lore*, published by Roald Dahl, a Royal Air Force flight lieutenant, in 1942. Pilots had taken to blaming male gremlins for unexplained aircraft malfunctions, the kind that happened in flight but could not be duplicated for the ground mechanics. Unlike her ugly brothers, Fifinella was said to bring good luck to pilots and "for a whiff of perfume, Fifinella will practically do your navigating." Her job specifically was to scare off the male gremlins.

After World War II a group of former WASPS who had been stationed at Marshall Field, Alabama, organized the Order of Fifinella to commemorate their services during World War II. The order kept address files and other archives for the group, organized reunions, and toured the country to reeducate the American public about the WASPS' contribution to the war effort.

See also
Order of Fifinella; Women's Airforce Service Pilots (WASPS)
References
Holden and Griffith, *Ladybirds: The Untold Story of Women Pilots in America* (1991); Rawls, *Disney Dons Dog Tags: The Best of Disney Military Insignia from World War II* (1992)

Finch, Linda

The woman who finally re-created Amelia Earhart's exact flight path around the equator in an exact replica of her plane, Finch was born in Highland Hills, Texas, in March 1951. She was married at 16, dropped out of high school, and had her first child in 1969. She was a month shy of 18 and a year shy of divorce.

After the divorce Finch earned her high school equivalency and became a bookkeeper for various businesses, including nursing homes. She soon decided to save up enough money to start her own chain of nursing homes in neighboring states and also decided to learn to fly to make it easier to manage them all.

Finch began flying lessons in late 1973 and attained her private pilot's license in 1979. Then she purchased her first nursing home by borrowing against her inheritance from her grandparents. In 18 months she owned seven more and formed the Care Centers Management Corporation. By 1997 her company was clearing $14 million a year, which Finch used to finance her interest in restoring classic aircraft.

In the late 1980s Finch began racing and performing in air shows with her first restoration project, a World War II training aircraft. In 1991 Finch wanted an even bigger challenge and decided to re-create not just a famous plane but a famous flight. She chose to re-create Earhart's 1937 world flight as a message to young girls in 1997 that with hard work and the right attitude, anything is possible, a sentiment first attributed to Earhart.

There were only two Lockheed Electras still operational in the world when Finch had the idea for what would be called World Flight 1997. Her past work at restoring planes became an asset. In the end World Flight, which took place between March 17 and 28, 1997, would cost $4 million. Finch's flight was underwritten by Pratt and Whitney, who had manufactured the engine for Earhart's original plane.

As to how she managed to put the whole event together, Finch said: "I have always figured out how to get what I wanted. I always believe that God takes care of me and will be with me every day. But you have to help yourself, too."

See also
Earhart, Amelia Mary
References
Nagy, "Linda Finch: A Woman Amelia Earhart Would Admire" (1997)

Fisher, Anna L.

A member of the first group of women astronauts chosen by the National Aeronautics and Space Administration (NASA), in 1978, Fisher was the first mother to go into space. She was born on August 24, 1949, in New York City, but she grew up in San Pedro, California. She always wanted to work in space.

Fisher's plan was to become a doctor on a space station, so she worked toward a bachelor of science degree in chemistry and an M.D. from the University of California, Los Angeles (UCLA), receiving her degrees in 1971 and 1976, respectively. In 1977 Fisher completed a year-long internship at Harbor General Hospital in Torrance, California, and in 1987 she received a master of science degree in chemistry from UCLA. After completing her internship Fisher specialized in emergency medicine and worked in several hospitals in the Los Angeles area.

Anna Fisher married Bill Fisher, also a physician, of the astronaut class of 1980. They spent their honeymoon going through the NASA physical exams. To keep their medical knowledge up-to-date while at NASA they worked one day a month in a local emergency room and were the recovery room doctors at Edwards Air Force Base during shuttle missions.

Anna Fisher was selected as an astronaut candidate by NASA in January 1978 and completed the one-year training and evaluation in 1979. Before flying on the

Anna L. Fisher (1985)

space shuttle, she was assigned as a crew representative for missions STS-5 through STS-7. It was her job to support vehicle-integrated testing and payload testing at the Kennedy Space Center.

In 1981, for the first flight of the *Columbia* space shuttle, Fisher was assigned to the alternate landing site at White Sands, New Mexico, in case medical assistance was needed at an emergency landing. She was also an on-orbit spacecraft communicator (CAPCOM) for the STS-9 mission.

In 1983, at 34, Fisher gave birth to a daughter, Kirstin Fisher, and at 35 she was a crewmember on NASA's first satellite rescue mission. On November 8, 1984, Fisher was a mission specialist on STS-51A, the second flight of the *Discovery* space shuttle. This mission was the first space salvage mission in history. Fisher and the crew retrieved for return to earth the Palapa B-2 and Westar VI satellites before landing on November 16, 1984.

Fisher was assigned as a mission specialist on STS-61H prior to the *Challenger* space shuttle accident. Following the accident she worked as the deputy of the Mission Development Branch of NASA's Astronaut Office. In 1987 Fisher served on NASA's Astronaut Selection Board for the 1987 class of astronauts and as the crew representative supporting space station development. After a few years' leave of absence to raise her family Fisher returned to the Astronaut Office in 1996, working on the operational flight data file and training issues in support of the International Space Station.

Fisher feels space flight is very important to the human race: "As a species we need to go one step beyond where we are. We need a frontier. Without it, I think life would be very confining."

See also
Challenger Disaster Investigation; *Challenger* Space Shuttle; *Discovery* Space Shuttle
References
Biographical Data Sheets, Lyndon B. Johnson Space Center (1997); Oberg, *Spacefarers of the 80's and 90's: The Next Thousand People in Space* (1985); O'Connor, *Sally Ride and the New Astronauts: Scientists in Space* (1983)

586th Fighter Regiment, 587th Bomber Regiment, and 588th Night Bomber Regiment
Although British and U.S. military strategists debated the need to use women as ferry pilots in their Air Transport Auxiliary (ATA) and Women's Airforce Service Pilots (WASPS) programs, the Soviet Union had no such luxury. They had lost so many male pilots by 1941 as the Germans advanced into the Ukraine that they desperately needed experienced women pilots to fill the void.

In October 1941 Marina Raskova was asked by Soviet High Command to recruit 200 women flyers for combat missions and as many female mechanics and armament fitters as possible. After she broadcast an appeal over Radio Moscow, Raskova received more than 2,000 applications. Applicants had to be between 18 and 22 and had to already have a pilot's license. Thanks to the existence of the many flying clubs before the war, there were experienced female pilots available. Many had been flight instructors by trade, and some had been employed as pilots of small airlines.

The chosen recruits began training in the town of Engels on October 15, 1941, wearing oversized men's uniforms, as no women's military uniforms existed. They were organized into three combat units, the 586th Fighter Regiment, with Olga Yemshokova as squadron leader; the 587th Bomber Regiment, under the command of Raskova herself; and the 588th Night Bomber Regiment, commanded by Yevdokia Bershanskaya, who became the only woman to remain in command of a woman's regiment for the full course of the war.

The 586th included fighter ace Lily Litviak, who served with the all-female regiment until September 1942, when she was transferred to the 73rd Fighter Regiment, an otherwise all-male battalion, assigned to defend Stalingrad.

Raskova's 587th eventually joined the fight for Stalingrad. In 1943 they bombed German troop concentrations around Smolensk. Members of their unit who were downed over German lines ended up at concentration camps rather than prisoner-of-war camps, since the Germans refused to consider women soldiers.

In their 125 separate battles, the 586th and 587th Regiments fought in the Ukraine, Crimea, and eventually Germany. They were successful at bombing German supply trains and ammunition dumps and helped bring about the fall of Berlin.

On June 8, 1942, the 588th flew their first combat mission. In January 1943,

after eight months of combat flying, they were honored by being renamed the 46th Guards Regiment, the first women's air regiment to receive such an honor.

Under the direction of squadron commander Major Mariya Smirnova, the women of the renamed 46th Guards Regiment frequently flew 15 to 18 bombing missions a night, for a total of 24,000 combat missions dropping 23,000 tons of bombs. By the end of the war 23 members of the regiment had been honored as Hero of the Soviet Union.

In 1943 Raskova was killed in combat, and she was given the first state funeral since the beginning of World War II. Her ashes were interred in the Kremlin wall with full military honors and the 587th Bomber Regiment was renamed the 125th M. M. Raskova Borisov Guards Bomber Regiment in recognition of her work.

See also
Air Transport Auxiliary (ATA); Litviak, Lidiia "Lily" Vladimirovna; Raskova, Marina; Smirnova, Mariya; Women's Airforce Service Pilots (WASPS)
References
Moolman, *Women Aloft* (1981); Myles, *Night Witches: The Untold Story of Soviet Women in Combat* (1981); Noggle, *A Dance with Death: Soviet Airwomen in World War II* (1994)

587th Night Bomber Regiment

See 586th Fighter Regiment, 587th Bomber Regiment, and 588th Night Bomber Regiment

Flinn, Kelly

The first woman to pilot a B-52 bomber for the U.S. Air Force, Flinn was born in Creve Coeur, Missouri, on December 23, 1970. Her first experience with flying was going with her mother to pick up her father at the local airport from one of his many business trips. Flinn became so enamored of flight that in high school she attended the U.S. Space Camp twice.

After high school Flinn attended the U.S. Air Force Academy, where she took her first flight lessons on a variety of military aircraft. In her sophomore year Flinn soloed in a glider. In her senior year she joined an exchange program and studied engineering and survival training at the French Air Force Academy. Flinn graduated from the academy with the rank of second lieutenant on June 2, 1993.

Flinn had earned a place in the T-38 combat pilot training program and was transferred to Columbus Air Force Base in Columbus, Mississippi, after graduation. There she soloed in her first jet and studied air acrobatics. As the distinguished graduate of her class, Flinn earned the right to choose her next assignment. She chose flying the B-52 bomber. To qualify for the B-52 Flinn moved to the Barksdale Air Force Base in Shreveport, Louisiana, in April 1995.

As the air force's first female bomber pilot Flinn was inundated with media attention. Her superiors indicated that they welcomed the good publicity for the air force, so Flinn accommodated the media, preparing statements and taking press conferences on top of the heavy course load. After being named distinguished graduate of the B-52 Formal Training Unit, Flinn took off for the Minot Air Force Base in Minot, North Dakota, home of the B-52s.

On November 24, 1996, Flinn was accused of adultery, fraternization, and conduct unbecoming an officer for having entered into an affair with the husband of an enlisted woman on the base. If convicted, Flinn would have faced nine and a half years in military prison.

During the course of the investigation Flinn was grounded from flying. She was placed in charge of writing achievement medals for others stationed at Minot. Her court-martial began on May 20, 1997. Rather than face a prison term Flinn resigned from the air force on May 28, 1997.

Her case caused such turmoil within the highest ranks of the air force that the first female secretary of the air force, Dr. Sheila Widnall, resigned as well.

See also
U.S. Air Force (USAF); U.S. Space Camp; Widnall, Sheila E.
References
Flinn, *Proud to Be: My Life, the Air Force, the Controversy* (1997)

Fornes, Patricia

The first woman to lead a U.S. Air Force ICBM unit, Fornes had the air force in her blood: Her father was an air force man.

In 1977 the U.S. Air Force opened Titan II missile training to women, and Fornes was the first to qualify for the program.

On June 17, 1993, Fornes took command of the 740th Missile Squadron at Minot Air Force Base, North Dakota. She also became the first woman to take over the command of a squadron once commanded by her own father.

As the first woman assigned to a crew position on the missile program, Fornes once said: "There were still some reservations among the men I worked for. They weren't sure if I'd get raped the first week or whether I'd rape someone."

See also
U.S. Air Force (USAF)
References
Boyne, *Beyond the Wild Blue: A History of the U.S. Air Force, 1947–1997* (1997); Holm, *Women in the Military: An Unfinished Revolution* (1982)

Fort, Cornelia

The first Tennessee woman to qualify for her commercial pilot's license, Fort was born on February, 5, 1919, in Nashville, Tennessee. She attended Sarah Lawrence College, majoring in music and journalism. She took her first ride in an airplane after graduation and soloed in April 1940. In June she had earned her private pilot's license, and before the year was out Fort qualified for her commercial license.

Her first job as a flight instructor was with the Civilian Pilot's Training Program (CPTP) at the Massey Ransom Flying Service in Colorado in 1941. In October of that year Fort transferred to an instructor's position with the Andrew Flying Service at the John Rogers Airport in Hawaii.

On December 7, 1941, she was in the air with a student when a Japanese Zero flew by their plane as part of the bombing of Pearl Harbor, the act that brought the United States into World War II. Fort and her student landed safely, though other civilians at their airport were killed in the bombing.

Three months later Fort left Hawaii and joined the Nashville wing of the Civil Air Patrol, giving speeches about aviation to potential pilots. On September 6, 1941, Fort was one of the few American women pilots to receive telegrams from Nancy Harkness Love regarding the formation of the Women's Auxiliary Ferrying Squadron (WAFS). At the age of 23 Fort became the second woman, after Betty Huyler Gillies, to volunteer to ferry military planes from manufacturing sites to air force bases.

Fort trained with the other original WAFS at New Castle Army Base in Wilmington, Delaware, and then was posted to Lock Haven, Pennsylvania, and eventually to Long Beach, California.

On March 21, 1942, Fort was on a ferrying mission from San Diego, California, to Texas, flying in formation with several other pilots. A male pilot was demonstrating his fancy maneuvers too close to Fort's plane. His landing gear hit her left wing, snapped it off, and forced her into the crash landing that killed her.

Fort described her love of flying to her mother in a letter, saying: "I was happiest in the sky—at dawn when the quietness of the air was like a caress, when the noon sun beat down and at dusk when the sky was drenched with the fading light. Think of me there and remember me, I hope as I shall you, with love."

See also
Civil Air Patrol (CAP); Gillies, Betty Huyler; Love, Nancy Harkness; Women's Airforce Service Pilots (WASPS)
References
Simbeck, "Daughter of the Air: The Soaring Life of Cornelia Fort" (1996); Van Wagenen Keil, *Those Wonderful Women in Their Flying Machines: The Unknown Heroines of World War II* (1979); Verges, *On Silver Wings: The Women Airforce Service Pilots of World War II, 1942–1944* (1991)

Funk, Mary Wallace

The first woman to qualify as an air safety investigator for the National Transportation Safety Board (NTSB), Funk was also the first female Federal Aviation Administration (FAA) inspector.

Funk was born in 1938, grew up in Taos, New Mexico, and made a name as a downhill and slalom skier while still in her teens. She excelled in academics and was able to enter Stephens College in Columbia, Missouri, at the age of 16. She graduated in 1958, taking a job at age 20 as the first female flight instructor at Fort Sill, Oklahoma. There she taught male U.S. Army trainees as well as officers how to fly.

In 1961 Funk was one of 13 women, including Jerrie Cobb, chosen to secretly undergo astronaut training funded by Jacqueline Cochran. As part of the Mercury 13, Funk was the first woman at El Toro Marine Corps Base to experience the Martin-Baker seat ejection test and the 39,000-foot high-altitude-chamber test. Though two of her test results surpassed those of John Glenn and she set a record in the sensory deprivation chamber, women were not allowed in the space program until 1972.

Instead of entering the National Aeronautics and Space Administration (NASA) astronaut ranks, Funk became a Good Will Flying Ambassador for the next three years. She flew over 80,000 miles to 50 countries. In 1964 Stephens College made her the youngest woman in the college's history to receive the distinguished Alumni Achievement Award.

In 1971 Funk became the first female FAA inspector. She joined the NTSB in 1974. Her experiences at her first crash site led Funk to initiate psychological training along with the technical education provided for investigators. In her ten-year career with the NTSB Funk solved 350 accidents. She quit the department to begin a lecture series on flying safely that stresses pilot attitude and preflight training.

On the cancellation of women's testing for the astronaut program, Funk said: "I'd have given my life for the space program. We served as human guinea pigs in a sense, but in doing so I believe we served a definite purpose and substantially aided the male-dominated space efforts."

See also
Cobb, Geraldyne "Jerrie"; Cochran, Jacqueline; Mercury 13
References
Holden and Griffith, *Ladybirds II: The Continuing Story of American Women in Aviation* (1993)

Gentry, Viola

The first woman to make a formal attempt to beat a man's aviation record, Gentry (born circa 1900) went after the endurance record on December 2, 1928, despite the fact that a storm was brewing off the coast. Considering 13 a lucky number, she planned to stay aloft 13 hours, 13 minutes, 13 seconds.

She left Curtiss Field on Long Island wearing two flying suits to protect her from the winter weather. Although her body was protected, the plane could not withstand the storm, and Gentry was forced to land too early to clinch the record. She managed 8 hours, 6 minutes, 37 seconds, which set the first woman's endurance record sanctioned by the Fédération Aéronautique Internationale (FAI) and challenged women like Bobbi Trout, Elinor Smith, and Louise Thaden eventually to beat it.

Gentry died in 1988.

See also
Fédération Aéronautique Internationale (FAI); Smith, Elinor Patricia; Thaden, Louise McPhetridge; Trout, Evelyn "Bobbi"
References
Holden and Griffith, *Ladybirds: The Untold Story of Women Pilots in America* (1991)

Gibson, Julie Ann

The first female pilot in the history of the Royal Air Force (RAF), Gibson was born into the family of a Royal Navy lieutenant commander. Her interest in flying came early in life. She was educated in a variety of places, including Malaya, England, and Scotland, as her father's military career kept the family on the move.

In 1983 Gibson graduated from the City University of London with a degree in aeronautical engineering. During her college years she learned to fly, soloed, and joined the university air squadron. She was accepted into the Royal Air Force

College in 1984. After training, her first posting was at the RAF Fighter Base in Suffolk, England, where she served as the officer commanding the general engineering flight over 75 men. In her next position she had 160 men under her command as well as all the bombs and missiles used by the tactical weapons unit of the McDonnell Phantom Squadron.

She applied for pilot training on single-jet engines in Yorkshire, England, then graduated to the Advanced Flying Training Squadron of the Multi-Engined Training Wing. On June 14, 1991, at the age of 29, Gibson became the first female pilot in the history of the RAF.

Gibson has never seemed as awed by her accomplishments as her interviewers are, describing her success simply by saying: "I remember looking up at the aeroplanes when I was little, and thinking, I can do that."

References
Cadogan, *Women with Wings: Female Flyers in Fact and Fiction* (1993)

Gilbert, Jeanne Genier

The first woman pilot in British Columbia, Gilbert was born in 1902 in Kamloops. She was fascinated with aviation during her entire childhood, but it was not until she was 26 years old that she could begin lessons. That year she moved to Vancouver and married Royal Canadian Air Force (RCAF) pilot Walter Gilbert. Because his career required them to move frequently, it was hard for Gilbert to join any aero club long enough to receive flying lessons, but she logged many hours in a variety of planes helping her husband unofficially.

On November 29, 1929, Gilbert earned her private pilot's license after snatching bits of lessons at all the different military posts her husband was sent to. She was the thirteenth woman in Canada to receive a private license. When her husband went to work as a pilot for Western Canada Airways in 1939, Gilbert earned her radio operator's license and began training for her commercial pilot's license. She was forced to stop her training, however, when the government banned unnecessary civilian flying after war was declared with Germany.

Gilbert tried to join the RCAF as a pilot, but like many other women pilots of the day she was turned down because of her sex. She appealed the decision, but her appeal was denied. Soon after, her marriage failed. Gilbert quit aviation after the divorce. She died in 1986.

In her opinion: "Flying was no trivial sport, but a tremendous field for women if the stubborn prejudice of the average man could be overcome."

References

Render, *No Place for a Lady: The Story of Canadian Women Pilots, 1928–1992* (1992)

Gillies, Betty Huyler

One of the earliest women to be employed as an aviator, Gillies later became a member of the Women's Airforce Service Pilots (WASPS) and was one of the founders and a president of the Ninety-Nines. Born in 1910, she decided to learn to fly in 1928 after reading Amelia Earhart's famous "Try Flying Yourself" article in *Cosmopolitan* magazine. Her lessons began on November 10, 1928, at Roosevelt Field in Long Island, New York, while she was a student nurse at a local hospital. She soloed on December 23, 1928, after only seven and a half hours of instruction and received her private license on May 6, 1929.

In November 1929 Gillies cofounded the Ninety-Nines along with Earhart and 97 other women pilots. The next month, on December 1, 1929, Gillies received her commercial license. She was then employed by the Curtiss-Wright Corporation of Long Island to demonstrate the curriculum of their flying school and the planes available to potential students.

On January 18, 1930, she married Brewster A. "Bud" Gillies, an executive with the Grumman Aircraft Corporation, where he was instrumental in hiring women, including his wife, as test pilots for the company. Her height, 5 foot 1 $1/2$ inches, was never a problem as long as she could adjust the seats in the plane. On June 16 she received her transport license.

In 1939 Gillies became president of the Ninety-Nines. As president, she was one of the first to alert her members to the fact that their flying skills might be useful to the coming war effort. She also created the Amelia Earhart Memorial Scholarship Fund and challenged and beat a long-standing rule of the Civil Aeronautics Administration that denied pregnant women the right to fly.

On September 21, 1942, she became one of the earliest recruits to the Women's Auxiliary Ferrying Squadron (WAFS) (later WASPS), second in command under Nancy Harkness Love. Stationed at the New Castle Army Air Base in Wilmington, Delaware, Gillies found herself flying military planes with seats that could not be adjusted. She phoned a male pilot she knew at Grumman who was her height and learned that he flew with special wood blocks strapped to the rudder pedals. She then had a set of such blocks fashioned for herself. Gillies was one of only five other WAFS to qualify for flying the highest level of airplanes. When Jacqueline Cochran, director of women pilots, succeeded in convincing the military to let WASPS do more than ferry planes, Gillies was one of the first to be given tougher assignments.

When Love received a promotion in December 1942 she promoted several WAFS to commanding officer positions. Gillies was promoted to commanding officer of the base at New Castle. On August 15, 1943, Gillies and Love became the first women to qualify as pilots of the B-17 Flying Fortress. They were training to be the first women to ferry a bomber across the Atlantic, but their mission was cut short by a top-ranking male general who was firmly against female pilots entering the combat arena.

On April 14, 1944, Gillies was a member of the first class of women allowed to take the officer training classes offered by the U.S. Air Force. The WASPS were deactivated in December 1944.

After the war Gillies and her family moved to San Diego, California. Gillies was one of the few women who could obtain employment as a pilot, once again through the position of her husband, who was now the head of the test program for Ryan Aeronautical Corporation. In May 1945 Gillies began training new test pilots in instrument flight and flight testing the Ryan Fireball herself.

In 1949 Gillies received a commission to the Air Force Reserve as a major in recognition for her work as a WASP. In the reserve she trained with the 9083rd VAR Training Group in San Diego. The commission was retracted, however, when new military rules banned women with children under the age of 18 from being officers.

From 1949 through 1952 Gillies flew private charters for pay and participated in the All-Women's Transcontinental Air Races (AWTAR) for fun. In 1953 Gillies was put in charge of the AWTAR; she raised the requirements for participation to keep the race as professional as possible. She held the position of chair of the board of AWTAR until 1961 and was then appointed by President Lyndon Johnson and served for three years on the first Women's Advisory Committee to the Federal Aviation Administration (FAA).

In 1981 Gillies received the Elder Statesman of Aviation Award from the National Aeronautic Association of the United States.

As far as her flying days with the WASPS were concerned, Gillies once said: "The fighter pilots fresh out of school would let it be known how difficult the planes were to fly. They resented the girls flying those aircraft, and I can't blame them."

See also
All-Women's Transcontinental Air Race (AWTAR); Cochran, Jacqueline; Earhart, Amelia Mary; Love, Nancy Harkness; Ninety-Nines; Women's Airforce Service Pilots (WASPS)

References
Douglas, *United States Women in Aviation, 1940–1985* (1990); *History of the Ninety-Nines, Inc.* (1979); Moolman, *Women Aloft* (1981); Van Wagenen Keil, *Those Wonderful Women in Their Flying Machines: The Unknown Heroines of World War II* (1979)

Gillies, Brewster A. "Bud"

As an executive with the Grumman Aircraft Corporation Gillies was instrumental in hiring women as test pilots for the company during and after World War II. Citing the shortage of civilian men as his reason, Gillies convinced company management to use women as test pilots, but the company required that they first be tested in safer jobs. Professional pilots like Cecil "Teddy" Kenyon, Barbara "Kibby" Jayne, and Elizabeth Hooker had raced and made money on the air show circuit before the war. They were overqualified for ferrying, but in 1942 they took the positions for the promise of better work.

After the war Bud Gillies was able to hire his wife, Betty Huyler Gillies, second in command of the then-defunct Women's Auxiliary Ferrying Squadron (WAFS), as a test pilot.

See also
Gillies, Betty Huyler; Hooker, Elizabeth; Jayne, Barbara "Kibby"; Kenyon, Cecil "Teddy"; Women's Airforce Service Pilots (WASPS)
References
Douglas, *United States Women in Aviation, 1940–1985* (1990); Van Wagenen Keil, *Those Wonderful Women in Their Flying Machines: The Unknown Heroines of World War II* (1979)

Godwin, Linda M.

The woman who performed the first spacewalk while docked to an orbiting space station, Godwin was born July 2, 1952, in Cape Girardeau, Missouri. She received a bachelor of science degree in mathematics and physics from Southeast Missouri State University in 1974 and a master of science degree in 1976 and a doctorate in physics in 1980 from the University of Missouri. Her first job out of college was with the National Aeronautics and Space Administration (NASA) in the Payload Operations Division, where she worked in payload integration and as a flight controller and payloads officer for several shuttle missions.

In 1986, after a year of training, Godwin became an astronaut. From April 5 to April 11, 1991, as a mission specialist and member of the crew of the *Atlantis* space shuttle, Godwin deployed the gamma ray observatory (GRO) to study gamma ray sources in the universe. *Atlantis* also carried amateur radio equipment for voice contact, fast scan and slow scan TV, and packet radio. Several hundred contacts were made with amateur radio operators around the world.

From April 9 to 20, 1994, Godwin was again in space, this time as a payload commander aboard the *Endeavor* space shuttle. She was responsible for the three large radars and a carbon monoxide sensor that were used to enhance studies of the earth's surface and atmosphere.

On March 22, 1996, with a crew of six aboard *Atlantis*, Godwin took part in STS-76, the third docking mission to the Russian space station *Mir*. Following rendezvous and docking with *Mir* a NASA astronaut, Shannon Lucid, was transferred to *Mir* for her record-breaking five-month stay.

It was on this mission that Godwin performed a six-hour spacewalk, the first while docked to an orbiting space station, to mount experiment packages on the *Mir* docking module to detect and assess debris and contamination in a space station environment. STS-76 landed on March 31, 1996.

Godwin's ground assignments between shuttle flights have included working with flight software verification in the Shuttle Avionics Integration Laboratory (SAIL) and serving as chief of the Mission Development Branch of the Astronaut Office of NASA, and as the astronaut liaison to its Educational Working Group.

See also
Atlantis Space Shuttle; *Endeavor* Space Shuttle; Lucid, Shannon W.; *Mir* Space Station
References
Biographical Data Sheets, Lyndon B. Johnson Space Center (1997)

Gokcen, Sabiha

The first woman to fly in active combat, Gokcen was also Turkey's first female

Sabiha Gokcen (1953)

In 1938 Gokcen began a series of tours as the unofficial ambassador of Turkey. She flew her own plane to the various Balkan states she visited and lectured at each stop. Gokcen gained steady employment as a flight instructor and executive at the Turkish Air School and retired from teaching in 1955. She retired from flying in 1966 after more than 4,000 hours in the air.

References

Cadogan, *Women with Wings: Female Flyers in Fact and Fiction* (1993); Lomax, *Women of the Air* (1987); Moolman, *Women Aloft* (1981)

Gower, Pauline

The woman who headed the British Air Transport Auxiliary (ATA) during World War II and the first woman to attain the rank of commander in the British Royal Air Force, Gower was born in 1910 in Kent, England. The daughter of Sir Robert Gower, she attended convent school in England and finishing school in Paris before asking for permission to attend flight school. Her father denied permission so Gower paid her own way by holding violin recitals and writing aviation articles for magazines.

She received her pilot's license in 1930 and teamed up with Dorothy Spicer, who had a ground engineer's certificate. They asked Amy Johnson to join them, but Johnson preferred to focus on breaking aviation records. In 1931 they purchased their first plane and opened a joyriding business, offering flights to tourists in and around Gower's hometown of Kent.

At the end of summer 1931 they were invited to attend the first British All-Women's Flying Meeting held at the Sywell Aerodrome in Northhampton sponsored by the Duchess of Bedford. Gower entered a race on a triangular course and had the lead until her engine died and she had to make a forced landing.

pilot and the first woman admitted into the army as a pilot. She was born in Bursa, Turkey, in 1919 and was orphaned early in life. Then luck stepped in, and Gokcen was adopted by the country's new leader, Kemal Atatürk, in 1925.

Gokcen was educated at the American Girl's College in Istanbul, Turkey. She learned to fly at the Turkish Aviation School and learned to fly gliders in the USSR. Through her father's influence she was then admitted to Eskisehir Military Air School, the Turkish Army's air cadet program, in 1935. There Gokcen led an all-female squadron, as it would have been socially unacceptable for a woman to give orders to male pilots.

In 1937 she flew as part of a nine-plane bombing mission to quell a revolt by Kurdish tribesmen. She gained the nickname "Amazon of the Air" for having survived the combat situation.

Together Gower and Spicer joined various air circuses in 1932 and 1933, flying with the likes of Mary Petre, the Honorable Mrs. Victor Bruce. They continued to work on their flying skills, and Gower became the third woman in England to hold a commercial pilot's license.

Gower wrote fiction for *Girl's Own Paper* to earn extra cash. In 1934 she wrote her first book, *Piffling Poems for Pilots*, a collection of short poems. In 1934 and 1935 she and Spicer were on their own again. They formed the Air Trips Ltd. company giving joyrides out of a field near Hunstanton, England, and they had a steady stream of tourists as customers. Gower worked for and earned her navigator's and instrument licenses in 1936. She became the first woman in the world to obtain the complete list of pilot's certificates.

In the summer of 1936 the women joined Tom Campbell Black's Air Display, where Gower's plane was hit on takeoff by another plane performing a landing. She was hospitalized for a week, and the experience ended her enthusiasm for air circuses. When the season ended in September 1936 she was glad to end her time as a stunt flyer.

As World War II approached Gower was elected president of the Gillingham Corps of the St. John's Ambulance Brigade and was awarded the Order of St. John of Jerusalem for her work with the group.

In 1938 Gower was the only woman invited to join the Committee on the Control of Flying, where she met the men who would create the ATA, which recruited civilian pilots to ferry planes from manufacturers to air bases to save military pilots for battle in World War II. The ATA excluded female pilots until Gower publicly protested this policy. Gower's objections won her permission to form a women's section of the ATA, starting with eight pilots who were permitted to fly only the smallest planes. She began her work for the ATA on December 1, 1939, at the age of 29 and for a salary of 400 pounds a year. She and the first group of eight recruits were stationed at the Hatfield Air Base in England.

As the war continued, Gower received permission to recruit more women. Lady Mary Bailey flew with the ATA, as did Gower's old flight school classmate Amy Johnson, who had in fact gained fame as a long-distance flyer. In 1942, while the United States debated admitting women to their ferry programs, Jacqueline Cochran recruited fellow American women for the ATA. In total she brought 25 women pilots to Britain during 1942. Gower's group was also visited by Eleanor Roosevelt and Oveta Culp Hobby on a tour to study the activities of women in wartime Britain.

Meanwhile, the performance of the Women's Section of the ATA earned Gower induction into the Order of the British Empire and made her a fellow of the Royal Meteorological Society. It also earned the female pilots the right to fly larger planes and allowed Gower to recruit even more women. Before the war's end, her roster numbered 100 women from around the world. These women ferried planes to more and more dangerous arenas of the war as the Allies advanced on Germany in 1943 and 1944.

During this time Gower joined the board of the British Overseas Airways Corporation, the first woman to be appointed to the board of an airline.

In 1944 Gower married Wing Commander Bill Fahie. The ATA was dismantled in November 1945 at war's end. Gower died in childbirth in March 1947.

Regarding her love of flying, Gower said: "For me, aviation is top-ranking among all the careers open to women. More than that, I would say that every woman should learn to fly. Psychologically, it is the best antidote to the manifold neuroses which beset modern woman."

Gray, Marjorie

A member of the first class of the Army
Air Force's Women's Auxiliary Ferrying
Squadron (WAFS), Gray was born in
Cliffside Park, New Jersey. She gained
her pilot's license in 1938 as World War
II was raging across Europe. She received
her commercial certificate in 1942 as the
United States entered the war.

Gray volunteered immediately for the
first class of WAFS, training at Howard
Hughes Field in Houston, Texas, where
the WAFS were based before Jacqueline
Cochran moved the group to Avenger
Field. Gray spent 25 months ferrying and
flew 19 different types of military aircraft
during her enlistment.

When the WAFS disbanded in December of 1944 Gray, like other officers
of the WAFS, was awarded a commission
in the Air Force Reserve but was never
called to action. Instead she became one
of the first women to open her own fixed-
base flight operation, opening the Marjorie M. Gray Inc. Aero Services in
Teterboro, New Jersey, in 1946.

In 1956 Gray was awarded the Lady
Hay Drummond-Hay Award for outstanding achievement in aviation. In
1966 she sold her Aero Services company
to take a job as a technical writer on aviation for the Curtiss-Wright Corporation. She also worked as an associate editor for *Flying* magazine after her time at
Curtiss-Wright and became a member of
the Ninety-Nines.

In 1992 Gray was inducted into the
Aviation Hall of Fame in New Jersey
with fellow former WASPS, including
Kay Brick and Jacqueline Cochran.

Grizodubova, Valentine

One of Russia's female combat aces in
World War II, Grizodubova was born in
1916 in Kharkov, Russia, to a seamstress
mother and aircraft-building father. Her
father introduced her to flying.

At 18 Grizodubova enrolled at the
Kharkov Technological Institute to study
science and mechanics to further her flying skills. As a student she had the chance
to meet government officials and used
her contacts to gain admission to various
flying schools, including the Osoarviakhim, one of the largest.

After gaining her license Grizodubova
became an instructor at the Osoarviakhim herself while continuing her education in flight mechanics. Her next job
was with the Maxim Gorky Escadrille,
with which she flew to remote areas of
Russia performing in air shows and then
distributing educational pamphlets and
giving lectures on everything from agriculture to science. She was the first
woman admitted to the group.

During these air shows Grizodubova
began her career as a record breaker, setting speed records in various planes. For
her efforts she was elected to the
Supreme Soviet, a collection of experts in
many fields who advised the Soviet Congress. Grizodubova soon met Marina
Raskova, another famous Soviet female
pilot, and together with Polina Osipenko

Valentine Grizodubova (1938)

they established a 6,450-kilometer distance record for women in September 1938. Together they were known as the Winged Sisters.

The three attempted to fly from Moscow to Komsomolsk-na-Amure. An hour before arrival, a snowstorm struck. Ice accumulated on the wings, and Grizodubova, who was piloting the craft, could not keep the plane at its prescribed flying height. They jettisoned everything they could, and finally Raskova even parachuted out to lighten the load. Grizodubova landed the plane, and Raskova was found ten days later. For their efforts each was honored as a Hero of the Soviet Union. They were the first Soviet women to receive this honor.

Soon after the flight Grizodubova married and had a son, and then World War II began. Russia lost so many men and so much aircraft to German bombers that Raskova was recruited to create several women's combat units. Grizodubova joined the Long-Range Air Regiment, which flew supplies and fresh recruits to the military units inside German lines. She received the Hero of the Soviet Union Medal for her combat work.

Regarding women's contribution to the world, Grizodubova said: "There are no special female professions in our country, no 'women's' business. There is no sphere, no branch of industry, culture or life in general where women are not a mighty force."

See also
Raskova, Marina
References
Knapp, *New Wings for Women* (1946); Myles, *Night Witches: The Untold Story of Soviet Women in Combat* (1981); Noggle, *A Dance with Death: Soviet Airwomen in World War II* (1994)

Haizlip, Mae (Mary)

The first woman pilot to be engaged as a traffic manager for a major airline, Haizlip was born in St. Louis, Missouri, circa 1905. She learned to fly from her pilot husband, Jimmy Haizlip. Her first public flight was as a member of a 5,000-mile air tour of the United States and Canada in 1929.

In 1930 Haizlip entered the Women's Dixie Derby but crashed near Greenwood, South Carolina. After a brief hospital stay, Haizlip was recovered enough to enter a 25-mile women's speed race, which she won by flying 121 miles per hour over the course. The prize was $500.

In June 1931 Haizlip set a women's altitude record of 18,097 feet, and in August of that year she won second place, after Phoebe Omlie, and $1,800 in the All-Women's Transcontinental Air Race. She entered the National Air Race in 1932 and won, setting a new women's speed record of 252 miles per hour.

In 1933 Haizlip won first place in both the Los Angeles Aero Trophy Race and Chicago's Walter E. Olsen Trophy Women's Race. This ensured her place as one of six recipients of the Outstanding American Flier of the Year Award from the National Aeronautic Association that year. Her husband was also a recipient that year, along with Amelia Earhart, Frances Marsalis, Louise Thaden, and Major James Doolittle.

Haizlip retired from active flying after 1933, taking a position as traffic manager for the Midwestern Division of Columbia Airlines. In 1936 she moved to Europe.

Regarding the many races in which she participated, Haizlip said: "I think these trials are more than sporting events. We have a laboratory of speed here at the races which certainly stimulates the making of better planes and engines for transportation."

See also
All-Women's Transcontinental Air Race (AWTAR); Earhart, Amelia Mary; Marsalis, Frances Harrell; National Air Races; Omlie, Phoebe Fairgrave; Thaden, Louise McPhetridge; Women's Air Derby
References
Adams and Kimball, *Heroines of the Sky* (1942)

Hamilton, Kelly

The first woman to fly a fighter aircraft since the Women's Airforce Service Pilots (WASPS) were deactivated at the conclusion of World War II, Hamilton (born 1955) also led the first all-female flight crew. In 1995 she was the most senior female aviator in the U.S. Air Force. She became a second lieutenant upon graduation from the Air Force's Officer Training School in 1973 though the air force was still not allowing women into their flight school. Instead, Hamilton became an evaluation officer, which involved working in all the aircraft she hoped to someday pilot.

When the air force opened pilot training to women, Hamilton was in the first group of 20 chosen. After graduation one of the first planes she flew was an F-5A Aggressor. After further combat crew and pilot training from 1978 through 1980, in 1981 Hamilton was given the chance to become the first woman to land a military aircraft in the United Kingdom since World War II. In 1982 she piloted a historic refueling flight, commanding the first all-female crew in the history of the air force.

In 1985 Hamilton took an assignment to the U.S. Air Force Academy as squadron commander and flight instructor to Cade Squadron 28. Hamilton became involved in the legal battle to topple the USC Title 10 Combat Exclusion Law, which kept women from the same combat flying assignments she was training the men to complete.

While this legal battle continued, Hamilton was rewarded for her efforts by the Women Military Advisors, who elected her president in 1988 and 1989.

Women were not allowed in combat flying until Desert Storm in 1990, and then, as before, Hamilton was among the first. Although they were still banned from flying fighters, bombers, and attack aircraft, she did log over 200 hours of fighter aircraft cover formation flying, for which she won the Aerial Achievement Medal.

It was not until July 31, 1991, that Hamilton's battle against the USC Title 10 Combat Exclusion Law was won.

About her attitude toward flying and her hard-won legal triumph, Hamilton said: "I've spent my adult life being told by people in the system that you can't do that, you're a woman. I have always taken great pleasure in proving them wrong. When it comes to flying, the airplane does not know my gender, it only respects my talent as an aviator."

See also
U.S. Air Force (USAF)
References
Holden and Griffith, *Ladybirds II: The Continuing Story of American Women in Aviation* (1993)

Hancock, Joy Bright

The first woman to become chief yeoman in the U.S. Navy (USN), Hancock

enlisted during World War I. She was born on May 4, 1898, in Wildwood, New Jersey. She was class historian and participated in athletics at Wildwood High School, eventually becoming president of the school's athletic league.

While Hancock was attending business school in Philadelphia in 1917, the USN began accepting women to serve as yeomen to release men for combat duty. Hancock applied, passed the physical, and was accepted. At that time women were not yet permitted to fly for the navy so Hancock's duties involved messengering confidential paperwork and handling Liberty war bond sales.

Between the wars female yeomen were mustered out of the service. Hancock married a World War I flyer and moved to England. Her husband died during peacetime duties, however, and in 1921 Hancock took a civilian job with the Bureau of Aeronautics in Washington, D.C., where she set up the first naval aviator files for the personnel department.

When she married again in June 1924 she quit her job. But her second husband died a year later while testing an experimental airship. Hancock took up flying to cure herself of her fear of flying after experiencing the two back-to-back tragedies. Hancock earned her pilot's license but truly excelled in the ground maintenance course.

Because jobs in aviation were hard to find for women, Hancock put her new knowledge to work at an old job: She rejoined the Bureau of Aeronautics but this time worked in the General Information Section, handling public relations and eventually creating the monthly *Naval Aviation News*.

In 1941 Hancock was employed as the head of the editorial and research division of the Bureau of Aeronautics. With the approach of yet another world war Hancock was sent to Canada to study the way women were incorporated into the Royal

Canadian Air Force. Her department then wrote a proposal outlining ways that women could participate in naval aviation to free the male civilians for combat flying.

Because of that report and much lobbying by Congresswoman Edith Nourse Rogers, the Women Appointed for Volunteer Emergency Service (WAVES) was created by act of Congress in July 1942 as a branch of the USN. Mildred McAfee was chosen as director and Hancock was appointed women's representative to the chief of the Bureau of Aeronautics, putting her in charge of all WAVES assigned to that organization.

Hancock arranged training for all new WAVES in a variety of different positions, including air traffic control, engineering, celestial navigation, and both gunnery and flight instruction. Once the recruits were given their assignments she quickly found herself involved in touchy discussions with the commanders of the various naval stations. Many commanders failed to assign the WAVES to duties commensurate with their specialized training, falling back on using them in clerical and messenger work, and it was Hancock's job to convince them to trust their new recruits.

After the war McAfee returned to her postwar position as president of Wellesley College. Captain Jean Palmer was made acting head of the WAVES until July 26, 1946, when Hancock took the appointment. Her postwar work with the WAVES involved pressing for legislation that would allow women to stay in the navy after the war emergency had passed. On June 12, 1948, the U.S. Congress approved the Women's Armed Services Integration Act thanks to Hancock's diligence.

Hancock's duties then revolved around organizing women's training within the boundaries of existing all-male training centers and touring U.S. bases in Europe to study the needs for postwar WAVES there. While in England Hancock had an audience with Queen Elizabeth II, who was impressed with the WAVES' war record.

Hancock stayed in the navy, serving as assistant chief of naval personnel for women until her mandatory retirement on June 1, 1953. On May 29, 1953, Hancock was awarded the Legion of Merit by the secretary of the navy. In 1954 she married a naval aviator and vice admiral in charge of the Sixth Fleet, stationed in the Mediterranean. Hancock traveled with him on his official visits to the fleet and visited with the navy women assigned to his command.

Hancock wrote her autobiography in 1972 and died in 1986. In her honor the National Women Officers Professional Association (WOPA) established the Captain Joy Bright Hancock Leadership Award the following year, which is awarded to a USN woman, officer, or enlisted member on active duty or reserve who has provided inspirational leadership.

See also
McAfee, Mildred; Rogers, Edith Nourse; U.S. Navy (USN); Women Appointed for Volunteer Emergency Service (WAVES)
References
Douglas, *United States Women in Aviation, 1940–1985* (1990); Hancock, *Lady in the Navy: A Personal Reminiscence* (1972)

Harrell, Francis
See Marsalis, Francis Harrell

Harris, Grace McAdams
One of the first women to attain an executive position with an aircraft company, Harris (born circa 1905) also learned to fly—and race—everything from hot air balloons to biplanes to motorcars. She was born in Newark, Missouri, and took her first flight in her early teens with a traveling barnstormer. She graduated from Kirksville State College in 1923 and

received her graduate degree in business and advanced accounting in 1925.

She landed a job in what was then referred to as the motorcar business and held it for six years, until her marriage to Gerald Harris on July 12, 1932. True to the customs of the times, Grace Harris retired from business to become a housewife. She became disenchanted with her life, however, and began taking a series of lessons that ranged from French to ice-skating. Then she and her sister enrolled in a local flying school and began working toward their pilots' licenses at Richards Field just outside of Kansas City. Harris received her private pilot's license in 1941.

That same year she worked three days a week as an accountant for the Ong Aircraft Corporation, an airplane distributor that owned Richards Field, as a way both to assist the war effort and to help pay for her advanced flying lessons. In 1942 Ong donated planes to and thus became a member of the Civilian Pilot Training Program, which trained men and women as certified private pilots. This led to Harris's involvement in the National Aviation Training Association and frequent trips to Washington, D.C., where she met a young Harry Truman in his first years as a Missouri senator.

In 1942 Harris, with her many hours in the air and experience with varied aircraft, was a prime candidate for the Women's Airforce Service Pilots (WASPS). She was faced with the choice of joining them or continuing her work in managing the training of new pilots. She chose to continue training.

After World War II Ong Aircraft's business grew rapidly. They were distributors for many of the major manufacturers, selling everything from Piper to Stinson planes. Their territory covered Kansas and western Missouri. Harris's job at Ong frequently required her to ferry new planes from the factories around the country where the planes were completed to the customers in their territory.

Soon she decided to enter the National Air Races of 1947. Her friend and business associate, Bill Ong, who had won several trophies of his own, offered to train her. They practiced and even entered several smaller races in their area. Their efforts resulted in Harris placing second in the 1947 Women's Trophy Race of the National Air Races. In 1948 she not only won the race but established a new record for women's closed course racing at Cleveland. She followed that triumph by coming in second at the All-Women's Air Show in Florida in 1949.

Sadly, her husband Gerald died of a heart attack a month later, only a few weeks before that year's National Air Race competition. Harris decided to compete anyway, using her work to help survive her grief, and she won the race again. It turned out to be the last year she could compete in the National Air Races, as the military took over the race in 1950.

There were other changes in her life as well. By 1956 Richards Field was sold to make room for a new housing development, and Harris and Ong found themselves out of airplane distribution and into airplane financing. During this pause in her flying career Harris developed an interest in sports car racing. She won several division championships and did some touring through Europe before she returned to the United States.

As a member of the Ninety-Nines Harris competed in the All-Women's Transcontinental Air Races and won several trophies. At the 1952 annual convention of the Ninety-Nines she met a young Jerrie Cobb, soon to break her own speed records, when the two women shared a hotel room. They became such good friends that Cobb asked Harris to be her Fédération Aéronautique Internationale (FAI) officiate at the World Congress Flights in Las Vegas in 1959. When Cobb broke the 2,000-kilometer speed record in an Aero Commander, it was Harris who verified her friend's accomplishment to the FAI.

Acting as Cobb's FAI officiate led to further FAI work involving the verification of the new flight records being set every day, which included studying the aircrafts to make sure no illegal modifications had been made, collecting other evidence, and witnessing record attempts in order to certify them. After Harris had verified a record for Max Conrad he invited her to copilot his next ferrying job from Boston to Paris in April 1960, her first trans-Atlantic flight. In 1961 she flew in her first European race, the Aero Club of Italy's Race and Rally, in which she placed sixth. Later that year she placed twenty-fifth out of 87 contestants in the FAI European Air Rally.

In 1962 she finished first in the All-Women International Air Race at Nassau in the Bahamas. In 1962 she was also introduced to ballooning, and in November she organized and was the first woman in the American Montgolfier Society, dedicated to the advancement of the sport of ballooning. A month later she took her first solo flight in a hot air balloon, making her the first female Federal Aviation Administration–licensed balloon pilot in the United States.

In 1963 she decided to try the European Air Rally again, with Virginia Britt of Fort Lauderdale, Florida, as her copilot. The team placed fifth out of more than 100 contestants. When Harris served as a delegate to the FAI World Conference at Mexico City later that year, she met General Cecil Childre and discussed her interest in flying jets. On their return to the United States the general arranged for Harris to take a jet indoctrination course at the air force base near her home, which he com-

manded. She trained for and flew a Lockheed F-80.

Harris and Britt again competed in the 1965 European Air Rally, this time without placing, and had plans to compete again in 1967 until Harris's business with Ong Aircraft suddenly began to grow rapidly. With the backing of a local railroad company, Harris's company expanded into the commuter airline business, and she was appointed executive vice president of Ong Airlines. Harris also frequently flew one of the airline's original seven planes in order to hold down salary expenditures. This enterprise lasted only 18 months because of legal actions against the railroad that had backed them, and Harris was soon free to officiate at FAI races again.

Harris flew to Austria for the 1969 FAI European Air Rally to serve as copilot of the official FAI plane in the event, the first one held with the cooperation of the Soviet Union, allowing some of their cities to serve as sites on the tour. This gave her the chance, rare for Americans of her day, of seeing East Germany. Further rallies and convention work for FAI offered her the opportunity to travel to Russia, South Africa, Tahiti, New Zealand, and Samoa.

In 1975 Harris was honored as an Aviation Great at the Experimental Aircraft Association's annual convention. To celebrate she treated herself to a flight on the then-controversial supersonic Concorde and was invited by the pilot to sit in the cockpit. In 1977 she rode with Jerrie Cobb in the commemorative flight of the All-Women's Transcontinental Air Race, the last year the race was sponsored by the Ninety-Nines.

In her autobiography Harris proudly wrote: "America's history clearly establishes that women, too, are pathfinders. Your happiest moment comes as you reach yet another frontier after a long, difficult, and often discouraging journey."

References
Harris, *West to Sunrise* (1980)

Harrison, Helen Marcelle

The first Canadian woman to qualify for her seaplane rating, Harrison was also a military flight instructor in Canada both before and after World War II. She was born in Vancouver, British Columbia, on December 7, 1909. After a childhood spent touring the world she took her first small plane ride on a vacation to England in 1933.

Though she had been training for a career as a beautician, Harrison turned her sights to aviation and began flying lessons when she returned home to Canada. She qualified for her private pilot's license on March 4, 1934, after six and three-quarters hours of instruction. On a trip to Singapore she qualified for her seaplane rating. Then Harrison returned to England and earned hours toward her commercial license, which she received on November 12, 1936. Then she studied for an instructor's certificate, qualifying for it (as well as for her multi-engine and instrument ratings) on September 10, 1937. With this certificate Harrison became the first woman in Canada and the second in the English empire to qualify as an instructor.

Well-paying jobs in aviation for women were scarce in England, so in the mid-1930s Harrison moved to South Africa, where the government was starting a pilot-training program to build up their Air Force Reserves. Harrison was the first female instructor in South Africa; she taught classes in Grahamstown, Pretoria, and the Orange Free State. This job made her the only Canadian woman to be paid to fly before 1940 and the first woman in the British Empire to fly and instruct on military aircraft.

During her time in South Africa Harrison also performed in air shows and carried medical teams to remote sites when emergencies arose. Harrison's longest flight was the 4,500-mile hop from Cape Town, South Africa, to Cairo, Egypt.

Harrison returned to Canada in 1940 and became a test pilot for the Cub factory in Hamilton, Canada. She then taught flying at the Kitchener-Waterloo Flying Club and at the Air Transport and Training Company Limited at the Toronto Island Airport.

In 1941, at the start of World War II, Harrison offered her skills to the Canadian military, but they refused to hire her to instruct pilots or to ferry planes. Instead, she started her own women's flying classes in the hope of creating a women's auxiliary air force as existed in the United States and other countries.

The Canadian government never accepted the idea, but in England the Air Transport Auxiliary (ATA) was instituted to ferry planes from manufacturing sites to military bases to free military pilots for combat service. These duties were reserved for civilian men until Pauline Gower, a prominent British aviator, protested and was given the right to recruit a women's section of the ATA.

When Harrison saw that she would not be able to use her aviation skills in her home country, she joined a group of similarly frustrated American women recruited by Jacqueline Cochran to join the British ATA. When she joined in 1942 Harrison was the first Canadian flyer in the ATA. She logged 500 hours in flight with the ATA and earned the rank of first officer before being discharged.

When the war ended Harrison returned to Canada. So many male pilots had come back to work after the war that she found it impossible, as a woman, to obtain employment in aviation. Harrison took a job driving a taxi at Montreal's Dorval Airport until an old acquaintance from the military found her a job testing and demonstrating Percival Proctor aircraft. In 1946 she made a cross-Canada solo flight in a Percival on one of her publicity tours. In 1949 she was hired to fly lumbermen and company officials for the Kent Logging Company of Vancouver.

From 1950 to 1969 Harrison managed a succession of flying clubs, but management never intrigued her. She also trained airline pilots but was refused employment as an airline pilot by all the major carriers in Canada. On August 26, 1969, Harrison retired from flying completely. In 1973 she was entered in Canada's Aviation Hall of Fame.

Though she had finished with flying, Harrison remained a part of the world of aviation by becoming the first woman director of Canada's Aviation Hall of Fame in 1981. The University of Calgary instituted a scholarship, funded each year by Spar Aerospace, in Harrison's name for a senior female engineering or science student.

Regarding the attitude her male students might have shown her through the years, Harrison said: "If they didn't like a woman instructor, they didn't show it. I was the first one these military pilots had ever had. I got on very well with my men students, but of course, they were under military discipline and couldn't very well object."

See also
Air Transport Auxiliary (ATA); Gower, Pauline
References
Knapp, *New Wings for Women* (1946); Render, *No Place for a Lady: The Story of Canadian Women Pilots, 1928–1992* (1992); Spring, *Daring Lady Flyers: Canadian Women in the Early Years of Aviation* (1994)

Hart, Marion Rice
The first woman to graduate as a chemical engineer from the Massachusetts Institute of Technology (MIT), in 1914, Hart (born 1892) also wrote a book on celestial navigation that she researched by sailing a 72-foot ketch around the world. However, she did not learn to fly until she was 54 years old.

Hart began flying lessons in 1945 at the Happy Landings Aviation Academy in New Jersey. She received her license in July 1946, and she promptly purchased a Cessna in which she flew from New Jersey through Key West, Florida, to Cuba. Eventually she traveled cross-country several times, including making a trip to Alaska.

In 1953 Hart published *I Fly as I Please*, a chronicle of her adventures, including her first flight across the Atlantic, which she took with another pilot. The book described her many trips and detailed lessons learned as an aviator and as a woman enjoying what was then considered a rich man's hobby.

Hart entered the All-Women's Transcontinental Air Race just once, just for the fun of it. In her later years she settled in southern California and learned to fly gliders.

In 1966, at 74 years old, Hart became the oldest woman to fly the Atlantic solo. In 1976 she was awarded the Harmon Trophy for her achievements in aviation.

See also
All-Women's Transcontinental Air Race (AWTAR)
References
Douglas, *United States Women in Aviation, 1940–1985* (1990); Hart, *I Fly as I Please* (1953)

Hatfield Air Base
The Women's Section of the Air Transport Auxiliary (ATA) was housed at Hatfield Air Base during World War II. They

were the first group of women recruited to ferry planes from manufacturing plants to military bases during the war.

In 1940 Pauline Gower received permission to form a women's section of the ATA, starting with eight pilots, who were permitted to fly only the smallest planes. These women were Winifred Crossley, Margaret Fairweather, Rosemary Rees, Marion Wilberforce, Margaret Cunnison, Gabrielle Patterson, Mona Friedlander, and Joan Hughes. They came through the first winter at Hatfield Air Base without losing a plane or a pilot to accidents.

See also
Air Transport Auxiliary (ATA); Gower, Pauline
References
Curtis, *The Forgotten Pilots: A Story of the Air Transport Auxiliary, 1939–45* (1971)

Hayes, Marcella

The first African American woman to graduate from the U.S. Army Aviation School, Hayes was born in Centralia, Missouri, in 1956. She joined the Reserve Officers' Training Corps (ROTC) while attending college at the University of Wisconsin. After graduating with a degree in English in 1978, Hayes joined the army full time. Soon she qualified for entrance into the U.S. Army Aviation School.

After studying meteorology, aerodynamics, communications, and navigation and completing five 1,250-foot parachute jumps, Hayes earned her army aviator's wings in November 1979.

Of her success, Hayes said: "The drawback in the past was that women had a fear of failure. But if you pass the Flight Aptitude Selection Test and the flight physical, you can have the same opportunity as the men and you can learn to fly."

See also
U.S. Army

References
Holden and Griffith, *Ladybirds: The Untold Story of Women Pilots in America* (1991)

Heath, Lady Sophie Mary

The first woman to qualify for her ground engineer's license and the holder of several records, Heath was born Sophie Mary Pierce Evans in County Limerick, Ireland, in 1896. She obtained a degree in science from the University of Dublin, spent time lecturing at Aberdeen University, and was both married and widowed before discovering her interest in aviation at the age of 29.

Among her many "firsts" was her flight, as Mrs. Eliott Lynn, as the first passenger in the first aero club in existence, the London Aeroplane Club. She was also the first woman pilot trained by the club in 1925.

Heath had decided to support herself as a pilot, but after qualifying for her private, or A, license she was told not to bother trying for the commercial, or B, license. In April 1924 the International Commission for Air Navigation revoked women's rights to commercial licenses, which allowed the transport of passengers, and refused to grant any more. Lady Heath and other female pilots of high social position began a protest against this ban immediately. Heath wrote personally to the International Commission for Air Navigation in November 1925. She cited the commission's lack of data on which to base a decision. Heath offered statistics that she herself had gathered while on the medical subcommission of the Olympic Congress to prove that women were able to compete at the games. Since that effort had been a success and women were accepted for competition in the games in 1928, Heath offered to act as a medical guinea pig and to let the commission run any tests they felt a woman needed to pass to earn a

Lady Heath (undated photo)

pilot's license. The commission took her up on her offer.

In January 1926 Heath reported to the Stag Lane Aerodrome, where she spent three months studying navigation, meteorology, and the theory of flight for the B license. When she received it she began a series of public performances to highlight her talents and to earn money. In the face of her example the ban on commercial licenses for women was rescinded in May 1926. In 1927 she set a new altitude record for women by flying to 16,000 feet. Her passenger on that flight was fellow female British pilot Lady Mary Bailey. In July of that year she made a publicity tour of the 79 different aerodromes in the British Empire, flying 1,300 miles and 13 $1/_2$ hours in one day. She married Sir James Heath in October 1927 and began planning her biggest publicity stunt.

On January 5, 1928, after much planning, Heath took off from Cape Town, South Africa, in an attempt to be the first woman to fly solo to England. Two weeks later Lady Mary Bailey would take off from London for Cape Town, causing much discussion in the society press over their semicompetitive aviation careers. After refueling stops in Port Elizabeth, Durban, and Dundee, Heath reached Johannesburg on the afternoon of January 22, 1928. Along the way she was hosted by and gave lectures and joyrides to the various flying clubs in each town, earning money she later donated to aeroplane clubs throughout South Africa. From Johannesburg Heath flew across Central Africa. She had to make an emergency landing at Fort Usher when she blacked out due to sunstroke. When she recovered she continued on to Livingstone and Nairobi, and she arrived in Khartoum, where she rendezvoused with Lady Bailey on April 1, 1928.

Heath cabled the British Air Ministry for an escort plane to lead her across the Mediterranean Sea but was denied. The Air Ministry did not approve of her precedent-setting flight. So Heath cabled Benito Mussolini of Italy, and he sent an escort to meet her in Tripoli. When she arrived in Rome Mussolini asked only that she share her experiences with him. From Rome she flew across Europe and returned to London.

Heath died in 1939. Her dedication to the field of aviation was never more evident than in her letter to the International Commission for Air Navigation. She wrote: "Having dealt for some years with hundreds of girls and women of all ages and nationalities, I have seen that when a women is sufficiently fine and healthy to enter the first class of athletics her periods of nervous difference are imperceptible."

See also
Bailey, Lady Mary
References
Heath and Murray, *Woman and Flying* (1929); Lomax, *Women of the Air* (1987)

Helms, Susan J.

The first U.S. military woman in space, Helms was born February 26, 1958, in Charlotte, North Carolina. Her father was a lieutenant colonel in the U.S. Air Force (USAF), so Helms's interest in aviation started early. After high school graduation in 1976 she entered the U.S. Air Force Academy and received a bachelor of science degree in aeronautical engineering in 1980.

Helms was then assigned to Eglin Air Force Base, Florida, as an F-16 weapons separation engineer with the Air Force Armament Laboratory. In 1982 she became the lead engineer for F-15 weapons separation and was named the Air Force Armament Laboratory Junior Engineer of the Year in 1983.

Helms attended Stanford University from 1984 to 1985, earning her master of science degree in aeronautics and astronautics. The air force assigned her to be an assistant professor of aeronautics at the U.S. Air Force Academy for the next two years.

In 1987 she attended the Air Force Test Pilot School at Edwards Air Force Base, California, where she was named a distinguished graduate and was the recipient of the R. L. Jones Award for Outstanding Flight Test Engineer, Class 88A.

After completing one year of training as a flight test engineer, Helms served as a USAF exchange officer to the Aerospace Engineering Test Establishment at the Canadian Forces Base in Lake, Alberta, Canada.

Helms was selected by the National Aeronautics and Space Administration (NASA) in January 1990 and after training became an astronaut in July 1991.

On January 13, 1993, Helms flew on the crew of the *Endeavor* space shuttle for STS-54. Among their other duties, Helms and her fellow astronauts demonstrated the physics principles of everyday toys to an interactive audience of elementary school students across the United States. They landed on January 19, 1993.

Her next shuttle mission was less than a year later. Helms served as the flight engineer for orbiter operations and the primary Remote Manipulator System (RMS) operator aboard the *Discovery* space shuttle for mission STS-64 from September 9 to September 20, 1994.

From June 20 to July 7, 1996, Helms was the payload commander and flight engineer aboard the *Columbia* space shuttle on the longest mission to date, STS-78. The mission included studies sponsored by ten nations and five space agencies and was the first mission to combine both a full microgravity studies agenda and a comprehensive life science investigation.

Between flights on the space shuttles Helms has worked on RMS/robotics issues in the Mission Development Branch of the Astronaut Office of NASA; as a CAPCOM (spacecraft communicator) for STS-57, STS-51, STS-58, STS-60, and STS-61; and as the branch chief for payloads/habitability for the Astronaut Office.

See also
Columbia Space Shuttle; *Discovery* Space Shuttle; *Endeavor* Space Shuttle
References
Biographical Data Sheets, Lyndon B. Johnson Space Center (1997)

Herity, Marjorie Chauvin
See Chauvin, Marjorie

Hewlett, Hilda
The first British woman to receive a pilot's license, Hewlett did so in 1911, though she had been performing in air shows for over a year. She took the test in Brooklands on August 29, 1911.

Then Hewlett, who was married to novelist Maurice Hewlett, established a pilot-training school of her own where she taught future flyers for the Royal Air Force. Her most notable student was her son, a naval airman and wing commander in World War I. She also operated an aircraft factory at Brooklands during the war, assisting the English government in constructing planes.

See also
Quimby, Harriet

Higginbotham, Joan E.

An astronaut candidate in 1996, Higginbotham was born August 3, 1964, in Chicago, Illinois. After high school graduation in 1982, she received a bachelor of science degree in electrical engineering from Southern Illinois University in 1987.

She was then hired by the Kennedy Space Center in Florida as a payload electrical engineer in the Electrical and Telecommunications Systems Division. Within six months she became the lead engineer for the orbiter experiments (OEX) on OV-102, the *Columbia* space shuttle. Soon Higginbotham was working on the reconfiguration of the shuttle payload bay for all shuttle missions. With the upper-level management at the Space Center she handled several special assignments; she served as the executive staff assistant to the director of shuttle operations and management, led a team of engineers in performing critical analysis for the space shuttle flow in support of a simulation-model tool, and helped create an interactive display to show detailed shuttle processing procedures at Spaceport USA.

During this time Higginbotham also attended the Florida Institute of Technology, receiving her master's degree in management in 1992 and a master's degree in space systems in 1996.

Higginbotham was promoted to lead orbiter project engineer for OV-102 after two years as an orbiter project engineer for OV-104 for the *Atlantis* space shuttle.

Higginbotham was one of the first women to hold the technical lead government engineering position in the firing room, where she supported and managed the integration of vehicle testing and troubleshooting. This hands-on exposure to the National Aeronautics and Space Administration (NASA) led her to apply to the astronaut program. In 1996 she was selected for training as a mission specialist. "I probably won't feel I really am [an astronaut] until I'm strapped in the seat and they say, 'You're ready to go to launch.'"

See also
Atlantis Space Shuttle; *Columbia* Space Shuttle
References
Beatty, "Meet the Astronauts of the 21st Century" (1997); Biographical Data Sheets, Lyndon B. Johnson Space Center (1997)

Hilsz, Marie-Louise

The first woman to fly from Paris to Saigon and back, Hilsz was born in 1903 and started her aviation career as a professional parachute jumper in her native France.

In 1930 she flew from France to Indochina. In 1931 she made the record-setting flight from Paris to Saigon, though it took three months because of engine problems with her Gypsy Moth. She flew from Paris to Japan in 1933 and later that year bettered her Paris-to-Saigon record by making the trip again, this time managing it in only 5 days, 9 hours.

In 1935 Hilsz set a women's altitude record by flying to a height of 36,000 feet. She entered and won the Buc-Cannes Air Race in 1936. She died in 1946.

See also
Batten, Jean

References

Boase, *The Sky's the Limit: Women Pioneers in Aviation* (1979); Moolman, *Women Aloft* (1981)

Hire, Kathryn P. "Kay"

The first female in the United States assigned to a combat aircrew, Hire was born August 26, 1959, in Mobile, Alabama. After graduating from high school in 1977 she earned a bachelor of science degree in engineering and management from the U.S. Naval Academy in 1981.

Hire learned to fly in the navy, receiving her naval flight officer wings in October 1982. Her first posting was at the naval air station in Patuxent River, Maryland, flying worldwide airborne oceanographic research missions with Oceanographic Development Squadron Eight. Later she was promoted to oceanographic project coordinator, mission commander, and detachment officer-in-charge on board the specially configured P-3 aircraft.

At her next posting, at California's Mather Air Force Base, Hire instructed student naval flight officers in the classroom, on the simulator, and on board the T-43 aircraft at the Naval Air Training Unit. She was promoted from navigation instructor to curriculum manager and won the Air Force Master of Flying Instruction Award for her work.

In January 1989 Hire joined the Naval Air Reserve at Naval Air Station (NAS) Jacksonville, Florida, while working on a master of science degree in space technology from the Florida Institute of Technology. In May 1989 she was assigned to the Kennedy Space Center as an activation engineer, and she later served as a space shuttle orbiter mechanical systems engineer for Lockheed.

In 1991 Hire received her master's degree and her certification as a space shuttle test project engineer (TPE), which placed her in charge of all technical aspects of the space shuttle from the moment each landed through its next launch.

On May 13, 1993, Hire became the first female in the United States assigned to a combat aircrew when she was assigned to Patrol Squadron 62 as a patrol plane navigator/communicator. The squadron was deployed to Iceland, Puerto Rico, and Panama.

She was accepted by the National Aeronautics and Space Administration (NASA) as an astronaut in 1994, beginning as supervisor of space shuttle orbiter mechanisms and launchpad swing arms. In April 1996, she became a spacecraft communicator (CAPCOM). Her first shuttle flight was as mission specialist 2 on STS-90 from April 17 to May 3, 1998.

See also

U.S. Navy (USN)

References

Biographical Data Sheets, Lyndon B. Johnson Space Center (1997)

Hobby, Oveta Culp

A full colonel in the U.S. Army, Hobby was best known as the head of the Women's Auxiliary Army Corps (WAAC) during World War II. She was born Oveta Culp on January 19, 1905, in Killeen, Texas. She attended public school but received the assistance of private tutors as well. Hobby attended college at Mary Hardin-Baylor College until her father was elected to the Texas House of Representatives and the family moved to Austin, Texas, in 1921. There Hobby audited law courses at the University of Texas.

In 1925 Hobby was hired as an assistant city attorney in Houston and served as parliamentarian for the Texas House of Representatives. In 1929, with the encouragement of her suffragist mother, Hobby ran for the House of Representatives herself but was defeated by a candidate who was also a member of the Ku Klux Klan. She later wrote *Mr. Chairman*, a textbook about parliamentary procedures, for the public schools.

In 1930 Hobby began working for the Houston *Post*, which was presided over by a former Texas governor, William Pettus Hobby, whom she married in 1931. They had their first child in 1932. Six years later, after the birth of their second child, Hobby worked her way from an assistant editorship to the position of executive vice president of the *Post*.

Hobby joined the War Department's Bureau of Public Relations in 1941 as head of a new women's division for the patriotic salary of a dollar a year. After the bombing of Pearl Harbor brought the United States into World War II, Hobby helped create the Women's Auxiliary Army Corps. She was appointed its director on May 14, 1942, placing her in command of the first women to serve in the U.S. Army. (On an interesting side note, while Hobby worked in Washington, her former home in Texas was used as a boardinghouse for female pilots of the Women's Flying Training Detachment, the WFTD, the first women to fly for the U.S. Air Force.)

One of Hobby's first duties as WAAC director was to fly to England with First Lady Eleanor Roosevelt to study the women pilots flying for the British Air Transport Auxiliary (ATA).

Back in the United States Hobby operated her group under military codes and ethics, though the military's rules did not always suit the women. Until Hobby fought for the rights of recruits who became pregnant while unmarried, they were dishonorably discharged. Using her prior legal experience, Hobby argued that the men who impregnated them were not discharged and that therefore the women were not being treated equally. Upon winning that battle, the pregnant women were given honorable discharges.

In 1945 Hobby retired from the WAACS and was awarded the Distinguished Service Medal, the first woman so honored. Hobby returned to her postwar position at the Houston *Post* and became publisher in 1952. In the same year she was appointed head of the Federal Security Agency under President Dwight Eisenhower. In 1953 the Federal Security Agency became part of the president's cabinet and was renamed the Department of Health, Education, and Welfare. Hobby therefore became its first secretary and the second woman ever to sit on a president's cabinet.

Hobby kept the position until 1955 when she returned to Houston to care for her ailing husband and take over his duties as publisher of the *Post*. In 1960 Hobby won the Publisher of the Year Award. Her husband died in 1964, and Hobby became chairman of the board of the Houston *Post* in 1965.

The George Catlett Marshall Medal for Public Service for "selfless and outstanding service to the nation" was awarded to Hobby by the Association of the United States Army in 1978.

In 1983 Hobby sold the paper and retired. She died in 1995.

See also
Air Transport Auxiliary (ATA); U.S. Air Force (USAF); U.S. Army; Women's Airforce Service Pilots (WASPS)
References
Magill, *Great Lives from History: American Series* (1987); Weatherford, *American Women's History: An A to Z of People, Places, Organizations, Issues, and Events* (1994)

Holm, Jeanne M.

Former director of the Women's Air Force (WAF) and one of the first two women promoted to the rank of colonel in the U.S. Air Force, Holm was born in Portland, Oregon, in 1921. She joined the Women's Auxiliary Army Corps (WAAC) in 1942 and was promoted to the rank of second lieutenant a year later. By the end of World War II Holm was a captain in charge of a women's training regiment. Like most women of the day, she returned to civilian life after the war.

Holm rejoined the air force in 1948. She served at the headquarters of the Allied forces for southern Europe in Naples, Italy, from 1957 to 1961. She was appointed director of women in the air force in November 1965. In this capacity she expanded assignments for women and modernized their uniforms, which doubled recruitment. On July 16, 1971, she became the first woman to reach the rank of brigadier general, and on June 1, 1973, she became the first woman to reach the rank of major general. With this new authority Holm succeeded in getting women admitted to flying school in 1975.

After retirement, Holm worked as adviser to the Defense Manpower Commission and to the president from 1976 to 1977. She remained on the Advisory Committee on Women in the Services through 1980.

References

Boyne, *Beyond the Wild Blue: A History of the U.S. Air Force, 1947–1997* (1997); Holm, *Women in the Military: An Unfinished Revolution* (1982); Uglow, *The Continuum Dictionary of Women's Biography* (1989)

Hooker, Elizabeth

One of the earliest female test pilots for a large aviation corporation, Hooker started out studying medicine until the lure of the air captured her. She was a flight instructor on the Link trainer when she was hired along with Cecil "Teddy" Kenyon and Barbara "Kibby" Jayne by Brewster A. Gillies, vice president of the

Grumman Aircraft Corporation during World War II.

Citing the shortage of civilian men as his reason, Gillies convinced company management to use women as test pilots, but the company required that they first be tested in simpler, safer jobs. Though Hooker and the others had flown races and earned money on the air show circuit before the war, they accepted jobs as ferry pilots for the promise of better work. It soon came. After serving without incident they were all promoted to test pilot status, with restrictions.

See also
Gillies, Brewster A. "Bud"; Jayne, Barbara "Kibby"; Kenyon, Cecil "Teddy"
References
Douglas, *United States Women in Aviation, 1940–1985* (1990)

Horton, Mildred McAfee
See McAfee, Mildred

Howard-Phelan, Jean Ross

The founder of the Whirly-Girls, the international organization of women helicopter pilots, Howard was born on September 5, 1916, in Washington, D.C. She attended George Washington University and there she learned to fly as part of the Civilian Pilot Training Program. She was a trainee for the Women's Airforce Service Pilots (WASPS) in World War II, but she balked at the strict army discipline applied to the civilian flyers. She left the WASPS and joined the Civil Air Patrol. She worked for the Red Cross overseas for a time and then returned to the United States to work for the Aeronautical Chamber of Commerce promoting aviation among women.

In 1954 Howard was assistant to the director of the Helicopter Council Aircraft Industries Association. In that capacity she met Lawrence Bell, manufacturer of the first commercial helicopter. Knowing he had taught Jacqueline Auriol, the famous French test pilot, to fly one, Howard asked for lessons. She took her license test after 18 days of lessons and became the eighth woman in the United States to receive helicopter accreditation.

When Bell called her a "whirly-girl" the name of her new organization was born. Howard began corresponding with other female helicopter pilots to see if they were interested in forming a group to provide support and networking opportunities and to foster the exchange of technical information. The Whirly-Girls were born in 1955 with Howard as their only officer, the recording secretary.

In 1964 she was invited to join the Women's Advisory Committee on Aviation by President Lyndon B. Johnson.

Regarding aviation as a career, Howard-Phelan has said: "I don't think everybody wants to fly. But I think it opens a whole new everything for you, socially and careerwise. Now the careers are super. I think as Jacqueline Cochran said, that everything good in her life had come about because of aviation, and I can certainly say that."

See also
Auriol, Jacqueline; Cochran, Jacqueline; Civil Air Patrol (CAP); Whirly-Girls; Women's Airforce Service Pilots (WASPS)
References
Holden and Griffith, *Ladybirds: The Untold Story of Women Pilots in America* (1991); Russo, *Women and Flight: Portraits of Contemporary Women Pilots* (1997)

Howell, Emily Warner

One of the first women hired to fly as a pilot for a major airline, Howell, who was born in 1943, had been planning on becoming a stewardess. Her first flight convinced her she wanted to be a pilot instead. She started flying lessons in Denver in 1958, became a flight instructor at the school in 1961, and became the manager of the school in 1969. She also held jobs as a flying traffic reporter, a Federal Aviation Administration (FAA) examiner, and chief pilot for the Clinton Aviation Company in Denver before applying to Frontier Airlines.

Howell was hired by Frontier on January 29, 1973, the same week Bonnie Tiburzi was being interviewed and tested to become the first woman pilot at American Airlines. Howell served as first officer on a Convair 580 and eventually flew Boeing 737s for Frontier.

See also
Tiburzi, Bonnie Linda
References
Holden and Griffith, *Ladybirds II: The Continuing Story of American Women in Aviation* (1993)

Hughes-Fulford, Millie

A veteran of one shuttle flight, Hughes-Fulford was born December 21, 1945, in Mineral Wells, Texas. She graduated from Mineral Wells High at the age of 16 in 1962 and entered college immediately. Hughes-Fulford earned her bachelor's degree in chemistry and biology from Tarleton State University in 1968 and a Ph.D. in plasma chemistry from Texas Woman's University in 1972.

After graduation, Hughes-Fulford joined the medical school faculty of the University of Texas, focusing on the study of the regulation of cholesterol metabolism.

Hughes-Fulford became an astronaut in May 1991, conducting experiments aboard the Spacelab on the first Spacelab mission dedicated to biomedical studies. During the nine-day mission the crew completed over 18 experiments and brought back more medical data than had any previous National Aeronautics and Space Administration (NASA) flight.

In 1991 Hughes-Fulford was appointed scientific advisor to the undersecretary of the Department of Veterans Affairs. In 1994 she joined the California Medical Center at San Francisco as a professor while also continuing her research at the Department of Veterans Affairs Medical Center as director of the Laboratory for Cell Growth and Differentiation.

Keeping her hand in at NASA, Hughes-Fulford designed a series of Spacehab/Biorack experiments that examine the regulation of osteoblast (bone cell) growth regulation. The first experiment, OSTEO, flew on STS-76 in March 1996. The second, OSTEOGENE, was on STS-81, which flew in January 1997. The third, OSTEOMARS, was on STS-84 in May 1997. The experiments will help scientists understand the osteoporosis that occurs in astronauts during spaceflight.

References

Biographical Data Sheets, Lyndon B. Johnson Space Center (1997)

Hultgreen, Kara

The U.S. Navy's first female F-14 Tomcat pilot, Hultgreen was born in 1966. Her first goal in life was to go as fast as possible, which meant growing up to be a pilot. She joined the Reserve Officers' Training Corps (ROTC) while attending the University of Texas. Then she entered Aviation Officer Candidate School in Pensacola, Florida, and earned her wings in 1989. Hultgreen's career path was stopped when it came to flying combat-ready planes because of the prohibition then in effect against women in combat. She and other women aviators lobbied Congress to lift the prohibition. In 1991 she attended the Tailhook Convention in Las Vegas, Nevada, hoping to speak to her superiors about ending this prohibition. Instead, she became embroiled in what was soon to be known as the Tailhook Sexual Harassment Scandal.

Hultgreen chose not to prosecute her harassers as Lt. Paula Coughlin and others tried to do because she felt that to be listed among a group of victims was demeaning. But the harassment did not stop in Las Vegas. For the rest of her career Hultgreen had to deal with the rumor that she had been moved ahead in F-14 training not for her abilities but as a public relations ploy in the wake of the scandal to show that the navy did not discriminate against women. In 1993 she was assigned to Carrier Air Wing 11, where she finally trained on combat-ready Tomcats at the Miramar Navy Air Station.

Hultgreen was assigned to the Black Lion Squadron, VF-213. She was assigned to the *Lincoln* aircraft carrier stationed in the Pacific Ocean and was preparing to deploy to the Persian Gulf War when she died on October 25, 1994, while attempting a daylight landing. Due to intense controversy over the cause of the crash, Hultgreen's plane was salvaged. After studying it, the navy released a report stating that the crash was caused by the left engine stalling on its landing approach, that is, a technical malfunction, not pilot error.

Reflecting on the death of a male pilot in her squadron, Hultgreen once said: "It's not that big a deal that he died—the hard part about all that is when you have to go to the funeral and see his parents. And you just sit there and you think, 'That could be my parents.' But I don't feel half as bad for him, because he died doing something that he really loved doing."

See also

Coughlin, Paula; Tailhook Sexual Harassment Scandal; U.S. Navy (USN)

References

Perry, "Navy Not Biased against Women, Report Finds" (1997); Vistica, *Fall from Glory: The Men Who Sank the U.S. Navy* (1995); Zimmerman, *Tailspin: Women at War in the Wake of Tailhook* (1995)

Ingalls, Laura

The first woman to fly the United States nonstop from coast to coast and the first to cross the Andes, Ingalls was born circa 1900 into a wealthy family in New York City. She studied music and art in Europe before returning to the United States in 1928 to learn to fly.

In April 1930 Ingalls graduated from the Roosevelt Field Aviation School in Long Island. In May she celebrated by flying 980 consecutive loop-the-loops. At an air meet in August she flew 714 barrel rolls, beating both the men's and women's records for the stunt. No one has ever beaten Ingalls's records.

On October 9, 1930, she set a new distance record for women, flying coast to coast in a time of 30 hours, 27 minutes. She wanted to be the first woman pilot to fly the Atlantic solo, but many women were making similar plans in 1931. Ruth Nichols tried first and failed. Then Ingalls got her opportunity. Unexpected plane repairs and unsafe weather delayed her until it was too late in the year to make the attempt. She put off the idea until 1932, but by then Amelia Earhart had become the first female pilot to cross the Atlantic alone.

Instead, Ingalls became the first woman to cross the Andes Mountains when she circled South and Central America in a 17,000-mile flight. She took off from Peru on March 14, 1934, and landed in Brazil and then in Cuba before returning to the United States on April 26, 1934. For her effort she was awarded the 1934 Harmon Trophy as the world's outstanding flyer.

On July 11, 1935, Ingalls became the first woman to fly the United States nonstop from coast to coast. She flew from New York to Los Angeles in 18 hours, 20 minutes, 30 seconds. She stayed in California long enough to plan her flight

back, which would be an attempt to break Amelia Earhart's west coast–to–east coast record. With Earhart's cooperation and help in planning, Ingalls broke that record by nearly three and a half hours on September 13, 1935. Ingalls's time on the flight was 13 hours, 34 minutes, 5 seconds.

In 1936 Ingalls entered the Bendix Transcontinental Air Races. It was the first year women were allowed to compete, and Ingalls came in second behind a team of Louise Thaden and Blanche Noyes. Ingalls won $2,500.

At the start of World War II in Europe, Ingalls joined the America First movement with famed aviator Charles Lindbergh and his wife, Anne Morrow Lindbergh. On September 26, 1939, as a member of the movement, she volunteered to fly over the White House and drop antiwar leaflets protesting U.S. involvement in the war. But the White House was a strict no-flying zone, and her license was revoked by the Civil Aeronautics Administration (CAA) the moment she landed. Ingalls appealed, retested, and won her license back.

In 1942, before she could secure funding for another record-breaking flight, Ingalls was arrested on suspicion of being

Laura Ingalls (1964)

a paid agent of Germany and failing to register as such. She defended herself, saying she was on the payroll of the German embassy but insisting that she was a double agent attempting to obtain information helpful to the Allies. Ingalls was convicted and sent to prison. She was released in 1943, but her flying career was ruined.

See also
Civil Aeronautics Administration; Earhart, Amelia Mary; Lindbergh, Anne Morrow; Nichols, Ruth Rowland; Noyes, Blanche Wilcox; Thaden, Louise McPhetridge
References
Adams and Kimball, *Heroines of the Sky* (1942); Roseberry, *The Challenging Skies: The Colorful Story of Aviation's Most Exciting Years, 1919–1939* (1966)

International Society of Women Airline Pilots (ISA + 21)

Like the Ninety-Nines, the International Society of Women Airline Pilots (ISA) arose through the efforts of one or two dedicated female pilots, in this case, Stephanie Wallach and Beverly Bass, who attended a Zonta Club event honoring Amelia Earhart in January 1978. There they met with a small group of other female airline pilots and discussed creating an organization where women could share their common professional interests.

In May 1978, 21 women met in Las Vegas at the home of Claudia Jones, a Southwest Airlines first officer. There they chose an acronym, ISA, which stood for the International Society of Women Airline Pilots as well as for an altitude pressure conversion that many worked with in their flying. The "+ 21" was in honor of their first set of members and a tribute to the way the Ninety-Nines had named themselves.

The goals of the group continue to be to provide networking, mentoring, and service projects for their members and to fund a series of scholarships to help other women pursue aviation as a career.

See also
Earhart, Amelia Mary; Ninety-Nines
References
Holden and Griffith, *Ladybirds: The Untold Story of Women Pilots in America* (1991)

International Women's Air and Space Museum

The International Women's Air and Space Museum (IWASM) is dedicated to "the preservation of the history of women in aviation and space and the documentation of their continuing contributions today and in the future." It was created under the auspices of the Ninety-Nines by a board that included aviation pioneer Nancy Hopkins Tier, who became the museum's first president.

The IWASM opened its doors to the public in March 1986 in Centerville, Ohio, in the historic home of Ashahel Wright, a great-uncle of Katherine

Wright. The museum is also a designated stop on the Dayton, Ohio, Aviation Trail.

The IWASM hosts displays of famous women in aviation, including Madame Blanchard, a French balloonist who served as Napoleon's chief minister of air; Jacqueline Cochran, the first woman to break the sound barrier; Valentina Tereshkova, the first woman in space; and Sally Ride, the first American woman astronaut. It also celebrates the contribution of women in wartime aviation, especially the Women's Airforce Service Pilots (WASPS), who ferried planes from manufacturers to air bases in World War II, freeing men for combat duty.

See also
Auriol, Jacqueline; Blanchard, Marie Madeleine Sophie Armont; Cochran, Jacqueline; Ride, Sally Kristen; Tereshkova, Valentina Vladimirovna; Tier, Nancy Hopkins; Women's Airforce Service Pilots (WASPS); Wright, Katherine
References
International Women's Air and Space Museum

Ivins, Marsha S.

A member of the National Aeronautics and Space Administration (NASA) Astronaut Class of 1984 and a veteran of four spaceflights, Ivins was born on April 15, 1951, in Baltimore, Maryland. Her family soon moved to Wallingford, Pennsylvania, where Ivins graduated from Nether Providence High School in 1969. She then entered the University of Colorado, where she received a bachelor of science degree in aerospace engineering in 1973.

Along the way Ivins qualified for a multiengine airline transport pilot license with Gulfstream-1-type rating; single-engine airplane, land, sea, and glider commercial licenses; and airplane, instrument, and glider flight instructor ratings.

Ivins joined the Lyndon B. Johnson Space Center in July 1974 as an engineer working on orbiter displays and controls and man-machine engineering. Her major assignment in 1978 was to participate in the development of the orbiter head-up display (HUD). In 1980 Ivins was assigned to be a flight engineer on the shuttle training aircraft (Aircraft Operations) and a copilot in the NASA administrative aircraft (Gulfstream-1).

From January 9 to January 20, 1990, Ivins was a mission specialist for STS-32, an 11-day flight on board the *Columbia* space shuttle. Ivins and the other crewmembers successfully deployed a Syncom satellite and retrieved the 21,400-pound long-duration exposure facility (LDEF).

From July 31 to August 8, 1992, Ivins was part of STS-46, an eight-day mission on board the *Atlantis* space shuttle, during which she and her fellow crewmembers deployed the European Retrievable Carrier (EURECA) satellite, and conducted the first Tethered Satellite System (TSS) test flight.

Ivins's third flight was on board the *Columbia* space shuttle for mission STS-62 from March 4 to March 18, 1994, a 14-day mission involving the U.S. Microgravity Payload 2 (USMP-2) and Office of Aeronautics and Space Technology 2 (OAST-2) payloads. These payloads studied the effects of microgravity on materials sciences and other spaceflight technologies. Other experiments on board included demonstration of advanced teleoperator tasks using the remote manipulator system and studies of protein crystal growth and the dynamic behavior of space structures.

Ivins's fourth spaceflight was the fifth mission to dock with Russia's *Mir* space station and the second to exchange U.S. astronauts with *Mir*. From January 12 to January 22, 1997, Ivins was again a mission specialist, on STS-81, a ten-day mission. The mission also carried the Spacehab double module, which provided additional middeck locker space for secondary experiments. In five days of docked operations more than three tons of food, water, experimental equipment, and samples were moved back and forth between the two spacecraft.

On the ground Ivins's technical assignments between flights have included crew support for orbiter launch and landing operations; review of orbiter safety and reliability issues; avionics upgrades to the orbiter cockpit; and software verification in the Shuttle Avionics Integration Laboratory (SAIL). She has served as a capsule communicator (CAPCOM) in Mission Control and a crew representative for the orbiter photographic system and procedures and for orbiter flight crew equipment issues. Ivins has also headed the Astronaut Support Personnel Team at the Kennedy Space Center in Florida, supporting space shuttle launches and landings.

Regarding the competition to get into the space program, Ivins has said: "I've never seen the need to separate men and women as far as what they do, and how they do it. They [NASA] were going to hire people and I wanted to be one of them."

See also
Atlantis Space Shuttle; *Columbia* Space Shuttle; *Mir* Space Station

References
Biographical Data Sheets, Lyndon B. Johnson Space Center (1997); Russo, *Women and Flight: Portraits of Contemporary Women Pilots* (1997)

Jayne, Barbara "Kibby"

One of the first female tests pilots in the United States, Jayne was hired by Brewster A. "Bud" Gillies, vice president of the Grumman Aircraft Corporation, during World War II and continued working for them after the war. Jayne was hired at the same time as Cecil "Teddy" Kenyon and Elizabeth Hooker, all professional pilots who had flown races and made money on the air show circuit before the war.

Citing the shortage of civilian men as his reason, Gillies convinced company management to use women as test pilots. But the company would not hire them first as test pilots, requiring them to prove their ability in simpler, safer jobs first. So Jayne and the others were hired as ferry pilots, picking up planes and other materials from around the country and delivering them back to Grumman.

The women hired were overqualified for ferrying, but in the winter of 1942 Jayne and the others took the positions for the promise of better work. During her work for Grumman, Jayne met and married a navy flyer who flew Hellcats, the same planes she tested.

See also

Gillies, Brewster A. "Bud"; Hooker, Elizabeth; Kenyon, Cecil "Teddy"

References

Douglas, *United States Women in Aviation, 1940–1985* (1990)

Jemison, Mae C.

Jemison was the first African American woman in space as a mission specialist on the space shuttle *Endeavor*. She was born in Decatur, Alabama, on October 17, 1956, but her family relocated to Chicago, Illinois, before she started school, so she has always identified herself as a Chicagoan.

Her interests in science and space started early in life. Her dreams of traveling in space as a scientist were encouraged and supported by her parents and her two older siblings. It was in the outside world that Jemison found discouragement. Society in the early 1960s still believed that African Americans could only work in certain support fields; therefore Jemison's teachers tried to channel her interest in science into a career in nursing. However, she was not to be deterred.

Jemison excelled in science and math in high school, and her high grades earned her acceptance into Stanford University's chemical engineering department. She also majored in Afro-American studies and was active in various student organizations, serving as president of the Black Student Union.

After graduation from Stanford University Jemison focused her interest in science on a career in medicine and applied to the Cornell University Medical College of New York. Here her traveling days began. As part of her medical training Jemison worked in Cuba, rural Kenya, and Thailand. She graduated medical school in 1981 and moved to Los Angeles to complete her internship and to start her own practice.

Jemison soon missed traveling, so she joined the Peace Corps. At the age of 26 Jemison became the area Peace Corps medical officer for Sierra Leone and Liberia, which put her in charge of the health of Peace Corps volunteers and embassy officials in those provinces in Africa.

On her return to Los Angeles after a two-year tour of duty, Jemison continued her medical practice by day and her engineering studies by night. Having never forgotten her dream of space travel, Jemison had kept her eye on the National Aeronautics and Space Administration (NASA). In 1977 they had begun accepting women for astronaut training. After the barrage of background checks, medical tests, and psychological interviews were over, Jemison became an astronaut in training in 1987.

On September 12, 1992, Jemison was the mission specialist for the space shuttle *Endeavor*. During the eight-day mission Jemison experimented with and studied everything from the effects of weightlessness on the loss of bone cells to motion sickness to frog fertilization. The last experiment involved fertilizing frogs, watching the tadpoles hatch, and studying them to see if they would develop normally in space. They did. The shuttle crew, complete with its new complement of frogs, landed back on earth on September 20, 1992.

For becoming the first African American woman in space Jemison was given the Trailblazer's Award at the American Black Achievement Awards in 1992. In 1993 she was inducted into the National Women's Hall of Fame.

Her postastronaut work has included teaching and research at Dartmouth College, the founding of an international summer science camp, and the formation of the Jemison Group, whose goal is to improve conditions in developing countries through the use of science and technology. She also speaks to groups around the country, and she wrote the introduction for Doris Rich's autobiography of Bessie Coleman, the first African American woman pilot.

Regarding her position as the first African American woman in space, Jemison says: "I'm very aware of the fact that I'm not the first African American woman who had the skills, the talent, the desire to be an astronaut. I happen to be the first one that NASA selected."

See also
Coleman, Bessie
References
Sakurai, *Mae Jemison: Space Scientist* (1995)

Jenkins, Louise

Known as "The Daring Lady Flyer" of Prince Edward Island, Canada, Jenkins was actually born in Pittsburgh in the United States in 1890. She went to England as a nurse and ambulance driver during World War I and met and married Dr. Jack Jenkins in 1918. When the war was over they returned to his family estate, Upton Farm, on Prince Edward Island.

As a way to promote more tourism in the literary home of Anne of Green Gables, Jenkins and her husband decided to build the first commercial airport on the island in 1929. Pilots from all over began to visit the island, and meeting them intrigued Jenkins. She took flying lessons both in Canada and in their summer home in Sarasota, Florida, soloing in December 1931. She received her license the following March, making her the first woman pilot on the island. She did her early flying on the mainland of Canada near Toronto, Ontario.

On February 23, 1932, Jenkins made the first nonstop flight from Montreal on the mainland to Charlottetown on Prince Edward Island. Construction of the commercial airport on their property had just been completed, so Jenkins landed on her own airstrip. On that flight Jenkins also set a new speed record, traveling 540 miles in 4 hours, 8 minutes.

To celebrate the airport's completion Jenkins hosted an air pageant in the spring; it attracted upwards of 8,000 tourists. After flying at a few other air meets, Jenkins's plans to continue her career in aviation were cut short by family demands and obligations. Her husband became ill and needed full-time care. Jenkins flew her own plane for the last time on November 8, 1932, before selling it to a minister in Nova Scotia.

After Jenkins's husband died and her children had grown up and moved off the island, she retired to Old Lyme, Connecticut, where she died in 1986.

When asked why she had begun flying in the first place, Jenkins said: "I flew to cleanse the spirit and to get away from problems and to add excitement to my life."

References

Render, *No Place for a Lady: The Story of Canadian Women Pilots, 1928–1992* (1992); Spring, *Daring Lady Flyers: Canadian Women in the Early Years of Aviation* (1994)

Jernigan, Tamara E.

A member of the National Aeronautics and Space Administration (NASA) class of 1985, Jernigan was born on May 7, 1959, in Chattanooga, Tennessee. Her family eventually moved to California, where Jernigan graduated from Santa Fe High School in Santa Fe Springs in 1977. She attended Stanford University, receiving a bachelor of science degree in physics (with honors) in 1981.

Jernigan became a research scientist in the Theoretical Studies Branch at NASA's Ames Research Center in June 1981. She continued to study for her master of science degree in engineering science and received it in 1983, also from Stanford. Then she transferred to the University of California at Berkeley for her master of science degree in astronomy, which she earned in 1985.

Jernigan became an astronaut in July 1986 and worked at the Lyndon B. Johnson Space Center while completing her doctorate in space physics and astronomy, which she earned from Rice University in 1988. Her first mission was STS-40, a dedicated space and life sciences mission. Jernigan was a mission specialist on board the *Columbia* space shuttle from June 5 to June 14, 1991, working with Spacelab Life Sciences (SLS-1) to perform experiments that explored how humans, animals, and cells respond to microgravity and readapt to earth's gravity on return. Other experiments were designed to investigate materials science, plant biology, and cosmic radiation.

For STS-52, from October 22 to November 1, 1992, Jernigan was again a mission specialist. She and the crew deployed the Italian Laser Geodynamic Satellite (LAGEOS), which measures movement of the earth's crust, and operated the U.S. Microgravity Payload 1 (USMP-1). Jernigan was also instrumental in working with the space vision system (SVS), developed by the Canadian Space Agency, which will be used for space station construction. Numerous other experiments were performed by the crew in the areas of geophysics, materials science, biological research, and applied research for the space station.

From March 2 to March 18, 1995, Jernigan was the payload commander on the STS-67 Astro-2 mission aboard the *Endeavor* space shuttle. She was in charge of the second dedicated Spacelab mission to conduct astronomical observations in the ultraviolet spectral regions to fill in large gaps in astronomers' understanding of the universe. She also oversaw an experiment sponsored by the Australian

Space Office to make ultraviolet observations of deep space or nearby galaxies. It was the longest NASA mission to date.

Jernigan's fourth mission was aboard the *Columbia* space shuttle, for STS-80, from November 19 to December 7, 1996. As a mission specialist she helped to successfully deploy and retrieve the wake shield facility (WSF) and the orbiting retrievable far and extreme ultraviolet spectrometer (ORFEUS) satellites. She had been scheduled for two spacewalks, which were canceled because of a jammed outer hatch on the airlock.

Between space missions Jernigan's assignments for NASA have included software verification in the Shuttle Avionics Integration Laboratory (SAIL) and operations coordination on secondary payloads. She has been a spacecraft communicator (CAPCOM) in Mission Control for several other shuttle flights, including missions STS-30, STS-28, STS-34, STS-33, and STS-32. Jernigan has been lead astronaut for flight software development and chief of the Astronaut Office Mission Development Branch. In 1997 Jernigan was the assistant to the chief of the Astronaut Office, a job that required her to direct crew participation in the development and operation of the future space station.

See also
Columbia Space Shuttle; *Endeavor* Space Shuttle
References
Biographical Data Sheets, Lyndon B. Johnson Space Center (1997)

Johnson, Amy
The first woman to fly solo from England to Australia, Johnson was born in 1903 in Yorkshire, England. Her mother was a housewife and her father a successful fish merchant. Johnson excelled in school, to the point of becoming bored with her classes. At the age of 12 she was

Amy Johnson (May 19, 1930)

transferred to a more challenging private school, where she performed well in classes and at hockey practice and violin lessons. At 16 Johnson saw her first airplane in a movie newsreel, and she was hooked. Johnson took her first ride with an out-of-work World War I pilot in 1919, but it was almost ten years before she took another.

Johnson tested and qualified with honors for the Oxford and Cambridge Senior Local Examinations, but her father kept her from college until she was 19. Then she attended Sheffield University, where she studied economics. Johnson received her degree in three years but could not find a job in the business world. She tried to bolster her office skills by attending business college to study typing and shorthand, but she stayed only three months.

Johnson took her first job as an advertising copywriter, but she stayed only long enough to pay back her college debts and her parents before she ran away to London for a taste of big-city life. The experiment nearly failed when she lost her job as a salesgirl while still in the training period. Through an old family friend she found work as a legal secretary, which finally provided her the funds to join the London Aeroplane Club in September 1928.

Johnson had her first flying lessons at the London Aeroplane Club and she flew her first solo in June 1929. She received her A license at the end of the month, the thirty-seventh woman in England to receive one. She immediately began to work toward the B license, which would allow her to carry passengers. She also studied for her ground engineer's certificate—something no other woman had yet qualified for in England.

Johnson obtained her ground engineer's certificate in January 1930. She was invited to join the only two other female students at the Stag Lane School, Dorothy Spicer and Pauline Gower, who wanted to start a joyriding business. Johnson preferred to make a name for herself breaking records. Realizing that any career in aviation was difficult for a woman, Johnson knew that she had to engage the public's interest in her career. With the backing of the director of civil aviation, Sir Sefron Brancker, she acquired enough funds to buy a Gypsy Moth airplane and the supplies necessary for a solo flight from England to Australia. Johnson wanted to challenge the record of former Royal Air Force officer Bert Hinkler, who had made the trip in 15 days.

Johnson took off from Croydon Airport in London on May 5, 1930. After refueling and maintenance stops in Vienna, Constantinople, and Calcutta she landed successfully at Port Darwin, Australia, on May 27, 1930. The first money she earned in aviation was the 10,000 pounds *The Daily Mail* paid for the exclusive rights to publish her story, quite an increase from the three pounds a week she

had made as a legal secretary. For her triumph Johnson also received the Commander of the British Empire from King George VI himself in a reception at Buckingham Palace.

Even before all the heady excitement had died down Johnson was already planning her next feat. On July 28, 1931, Johnson became the first pilot to fly from England to Moscow in one day, traveling the 1,760 miles in approximately 21 hours.

Johnson met her future husband, Jim Mollison, a record-breaking flyer himself, when she was recuperating from an appendectomy in Cape Town, South Africa. Mollison was challenging the England–to–South Africa speed record, and Johnson met him at the airport at the end of his flight. Their competing careers kept them from meeting again until they had lunch in London later in 1931. Mollison impulsively proposed, and Johnson equally impulsively accepted.

The next day the announcement of the engagement of two such famous and daring pilots was reported across the English empire. They were married in July 1932 and spent their honeymoon in a castle in Scotland making plans for Mollison's next record-setting solo flight, across the Atlantic from east to west. He took off three weeks after their wedding and survived the crossing.

In November 1932 Johnson challenged and broke an earlier record of Mollison's by flying from England to South Africa. She had also bettered the Duchess of Bedford's time by nearly two days, and Johnson became the first solo pilot to make the round-trip, breaking records both ways. Her flying record and her romantic marriage were soon immortalized in the song "Amy, Wonderful Amy."

To capitalize on their success Johnson and Mollison decided to fly the Atlantic together. They purchased and equipped a de Havilland Dragon, named it *Seafarer,* and crashed on takeoff on June 8, 1933. Neither was hurt, so they had *Seafarer* repaired and tried again June 22, 1933. This time they made it across the Atlantic, but they were just a few gallons short of enough fuel to reach New York. They crashed at Bridgeport airport just outside the city. Though the plane was destroyed they survived this second crash and were feted by a ticker tape parade down Broadway. Several days later they had lunch at the White House with President Franklin Delano and First Lady Eleanor Roosevelt.

While in the United States, Johnson met Amelia Earhart and had the opportunity to fly a three-engine airplane compliments of the Trans-Continental and Western Air Lines. They invited her to copilot a cross-country flight in honor of her Atlantic crossing.

Meanwhile Mollison returned to England to purchase a plane in which to make the flight from America to England to clinch the record both ways. But this flight never happened. He returned to the United States with *Seafarer II*, which was destroyed on takeoff from Canada's Wasaga Beach. Before it could be repaired the weather changed, and the flight was postponed.

Johnson made money for the purchase of a new plane by writing a weekly column of aeronautical stories for *The Daily Mail*. Like many pilots of her day, she also demonstrated planes to potential customers for American Beechcraft and even flew as a commercial pilot for Hillman Air, the first daily service between London and Paris.

To commemorate the centenary of the founding of the State of Melbourne, Sir MacPherson Robertson, one of Australia's wealthiest citizens, sponsored a race from England to Australia with a prize of 15,000 pounds. Johnson and Mollison decided to fly it as a team. Technical malfunctions kept them from finishing the race, but they did create a new record for flying from England to India by making this first leg of the race in 22 hours.

Johnson and Mollison separated after the Robertson race. It was the end of their marriage and the end of the era of pioneering flights. To earn a living Johnson now relied on her writing and lecturing and on her position as president of the Women's Engineering Society. To renew interest in herself as a solo flyer, Johnson set out to regain her England–to–South Africa record in spring 1936.

She succeeded in breaking the existing records on both legs of the flight, flying 14,000 miles in 12 days. She also became the first pilot to use both the east and west routes during a record-breaking attempt. When she landed in London on May 14, 1936, Johnson was awarded the Gold Medal of the Royal Aero Club. That year she also wrote the book *Sky Roads of the World* about her many travels to exotic countries.

In 1938 Johnson divorced Mollison and went back to the use of her maiden name. She had to find a way to support herself, but she also wanted to contribute to her country's war effort against the Axis powers of World War II. Johnson tried to join the Royal Air Force as a pilot, but she was turned away because of her sex. The Secret Service turned her away for the same reason. In 1940 the Air Transport Auxiliary (ATA), an organization of civilian pilots who relieved the military from mundane flight tasks, opened a women's section. After exhausting the other outlets of war work, Johnson joined the ATA women's section.

Normally ATA pilots would ferry a new plane to an airfield and return to their base by train. On one trip, however, Johnson was offered the chance to fly back to base in an Airspeed Oxford. It was January 5, 1941, the anniversary of the first ferry trips made by women of the

ATA, and celebrations were scheduled at the main base. Johnson took off from Blackpool, England, in cloudy weather. The plane's engine failed over the Thames River off Herne Bay, and Johnson crashed into the water. Like her American friend Amelia Earhart, Johnson's body was never found. The anniversary party was canceled in her honor.

Of flying, Johnson once wrote: "There is nothing more wonderful and thrilling than going up into the spaciousness of the skies in a tiny plane where you feel alone, at peace with everyone, and exactly free to do what you want and go where you will."

See also

Air Transport Auxiliary (ATA); du Caurroy, Mary Tribe, Duchess of Bedford; Earhart, Amelia Mary; Roosevelt, Eleanor

References

Curtis, *The Forgotten Pilots: A Story of the Air Transport Auxiliary, 1939–45* (1971); Grey, *Winged Victory* (1966); Johnson, *Sky Roads of the World* (1939)

Karasova, Nina

A teenage Russian navigator during World War II, Karasova was captured by the Nazis. After a lengthy interrogation she was sent to the Ravensbruck concentration camp and later to the camp at Buchenwald. Karasova survived for 18 months until the war ended and Allied troops liberated the camp.

References
Cadogan, *Women with Wings: Female Flyers in Fact and Fiction* (1993)

Kavandi, Janet

An astronaut candidate in the National Aeronautics and Space Administration (NASA) class of 1994, Kavandi was born July 17, 1959, in Springfield, Missouri. After graduating as class valedictorian from Carthage Senior High School in 1977, she attended Missouri Southern State College in Joplin, Missouri, on a Presidential Scholarship. In 1980 she received a bachelor of science degree in chemistry and transferred to the University of Missouri, where she earned her master of science degree in chemistry in 1982.

Following graduation in 1982 Kavandi accepted a position at Eagle-Picher Industries in Joplin, Missouri, as an engineer in new battery development for defense applications. In 1984 she accepted a position as an engineer in the Power Systems Technology Department of the Boeing Company. During her ten years at Boeing Kavandi supported numerous programs and proposals regarding energy storage systems through performing power analyses, trade studies, sizing, selection, development, testing, and data analysis.

Kavandi was lead engineer of secondary power for the Short Range Attack Missile II and principal technical staff representative in the design and develop-

ment of thermal batteries for Sea Lance and the Lightweight Exo-Atmospheric Projectile. Other programs she has supported include the space station; Lunar and Mars Base studies; Inertial Upper Stage, Advanced Orbital Transfer Vehicle; Get-Away Specials; Small Spacecraft; the Air-Launched Cruise Missile; and the Minuteman and Peacekeeper missiles.

In 1986, while still working for Boeing, Kavandi was accepted into graduate school at the University of Washington. She began working toward her doctorate in analytical chemistry, which she received in 1990. Kavandi wrote her doctoral dissertation on the development of a pressure-indicating coating that uses the oxygen-quenching properties of porphyrin photoluminescence to provide continuous surface pressure maps of aerodynamic test models in wind tunnels. Her work on pressure-indicating paints has resulted in two patents to date.

In December 1994 Kavandi was selected as an astronaut candidate by NASA, and she reported to the Johnson Space Center in March 1995. Following an initial year of training she was assigned to the Payloads and Habitability Branch, where she currently supports payload integration for the International Space Station.

References
Biographical Data Sheets, Lyndon B. Johnson Space Center (1997)

Kenyon, Cecil "Teddy"

One of the first female test pilots, Kenyon was born circa 1910 and grew up in Kent, Connecticut. She was educated at the Scarsdale School and attended Boston College. There she met her future husband, Theodore Kenyon, a barnstorming pilot in his own right and a student at the Massachusetts Institute of Technology. Before marrying, however, Cecil Kenyon spent two years living in France. When she returned to the United States, Cecil and Theodore were married.

Kenyon learned to fly from her husband, who had taken a job as a pilot for Colonial Airlines. On return trips when there were no paying passengers aboard, Kenyon earned time in the air by flying the ship back herself.

In 1930 Kenyon entered her first air meet. She won the $300 first prize in the contest, which was sponsored by the American Legion. In 1933 she entered a charity air show on Long Island and competed against 39 men and women for a chance to be named "champion sportsman" and win a $5,000 prize. Kenyon won again.

Kenyon was invited to join her husband at the Sperry Instrument Company, where they tested new aviation devices, including antiaircraft locators, and demonstrated them for customers. In 1937 Kenyon was testing an automatic pilot device that was still used in airplanes some 40 years after she had completed her testing. She demonstrated the device to the army the next year, becoming one of the first women to fly before military officials.

During World War II Kenyon joined the Civil Air Patrol to help train pilots for the military. Soon, however, she learned of more interesting work: The Grumman Aircraft Corporation needed pilots to pick up and deliver parts up and down the East Coast. Kenyon became one of three women—along with Elizabeth Hooker and Barbara "Kibby" Jayne—hired by Brewster A. "Bud" Gillies, Grumman vice president, in the spring of 1942. In the course of the war Kenyon logged over 4,000 takeoffs and landings in a wide variety of military aircraft.

Kenyon died in 1985. Of her love of flying, she said: "Flying gives you a wholly different perspective on life, a sort of spiritual something that makes you feel good inside. It's strange, but all pilots feel that way."

See also
Gillies, Brewster A. "Bud"; Hooker, Elizabeth; Jayne, Barbara "Kibby"
References
Adams and Kimball, *Heroines of the Sky* (1942); Knapp, *New Wings for Women* (1946)

King, Alison

A member of the third wave of pilots recruited by Pauline Gower for the Women's Section of the British Air Transport Auxiliary (ATA) during World War II, King (born circa 1910) had learned to fly as a member of the Essex Flying Club in 1938. The group provided flying lessons and flight time to members at a minimal price. To keep costs down, members took turns using the few planes available, which made it hard to accumulate flying hours.

When the Women's Section began King did not have enough flying hours to qualify. However, she took a secretarial job as underassistant to the adjutant at Hatfield Air Base to help the war effort and to be with her friend, Margot Gore, who had qualified as a pilot. Gore and King had taken their lessons together at Essex, and it was Gore who recommended King for the job at the Hatfield Air Base.

In 1940, when her boss, Marion Wilberforce, Hatfield's commanding officer (CO), began being away from base on her own flights, King took over her duties. She became the first woman's operations officer. While at the base she had the chance to fly with Amy Johnson, the famous long-distance flyer who had just joined the ATA. Sadly, in January of that year the plane Johnson was ferrying crashed into the Thames River, and one of King's new duties was to take charge of the accident investigation.

In September 1941 the ATA had grown to more than 50 pilots, and another pilot pool was started at a previously all-male air base, Hamble. Gore was made CO and King was promoted to operations officer for the new unit. They started with five engineers and ten Women's Section pilots, one of whom was Ann Welch, founder of the Surrey Gliding Club. Soon Gore and King built the group up to 30 pilots and 20 engineers, recruited from several countries in the United Kingdom. It was King's job to schedule the pilots into planes for which they were qualified and to arrange for their return to base when their missions were complete. It was also her job to attend the funerals of any pilots who died in the line of duty.

In 1942 King was promoted to flight captain. The Operations Office she headed at Hamble now included a meteorology department and a sick bay staffed by volunteer medical personnel.

In April 1942 King successfully coordinated the delivery of 99 planes to the defense of Malta. Then, as the ATA began to train new recruits to keep the unit operational, she was offered the chance to become a full-time pilot herself. She chose to pass up the opportunity in order to remain at her post in Operations. By 1943 the ATA was responsible for ferrying larger and larger aircraft closer and closer to the combat lines. The pilots were constantly in training to fly the various aircraft.

In the spring of 1944 King helped coordinate the delivery of aircraft necessary for the Allied invasion of Europe from her post at Hamble Air Base. In September 1945 King's unit was decommissioned. Over the course of the war King was responsible for the successful delivery of 9,611 airplanes, compared to the 7,811 delivered by the male unit also stationed at Hamble.

After the disbanding of the Women's Section of the ATA King remained active in aviation by becoming the director of the Women's Junior Air Corps. She also spent some time as the chairman of the British Women Pilot's Association. In 1956 she wrote a book about her wartime experiences.

In her book King noted that despite the many achievements of women in aviation in World War II, ten years after the war women pilots faced continued discrimination: "How ridiculous it now seemed that the Brontës had to write under the names Currer, Ellis and Acton Bell, partly because they felt their books would have a better chance ambiguously sexed. Surely women pilots were not, a hundred years later, back in the parsonage with those writers of genius? I knew in my heart it was not so. Much had happened and they were now on the way to being accepted, if they had the qualifications and the training, as 'just one of the pilots.'"

See also
Air Transport Auxiliary (ATA); Gower, Pauline; Johnson, Amy; Welch, Ann Walker
References
King, *Golden Wings: The Story of Some of the Women Ferry Pilots of the Air Transport Auxiliary* (1956)

Kondakova, Elena V.

A Russian cosmonaut, Kondakova was born on March 30, 1957, in Mitischi, near Moscow. She graduated from Moscow Bauman High Technical College in 1980 and was hired as a researcher by RSC-Energia. She spent the next eight years working on science projects, experiments, and research.

In 1989 Kondakova was selected as a cosmonaut candidate by the RSC-Energia Main Design Bureau. She entered the Gagarin Cosmonaut Training Center for her general space training, which she finished in March 1990.

Kondakova spent early 1994 training for the seventeenth main mission and Euromir-94 flight as a flight engineer of the prime crew. Her first mission in space was on board the spacecraft *Soyuz TM-17*, and the orbital complex *Mir* as a flight engineer of the seventeenth main mission from October 4, 1994, through March 9, 1995. This six-month stay in space set a new women's space endurance record that stood until American astronaut Shannon Lucid spent seven months on *Mir* in 1996.

On her second space mission Kondakova was a mission specialist on STS-84 from May 15 to May 24, 1997. It was the sixth National Aeronautics and Space Administration (NASA) shuttle mission to rendezvous and dock with the Russian space station *Mir*. For her work in space Kondakova has been designated a Hero of Russia.

See also
Lucid, Shannon W.
References
Biographical Data Sheets, Lyndon B. Johnson Space Center (1997)

Lambine, Janna

The first female helicopter pilot in the U.S. Coast Guard, Lambine was born in 1951 and grew up in Walpole, Massachusetts. She attended Bates College in Lewiston, Maine, and earned a degree in geology. Rather than attend graduate school Lambine enlisted in the Coast Guard and qualified for their 18-month officers' candidate training school the first year women were considered for flight training in that branch of the military. She was the only woman in a class of 400.

After training and earning her gold pilot's wings on fixed-wing aircraft on March 4, 1977, Lambine was assigned to Whiting Field Naval Air Station as a naval aviator. She was 26 years old. Lambine soon transferred to the Mobile, Alabama, base to train on Sikorsky-61 helicopters, which are used in search-and-rescue work. Lambine earned her helicopter license in June 1977 and was transferred to the Coast Guard base in Astoria, Oregon.

On dealing with the still male-dominated military Lambine said: "I know I can do just as good a job as men. And I don't have to go around telling everybody about it."

References
Easterling, "The Woman Pilots a Helicopter" (1977); Holden and Griffith, *Ladybirds: The Untold Story of Women Pilots in America* (1991)

Laroche, Baroness Raymonde de

The first woman to obtain a pilot's license, Laroche was born in 1889 into French high society. She had already dabbled in art, theater, balloons, and racing cars when she asked Charles Voisin to teach her to fly the plane he created and named for himself. Lessons began in October 1909 at Chalons airfield.

The Voisin plane had only one seat, for the pilot, so Laroche was also the first woman to solo. On her very first lesson she piloted the plane as her teacher shouted instructions from the ground. Her first flight took her to an altitude of 15 feet. Laroche passed her license test on March 8, 1910, at the age of 23.

In July 1910, as the only woman in an all-male air show, Laroche was one of the first pilots to crash because of what would later be analyzed as the prop wash from the plane in front of her. The accident left her with a broken arm and two broken legs, internal injuries, and head wounds. It was predicted that she neither would nor should fly again.

In 1913 Laroche won the Coupe Femina, a race set aside for women. Later that year she experienced a near-fatal crash that broke many of her bones, but she recovered and continued flying until World War I, when the government banned private flying. She went back to flying immediately after the war, however, setting another altitude record for women.

In 1919 she agreed to ride as a passenger in the test flight of a new experimental plane. Her pilot lost control and Laroche died in the crash.

In response to a comment that flying was a dangerous occupation for a woman,

Raymonde de Laroche (undated photo)

Laroche said: "Most of us spread the hazards of a lifetime over a number of years. Others pack them into minutes or hours. In any case, what is to happen, will happen. It may be that I shall tempt Fate once too often, but it is to the air that I have dedicated myself and I fly always without the slightest fear."

See also
Chalons Airfield
References
Moolman, *Women Aloft* (1981)

Law, Ruth

The first woman to fly at night, Law was also the first to loop-the-loop. Aviation ran in her family; her brother was a well-known flyer and parachutist. Law took her first solo flight on the day Harriet Quimby fell to her death, and, along with Blanche Stuart Scott, she witnessed the accident. She received her license a month later in November 1912.

Law made a living that winter by taking Florida tourists on joyrides for $50 apiece and performing in aviation exhibition shows. Her first memorable stunt was a 20-minute moonlit flight around Staten Island, New York, in November 1913, which made her the first woman to fly at night. In the spring of 1915 she made her first exhibition of acrobatic flying, in Daytona Beach, Florida. It was here that she first looped-the-loop, a stunt also performed by her occasional exhibition partner, Katherine Stinson.

In 1916 in Sheepshead Bay, New York, Law took second place at an altitude contest and won $250 by flying to a height of 11,200 feet. She was also invited back to New York to celebrate the lighting of the Statue of Liberty by performing another night flight around the famous landmark while towing a banner proclaiming "LIBERTY." On November 19, 1916, Law broke both the U.S. and the world nonstop cross-country flight records for either men or women by flying 590 miles from Chicago, Illinois, to Hornell, New York. When she arrived in New York City for the celebration, Law was congratulated by President and Mrs. Woodrow Wilson, as well as by the men who had discovered both the North and South Poles, Admiral Robert Peary and Captain Roald Amundsen, respectively.

Law was renowned as an inventor as well as for her solution to the problem of keeping a map readily accessible: She cut the map of her route into eight-inch-wide strips and affixed them to cloth, creating a cloth map roll that she could tie to her knee during the flight and roll out one section at a time, thus keeping her hands free to operate the controls. After breaking the cross-country record, Law commanded a salary of nearly $9,000 a week for her exhibitions.

At the outbreak of World War I Law was hired by *World Magazine* in January 1917 to go to Europe and report on the use of aviation at the front. When she returned to the United States in April of that year, Law volunteered to fly for the U.S. Army but was refused because of her gender. Instead, Law helped raise money for the war effort by performing in charity exhibitions for the Red Cross. For this she was honored as the first woman allowed to wear an army noncommissioned officer's uniform.

Still angered by her rejection from the military, Law wrote an article for *Air Travel Magazine*, "Let Women Fly!," which was published in 1918 and which denounced the military for falling prey to the ages-old controversy of whether or not a woman is suited for "man's work" when women like Law and her contemporaries were proving every day that they were.

After the war Law and her husband and business manager, Charles Oliver, formed Ruth Law's Flying Circus and toured the Orient performing acrobatic aviation exhibitions. Law was famous for racing her plane against cars on a racetrack and making car-to-plane transfers in which a stunt girl would leap off the car and grab onto a rope ladder dangling from the nearby plane. In an incident that reflected the many risks early aviators took to excite an audience, one such attempt ended tragically when her stunt girl missed the ladder and fell to her death.

In another risky trick Law would fly with a copilot, climb out of the cockpit, and stand on the wing of the plane while her copilot looped-the-loop as many as three times. Apparently, this so frightened her husband that, without her permission, he announced her retirement to the press.

Ruth Law (August 12, 1913)

How she honestly felt about this forced retirement is unknown, although she was quoted in later years as saying: "Things are so proper now. . . . A pilot has so many rules and regulations to follow, it wouldn't be much fun. I couldn't skim over the rooftops or land in the streets or on a racetrack. The good old days of flying are gone."

See also
Quimby, Harriet; Scott, Blanche Stuart; Stinson, Katherine
References
Adams and Kimball, *Heroines of the Sky* (1942); Lomax, *Women of the Air* (1987); Moolman, *Women Aloft* (1981)

Lawrence, Wendy
A member of the National Aeronautics and Space Administration (NASA) class of 1992, Lawrence was born on July 2, 1959, in Jacksonville, Florida. Her father's career as an admiral in the U.S. Navy took the family to Alexandria, Vir-

ginia, where Lawrence graduated from Fort Hunt High School in 1977. She joined the navy and graduated from the U.S. Naval Academy in Annapolis, Maryland, in May 1981 with a bachelor of science degree in ocean engineering.

Lawrence was designated as a naval aviator in July 1982 and learned how to fly six different types of helicopters. While stationed at Helicopter Combat Support Squadron 6, she was one of the first two female helicopter pilots to make a long deployment to the Indian Ocean as part of a carrier battle group. In 1986 Lawrence was awarded the National Navy League's Captain Winifred Collins Award for inspirational leadership.

Lawrence received a master of science degree in ocean engineering from the Massachusetts Institute of Technology (MIT) and the Woods Hole Oceanographic Institution (WHOI) in 1988. She was then assigned to Helicopter Anti-Submarine Squadron Light 30 as officer-in-charge of Detachment Alfa.

In October 1990 Lawrence was reassigned to the U.S. Naval Academy, where she served as a physics instructor and the novice women's crew coach.

Lawrence was selected by NASA in March 1992. She flew as the ascent/entry flight engineer and blue shift orbit pilot on STS-67 in March 1995. This record-setting 16-day mission was the second flight of the Astro observatory, a unique complement of three telescopes. During this mission the crew conducted around-the-clock observations to study the far-ultraviolet spectra of faint astronomical objects and the polarization of ultraviolet light coming from hot stars and distant galaxies.

On the ground Lawrence's technical assignments have included flight software verification in the Shuttle Avionics Integration Laboratory (SAIL) and serving as the assistant training officer at the Astronaut Office of NASA. She served as di-

rector of operations for NASA at the Gagarin Cosmonaut Training Center in Star City, Russia, where she was responsible for the coordination and implementation of mission operations activities in the Moscow region for the joint U.S./Russian shuttle/*Mir* program.

On July 30, 1997, Lawrence was announced as the next American astronaut to be posted on the *Mir* space station. One day later that posting was revoked. *Mir* contained only two Russian-made flight suits for spacewalks and Lawrence, at 5 foot 3 inches tall, was too short to fit into them. Normally only the cosmonauts are assigned spacewalks, but after *Mir* suffered extensive damage from a collision with a supply ship officials wanted everyone on board to be able to perform the exterior repairs.

See also
U.S. Navy (USN)
References
Biographical Data Sheets, Lyndon B. Johnson Space Center (1997)

Lindbergh, Anne Morrow

The first American woman to earn a glider pilot's license, Lindbergh was also a best-selling author. She was born Anne Spencer Morrow on June 22, 1906, in Englewood, New Jersey. In 1924 she entered Smith College with an interest in writing and had several early pieces published in the *Smith College Monthly*.

Her father became U.S. ambassador to Mexico in 1927 while Lindbergh was still in college. She spent that year's Christmas break with her parents, and there she met famed aviator Charles Lindbergh, who had just made the first nonstop flight from New York to Mexico. During this visit he took her family for a plane ride that was probably Lindbergh's first flight. Two years later, on May 27, 1929, they were married.

The couple had their first public aviation event when Charles piloted the inaugural flight of Transcontinental Air Transport (later TWA) on July 7, 1929, with such well-known passengers as Amelia Earhart and silent screen star Mary Pickford. Anne rode with them in the passenger cabin to explain to the less experienced riders the dynamics of the plane and to assuage their fears. The Lindberghs' first long flight together was in September of that year, when they inaugurated airmail service from Puerto Rico to Dutch Guiana.

The couple also delighted in experimenting with new types of aircraft. In the middle of her first pregnancy Lindbergh took her first solo flight in a glider. After one day of instruction she became the first American woman to earn a glider pilot's license. Later in the pregnancy Lindbergh accompanied her husband when he broke the U.S. transcontinental speed record in April 1930. The couple flew from Los Angeles to New York City in 14 hours, 45 minutes. On June 22, 1930, Lindbergh gave birth to Charles Augustus Lindbergh Jr.

In May 1931 Lindbergh received her pilot's license after instruction from her husband in everything from aerodynamics to navigation to radio transmission. Then the Lindberghs began planning for their first adventure together as pilot and copilot. On July 27, 1931, they set off on a flight from Long Island, New York, to China via Canada and Alaska. They had been hired by Pan American Airways to pioneer a new route to the Orient to increase commercial air travel for the company.

The Lindberghs made it safely to the Yangtze River region of China, where floods had recently devastated the population. There they interrupted their trip to assist with delivering medicine and food to isolated locations. On one delivery their plane was badly damaged by a crane. Before they could complete repairs and finish the last lap of the trip, Lindbergh received the news that her father had died. The couple returned to the United States by boat immediately.

At home Anne gave a speech on the radio about their humanitarian work in China on behalf of the China Flood Relief. Lindbergh also began writing a book about the trip, *North to the Orient.*

Tragedy struck the Lindberghs on March 1, 1932, when their son was kidnapped from his nursery for a ransom of $50,000. On May 12, after nine weeks of false leads and continuous press coverage, the child was found dead not far from the family home. On August 15, 1932, Anne gave birth to a second son, Jon Lindbergh.

On July 9, 1933, after a year of mourning, the Lindberghs took off from Long Island on a five-month survey flight studying new cargo routes for the Transcontinental Air Transport. They flew 30,000 miles, including to Greenland, Iceland, Russia, England, Spain, Africa, and Brazil, searching for potential air bases.

During this trip Lindbergh established a world record for radio communications between an airplane and a ground station when she made contact with Sayville, Long Island, while flying off the coast of West Africa. On March 31, 1934, Lindbergh was the first woman awarded the National Geographic Society's highest award, the Hubbard Gold Medal, for her achievements as copilot and navigator on the flight.

The trial of her son's kidnapper, which began on January 3, 1935, kept the Lindberghs from much flying work that year. Anne used the time to finish her book *North to the Orient* and find a publisher. On August 15, 1935, Harcourt Brace published the book, and it became an immediate best-seller that remains in print to this day.

The Lindberghs moved to England in December 1935 because of threats on their son Jon's life. There she wrote her second book, *Listen! The Wind*. When the U.S. ambassador to Germany invited the Lindberghs to visit him at his home there and study the German military machine, they accepted. They flew to Germany on July 22, 1936, which angered Americans on the verge of war with Germany. In February 1937 they flew to Italy and India. On May 12, 1937, Lindbergh gave birth to her third son, Land Lindbergh.

In August 1938 the Lindberghs flew to Russia to study their air strength and report their findings to U.S. intelligence agencies. In October they returned to Germany on a similar mission, but to the U.S. public it looked as if the Lindberghs were supporting Hitler's regime, and their reputations were at risk.

They returned to live in the United States on April 19, 1939, so that Charles could take a commission with the U.S. Army Air Corps in preparation for World War II. Lindbergh used this time to write her third book, *The Wave of the Future*, which attempted to persuade the United States not to enter the war in Europe. On October 2, 1940, she gave birth to her fourth child, a daughter named Anne Spencer.

The Steep Ascent, Lindbergh's fourth published book and her first fictional piece, was published in March 1944. It told the story of a husband-and-wife flying team facing a perilous landing in the Alps. Despite the Lindberghs' reputation in the United States, it was well received and was both critically and financially a success. In 1955 Lindbergh published *Gift from the Sea*, her most successful book, and in 1962 she published *Dearly Beloved: A Theme and Variations*.

Earth Shine came out in 1969 and included an essay describing the launch of the first moon-orbiting space mission, *Apollo 8*, to which Lindbergh and her

husband had been invited. After her husband died on August 26, 1974, she published five volumes of diaries detailing her life. She died in 1993.

See also
Earhart, Amelia Mary
References
Herrmann, *Anne Morrow Lindbergh: A Gift for Life* (1992)

Litviak, Lidiia "Lily" Vladimirovna

One of the few women to fly combat missions during World War II, Litviak was born on August 18, 1921, Aviation Day in the Soviet Union. Though she became interested in flying at the age of 15, aero clubs would not take members under the age of 17. Litviak studied books on aviation to impress the chief instructor of the Chklav Aeroclub of Moscow with her abilities and succeeded in being allowed to join at the age of 16.

Litviak attempted a career in geology but could not resist flying. After gaining her flight instructor certificate at the Kherson Flight Academy, she was hired by the Moscow aeroclub.

After the great losses of men and machines in the German surprise attack on the Soviet Union in October 1941, Marina Raskova organized three regiments of women combat pilots. Litviak was recruited into the all-female 586th Fighter Regiment, which began training at the Engels Military Base on October 15, 1941. Her regiment was deployed on May 18, 1942, and was based at the Saratov Military Base. She was given the nickname "Lily" when she painted a white lily on the side of her plane. Litviak served with the all-female regiment until September.

Then Litviak was transferred to the 73rd Fighter Regiment, an otherwise all-male battalion, assigned to defend Stalingrad. At first her new commander refused to let her fly, assigning her plane to a male pilot and assigning Litviak to ground crew work. Eventually Litviak convinced the commander to let her fly one mission with him as a test. This tangible evidence of her skills succeeded in convincing him to let her fly with the 73rd, and the next day, September 13, 1942, she claimed her first kill.

By the end of the year Litviak had completed 20 combat missions. On February 17, 1943, she was awarded the Order of the Red Banner and promoted to junior lieutenant. Litviak's flying career made her famous in her own country and also in Germany. On March 15, 1943, she was wounded in the leg during an air battle. When she returned to her regiment in May she was promoted to the rank of flight commander. Wounded again, she crashed behind German lines but managed to walk back to base without being detected by German soldiers. Tragedy followed her success, however, when her fiancé, Aleksei Salomatin, another flying ace in their regiment, was shot down on May 21.

Litviak destroyed 12 German planes in the course of her career before being downed by one on July 31, 1943, near Krasny Luch. She was 22 years old.

Her aircraft and remains were not found until 1989, and she was then posthumously named a Hero of the Soviet Union.

See also
Raskova, Marina
References
Mellinger, "Lidiia Litviak" (1997); Moolman, *Women Aloft* (1981); Myles, *Night Witches: The Untold Story of Soviet Women in Combat* (1981)

Lockness, Doris

A member of the Women's Airforce Service Pilots (WASPS) as well as the United Flying Octogenarians, Lockness was born on February 2, 1910. She was 29 years old and the mother of four children when she began taking flying lessons at a small airport near her home in Wilmington, California, in 1938. Her husband did not want her to fly, so to pay for the lessons Lockness would wash, fuel, and tie down aircraft in exchange for flying time with the owners.

With her pilot's license in hand Lockness got a job as a liaison officer for C-47s for the Douglas Aircraft Company. At the outbreak of World War II Lockness applied to the WASPS, hoping to help ferry planes from manufacturers' warehouses to air force bases to free up male flyers for the military. The group was created and run by Jacqueline Cochran. When Lockness was accepted her husband divorced her. She flew through the whole time the WASPS were in existence.

After the war Lockness worked to promote flight safety among pilots. In 1963 she became the fifty-fifth woman in the world to earn her helicopter license, after which she joined the Whirly-Girls. In 1988 she studied for and received her commercial rating in a constant-speed propeller-driven gyroplane. Lockness was the second woman in the United States to receive this rating.

In 1984 she was honored as the only female pilot ever to receive the Legion of Merit Award from the OX5 Aviation Pioneers. In 1987 they selected her for the Outstanding Women's Award of the year, and in 1989 they inducted her into their Aviation Pioneers Hall of Fame. Lockness was honored with the Elder Statesmen of Aviation Award from the National Aeronautical Association in 1996. She also received the Katherine B. Wright Memorial Trophy from the Ninety-Nines in 1997 for her personal contribution to the advancement of the art, sport, and science of aviation over a lifetime.

About the adversity she faced in getting her pilot's license, Lockness said: "I really didn't have that good a support background when I was twenty-nine that a lot of pilots have, but I just made up my mind that was something that I wanted to do. There wasn't anything that could stop me, not even an angry husband and four youngsters."

See also
Cochran, Jacqueline; Ninety-Nines; Whirly-Girls; Women's Airforce Service Pilots (WASPS); Wright, Katherine
References
Holden and Griffith, *Ladybirds II: The Continuing Story of American Women in Aviation* (1993); Russo, *Women and Flight: Portraits of Contemporary Women Pilots* (1997)

London, Barbara Erickson

A commanding officer (CO) of the Women's Auxiliary Ferrying Squadron (WAFS), London was stationed in Long Beach, California, under Nancy Harkness Love during World War II. She had been studying home economics in college in 1939 when the University of Washington started a Civilian Pilot Training Program. London applied and was accepted. She earned her pilot's and flight instructor's licenses in 12 months and began teaching students.

In 1942 London received a letter from Love inviting her to join the WAFS. London went to the nearest base, in Wilmington, Delaware, to take her physical. Soon after London joined the WAFS Love was transferred to headquarters back in Washington, D.C. She promoted several of her top pilots to commanding officer status. In her short time with the WAFS London had earned enough of a reputation to be made CO of the Long Beach squadron, the Sixth Ferry Group. London had the distinction of testing for and qualifying to fly more than 36 different types of planes. She could also take pride in the fact that her squadron only lost five pilots during the course of the war and in the fact that she was one of five women who reached the highest level of pilot qualifications, Class 5.

In 1944 the WAFS were disbanded, and London married a fellow military pilot, Jack London. In March she was awarded the Air Force Medal for tireless flying, and President Franklin Delano Roosevelt sent her a personal citation for her exceptional service. In 1946 London herself took a commission as a major in the Air Force Reserves, which she kept for 20 years. After she retired in 1956 she was hired as the permanent executive secretary of the All-Women's Transcontinental Air Race (AWTAR).

In 1973 London became the owner and operator of Barney Frazier Aircraft in Long Beach, California, where she employed both her daughters as pilots.

In 1991 London was invited to speak to the graduating class of the U.S. Air Force Air Command and Staff College as a prominent aviation pioneer.

In discussing her long career in aviation London said: "The women of my era were so lucky to be flying during that period in our history. To be twenty-one and flying every piece of equipment being made was a pilot's dream come true and an opportunity that women will never have again."

See also
All-Women's Transcontinental Air Race (AWTAR); Love, Nancy Harkness; U.S. Air Force (USAF); Women's Airforce Service Pilots (WASPS)
References
Holden and Griffith, *Ladybirds II: The Continuing Story of American Women in Aviation* (1993)

Loper, Rose

The first woman to graduate with honors from the U.S. Army Flight School, Loper was born in 1948 in Eustis, Florida. She received a bachelor of science degree in education from Carson-Newman College in Jefferson City, Tennessee, and a master's degree in recreation administration from Florida State University. She graduated from the master's program in 1973 but found teaching not to her liking.

In 1974 Loper joined the U.S. Army. She tested for and was the fourteenth woman accepted to the U.S. Army Flight School, which she attended that fall. She graduated in 1975 with honors. Loper was the fourth woman to successfully complete the Aviation Maintenance Officer Corps Course, which qualified her as a test pilot.

Loper's first posting was as a production control officer with the Ninth Infantry Division. In 1978 she took command of the ground maintenance company stationed at Ft. Lewis, Washington. She was then promoted to the rank of captain.

In 1980 Loper retired from the army and became the first woman ever hired as a ground engineer for the Boeing Company in Seattle, Washington. She went on to become the first woman pilot at Boeing when she took a job as the company's corporate helicopter pilot. In 1986 Loper was promoted to the position of chief pilot for the flight test department. In 1990 she was made a production test pilot, responsible for performing system checks on brand-new planes just off the assembly line.

She maintained her connection with the army by test-flying a Boeing plane equipped for the Strategic Defense Initiative (SDI) in May 1990. Loper also served in the U.S. Army Reserves.

Regarding surviving as a female in the newly gender-friendly military, Loper said: "I came to realize that the doors were open for me if I was just smart enough to figure out a way to step through."

See also
U.S. Army
References
Holden and Griffith, *Ladybirds II: The Continuing Story of American Women in Aviation* (1993)

Love, Nancy Harkness

One of the first women to head a military unit of female pilots and an early commercial airline pilot, Love was born to a wealthy family in Philadelphia in 1914. She learned to fly in Houghton, Michigan, at the age of 16 while a boarding student at the Milton Academy in Massachusetts. She earned her commercial pilot's license during her college years at Vassar. In 1933, with the Depression depleting her father's wealth, Love left college without completing a degree to make her living flying.

Her first job was selling airplanes on commission at the East Boston Airport. In 1935 Love was among the many women who worked as pilots for the Works Progress Administration. She and two others were assigned to the air-marking project, which required them to negotiate fees with towns and landowners for the right to mark city names on water towers and barns to aid pilots in navigating cross-country. Love's territory was the state of New York. Then she worked with the Bureau of Air Commerce as a test pilot for experimental airplane safety features.

In 1936, with no prior racing experience, Love flew in the Amelia Earhart Trophy Race at the National Air Races, placing fifth. The same year she married Robert H. Love, with whom she founded an aviation corporation, Inter-City Airlines in Boston.

In 1937 Love left the Bureau of Air Commerce and took a job demonstrating and selling planes for the Gwinn Aircar Company in Buffalo, New York. When their regular test pilot took a new job in the West, Love lobbied for his old one. Through her work new landing gears were tested and adopted by Gwinn Aircar and many other aircraft designers. She also worked at Inter-City Airlines with her husband teaching flying classes and demonstrating and selling planes.

In June 1940 she joined other patriotic pilots in ferrying to Canada U.S. planes that would then be shipped to France for use against the approaching German Army.

Two weeks after the bombing of Pearl Harbor Love moved to Washington, D.C., when her husband was called to World War II military duty. Love took a civilian administration job with the Air Transport Command (ATC) in Baltimore and commuted to it by plane. She met with his superiors at the ATC to discuss her ferrying experience and the concept of a corps of women ferry pilots. Brigadier General Harold L. George liked the idea and asked Love to draft a proposal.

On Thursday, September 10, 1942, Love's proposal was announced in the newspapers. Women who filled the requirements were asked to apply to what was then called the Women's Auxiliary Ferrying Squadron (WAFS). Love was named director of the group, a position she held throughout the war. Although most of her duties were administrative, Love continued to be checked out on many of the new planes so that she would understand what she was asking of her recruits. On February 27, 1943, she became one of the first pilots to fly the P-51 Mustang. Love went so far as to station herself at a base in Long Beach, California, where most of these new planes were being designed.

In 1943 the Pentagon combined the WAFS with Jacqueline Cochran's Women's Flying Training Detachment (WFTD) and renamed them the Women's Airforce Service Pilots (WASPS). Cochran retained command of training, and Love of deployment. To support their efforts, Walt Disney created Fifinella, a female gremlin mascot, for the group.

On August 15, 1943, Love and one of her WAF COs, Betty Huyler Gillies, became the first women to qualify as pilots of the B-17 Flying Fortress. They were training to be the first women to ferry a bomber across the Atlantic Ocean, but their mission was cut short by a top-ranking male general firmly against female pilots entering the combat arena.

As the war in Europe seemed to be going well for the Allies, the WASP program was deactivated on December 20, 1944. In July 1946 Love was awarded the Air Medal for her leadership of the WAFS on the same day that her husband was awarded the Distinguished Service Medal, making them the first couple to be decorated for military service on the same day.

In 1947 Love had her first child. She and her family moved to Martha's Vineyard and commuted by plane from there to Boston whenever business called. She died of cancer in October 1976.

In a way Love lived her own vision of the future of women in aviation, which she stated at the end of World War II: "My goal is to see flying so safe that anybody's grandmother will just naturally take a plane to the sewing club meeting. I want to see flying become as commonplace in our generation as riding a trolley car was in grandmother's day."

See also
Fifinella; Gillies, Betty Huyler; National Air Races; Women's Airforce Service Pilots (WASPS)

References
Douglas, *United States Women in Aviation, 1940–1985* (1990); Knapp, *New Wings for Women* (1946); Van Wagenen Keil, *Those Wonderful Women in Their Flying Machines* (1979)

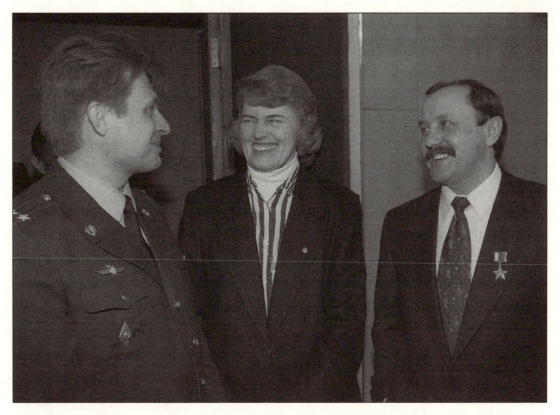

Shannon Lucid with Russian cosmonauts Yuri Onufriyenko (left) and Yuri Usachev (right), her crew members aboard Mir.

Lucid, Shannon W.

The American astronaut who has logged more continuous time in space than any other American astronaut, male or female, Lucid spent seven months on the *Mir* space station in 1996. She was also the first American woman to live on *Mir* and the first American woman to go into space five times. A member of the first class of National Aeronautics and Space Administration (NASA) astronauts to include women, and a classmate of both Sally Ride and Judith Resnik, Lucid was born on January 14, 1943, in Shanghai, China, where her parents were missionaries.

After World War II Lucid's family moved back to the United States. Lucid graduated from Bethany High School in Bethany, Oklahoma, in 1960. She saved up money from baby-sitting and house-cleaning jobs to take flying lessons and gained her pilot's license the summer after graduation.

In 1963 Lucid received a bachelor of science degree in chemistry from the University of Oklahoma. She became a teaching assistant in their Department of Chemistry from 1963 to 1964 and worked as a senior laboratory technician at the Oklahoma Medical Research Foundation from 1964 to 1966. During this time she applied for jobs as a commercial pilot but was continually turned down because of her sex. In 1966 Lucid joined Kerr-McGee, in Oklahoma City, Oklahoma, as a chemist.

Lucid served as a graduate assistant at the University of Oklahoma Health Science Center's Department of Biochemistry and Molecular Biology from 1969 to 1973. She earned a master of science degree in 1970 and a Ph.D. in biochemistry in 1973.

Lucid then worked as a research associate with the Oklahoma Medical Research Foundation in Oklahoma City from 1974 until her selection to the astronaut candidate training program in 1978. As a member of the first group of female astronauts selected by NASA, Lucid was not the typical astronaut candidate. She was married and had three children at the time of her appointment.

On June 17, 1985, Mission Specialist Lucid went into space for the first time aboard the *Discovery* space shuttle and landed on June 24, making her first foray into space her shortest. STS-51G was a seven-day mission during which the crew deployed communications satellites for Mexico, the Arab League, and the United States. They used the Remote Manipulator System (RMS) to deploy and later retrieve the *Spartan* satellite, which performed 17 hours of x-ray astronomy experiments while separated from the space shuttle. In addition the crew activated the Automated Directional Solidification Furnace and six Getaway Specials and participated in biomedical experiments.

On her second flight Lucid served as mission specialist for STS-34. She was a member of the crew of the *Atlantis* space shuttle from October 18 to October 23, 1989, helping the crew to deploy the *Galileo* spacecraft on its journey to explore Jupiter, operate the Shuttle Solar Backscatter Ultraviolet Instrument to map atmospheric ozone, and perform numerous secondary experiments involving radiation measurements, polymer morphology, lightning research, microgravity effects on plants, and a student experiment on ice crystal growth in space.

Once again on *Atlantis* for STS-43 Lucid's third flight was a nine-day mission. From August 2 to August 11, 1991, Lucid and the crew deployed the fifth Tracking and Data Relay Satellite, conducting 32 physical, material, and life science experiments, mostly relating to the Extended Duration Orbiter and Space Station Freedom.

In a preview of her future space endurance record, Lucid's fourth flight was as a member of a record 14-day mission on board the *Columbia* space shuttle. STS-58, which was in orbit from October 18 to November 1, 1993, was recognized by NASA management as the most successful and efficient Spacelab flight yet flown. Lucid and the crew performed neurovestibular, cardiovascular, cardiopulmonary, metabolic, and musculoskeletal medical experiments on themselves and 48 rats, expanding our knowledge of human and animal physiology both on earth and in spaceflight. In addition, they performed 16 engineering tests aboard the Orbiter *Columbia* and 20 Extended Duration Orbiter Medical Project experiments. At the completion of this flight Lucid had logged 838 hours, 54 minutes in space, which made her America's female space traveler with the most hours in space.

On March 22, 1996, Lucid hitched a ride aboard the *Atlantis* space shuttle for STS-76, which brought her to the *Mir* space station, where she served as board engineer 2 for seven record-setting months. Lucid performed numerous life science and physical science experiments during the course of her stay aboard *Mir.* She returned to earth on STS-79 on September 26, 1996. Lucid holds an international record for the most flight hours in orbit by any non-Russian and holds the record for the most flight hours in orbit by any woman in the world.

For her work on *Mir* Lucid became the first and only woman to have earned the Congressional Space Medal of Honor awarded by the president of the United States. Russian president Boris Yeltsin also awarded Lucid the Order of Friendship Medal, the highest award that can be presented to a noncitizen.

Between spaceflights Lucid's technical assignments have included the Shuttle Avionics Integration Laboratory and the Astronaut Office at Kennedy Space Center, where she participated in payload testing, shuttle testing, and launch countdowns. She has served as a spacecraft communicator (CAPCOM) in the Johnson Space Center (JSC) Mission Control Center during numerous space shuttle missions and as chief of mission support and chief of astronaut appearances, of which she herself has made many.

With regard to her position as a working mother, Lucid said: "Obviously, when I was raising the children in the sixties and the early part of the seventies, it was not looked on favorably for a woman to work, especially if she had children. So you had to justify in your own mind why you were going against the norm. I took all the kids flying by the time they were a week old so that they knew that they were living with me and I wasn't living with them."

See also
Atlantis Space Shuttle; *Discovery* Space Shuttle; *Mir* Space Station; Resnick, Judith Arlene; Ride, Sally Kristen

References
Begley, "Down to Earth" (1996); Biographical Data Sheets, Lyndon B. Johnson Space Center (1997); Oberg, *Spacefarers of the 80's and 90's: The Next Thousand People in Space* (1985); Russo, *Women and Flight: Portraits of Contemporary Women Pilots* (1997)

Lynn, Mrs. Elliott
See Heath, Lady Sophie Mary

MacGill, Elizabeth M. G.

The first Canadian woman to graduate with a degree in electrical engineering from the University of Toronto, MacGill was also the first female aeronautical engineer in the world. She was born in Vancouver, British Columbia, on March 27, 1905. After earning her bachelor's degree, MacGill took a job with the Austin Aircraft Company but soon decided to continue her education instead. MacGill entered the Massachusetts Institute of Technology and earned her master's degree in aeronautical engineering while battling polio.

Her first job after obtaining her master's degree was as assistant aeronautical engineer for Fairchild Aircraft Limited, where she researched stress analysis on airplane parts. In 1938 MacGill was hired as chief aeronautical engineer at the Fort William plant of the Canadian Car and Foundry Company Ltd. During World War II her primary responsibility was the production of the Hawker Hurricane fighter aircraft. A staff of more than 4,500 employees worked under MacGill and produced more than 2,000 airplanes for the war effort during her tenure. While at the Canadian Car and Foundry Company MacGill also designed the Maple Leaf II trainer airplane, which was the first airplane designed by a woman.

In 1937 MacGill became the first woman to be admitted to corporate membership in the Engineering Institute of Canada. For her paper "Factors Affecting the Mass Production of Aeroplanes" she received the Gzowski Medal in 1941.

During her career in aviation technology, MacGill was the first woman to serve as Canadian technical adviser to the UN International Civil Aviation Organization and helped draft the international airworthiness regulations for the design of commercial aircraft.

MacGill was given an honorary membership to the American Society of Women Engineers and was named Engineer of the Year by that group in 1953. In 1967 she was awarded the Centennial Medal by the Canadian government in recognition of her substantial contributions to her field. The Ninety-Nines awarded her the Amelia Earhart Medal in 1975, and in 1979 she was presented with the gold medal of the Ontario Association of Professional Engineers in recognition of her distinguished career.

MacGill died on November 4, 1980. She was posthumously inducted into Canada's Aviation Hall of Fame in 1983.

See also
Ninety-Nines
References
Render, *No Place for a Lady: The Story of Canadian Women Pilots, 1928–1992* (1992); Spring, *Daring Lady Flyers: Canadian Women in the Early Years of Aviation* (1994)

MacPherson, Jeanie

The Hollywood screenwriter who wrote *The Ten Commandments* for producer Cecil B. De Mille, MacPherson was a stunt pilot as well. She was born in Boston in 1883 to a wealthy family. Her first career goal was to sing in the opera.

MacPherson's parents sent her to Paris to study music, but when she returned to the United States she found straight acting jobs as well. These brought Mac-Pherson to the attention of famed director D. W. Griffith, who brought her to Hollywood to perform in his films in 1908.

MacPherson became a director and screenwriter at Universal Studios and then acted in a De Mille film in 1914. She permanently joined his staff of writers in 1918, earning a salary of $150 a week. This was enough to finance her newfound hobby, aviation. It was a hobby she shared with De Mille, who owned his own plane and had set up the first commercial airline in the United States offering regular passenger flights.

MacPherson was the only female pilot in the trio of pilots employed by Orme Locklear, who billed himself as the Man Who Walked on Wings during his performances at air shows in the early 1920s. Locklear had taught MacPherson to fly while he was teaching De Mille. On April 9, 1920, they were cited for reckless flying during one stunt event over the Ambassador Hotel in Santa Barbara, California.

MacPherson stopped flying and screenwriting full time in 1933. Her last film credit was *The Buccaneer*. She died of cancer in 1946.

References
Beauchamp, *Without Lying Down: Frances Marion and the Powerful Women of Early Hollywood* (1997); Boase, *The Sky's the Limit: Women Pioneers in Aviation* (1979); Edwards, *The DeMilles: An American Family* (1988); Ronnie, *Locklear: The Man Who Walked on Wings* (1973).

Magill, Eileen

Canada's second woman pilot, Magill was also the first woman elected to the board of directors of an aero club. She was also the first woman pilot in Manitoba and the first Canadian woman to fly across the border to the United States.

Magill was born in Halifax, Nova Scotia, in 1906 but moved with her family to Winnipeg, Manitoba, in 1919. She was known for being a bit of a tomboy, and it was no surprise to family and friends that she joined the Winnipeg Flying Club when it was founded in May 1928.

There Magill took ten hours of flying lessons from Michael DeBlicquy, and she then flew five solo hours before receiving her private pilot's license on October 24, 1928. Soon afterward she flew to St. Paul, Minnesota, and made the front page of the *Winnipeg Free Press* as the first Canadian woman to fly across the border.

Her dedication to aviation helped get her elected to the Winnipeg Flying Club Board of Directors. This was the only position in aviation that she was able to get, although she applied for many, including an administrative job with the Department of Civil Aviation.

Frustrated by her lack of success in aviation, Magill stopped flying. She died in 1964.

References
Render, *No Place for a Lady: The Story of Canadian Women Pilots, 1928–1992* (1992)

Magnus, Sandra

An astronaut candidate in the National Aeronautics and Space Administration (NASA) class of 1996, Magnus was born on October 30, 1964, in Belleville, Illinois. She graduated from Belleville West High School in 1982 and went on to receive a bachelor's degree in physics in 1986 and a master's degree in electrical engineering from the University of Missouri at Rolla in 1990. During that time Magnus worked as a stealth engineer for the McDonnell Douglas Aircraft Company, where she worked on internal research and development studying the effectiveness of radar signature-reduction techniques. She was also assigned to the navy's A-12 Attack Aircraft program, working primarily on the propulsion system until the program was canceled.

From 1991 to 1996 Magnus completed her thesis work, which was supported by the NASA-Lewis Research Center through a graduate student fellowship from the School of Material Science and Engineering at the Georgia Institute of Technology. Magnus received her doctorate in 1996.

She was selected by NASA in April 1996 for two years of training and evaluation.

References
Biographical Data Sheets, Lyndon B. Johnson Space Center (1997)

Mariner, Rosemary Conaster

The U.S. Navy's second most senior female aviator, in 1995 Mariner was on the staff of the Joint Chiefs and was instrumental in forcing the navy to deal with the Tailhook sexual harassment scandal of 1991. She was also the first woman to qualify for the aviation program at Purdue University in Indiana and the first woman to command a squadron of navy aircraft.

Born in 1953, Mariner grew up Rosemary Conaster in Orange County, California, in a career military family housed at the Miramar Naval Air Station. Her mother was a navy nurse; her father, an Army Air Force pilot, died in the line of duty when she was three.

In ninth grade Mariner began cleaning houses to earn money for flying lessons at Lindbergh Airfield. She also bartered for them by washing planes for her instructor, Fred Priest. She earned her private pilot's license in 1971, on her seventeenth birthday. Her further training, including her multiengine rating, was provided by a succession of former Women's Airforce Service Pilots (WASPS) living in the area.

At Purdue University Mariner studied under another former WASP. When she learned that the navy had lifted its ban on training for female pilots, she graduated early, at 19, with a degree in aviation technology. In 1972 she joined the first class of women at the navy's flight school in Pensacola, Florida. After graduating Mariner was commissioned as an officer in 1973. She was assigned to the Oceana squadron of A-6 pilots, the only female on the entire base. Her duties included towing targets for gunnery practice, a job many WASPS had held in World War II.

In 1975 Mariner was promoted to training on jets, and eventually she became one of the first women to land a jet on an aircraft carrier. In 1988 she became the executive officer at Point Mugu, California, and in July 1990 she was promoted to squadron commander, the navy's first female in that position.

In June 1995 Mariner reached another milestone, when she was promoted to commander and placed in charge of the naval air station in Meridian, Mississippi, the first navy woman to command a naval air station.

As to her experience in the first class of women in navy flight school, Mariner said: "While the newspapers were making heroines of us, our male counterparts were not so impressed. For the first time in many of our lives we were disliked by some people solely because of what we were; unwelcome outsiders invading a fraternity."

See also
Tailhook Sexual Harassment Scandal; U.S. Navy (USN); Women's Airforce Service Pilots (WASPS)
References
Ebbert and Hall, *Crossed Currents: Navy Women from WWI to Tailhook* (1993); Zimmerman, *Tailspin: Women at War in the Wake of Tailhook* (1995)

Markham, Beryl

The first woman to fly the Atlantic solo from east to west, Markham was also an accomplished horsewoman and author. She was born Beryl Clutterbuck in England in the county of Rutland on October 26, 1902, the second child of Charles and Clara Clutterbuck. Her father emigrated to East Africa intending to farm and raise horses in England's newly opened province. In 1905 Clara and the children, including Beryl, joined him. When Clara later separated from Charles and returned to England she took her son but left Beryl in Africa to grow up among the Kikuyu and Kipsigi tribes who worked her father's farm.

It was there Markham learned to ride horses, and she soon became an accomplished horsewoman, training and riding horses from her father's stables. She became the first woman in Kenya to obtain a horse trainer's license and to be trusted with training some of the finest racehorses in the country. She was so renowned that she received the Swahili name Memsahib wa Farasi, which translates into "Lady of Horses." On October 5, 1919, Markham married Alexander Laidlaw "Jock" Purves, an acquaintance from a neighboring farm, but the marriage only lasted two years. She left Purves after numerous arguments regarding her work outside the home.

She was married a second time, on September 3, 1927, to Mansfield Markham, a member of the high society of the province, providing her with money and a security she had not previously enjoyed. They honeymooned in England, where Beryl was presented to the queen, an unusual honor because divorced women were not then presented at Court. In 1928, on a royal safari to Nairobi, Prince Henry returned the visit and rode a horse that Beryl had personally trained. Sadly, her second marriage also lasted just over two years. It produced a son, Gervase

Markham, born on February 27, 1929. Before he reached his first birthday he was sent to his aunt, Lady Markham, to be raised while Beryl and Mansfield began a separation that would last 15 years.

During this time Beryl returned to England and began dating Prince Henry, third in line for the throne. The relationship was broken off by the queen herself, who promised Beryl a pension for life if she would leave the prince. She returned to Kenya and her horses in 1930. There she began yet another affair, with Denys Finch Hatton, longtime love of Karen "Tania" Blixen, also known as Isak Dinesen, author of *Out of Africa*.

It was Denys who first took Beryl flying and stirred her interest in taking the controls. She saw flying as a sensible way of reaching remote parts of the colony as well as a new and exciting challenge. She soloed after only eight hours of instruction, but, sadly, this success came on the day that Hatton died in a plane crash while scouting elephant herds by air.

Markham passed her A license test on July 13, 1931, and took her first solo cross-country flight just four days later. On April 24, 1932, she started from Nairobi and arrived in London seven days later. It had only been five years since the first professional pilots began making flights between Kenya and England. Soon she earned her Air Ministry's pilot's B license, which allowed her to "carry passengers in an aeroplane for hire or reward." Not only was she the first woman to receive such a license, she was also the first Kenya-trained pilot of either sex to do so. This allowed her to obtain her first professional flying work— scouting game herds by air for visiting hunters. She also provided message services for bush camps, flew mail and supplies to gold miners, and delivered medical supplies for doctors.

In 1936 Markham flew to London and took a job as chief pilot with Air Cruisers Limited, which mostly involved ferrying the company owner, François Dupre, to and from Paris on business trips. In September of that year she started the trip that made her famous. She wanted to be the first pilot to fly nonstop from London to New York City, crossing the Atlantic east to west. A miscalculation of her fuel supply caused her to run out of gas just off the eastern tip of Nova Scotia after 22 hours in the air. She managed a water landing and was flown to New York to meet Mayor Fiorello La Guardia in honor of her Atlantic crossing.

In 1937 she spent time at the home of fellow aviator Jacqueline Cochran, as they waited for Amelia Earhart to complete her second try at an around-the-world flight. This was the trip on which Earhart disappeared without a trace, and Markham quickly found herself in the midst of another media blitz.

In the United States Markham found it difficult to obtain work as a pilot. While visiting writer Anita Loos in the summer of 1939 Markham was hired by Paramount Pictures as a technical adviser for *Safari*, a film about scouting big game from biplanes. In 1940 she approached a literary agent about writing a book of her adventure crossing the Atlantic. In 1942 *West with the Night* was published to great critical praise but poor sales figures, so it was discontinued after the first printing. This was also the year Markham finally agreed to end her 15-year separation from Mansfield, and a divorce was granted to them on October 14, 1942. The following Saturday she married Raoul Schumacher. Concerned about the German advance into Africa, the couple decided to sell her family ranch in Kenya and move to southern California. Markham made a living as a writer of short, autobiographical fiction for magazines such as *Ladies' Home Journal* and *Collier's Weekly*.

In 1960 she divorced Schumacher and moved to England. She never returned to the United States but went from London back to Africa, living on the generosity of a string of old friends who provided her free housing in their various guest quarters. In 1956 she returned to the world of horse training with the monetary support of her father, who died of a heart attack in 1957.

On New Year's Day 1959, 33 years after a horse she had trained had won the Kenya St. Leger race, her newest horse won the very same race. A later horse, Niagara, won the Kenya Triple Crown the following year, cementing the success of her return to training.

In 1983 *West with the Night* was rereleased, this time to great success both critically and financially. Markham died on August 3, 1986, of pneumonia, just a month and a day shy of the fiftieth anniversary of her famous flight across the Atlantic.

She had lived her life with the motto "Never look back. You've got to keep looking forward. Something will always happen if you try to make it happen."

See also
Cochran, Jacqueline; Earhart, Amelia Mary
References
Lovell, *Straight on till Morning: The Biography of Beryl Markham* (1987); Markham, *West with the Night* (1983); Markham, *The Splendid Outcast* (1987)

Marsalis, Frances Harrell
Born in Texas circa 1900, Marsalis is known for twice breaking the refueling flight endurance record. She was employed as a credit manager for a Houston bank when she inherited enough money to quit that job and study aviation. Marsalis was first a student at Roosevelt Field and then of the Curtiss Flying

School. There she took flying lessons with William Marsalis, her future husband. Once she obtained her license, Marsalis was hired by the Curtiss Exhibition Team, demonstrating planes for the Curtiss-Wright Corporation at air shows.

From August 14 to August 22, 1932, Viola Gentry, an early pioneer of aviation, organized a publicity stunt for Curtiss-Wright. She invited Marsalis and Louise Thaden to beat the current refueling endurance flight record (set at 123 hours by Bobbi Trout). Marsalis was struck by a mild attack of appendicitis while in flight but refused to land and lose the record. She spent a day on board the plane packed in ice while Thaden flew, and she was able to fly again on their last day aloft.

Despite the appendicitis, a fierce storm, and a faulty oil gauge, Marsalis and Thaden spent 73 more hours in flight than Trout did for a total of 8 days, 4 hours, 5 minutes. For this feat they were celebrated at a dinner held at the White House with President Herbert Hoover. Marsalis was also elected governor of the New York chapter of the Ninety-Nines in celebration of this record.

After four months of lectures and air shows Marsalis decided to try to break her own record in December 1933. This time her partner was Helen Richey of Pennsylvania. The two managed 9 days, 21 hours, 42 minutes and succeeded in breaking the record. Marsalis's reputation earned her a job demonstrating Waco planes, which she flew for two first-place prizes in local air meets at the start of 1934.

On August 4, 1934, Marsalis was an entrant in the First National Air Meet for Women in Dayton, Ohio. While circling a pylon in the 50-mile free-for-all, Marsalis was caught in the slipstream of another contestant, Edna Gardner Whyte, and lost control of her own plane. Whyte veered to the left at the last minute and won the race, but she was disqualified for the erratic move because race rules only allowed passing on the right. Helen Richey was declared the winner. Marsalis died in the crash.

Discussing the danger of breaking records, Marsalis had once said to her friend Thaden: "When my time comes, I hope it's in a plane where I can crack up in one grand splurge, engine wide open. It's a sissy wish to want to die that way, but I don't want to lie on a bed for weeks or months suffering, knowing I would never be well again."

See also
Gentry, Viola; Ninety-Nines; Richey, Helen; Thaden, Louise McPhetridge; Trout, Evelyn "Bobbi"; Whyte, Edna Marvel Gardner
References
Adams and Kimball, *Heroines of the Sky* (1942); Thaden, *High, Wide, and Frightened* (1973)

Marvingt, Marie
Known as "the Fiancée of Danger," Marvingt was born in 1875, the daughter of a postmaster; like Helene Dutrieu, she became a prize-winning bicyclist. Later Marvingt mastered mountain climbing, skiing, swimming, boxing, wrestling, and judo. Marvingt was a war correspondent, nurse, surgeon, and balloonist before gaining her pilot's license.

On November 27, 1910, Marvingt set a world speed record for women, flying 45 kilometers in 53 minutes during the Coupe Femina race.

At 80 she was still active, piloting a jet-powered helicopter. Marvingt died on December 15, 1963, at the age of 88.

Explaining why she never married, Marvingt once said: "I don't think any man would put up with me for long. I'm more interested in mountain climbing than in washing dishes."

See also
Dutrieu, Helene
References
Villard, *Contact! The Story of the Early Birds* (1968)

McAfee, Mildred

The first director of the Women Appointed for Volunteer Emergency Service (WAVES), McAfee was born in Parkville, Missouri, in 1906. She graduated from prestigious Vassar College in 1920 and taught at secondary schools. She earned a master's degree in education from the University of Chicago and then taught at Tusculum College in Tennessee. In 1932 McAfee became dean of women at Centre College in Kentucky, and in 1934 she was hired as dean of women at Oberlin College, the first college in the United States to accept female students. In 1936 McAfee was selected as president of Wellesley College.

On July 30, 1942, the WAVES were created by an act of Congress. When she was appointed to lead them, McAfee became the first woman ever commissioned as an officer in the U.S. Navy. She was made a lieutenant commander and took a leave of absence from the college to handle her new responsibilities. In turn McAfee appointed Joy Bright Hancock, whose career in the navy had begun as a yeoman in World War I, as women's representative to the chief of the Bureau of Aeronautics.

McAfee retired from the WAVES as a full captain in December 1946. For her service she received the Distinguished Service Medal. Although she never publicly spoke out against it, McAfee angered some of her former recruits by refusing to testify before Congress in favor of permanently retaining women in the armed forces after World War II. She preferred to return to private life and her position at Wellesley.

McAfee was married to the Reverend Douglas Horton. When she retired from Wellesley in 1949 she became vice president of the National Council of Churches and also served as president of the American Association of Colleges. McAfee died on September 2, 1994.

In one of her speeches after the war McAfee defended the value of women in the military, saying: "Discussing manpower in a national emergency as though it were only male power puts women in the category of a national luxury instead of a national asset."

See also
Hancock, Joy Bright; Women Appointed for Volunteer Emergency Service (WAVES)
References
Ebbert and Hall, *Crossed Currents: Navy Women from WWI to Tailhook* (1993); "Mildred McAfee Horton Dies; First Head of WAVES Was 94" (1994); Weatherford, *American Women's History: An A to Z of People, Places, Organizations, Issues, and Events* (1994)

McAuliffe, Sharon Christa

The fourth mother in space and the winner of the National Aeronautics and Space Administration (NASA) 1985 Teacher in Space Program, McAuliffe perished in the explosion of the *Challenger* space shuttle. She was born Sharon Christa Corrigan on September 2, 1948, in Boston, Massachusetts. She graduated from Marian High School in 1966 and received her B.A. degree in education from Framingham State College in 1970. She married her high school sweetheart, Steve McAuliffe, on August 23, 1970.

McAuliffe worked as a substitute teacher at Benjamin Foulois Junior High School her first year out of college while her husband pursued a law degree. The next year, 1972, McAuliffe received her first full-time position teaching American history, civics, and English at Thomas Johnson Junior High in Lanham, Maryland, a job she held for six years. While she continued teaching, McAuliffe also studied for her master's degree in education supervision and administration at Bowie State College.

She had her first child, a boy, on September 11, 1976. In 1978 McAuliffe received her master's degree, and the family moved to Concord, New Hampshire, where she returned to substitute teaching. She had her second child, a girl, on August 24, 1979. Her next full-time position came that fall, teaching social studies and English at Bow Memorial School in Concord. Always interested in improving working conditions for teachers, she ran for and was elected president of the Bow teachers' union, a chapter of the National Education Association (NEA). She succeeded in convincing the local taxpayers to authorize a larger budget for the school system and to raise teachers' salaries.

In 1981 McAuliffe accepted a position teaching American history, law, and economics at Concord High School. She then developed the curriculum for "The American Woman," a history class told from the female perspective. On August 27, 1984, President Ronald Reagan inaugurated the Teacher in Space Program by announcing that NASA's first citizen in space would be "one of America's finest: a teacher." McAuliffe had been teaching for 14 years.

The idea caused controversy. The president of the NEA argued that it was just a gimmick and that sending teachers into well-equipped classrooms was better than sending them into space. A columnist for the *New York Times* bemoaned the fact that the teacher chosen would become nothing but another cut-rate celebrity and that his or her teaching career would be over. Nevertheless, McAuliffe applied. She saw the opportunity as a chance to humanize the space program that she had always admired and to elevate the status of teaching.

On June 28, 1985, McAuliffe made the list of ten finalists, all of whom then underwent strenuous physical and psychological tests similar to those given to astronauts. These included tests for claustrophobia and spatial disorientation.

On July 19 Vice President George Bush held a national news conference to announce that McAuliffe would be the first teacher in space. She was assigned to mission STS-51L, whose crew would also include Judith Resnick, the second American woman in space.

After a summer filled with hometown parades and guest spots on television interview shows, training began on September 9, 1985. This included flying in T-38s at faster than the speed of sound and learning how to fight fires inside a mock-up of the space shuttle.

McAuliffe's mission was first scheduled to launch on January 22, 1986, but was rescheduled because of a dust storm in the Sahara Desert. The flight was pushed back to January 26 and then 27, and it was finally rescheduled to January 28, 1986. That turned out to be the coldest launch weather ever attempted by NASA. Seventy-two seconds into the flight, the *Challenger* space shuttle suffered a booster rocket failure that resulted in the breakup of the vehicle. McAuliffe and the rest of the crew died in the crash.

In one of her many interviews during the months of training, McAuliffe explained her mission in space: "Any dream can come true if you have the courage to work for it. I would never say, 'Well, you're only a C student in English so you'll never be a poet!' You have to dream. We all have to dream. Dreaming is okay. Imagine me teaching from space, all over the world, touching so many people's lives. That's a teacher's dream! I have a vision of the world as a global village, a world without boundaries. Imagine a history teacher making history!"

See also
Challenger Space Shuttle; Resnick, Judith Arlene

References
Biel, *World Disaster Series: The Challenger* (1991); Corrigan, *A Journal for Christa: Christa McAuliffe, Teacher in Space* (1993); Hohler, *I Touch the Future: The Story of Christa McAuliffe* (1986)

McKillop, Peggy

Part of the first team of women to barnstorm across Australia, McKillop was born in 1916 in Orange, New South Wales. She took flying lessons in 1933 from Charles Kingsford-Smith, a record-breaking pilot who had opened a flying school in Mascot, Australia, that would years later grow into the Sydney International Airport. She earned her private pilot's license in 1932 and her commercial license in March 1935. In working toward her commercial license McKillop became one of the first two women in New South Wales to fly at night.

On April 3, 1935, she teamed up with the only other female student in Kingsford-Smith's class, Nancy Bird, on their first barnstorming tour of Australia. They were sponsored by the Shell Oil Company and *Woman* magazine. They flew for three months and 22,000 miles, offering rides for pay and giving lectures at local schools and town halls.

McKillop and Bird usually stayed by invitation at the homes of the wealthier members of the communities, as it was a novelty to host female pilots. One of their stays was at Malaraway, the home of Colin Kelman. Also along the barnstorming tour McKillop and Bird took time to hire themselves out as charter pilots, flying ranchers to the far corners of their property to count sheep or to other ranches to size up future purchases.

After their first tour, McKillop returned to her hometown to relax. Bird did some more charter flight work and met the Reverend Stanley Drummond. He headed the Far West Children's Health Scheme (FWCHS), a group dedicated to eradicating trachoma in small country towns. He asked them to fly various volunteer doctors on rounds to patients in the outlying districts, a task too difficult to do by car.

Between barnstorming and assisting Drummond, the women entered the Nar-romine Air Pageant in September 1935 and won the silver cup. In 1939 Kelman followed McKillop when she moved to England. They were married and flew together to Australia for their honeymoon.

See also
Bird, Nancy De Low
References
Bird, *Born to Fly* (1961)

McNabb, Betty

The namesake of the U.S. Coast Guard Auxiliary's Betty McNabb Aviation Award, McNabb was born on August 5, 1909. She did not learn to fly until she was 42 years old, and then she did so for business. In 1951 McNabb was a health records consultant in Georgia, traveling unpaved roads through the rural parts of the state at all hours of the day and night. Rather than drive those rounds, McNabb learned to fly them.

When she later moved to Florida McNabb became known at the local air force base. In 1958 the base commander invited her to fly with him on a sound barrier–breaking flight. On the flight McNabb took the controls as the plane crashed the barrier, making her the eighth woman in the Western Hemisphere to fly through the sound barrier.

In 1964 she graduated from the U.S. Air Force War College with the rank of lieutenant colonel. In June 1969 she joined the Coast Guard Auxiliary, flying missions for them for the next 20 years, well into her eighties. In 1990 the Coast Guard honored her by naming an award for her, and in 1991 they gave her their Award of Merit for exceptional personal dedication to the Coast Guard.

See also
U.S. Coast Guard (USCG)
References
Holden and Griffith, *Ladybirds II: The Continuing Story of American Women in Aviation* (1993)

Melroy, Pamela

One of the first women to qualify as a shuttle pilot, Melroy was born on September 17, 1961, in Palo Alto, California. Her family moved to Rochester, New York, where she graduated from Bishop Kearney High School in 1979. Melroy attended Wellesley College, where she earned a bachelor of science degree in physics and astronomy in 1983.

Melroy joined the U.S. Air Force Reserve Officers' Training Corps (ROTC) in 1983 and worked toward a master of science degree in earth and planetary sciences, which she received from the Massachusetts Institute of Technology in 1984. She then attended undergraduate pilot training at Reese Air Force Base in Lubbock, Texas.

Melroy graduated in 1985 and flew the KC-10 for six years at Barksdale Air Force Base in Bossier City, Louisiana, as a copilot, aircraft commander, and instructor pilot. She logged over 200 combat and combat support hours in Just Cause, a nonfunded group dedicated to "adopting" MIAs from the Vietnam War and working to discover the truth of their whereabouts, and Desert Shield and Desert Storm.

In June 1991 Melroy attended the Air Force Test Pilot School at Edwards Air Force Base, California. Upon graduation, she was assigned to the C-17 Combined Test Force, where she served as a test pilot until her selection for the astronaut program in December 1994.

Melroy completed a year of training and qualified for assignment as a shuttle pilot. She was then assigned to astronaut support duties for launch and landing while awaiting her first flight assignment.

See also
U.S. Air Force (USAF)
References
Biographical Data Sheets, Lyndon B. Johnson Space Center (1997)

Mercury 13

Mercury 13 was the nickname given to the group of 13 women whom the National Aeronautics and Space Administration (NASA) tested for the astronaut program in the early 1960s. Dr. Randolph Lovelace, chairman of NASA's Life Sciences Committee for Project Mercury, had tested the male Mercury astronauts. He wanted to study the effects of spaceflight on women, so he asked Jacqueline Cochran, America's premier female pilot, to speak to the most prestigious female pilots she knew. He wondered if any would be interested in undergoing the tests. In the end, 13 were. At 54 Cochran was too old for the tests herself, but she assisted the effort by helping to fund Lovelace's studies.

Jerrie Cobb, a pilot who had logged over 10,000 flight hours, was the first woman selected to report to the clinic for the first phase of the tests in 1960. Her preparation for the tests involved running 5 miles a day and riding 20 more on a stationery bike. The tests themselves were exactly the ones given to the Mercury astronauts, and Cobb matched the men's statistics on each test. For the isolation test Cobb was immersed up to her neck in an underground water tank; she stayed there for 9 hours, 40 minutes, exceeding the highest male astronauts' test time by just over three hours. Her test results were so extraordinary that Cobb was sent to phase two of the program, and the other women began phase one.

Among the others of the Mercury 13 there were members of the Women's Airforce Service Pilots (WASPS) from World War II, schoolteachers, and two identical twins. All test subjects accepted Cochran's invitation, despite the fact that they had to agree to pay their own way. Twelve of the women had phenomenal test results: Rhea Allison, Jane Hart, Mary Wallace "Wally" Funk, Jean Hixson, Myrtle Cagle, Irene Leverton, Sara

Gorelick, Jan and Marion Dietrich (the twins), Gene Nora Stumbough, B. Steadman, and Gerry Sloan Truhill.

For phase two Cobb underwent the usual navy pilot testing at the Navy School of Aviation. Overall the women proved to be less prone to heart attacks and less vulnerable to loneliness, cold, heat, pain, and noise. It was also discovered that NASA could save money by using women astronauts, since the cost of sending anything into space was nearly $1,000 per pound. Women weighed less and would therefore cost less in space.

Despite these advantages, and although Cobb passed her second phase of testing with flying colors as well, NASA did not allow her or the other 12 members of the Mercury 13 to become full astronauts in the Mercury program. Instead, Cobb was made a NASA consultant. The others were simply dismissed. On July 17, 1962, Cobb and a few others testified before Congress in favor of women being included in the astronaut corps. Astronaut John Glenn, the first man to orbit the earth, testified against. The Mercury 13 lost. In July 1961 NASA canceled all further testing of women for the Mercury program.

NASA decided that although women could pass the astronaut tests, they did not have the complete qualifications to take them. Women had never passed the jet aircraft testing at Edwards Air Force Base because women were not yet eligible for jet pilot training programs in the military (and they would not be eligible by law until 1973). Cobb requested the jet experience requirements be waived in lieu of her extensive flying hours and high scores in the naval tests at Pensacola. NASA refused to waive the requirement.

Jerrie Cobb left her token position at NASA and returned to private flying, focusing her energies on missionary work in South America. For years she flew supplies to Amazon tribes in her own plane. In 1981 she was nominated for the Nobel Peace Prize.

Among the other members of the Mercury 13, Jan Dietrich became a corporate jet pilot, and Wally Funk became the first female Federal Aviation Administration inspector. Thirty-four years later, seven of the Mercury 13 witnessed America's first woman pilot astronaut, Lt. Col. Eileen Collins, launch at Cape Kennedy on February 3, 1995, piloting the *Discovery* space shuttle on mission STS-63.

See also
Cobb, Geraldyne "Jerrie"; Cochran, Jacqueline; Collins, Eileen; *Discovery* Space Shuttle; Funk, Mary Wallace; National Aeronautics and Space Administration (NASA)

References
Life Magazine, June 28, 1963; *Ms.* magazine, September 1973

Meyer, Marta Bohn

The first woman to fly as a crewmember aboard a triple sonic flight, Meyer was born in Amityville, New York, on August 18, 1957. Her father was a test pilot for Grumman Aircraft, so she was surrounded by test pilots during her childhood. Meyer began flying at the age of 14 and earned her pilot's license before she was 16.

Meyer graduated from Rensselaer Polytechnic Institute in 1979 with a degree in aeronautical engineering. Her first job was with the National Aeronautics and Space Administration (NASA) Dryden Flight Research Facility, where she conducted research involving the thermal protection tiles of the space shuttle. In 1989 the U.S. Air Force decommissioned the SR-71 triple sonic aircraft, which was capable of flying three times the speed of sound, and Meyer's company was hired to study the possibility that the SR-71 might be used in NASA training programs. It was as part of her analysis that Meyer flew aboard the SR-71. Her husband, with whom she builds competitive aerobatic planes in their spare time, was another crewmember.

In 1990 Meyer won the California Championship title in the intermediate category of aerobatic competition. Nevertheless, Meyer considers her triple sonic flight the true highlight of her career: "Flying at Mach 3 is at the top of my list of experiences and there is nothing that could equal it for me. I had a grin on my face from ear to ear and we hadn't even left the pavement yet. If I ever get down or depressed, I just remember how great that feeling was and it gets me motivated again."

See also
U.S. Air Force (USAF)
References
Holden and Griffith, *Ladybirds II: The Continuing Story of American Women in Aviation* (1993)

Miles, Maxine

As director of the Miles Aircraft Company of Great Britain during and after World War II, Maxine Miles was her country's only aircraft designer for many years. The daughter of a famous stage actor, Miles was not introduced to aviation until she met and married Frederick George Miles, an airplane designer.

Together they started the Miles Aircraft Company with the manufacture of one two-seater training plane at the Reading Airport. Eventually they purchased the airport to keep it from going bankrupt and to ensure that they would have a location for their manufacturing plant. In 1935, when they were designing and building ten different types of planes (one of which they sold to Charles and Anne Lindbergh), they went public. Besides drafting designs Maxine was in charge of representing the company to the Aircraft Production Ministry officials

in London, and she sat on the company's board of directors.

At the approach of World War II the Mileses opened up a flight training school at their airport to prepare men for the Royal Air Force. They also began designing planes for the military. Because of the large numbers of men conscripted into the military, many of their plant employees were female. Maxine instituted a day nursery at the plant to provide the women with safe, free care for their children. The program was so popular it continued after the war.

See also
Lindbergh, Anne Morrow
References
Knapp, *New Wings for Women* (1946)

Milstead, Violet

Canada's first female bush pilot, Milstead was also a member of the British Air Transport Auxiliary (ATA) in World War II. Born in 1912, Milstead started her lessons at Pat Patterson's Flyers Limited School at Barker Field, Toronto, in 1939. She received her private pilot's license on December 20, 1939. During her first solo flight, to and from Barker Field through Lambeth and Jarvis, Milstead had to land the plane at Jarvis and obtain a local citizen's signature to certify her arrival.

Milstead received her commercial pilot's license in April 1940. Then Patterson offered to fund her work toward an instructor's license. The male instructors at his flying school were being recruited into the Royal Canadian Air Force (RCAF), and he wanted to ensure that he would have an employee who could not enlist.

Milstead found a partner to run her family's wool shop while she worked toward the instructor's certificate, which she received in July 1941. This made her eligible to be one of the five Canadian women, including Helen Harrison and

Marion Powell Orr, who were approved by the RCAF as flying instructors for male pilots at the start of World War II. At the same time, until civilian flying was grounded in November 1942, she was also instructing civilians at Patterson's school.

On April 19, 1943, Milstead moved to England. She had applied to the Women's Division of the ATA, which had just been formed by Pauline Gower. Women would be used to ferry new and repaired aircraft from manufacturers' sites to Royal Air Force bases to free up more male pilots for combat work. Milstead's experience was just what the ATA required.

The women in the ATA received some quick training in flying the various military aircraft and ground school classes so they could do elementary repair if they experienced any problems while en route. After this initial training, Milstead began her full-time ferrying duties in September 1943. During the war the women of the ATA continued training on more and more complex aircraft, and by the end of the war Milstead was qualified as a pilot in over 40 planes.

With victory for the Allies in sight, Milstead's last wartime ferrying mission was on May 4, 1945. After the war many women pilots resigned to return to their homes and families. Milstead chose to stay on, flying new planes to bases in invaded areas and returning to England with planes in need of repair. Once this work, too, was finished, Milstead returned to Canada on August 28, 1945.

Milstead's first postwar job in aviation was as an instructor for the Leavens Brothers Flying School in Toronto. There she met her future husband, Arnold Warren, who was the school's chief instructor. In 1947 the two moved on to Nickel Belt Airways, where Milstead operated the flying school while her husband took care of charter flights. During busy times Milstead also flew charters into the bush country. Her pas-

sengers were fly fishermen, prospectors, trappers, and even politicians looking to drum up votes. The first woman pilot in Canada to fly into the bush, she became known as "The Bush Angel."

In 1950 Nickel Belt was bought out by a larger company, and Milstead and her husband were hired by the Department of Transportation to manage the Windsor Flying Club. In 1952 they tried working in Indonesia, where her husband taught flyers at the Indonesian Aviation Academy. Milstead was the first woman to earn an Indonesian instructor's license, but she found no students, since Muslims were forbidden by their religion to accept instruction on any subject from females.

Back in Canada in 1954 they were both finding it difficult to obtain work flying. The Orenda Engine Plant in Toronto hired Milstead as their librarian and her husband as a public relations officer, jobs they held until 1959. She later worked as a librarian for the Ontario Water Commission. They both retired in 1973 and moved to Port Colborne, Ontario, flying only for personal enjoyment.

Milstead once described her love of flying by saying: "I felt alive in a way I had never before imagined. I seem to be blessed with a temperament which has enabled me to delight in the challenges of flight, to love its freedom, its self-sufficiency, its splendid loneliness, to marvel at the awesome beauty of sky-scapes, to pity the earthbound."

See also
Air Transport Auxiliary (ATA); Gower, Pauline; Harrison, Helen Marcelle; Orr, Marion Powell

References
Render, *No Place for a Lady: The Story of Canadian Women Pilots, 1928–1992* (1992)

Mir Space Station

Completed and launched on February 19, 1986, the *Mir* space station housed up to six astronauts running experiments and testing life in space. "*Mir*" is the Russian word for "peace" or "world"; the *Mir* space station was the world's first permanently manned space station. It would come to U.S. fame in 1996 when astronaut Shannon Lucid became the world's longest resident of space, spending seven months on board.

The first woman to work on *Mir* was cosmonaut Elena Kondakova, whose first mission in space was on *Mir* as a flight engineer of the seventeenth main mission from October 4, 1994, through March 9, 1995. This six-month stay in space set a new women's space endurance record.

On March 22, 1996, Lucid was ferried by the *Atlantis* space shuttle mission STS-76 to *Mir*, where she served as board engineer 2 for seven record-setting months. Lucid performed numerous life science and physical science experiments during the course of her stay aboard *Mir*. She returned to earth on STS-79 on September 26, 1996. Lucid holds an international record for the most flight hours in orbit by any non-Russian and holds the record for the most flight hours in orbit by any woman in the world.

For her work on *Mir* Lucid became the first and only woman to have earned the Congressional Space Medal of Honor awarded by the president of the United States. Russian president Boris Yeltsin also awarded Lucid the Order of Friendship Medal, the highest award that can be presented to a noncitizen.

See also
Kondakova, Elena V.; Lucid, Shannon W.
References
Vogt, *Space Library: Space Stations* (1990)

Misty Blues
An exclusive, invitation-only, all-female group of skydivers, the Misty Blues was started in 1985 by Sandra Williams.

Members must have achieved 1,000 parachute jumps on their own before being invited to join. There are no more than 14 members at any one time, and they perform all over the world. By 1993 they had logged over 30,000 jumps as a team, with each member achieving her own world parachuting record in the course of her career with the Misty Blues.

Misty Blues members continue in their full-time jobs while on the team. Past members have been everything from elementary school teachers to commercial artists to gemologists. Like participants in other team sports, they attend a spring training camp at their headquarters in Florida once a year where they create new parachuting stunts and practice their previous crowd pleasers, one of which is the cutaway, which simulates falling with a faulty parachute.

In 1991 the Misty Blues were voted the Best of the Best at the annual convention of the International Council of Air Shows.

References
Holden and Griffith, *Ladybirds II: The Continuing Story of American Women in Aviation* (1993)

Mock, Geraldine "Jerrie" Frederitz

In 1964 Mock (born 1925) became the first woman to fly around the world, 27 years after Amelia Earhart's disappearance in 1937. Joan Merriam Smith was flying with the same goal in mind and completed her trip successfully, but Mock had registered first with the Federal Aviation Administration (FAA) and therefore won the title. Her plane, a single-engine Cessna 180, was called the *Spirit of Columbus*.

Mock's flight took place from March 19 to April 17, 1964. Along the way she made maintenance and refueling stops in Casablanca, Cairo, Calcutta, Manila, and

Geraldine Mock (April 17, 1964)

Honolulu, frequently staying with local dignitaries. In all she traveled 23,000 miles in 29 ½ days. Part of the trip was funded by Mock's filing daily news reports of her progress from each stop.

The flight gave Mock a number of aviation firsts, including first woman to fly both the Atlantic and Pacific, first woman to fly the Pacific in both directions, and first woman to fly the Pacific in a single-engine plane.

On May 4, 1964, Mock received the FAA's Decoration for Exceptional Service, the country's highest civil aviation award, which was presented to Mock personally by President Lyndon Johnson. In celebration of her achievement the Pentagon offered Mock the chance to pilot an F-101 supersonic plane on July 14, 1964, something no other woman had yet done.

In 1964 Mock was also awarded the Amelia Earhart Memorial Award, the Ohio Governor's Award, and the American Institute of Aeronautics and Astronautics Special Award for her flight.

In 1965 Mock won the Louis Blériot medal, established by the Fédération Aéronautique Internationale (FAI) and awarded by the General Aviation Commission each year to the respective holders of the records for speed, altitude, and straight-line distance.

Mock continued to fly at air meets and events, setting new records in speed and distance in 1965, 1968, and 1969, when she was voted Sports Woman of the Year by the Columbus *Citizen-Journal*.

See also
Earhart, Amelia Mary; Fédération Aéronautique Internationale (FAI); Smith, Joan Merriam; U.S. Air Force (USAF)
References
Mock, *Three-Eight Charlie* (1970)

Moisant, Matilde

The second licensed female pilot in the United States and the first woman to fly to an altitude of 1,200 feet, Moisant qualified for her license after only 32 minutes of in-flight instruction. In so doing she established the record for the shortest time spent learning to fly, a record that, at least partly because of later federal requirements and regulations, has never been broken.

Born on September 13, 1886, Moisant learned to fly in Hempstead, New York, at the Moisant Aviation School. Her brother John, the first pilot to take passengers across the English Channel, died in a plane crash in 1911. His brother Alfred started the school in his honor. Matilde's instructor, however, was André Houpert.

Moisant began ground school lessons on July 13, 1911. After passing the written exam, she spent 32 minutes actually flying and received her license on August 13, 1911. She joined the Moisant International Aviators, her brother's exhibition flying team, with her friend and fellow student Harriet Quimby, the first licensed female pilot in the United States.

On September 13, 1911, her twenty-fifth birthday, Moisant won a women's altitude competition by flying to a height of 1,500 feet. She was the first American woman to be awarded an altitude prize. A few months later she set a new world altitude record for women when she piloted her plane twice as high, to a height of 3,000 feet. Together she and Quimby flew in exhibition shows throughout the United States and Mexico. On November 13, 1911, at the inauguration of President Francisco Madero, Moisant became the first woman to fly over Mexico City and the first person, man or woman, to land a plane in Mexico City.

After that tour Quimby went to England to attempt a channel crossing. For Moisant there followed a run of bad luck, from Shreveport, Louisiana, where she crashed and was pinned underneath the wreckage, to Wichita Falls, Texas, where her plane caught fire in a crash landing during a show on March 13, 1912.

The landing field in Texas had been swarmed by excited fans, and Moisant had to pull out of the landing to avoid them. The plane stalled and crashed. When Moisant was pulled from the wreckage her tweed flying suit was on fire. Luckily it was thick material and kept her skin from being burned. She retired from flying that day, at the age of 26.

Four years later, at the outbreak of World War I, Moisant volunteered as a pilot but was turned down because of her sex. Instead, she joined the Red Cross and worked with them in France until the armistice.

In 1953 she came out of retirement long enough to serve as official hostess to the Sixth Annual Air Fair in Los Angeles, her last public event in aviation. She died in Los Angeles, California, in 1964.

Many other women had survived crashes but kept on flying. When asked why she retired, Moisant said: "My flying career didn't last very long because in those days that was man's work and they didn't think a nice girl should be in it.

There were not many flying schools that would accept women. Goodness, they didn't want us driving motor cars, can you imagine airplanes?"

See also
Quimby, Harriet
References
Adams and Kimball, *Heroines of the Sky* (1942); Holden, *Her Mentor Was an Albatross: The Autobiography of Pioneer Pilot Harriet Quimby* (1993); Lomax, *Women of the Air* (1987); May, *Women in Aeronautics* (1962); Moolman, *Women Aloft* (1981)

Montgomery, Helen

One of the first women in the United States to earn her glider pilot's license, Montgomery was born in Fort Wayne, Indiana. She graduated from high school at the age of 16 and received a nursing degree from the University of Michigan School of Nursing in the middle of the country's worst economic depression.

At college she met and married a graduate student in the Physics Department, Lawrence Montgomery. They moved to Cleveland, Ohio, where the National Air Races were annually held and found a mutual interest in aviation. When they later moved to Ann Arbor, Michigan, they immediately joined the local glider club. Montgomery also joined the local chapter of the Ninety-Nines, which included Maude Squire Rufus among its members.

While in Michigan Montgomery earned her pilot's license in powered craft first, then gained her glider pilot license after two practice flights. She and her husband then started the XYZ Soaring Club of Michigan and went to their first soaring contest in 1936. In 1938 Montgomery set a women's national endurance record for gliders, flying 7 hours, 28 minutes. Later in the year she set an altitude record for American women, flying at a height of 4,183 feet, and a distance record for flying 15 miles in her glider. In

August 1940 Montgomery performed glider aerobatics at the annual air show in Pontiac, Michigan. She was the only woman entered in the competition, and she came in sixth in the group of 63 participating pilots.

At the start of World War II the government severely restricted civilian flying, so the Montgomerys disbanded the XYZ club and took jobs instructing army glider pilots at a school in Lamesa, Texas. Then Montgomery was called to be a flight instructor at the Women's Airforce Service Pilots (WASPS) training school in Sweetwater, Texas. She kept that position until the WASPS were disbanded just before the end of the war.

Montgomery returned to gliding as a sport after the war.

See also
National Air Races; Ninety-Nines; Rufus, Maude Squire; Women's Airforce Service Pilots (WASPS)
References
Knapp, *New Wings for Women* (1946)

Mosher, Leah

One of the first three women to fly with the Canadian Air Force (CAF), Mosher was born in 1955 in Sydney, Nova Scotia, to a military family. Both her mother and father had worked as fighter control operators. In 1973 Mosher joined the family business, enlisting as a supply technician and getting her name on the list for officers' training.

In 1975 Mosher was accepted to officers' training. A year later she graduated from officers' training and managed to complete her bachelor of arts in history at the university. She became a supply officer at the CAF base in Edmonton. In 1978 Mosher attained the rank of captain. She also began working toward her private pilot's license to be prepared for the day the CAF would accept women into the pilot training program, and, with

Nora Bottomley and Deanna Brasseur, she was one of the first three women allowed to train as pilots for the CAF.

Mosher received her air force wings in March 1981 and was immediately enrolled in three months of training on the Hercules jet. She also trained on the CF-18 jet but was initially barred from tactical airlift training on the basis that it was intended for pilots eligible for combat, which did not include women. Her base commander, however, supported her case, and Mosher was allowed to enroll.

After completing training Mosher traveled to 33 different countries for maneuvers and to supply Canadian embassies with personnel and property. In 1985 Mosher was transferred to the CAF base at Uplands, Ottawa, where she worked as a protocol officer until an opening came up for training on the Challenger jet in 1987. Mosher transferred to the 412 Squadron in Ottawa, Ontario, and flew the newest jet in the CAF until 1989.

Mosher was then promoted to staff officer for the Administration of Policy and then to director of recruiting services at the National Defense Headquarters in Ottawa. But, she says, flying will always be her first love. According to Mosher: "I enjoyed my work but I really dreamed of being a pilot. From my very first rides as a passenger in the Argus and the Herc, I knew that's what I wanted. As corny as it sounds, I love viewing the world from above."

See also
Bottomley, Nora; Brasseur, Deanna
References
Render, *No Place for a Lady: The Story of Canadian Women Pilots, 1928–1992* (1992)

Mumaw, Katrina

The first child, male or female, to pilot a plane through the sound barrier, Mumaw was born in Lancaster, California, in 1983. Federal Aviation Administration regulations do not allow anyone under the age of 17 to be issued a pilot certificate, but training can begin at any age. Mumaw fell in love with aviation at the age of three after she met Jeana Yeager and Dick Rutan of *Voyager* fame. She took her first plane ride at the age of five and began training with a flight instructor when she was eight.

Since then Mumaw has flown hot air balloons and a variety of military jets. She frequently participates in air combat dogfights with Edwards Air Force Base test pilots as her competition.

In 1994 Mumaw broke the sound barrier at the age of 11. At 13 she was both competing and speaking at air meets and aviation events around the state.

About breaking records, Mumaw told an interviewer in 1996: "There's not really any hurry. I would have done it [broken the sound barrier] if I was the first, the 21st or even the 121st."

Sally Murphy (1974)

See also
Yeager, Jeana
References
Callender, "Why Did They Take Off? Asks Lancaster Pilot, 13" (1996); Holden and Griffith, *Ladybirds II: The Continuing Story of American Women in Aviation* (1993)

Murphy, Sally

The first female aviator in the history of the U.S. Army, Murphy was born in 1949. Before she became an aviator, her background was in military intelligence. The first year the army accepted women to flight school she joined the first class to mix male and female students, Officer Rotary Wing Class 7414 at the Army Aviation Center in Fort Rucker, Alabama. The only woman among 24 men, Murphy received her wings on June 4, 1974.

After graduation Murphy was assigned to the 330th Army Security Agency Company, which flew intelligence missions. She was soon promoted to the 62nd Aviation Company, nicknamed "The Royal Coachmen," where she was in command of 200 soldiers, 37 helicopters, and two airplanes.

In April 1991 Murphy took command of a battalion in Japan.

Of her status as the first female army aviator, Murphy has said: "I'm never certain whether attitudes have changed, or whether I've toughened up (probably both). The challenge, however, was to perform to the best of my ability, every day as an officer and as a pilot. These are the same challenges faced by all lieutenants; by all beginners in their careers."

See also
U.S. Army
References
"Army's First Female Pilot Wins Helicopter Wings" (1974); Holden and Griffith, *Ladybirds: The Untold Story of Women Pilots in America* (1991)

Myers, Mary Breed Hawley

The first woman in the United States to pilot her own aircraft was Myers of Mohawk, New York. Her husband, Carl E. Myers, was researching ballooning, and Myers assisted him. Together they developed a new balloon fabric that was flexible enough to fold without cracking, so it lasted longer than the currently available fabrics and performed better on rough landings.

Myers began ballooning herself under the stage name of Carlotta Myers—Lady Astronaut. Her first solo flight took place on July 4, 1880, at Little Falls, New York. After that she was hired by resort hotels in Saratoga Springs to take tourists on balloon rides.

In Franklin, Pennsylvania, in 1886 Myers set a world altitude record for ballooning, flying to a height of nearly four miles (20,000 feet). She successfully made later ascents without the use of supplemental oxygen. In 1889 Myers and her husband moved to Franklin permanently. They established a Balloon Farm where they built and stored experimental balloons. Running the business became a drain on her time, and Myers retired from flying tourists in 1891. She test-flew her husband's inventions at the farm privately until about 1910.

References

Oakes, *United States Women in Aviation through World War I* (1978)

Naito, Chiaki

The first Japanese woman chosen as an astronaut, Naito was born in Tokyo on May 6, 1952. She received her medical degree as a surgeon from Keio University in Tokyo in 1977. After two years of general surgery residency at the Keio University Hospital she was promoted to the department of cardiovascular surgery as an instructor.

When the National Aeronautics and Space Administration (NASA) extended the shuttle program and its opportunities to the international community, one of their planned missions was the shuttle/Spacelab J mission, scheduled for January 1988. Naito qualified for the mission along with an aeronautical engineer and a physicist, both male.

On January 28, 1986, however, the *Challenger* space shuttle and its seven-member crew, including Judith Resnick and Christa McAuliffe, were lost 73 seconds after launch when a booster rocket failure resulted in the breakup of the vehicle. This disaster and the investigation that followed suspended all future Spacelab plans, including Spacelab J.

See also
Challenger Disaster Investigation; *Challenger* Space Shuttle; National Aeronautics and Space Administration (NASA)
References
Cassutt, *Who's Who in Space* (1987)

National Aeronautics and Space Administration (NASA)

Established in 1958 by President Dwight David Eisenhower, the National Aeronautics and Space Administration (NASA) first admitted female astronauts to serve as mission specialists in 1978.

The agency began with a $125 million allotment. On August 27, 1958, the Soviet Union successfully sent two dogs 281

miles above the earth and returned them safely to the ground, after which the president requested an additional $80 million to help NASA stay competitive.

Dr. Randolph Lovelace, chairman of NASA's Life Sciences Committee, was in charge of testing potential astronauts for the Mercury program. Once the male candidates were chosen, Lovelace wanted to study the effects of spaceflight on women, so he asked Jacqueline Cochran, America's premier female pilot, to speak to the most prestigious female pilots she knew.

Jerrie Cobb, a pilot who had logged over 10,000 flight hours, was the first woman selected to report to the clinic for phase one of the tests in 1960. The other women included WASPS from World War II and schoolteachers; two were identical twins. Overall, the women proved to be less prone to heart attacks and less vulnerable to loneliness, cold, heat, pain, and noise. It was also noted that NASA could save money by using women astronauts, since the cost of sending anything into space was nearly $1,000 per pound. Women weighed less and would therefore cost less in space.

Despite these facts, NASA did not allow Cobb or the other 12 members of the Mercury 13 to become full astronauts in the Mercury program. On July 17, 1962,

Cobb and a few others testified before Congress in favor of including women in the astronaut corps. Astronaut John Glenn, the first man to orbit the earth, testified against. The Mercury 13 lost. In July 1961 NASA canceled all further testing of women for the Mercury program.

NASA did not allow women into the space program until 1978, when that year's class included Sally Ride, Judith Resnick, Shannon Lucid, Rhea Seddon, Kathryn Sullivan, and Anna Fisher.

See also
Cobb, Geraldyne "Jerrie"; Cochran, Jacqueline; Fisher, Anna L.; Lucid, Shannon W.; Mercury 13; Resnick, Judith Arlene; Ride, Sally Kristen; Seddon, M. Rhea; Sullivan, Kathryn
References
Biographical Data Sheets, Lyndon B. Johnson Space Center (1997)

National Air Races
The race that gave birth to the famous Powder Puff Derby began as a ten-day extravaganza sponsored by the Cleveland Speed Foundation, headed by industrialist Frederick C. Crawford. It was managed by Clifford and Phil Henderson.

Men and women first competed together in the races in 1931. Phoebe Omlie won the sweepstakes prize of $2,500 and a new car that year, defeating an all-male group of competitors.

After World War II the races became a four-day event flooded by military aircraft, which kept civilians from truly being able to compete. In 1950 the races were exclusively open to the military, which left women out until the various services allowed them to begin training as aviators in the mid-1970s.

See also
All-Women's Transcontinental Air Race (AWTAR); Omlie, Phoebe Fairgrave
References
www.airrace.org

National Council for Women in Aviation and Aerospace (NCWA)
The National Council for Women in Aviation and Aerospace (NCWA) was founded in October 1992. Seven women met in Hilton Head, North Carolina, to discuss the need for a group linking women from all facets of aviation, from pilots to air traffic controllers to meteorologists to aviation lawyers. They agreed to form such a group, whose purpose would be to "provide a source of information and promote opportunities for women in all facets of aviation and aerospace through educational, charitable and scientific means."

Based in Lemont, Illinois, the NCWA was established in 1993; Marie Christensen was president. Open to anyone with an interest in aviation, the NCWA sponsors yearly scholarship programs and aviation exchanges in countries around the world.

References
National Council for Women in Aviation

Neuffer, Judith Ann
A member of the first class of women allowed to train at the U.S. Navy flight training program at Pensacola, Florida, Neuffer was born in Wooster, Ohio. She took her first flying lessons from her air force father when she was 15, and she soloed at 16.

After receiving her degree from Ohio State University, Neuffer enlisted in the naval air force, but pilot training was not available to women. Neuffer worked as a computer programmer until 1974, when women were first admitted to naval pilot training classes. Upon graduating from those classes, Neuffer asked to be assigned to the navy's Hurricane Hunter Squadron, whose pilots flew over, under, and through hurricanes with winds of up to 150 miles an hour.

Judith Neuffer, the first woman to fly a plane through the eye of a hurricane, tracking Hurricane Carmen in the Gulf of Mexico (1974).

Asked what the key to her success was, Neuffer said: "Motivation is the key. It's a lot of hard work. I've never worked harder in my life, but it's been worth it. I've seen the world from one pole to the other. I've certainly had opportunities that many women haven't had."

See also
U.S. Navy (USN)
References
Holden and Griffith, *Ladybirds: The Untold Story of Women Pilots in America* (1991)

Nevius, Colleen

The U.S. Navy's first female test pilot and the first woman to graduate from the Naval Test Pilot School in Patuxent River, Maryland, Nevius was also an executive director of the Whirly-Girls. She was born in Corpus Christi, Texas, on April 13, 1955, and graduated from Jeb Stuart High School in Falls Church, Virginia, in 1973.

Nevius joined the navy right out of high school, becoming one of the first women to receive a full Reserve Officers' Training Corps (ROTC) college scholarship, exchanging four years of military service for four years of free college tuition. She used that tuition to earn a degree in management from Purdue University in 1977.

In 1978 Nevius entered Aviation Officer Candidate School. She took her advanced flight training in Corpus Christi, Texas, which was also the base where her father had once been a flight instructor. Nevius learned to fly T-28 Trojans as well as helicopters, winning her naval aviator's wings on February 11, 1979. She was then assigned as helicopter aircraft commander at a helicopter combat support squadron in Norfolk, Virginia. There she became one of the first women to fly vertical replenishment helicopters to ships at sea, though women still could not be deployed to the all-male ships.

Nevius took the 11-month course at the Naval Test Pilot School and became its first female graduate in June 1983. After graduation she also became the first female member of the Society of Experimental Test Pilots. In her new role Nevius conducted tests on the first modified HH-46A Seaknight helicopter.

Nevius was hired as a consultant at the Johnson Space Center in Houston, Texas, and moved into the Naval Reserve. She attended the University of Houston to work on a master's degree in computer and systems engineering. She was elected executive director of the Whirly-Girls in 1991. She is married to National Aeronautics and Space Administration (NASA) astronaut William F. Readdy and has two sons and one daughter.

Of her selection into the Naval Test Pilot School, Nevius said: "I believe all individuals should have the choice to pursue their talents and desires without limits. And I look forward to the day when there aren't any restrictions on what women can and cannot do. I consider raising my kids as my 'second career,' and look forward to a third and maybe fourth career down the road a bit!"

See also
U.S. Navy (USN)
References
Christman, "Navy's First Female Test Pilot" (1985); Holden and Griffith, *Ladybirds: The Untold Story of Women Pilots in America* (1991)

Nichols, Ruth Rowland

The first woman to receive a hydroplane license and the first American woman to fly across the Irish Sea, Nichols was also the founder of Relief Wings. She was born in 1901. Her father was a stockbroker, which would prove lucrative until the stock market crash of 1929. Until then, Nichols spent her childhood in the family home in Manhattan. She took her first plane ride at an aviation show in Atlantic City in 1919 with World War I flying ace Eddie Stinson, brother of Katherine and Marjorie Stinson. It cost $10 for ten minutes' airtime.

Nichols was the first female in her family to attend college. She managed two years at Wellesley before her father insisted she "learn to be a lady." Nichols's parents sent her to Miami for a winter social season of dances and dates only to have her meet her first and favorite flying instructor, Harry Rogers, who taught her to fly for $60 an hour.

After a summer of lessons and a failed season as a debutante, Nichols returned to college. Rogers moved his flying business to New York and continued to instruct Nichols, who soloed in 1924, the same year she graduated from Wellesley. She became the first licensed woman pilot in New York State and the nineteenth in the country.

Before she could make any decisions about her future Nichols was invited to accompany her best friend on a grand tour of Europe. It was on this trip that she witnessed the intense poverty of India and became determined to help in some way. But on her return to the United States Nichols learned that both her father's health and the family's finances were failing. She took a job as an assistant to the treasurer of a large bank to help earn money for the family and for her continued flying lessons. She received her government transport license on June 4, 1927.

Two days into 1928 Nichols copiloted a Fairchild Aircraft monoplane in a test flight from New York to Miami for her friend Harry Rogers. He wanted to see if a commuter service between those cities would be viable. He already knew it could be lucrative considering the number of rich New Yorkers who spent their winters in Miami every year. The flight lasted 12 hours, and Nichols made headlines as the "Flying Debutante."

As a result of the publicity Sherman Fairchild, the president of Fairchild Aircraft, offered her a job in sales promotion for his company. Her duties entailed flying Fairchild aircraft around the country and making speeches to heighten the public's interest in airplanes as a new mode of transportation. Nichols became the first woman executive in a million-dollar-a-year aviation company. Also in 1928 she joined John Reaves and Darwin Adams in founding Aviation Country Clubs as a way to interest the rich in buying their own planes. A 46-state, 12,000-mile Aviation Country Club Tour was organized to publicize the club and to make a study of possible landing strips for future clubs. Nichols flew a Curtiss Fledgling plane from New York to Los Angeles and back over a period of six months in 1929.

Along the way Nichols stopped to compete in the first Powder Puff Derby, flying from Santa Monica, California, to Cleveland, Ohio, against all-female competition, including Thea Rasch, Phoebe Omlie, and Ruth Elder. She was forced into two emergency landings on her route to the starting point of the race and, unfortunately, crashed just 100 miles short of the finish line on August 27, 1929. Nichols survived the crash and went back to her Aviation Country Club Tour, in which she succeeded in forming two new clubs in California. All seemed well; flying was an ideal new hobby to interest the idle rich, until the stock market crash in October 1929.

The bright spot in the fall of 1929 was the formation of the Ninety-Nines, founded by Nichols, Amelia Earhart, and 97 other active, licensed female flyers. In the spring of 1930 Colonel Clarence Chamberlin began offering Nichols the chance to test-fly new airplanes. For him she piloted the first midnight flight from New York to Chicago to deliver New York newspapers by air. As a result of their association Nichols became a sales representative of his Crescent Aircraft Company, demonstrating and delivering new-model airplanes to customers.

In the summer of 1930 Nichols's celebrity earned her a place on American Airlines' inaugural nonstop coast-to-coast flight from Atlanta, Georgia, to Los Angeles, but she preferred doing her own piloting. On December 1, 1930, Nichols broke the transcontinental flight record by flying from Roosevelt Field to Burbank Airport in 16 hours, 59 minutes, 8 seconds.

On March 6, 1931, Nichols took off in her Lockheed Vega, trying to become the first woman to complete a solo flight across the North Atlantic. Engine failure forced her to return to the Jersey City Airport, where she learned that she had set a new women's altitude record of 28,114 feet, breaking the previous record set by Elinor Smith. Later that year Nichols broke Amelia Earhart's women's speed record by flying 210 miles per hour over a course in Detroit. In June she made her second solo trans-Atlantic attempt. On the advice of Charles and Anne Lindbergh she installed a radio, not yet required equipment on planes. Sadly, she never got the chance to use it on that flight. Nichols crashed outside of St. Johns, New Brunswick, breaking five vertebrae in her back. The doctors predicted the injury would take a year to heal.

Four months later Nichols had graduated from a plaster cast to a steel brace and was ready to make another trans-Atlantic attempt, but the weather over the ocean was uncooperative. Instead, she flew to an air meet in Charlotte, North Carolina, and from there took the southern route to California, which was longer than the trans-Atlantic passage, proving she could make the flight in her steel corset once the weather cleared. On her return trip she broke the women's world distance record then held by Maryse Bastie of France by flying 1,950 miles, landing in Louisville, Kentucky, on October 25, 1931. Two days later, at the beginning of her trip home, her trusted Lockheed Vega burst into flames on take-off. Though still fettered by her steel corset, Nichols jumped from the wreckage unharmed.

To earn money to repair her beloved plane Nichols wrote magazine articles, gave speeches, and eventually took a job as the International Congress of Women's "Air Ambassadress." Her assignment was to fly across the United States over a two-week period collecting signatures to petition foreign governments to send delegates to the congress. This was the beginning of her work in bettering international relations.

In November 1932 she was invited to attend the annual diplomatic reception given by President and Mrs. Herbert Hoover at the White House. On December 29, 1932, she piloted the inaugural flight of New York and New England Airways, which made her the first woman nonscheduled airline pilot. In June 1933 women were first allowed to take part in the Bendix Transcontinental Air Race, and Nichols was one of the first women invited to compete. Both she and her friend, Amelia Earhart, suffered from a series of mechanical failures, and neither placed that year.

The depression kept the field of aviation from moving along as quickly as originally anticipated, and Nichols found herself earning money in 1933 and 1934 by lecturing at women's colleges and even for a few men's engineering courses at smaller universities. In the summer of 1935 her friend Colonel Chamberlin again provided her an income from fly-

ing. He offered her the copilot position in a twin-engine Condor on a barnstorming tour intended to arouse the public's interest in flying and to demonstrate its safety. Sadly, the tour ended in tragedy on October 21, 1936, when the Condor she was copiloting crashed into a grove of elm trees, killing the pilot and leaving Nichols with a leg broken in nine places, a broken wrist, a fractured cheekbone, and a broken nose. By spring of 1937 Nichols had healed enough to retest for and regain her commercial pilot's license. That summer she was unable to compete again in the Bendix race but was invited to attend as an official.

A few months later Nichols approached the Emergency Peace Campaign with a request for financial support for an around-the-world flight promoting peace. They could not offer enough funds for such a flight, but they did offer her a job as a fund-raiser for the campaign, a job that satisfied her Quaker background and provided a steady salary.

On May 27, 1939, Nichols founded Relief Wings, created to enlist private planes for emergency and disaster relief work. In 1942 she offered the services of her group to the Civil Air Patrol (CAP) as her contribution to winning World War II. In return Nichols was made a life member of the CAP, eventually attaining the rank of lieutenant colonel.

In 1948 she was offered the chance to copilot a flight as a special volunteer correspondent to UNICEF. In each of the nations she visited she investigated the feeding and medical care of the world's neediest children. On the way home from Rome the commercial airliner on which she was a passenger crashed into the Irish Sea, killing nine passengers, but Nichols survived with 49 other passengers. They spent the night in a life raft until a rescue plane spotted them.

At home again she regrouped and decided to focus her future service to others through flight. In 1954 she was named adviser to the national commander on matters pertaining to aeronautical administration of the Civil Air Patrol. In this capacity she recruited and trained doctors and nurses for aeromedical procedures, which included ferrying medical personnel to remote accident sites and performing medical emergency procedures while in flight.

In 1958 Nichols flew a supersonic Delta Dagger at 51,000 feet at 1,000 miles per hour, faster than any other woman in the world to that date. She died in 1960.

In her autobiography, Nichols wrote: "The longer I live the more life has shown that if you just hold on long enough, there's always something wonderful around the corner."

See also

All-Women's Transcontinental Air Race (AWTAR); Bastie, Marie-Louise "Maryse"; Beech, Olive Ann Mellor; Civil Air Patrol (CAP); Earhart, Amelia Mary; Elder, Ruth; Lindbergh, Anne Morrow; Ninety-Nines; Omlie, Phoebe Fairgrave; Rasch, Thea; Smith, Elinor Patricia; Stinson, Katherine; Stinson, Marjorie

References

Adams and Kimball, *Heroines of the Sky* (1942); Nichols, *Wings for Life* (1957)

Ninety-Nines

The first Women's Air Derby in 1929 brought together the most experienced female aviators of their day. It inspired them to create the first organization for women "dedicated to the improvement of women's opportunities in aviation." Membership would be open to any woman with a pilot's license.

On November 2, 1929, 26 women met at Curtiss Field in Long Island, New York, to discuss the purpose of the group. By December 14, 126 licensed female pilots had been sent letters inviting them to participate. Ninety-nine accepted in all, hence the name of the group, as suggested by Amelia Earhart, one of the founding members. Other charter members included Viola Gentry, Betty Huyler Gillies, Lady Mary Heath, Blanche Wilcox Noyes, Gladys O'Donnell, Phoebe Fairgrave Omlie, Thea Rasche, Nancy Hopkins Tier, Evelyn "Bobbi" Trout, and Fay Gillis Wells.

Louise Thaden, winner of the first Women's Air Derby, served as club secretary during the first years. She oversaw such early publicity events as the one on December 19, 1930, when, to begin acting upon their charter, the flyers dropped leaflets over New York City appealing for contributions to the Salvation Army's unemployment relief fund.

In 1931 Amelia Earhart was elected the group's first president. In September 1933 another flyover was staged to promote President Franklin Delano Roosevelt's National Reconstruction Act. Elinor Smith led a team of planes that dropped fliers as well as bouquets while performing aerial stunts over New York City.

In 1935, at the suggestion of Phoebe Omlie, the group began promoting the idea of aerial markings to help guide pilots over popular air routes. In 1939 the Ninety-Nines created a scholarship to help women finance advanced flight training classes. They named the scholarship after their first president, Amelia Earhart, who had been lost at sea two years earlier.

In 1975 the Ninety-Nines began sponsoring the American Red Cross's "blood flights," which ferried blood donated from rural townships to processing centers in larger cities within a four-hour time period. In 1981, with Janet Green as president, the Ninety-Nines began sponsoring the U.S. Precision Flight Team and managing regional and national meets.

Today the Ninety-Nines carry on the tradition and fulfill the need for air markings by volunteering their time to paint the airport names, compass rose symbols, and other identifications on airports. Ninety-Nines air mark airports based on need, which many times takes them far from their local area. When members of the Ninety-Nines in Alaska did air markings, some traveling up to 330 air miles to meet at the airport.

Today the group continues to encourage female pilots through scholarships and awards such as the Amelia Earhart Research Scholar Grant and the Katherine B. Wright Memorial Trophy.

See also
Earhart, Amelia Mary; Gentry, Viola; Gillies, Betty Huyler; Heath, Lady Sophie Mary; Noyes, Blanche Wilcox; O'Donnell, Gladys; Omlie, Phoebe Fairgrave; Rasche, Thea; Smith, Elinor Patricia; Thaden, Louise McPhetridge; Tier, Nancy Hopkins; Trout, Evelyn "Bobbi"; Wells, Fay Gillis; Women's Air Derby; Wright, Katherine
References
Briggs, *At the Controls: Women in Aviation* (1991); Douglas, *United States Women in Aviation, 1940–1985* (1990); Lomax, *Women of the Air* (1987); Moolman, *Women Aloft* (1981)

Nowack, Lisa

A pilot who has logged over 1,100 flight hours in more than 30 different aircraft and an astronaut candidate in the National Aeronautics and Space Administration (NASA) class of 1996, Nowack was born on May 10, 1963, in Washington, D.C. She graduated from C. W. Woodward High School, in Rockville, Maryland, in 1981. Nowack received both a bachelor of science degree in aerospace engineering from the U.S. Naval Academy and her commission from the U.S. Naval Academy in May 1985.

After receiving her commission Nowack was assigned temporary duty from June to November 1985 providing engineering support for the Johnson Space Center's Shuttle Training Aircraft Branch at Elling-

ton, Texas. After the completion of that assignment Nowack reported to flight school. She earned her wings as a naval flight officer in June 1987. She then attended Electronic Warfare School at Corry Station, Florida, and initial A-7 training at Naval Air Station Lemoore, California. Nowack was then assigned to Electronic Warfare Aggressor Squadron 34 at Point Mugu, California, where she flew EA-7L and ERA-3B aircraft, supporting the fleet in small- and large-scale exercises with jamming and missile profiles. While assigned to the squadron she qualified as a mission commander.

At the same time Nowack was working toward a master of science degree in aeronautical engineering and an aeronautical and astronautical engineer degree from the U.S. Naval Postgraduate School, receiving both in 1992. She began working at the Systems Engineering Test Directorate at Patuxent River, Maryland. In 1993 she was selected for both aerospace engineering duty and U.S. Naval Test Pilot School. After graduation in June 1994 she stayed at Patuxent River working as an aircraft systems project officer at the Air Combat Environment Test and Evaluation Facility and at Strike Aircraft Test Squadron, flying the F/A-18 and EA-6B.

Nowack was then assigned to the Naval Air Systems Command, working on acquisition of new systems for naval aircraft, when she was selected for the astronaut program in April 1996.

See also
U.S. Navy (USN)
References
Biographical Data Sheets, Lyndon B. Johnson Space Center (1997)

Noyes, Blanche Wilcox

The first woman to head the first U.S. government program conceived, planned, and directed completely by women,

Noyes was born in 1900 in Cleveland, Ohio. She learned to fly by taking lessons from her husband, Dewey Noyes, whom she met at a dinner honoring Charles Lindbergh in 1927. He began giving her lessons two weeks after that meeting, and they were married a year later.

Noyes received her pilot's license in April 1929, becoming the first woman in Ohio, the home of the Wright Brothers, to do so. In October she participated in the first Women's Air Derby. A fire in the baggage compartment of her plane, which she put out with her bare hands, effectively ended her competition in the race. Nevertheless, Noyes managed to cross the finish line in fourth place.

In 1931 Noyes was hired by the Great Lakes Aircraft Corporation to demonstrate planes to potential buyers. This position offered her the chance to gain flying hours on a variety of aircraft, including, in 1933, an early helicopter called the autogiro.

In 1934 Noyes won the Leeds Trophy. In preparation for an around-the-world flight with her husband, Noyes studied instrument flying. But the flight was canceled when her husband died in an air fatality. His funeral was attended by such well-known aviators as Amelia Earhart.

In 1935 Phoebe Omlie asked Noyes to join the Air Marking Division of the Bureau of Air Commerce. At the suggestion of Eleanor Roosevelt, the bureau hired women pilots to negotiate with owners of tall buildings along various air routes to allow place-names to be painted on those buildings. Noyes moved to Washington, D.C., and took the job working with Omlie, Louise Thaden, and Helen Richey.

When Thaden was offered the use of an airplane by Olive Beech to fly in the Bendix Transcontinental Air Race, she asked Noyes to be her copilot and navigator. On September 4, 1936, they became the first female team to win against male competition.

After the race Thaden returned to her work as an airplane demonstrator for Beech Aircraft, and Noyes returned to the Air Marking Division. Federal money had dried up for the project, so Noyes's job became convincing local governments to fund the marking of local buildings.

In 1948 Noyes was elected president of the Ninety-Nines. In 1976 she received the Elder Statesman of Aviation Award from the National Aeronautic Association of the United States. She died in 1981.

See also
Beech, Olive Ann Mellor; Earhart, Amelia Mary; Ninety-Nines; Omlie, Phoebe Fairgrave; Richey, Helen; Thaden, Louise McPhetridge

References
Adams and Kimball, *Heroines of the Sky* (1942); Douglas, *United States Women in Aviation, 1940–1985* (1990)

Ochoa, Ellen

A veteran of two spaceflights, Ochoa was born on May 10, 1958, in Los Angeles, California. She graduated from Grossmont High School in La Mesa, California, in 1975.

She received a bachelor of science degree in physics from San Diego State University, where she was the valedictorian of the Class of 1980. She attended Stanford University on a Stanford Engineering Fellowship and an IBM Predoctoral Fellowship. In 1981 she earned her master of science degree and in 1985, a doctorate in electrical engineering.

In her doctoral studies at Stanford, and later as a researcher at Sandia National Laboratories and the National Aeronautics and Space Administration (NASA) Ames Research Center, Ochoa investigated optical systems for information processing, and she shares three patents in this field. As chief of the Intelligent Systems Technology Branch at Ames she supervised 35 engineers and scientists in the research and development of computational systems for aerospace missions.

Ochoa was selected by NASA in January 1990. In April 1993 she flew on STS-56 as a mission specialist aboard the *Discovery* space shuttle. During this nine-day mission the crew conducted atmospheric and solar studies in order to better understand the effect of solar activity on the earth's climate and environment. Ochoa used the Remote Manipulator System (RMS) to deploy and capture the *Spartan* satellite, which studied the solar corona.

From November 3 to November 14, 1994, Ochoa served as the payload commander on STS-66. The Atmospheric Laboratory for Applications and Science–3 (ATLAS-3) continued the series of Spacelab flights to study the energy of the sun during an 11-year solar cycle and to learn how changes in the sun's irradi-

ance affect the earth's climate and environment. This time Ochoa used the RMS to retrieve the CRISTA-SPAS atmospheric research satellite near the end of its eight-day free flight.

On the ground Ochoa's technical assignments have included flight software verification in the Shuttle Avionics Integration Laboratory, where she served as the crew representative for flight software and computer hardware development. She has also served as crew representative for robotics development, testing, and training.

In 1997 Ochoa became the assistant to the chief of the Astronaut Office of NASA, directing crew involvement in the development and operation of the International Space Station.

See also
Discovery Space Shuttle
References
Biographical Data Sheets, Lyndon B. Johnson Space Center (1997)

O'Donnell, Gladys

Born in 1904, O'Donnell did not take up flying until late 1928, after she married J. Lloyd O'Donnell, who owned a flying school in Long Beach, California. The couple had two children before O'Donnell started lessons in late 1928. She soloed after two months of lessons and entered the Women's Air Derby in 1929. With a mere 30 hours of solo flying time in her logbook O'Donnell came in second, behind Louise Thaden and ahead of Amelia Earhart, who came in third. Then O'Donnell competed in the women's events of the National Air Races and won both the 60-mile race and the Cleveland-to-Pittsburgh race.

O'Donnell worked as an instructor in her husband's aviation school on her return home. On June 18, 1930, she joined Thaden and Earhart in a trip to scout the route for the upcoming Women's Air Derby. O'Donnell also made time for more contests. On August 1, 1930, she placed second, after fellow Californian Pancho Barnes, in the Tom Thumb Derby, flying from Long Beach to Santa Paula, California, through fog. O'Donnell's time was 1 hour, 39 minutes, 14 seconds.

She came in first in the 1930 Women's Air Derby against six other racers. At that year's National Air Races O'Donnell won four of the five women's events, including the free-for-all, which earned her a $2,500 prize. On January 27, 1930, O'Donnell was awarded the Aero Trophy and a cash prize of $3,000 by the National Aeronautical Association.

In 1931 O'Donnell won two women's events at the National Air Races, and in 1932 she won the Aero Trophy again by reaching a speed of 185 miles per hour. In 1933 O'Donnell used her knowledge of aviation to host the radio show *Sky Doings*, and she flew a stunt plane in the movie *The White Sister*.

In 1935 O'Donnell was asked to be the managing director of the Pacific Air Pageant, a job that utilized her experience of the many previous air meets in which she had competed.

In 1936 she placed second in the Amelia Earhart Race at the National Air Races. Between air meets O'Donnell

continued teaching at the O'Donnell Flying School and helped her husband start O'Donnell Aircraft, selling and servicing planes at the Long Beach Airport.

She died in 1973.

See also
Earhart, Amelia Mary; Thaden, Louise McPhetridge
References
Adams and Kimball, *Heroines of the Sky* (1942)

Omlie, Phoebe Fairgrave

The first woman to win the National Air Races in Cleveland against male competition, Omlie won in 1931, the first year women were admitted to the race. She received the $2,500 prize and a car for her effort. Omlie was also the first woman to become a government aviation official and the first to receive her aircraft mechanic's license.

Born in Des Moines, Iowa, in 1902, Omlie quit a secure job with an insurance firm to take flying lessons at the Curtiss Field in St. Paul, Minnesota, in 1921. Her instructor was Vernon Omlie, who would one day become her husband. Jobs in aviation were scarce, so Omlie began her aviation career as a wing walker. She joined Glenn Messer's Flying Circus and was famous for dancing the Charleston on the wings of a plane; she later stood upright while the plane looped-the-loop.

Soon the Omlies broke from Glenn Messer's group and started their own flying circus. They also founded a flying school in Memphis. On June 30, 1927, she became the first woman to earn a transport license allowing her to fly packages for hire. When the Mississippi Valley was decimated by a flood the Omlies flew medical supplies and food to the victims. For her part in the rescue operation Omlie was invited to join the International League of Aviators, the first woman so honored.

Phoebe Omlie (1930)

In 1929 Omlie set an altitude record for women at 25,400 feet, and later in the year she flew in the first Women's Air Derby against such accomplished pilots as Pancho Barnes, Amelia Earhart, and Gladys O'Donnell. Unfortunately, the depression bankrupted most of the Omlies' steady customers at the Memphis airfield, and they had to close it. Her husband took a job as a pilot with a small airline, and Omlie entered air races for the prize money. Her first win was in 1930 in the Dixie Derby, in which she won $2,000. Her second was the National Air Races victory in 1931.

To publicize her own piloting skills, Omlie flew Sarah Fain across the United States during Franklin Delano Roosevelt's presidential campaign. For her efforts she asked for and was granted the job as liaison between the only two federal aeronautical agencies in existence at the time, making her the first female government aviation official.

In 1934 the Women's Air Derby sponsored a cross-country trip to help promote membership and to underscore Omlie's petition for equal pilot licensing standards for men and women.

From 1934 through 1936 she was on the National Advisory Committee for Aeronautics. At Omlie's suggestion the Ninety-Nines began promoting the idea of aerial markings to help pilots along popular air routes. In 1936 Omlie campaigned by air for President Roosevelt again. Her husband Vernon died that same year. Omlie resigned from her post in Washington and took a position with the chairman of Tennessee's Aviation Commission. Together they drafted legislation to make public funds available for training aviators, both male and female, a cause her husband had been working on before his death. When their measure passed, Omlie joined the Vocational Division of the Memphis School Board to organize the classes.

In 1941 Omlie returned to Washington as the private flying specialist for the Civil Aeronautics Authority (CAA) to help the country prepare for World War II. She was in charge of choosing flying schools across the country that could serve as training centers for military flyers. In 1942 she tried to convince the CAA to train women as flight instructors in preparation for assisting the war effort. They turned her down, so Omlie took her proposal to the Tennessee Bureau of Aeronautics, and they began with a class of ten women. Eventually other states began similar programs.

After World War II Omlie moved back to Washington, D.C., to research flight-training methods. She died in 1975 at the age of 72 in Indianapolis, Indiana.

Explaining her work training women to be flight instructors, Omlie said: "Naturally, the dashing uniformed woman pilot of a roaring warplane is going to get more attention than her flight instructor sister, just as the uniformed volunteer gets more publicity than her coveralled sister at the factory workbench. Just as naturally, however, women are finding their proper places as instructors, the position women have filled better than men for generations."

See also
Barnes, Florence Lowe "Pancho"; Earhart, Amelia Mary; National Air Races; Ninety-Nines; O'Donnell, Gladys; Women's Air Derby; Women's Air Reserve
References
Adams and Kimball, *Heroines of the Sky* (1942); Knapp, *New Wings for Women* (1946); Lomax, *Women of the Air* (1987); Moolman, *Women Aloft* (1981)

Order of Fifinella

This group was founded by Women Airforce Service Pilots (WASPS) stationed at Marshall Field, Alabama, to commemorate their services during World War II; it was named for Fifinella, the insignia designed for the WASPS by Disney during World War II. The Order of Fifinella kept address files and other archives for the group and organized their first reunion, on their thirtieth anniversary, in 1972. Since then they have held reunions every two years.

Under the direction of President Beatrice Haydu this group collected 25,000 signatures for a petition requesting formal military pensions for the WASPS. The WASP bill was sponsored by Congresswoman Lindy Boggs of Louisiana in September 1977. The proposed bill was hotly debated in Congress, since it raised fears that if the WASPS were awarded veteran status many other civilian branches of the military, such as the Merchant Marine, would request the same treatment. The Order of Fifinella solicited press inter-

views about the WASPS' wartime service and toured the country to reeducate the U.S. public on their existence. They also sent decals of Fifinella to new female graduates of the Air Force Academy.

The WASP bill became the only piece of legislation in history to be cosponsored by every female member of Congress. It passed and was signed into law by President Jimmy Carter on November 23, 1977.

In testifying for the legislation in 1977, William H. Tunner, former head of the Air Transport Command Ferrying Division, said: "Certainly someone today can partially correct the unfairness we showed by making veterans of these women who served so faithfully and well, and with little complaint."

See also
Fifinella; Women's Airforce Service Pilots (WASPS)
References
Leuthner and Jensen, *High Honor: Recollections by Men and Women of World War II Aviation* (1989); Van Wagenen Keil, *Those Wonderful Women in Their Flying Machines* (1979)

Orr, Marion Powell

The first Canadian woman to earn her helicopter pilot's license and the first to own and operate a flying school, Orr was also one of five Canadian female pilots to fly for the British Air Transport Auxiliary (ATA) during World War II. She was born in Toronto and was orphaned at 15, so she had to leave school to support herself. It took Orr six years to save up for flying lessons, which were held at Pat Patterson's Flyers Limited School at Barker Field. The only other female student was Violet Milstead.

Orr received her private pilot's license on January 5, 1940. To be able to continue working toward her commercial license Orr took a job with the de Havilland Aircraft Company as an aircraft inspector. Her instructor was Doug Orr, whom she soon married. On December 12, 1941, she qualified for her commercial license and was hired by the St. Catherine's Flying Club.

Because of a fire at the club and the grounding of civilian flyers in World War II, Orr's only aviation work for a while was as an air traffic controller at the Goderich Airport. She was the second woman in Canada to qualify for the job.

When the Royal Canadian Air Force needed extra instructors to teach new male recruits to fly, Orr was one of five Canadian women, including Milstead and Helen Harrison, who were approved. Soon pilot work was available again. On April 19, 1943, Orr moved to England. She had applied to the Women's Division of the British Air Transport Auxiliary (ATA), which had just been formed by Pauline Gower. Women would ferry new and repaired aircraft from manufacturers' sites to Royal Air Force bases to free up more male pilots for combat work.

The pilots were given some quick training in flying the various military aircraft and ground school classes so they could do elementary repairs if they experienced any problems while en route. Orr began her full-time ferrying duties on June 2, 1943.

In October 1944 Orr took a short leave from the ATA that became permanent as the war was nearing an end. She was honorably discharged after 700 hours flying over 67 different types of aircraft.

After the war she taught at a variety of flight schools until she decided to strike out on her own. In 1949 she was working for Aero Activities at Barker Field when they went bankrupt. She purchased the company at the bankruptcy sale, making her the first Canadian woman to own and operate a flying school. She made a point of hiring female instructors when she could.

In 1951 the field where her school was located was sold to a housing developer, and all tenants were given a year to close down or relocate. Despite bureaucratic problems, Orr managed to purchase some land and build a new airport in Maple, Canada, a town just north of Toronto. In January 1953 she was ready for customers. The business throve, but by 1956 Orr's health was failing from the strain of operating it. She sold her business and retired to Florida.

By 1960 Orr had revived, and she returned to flying, working as an instructor in Florida for half the year and Toronto the other half. The new Markham Airport Flying Club of Toronto hired her as chief flying instructor. Yet another tempting new offer presented itself: Vendaire Limited offered to pay for Orr's training for a helicopter license if she would agree to demonstrate them for Vendaire's customers. Orr qualified in 1961 and began taking up customers and students immediately. A crash later in the year resulted in a broken back that required six months of recuperation.

In 1976 Orr was awarded the Amelia Earhart Medallion for her many contributions to aviation, and in 1981 she was inducted into the Canadian Aviation Hall of Fame. In 1984 Queen Elizabeth II honored Orr and other female pioneers of aviation at the opening of the Western Canada Aviation Museum.

Orr continued for a while to instruct at other airports, but she was forcibly retired at the age of 65. She took part-time and freelance work until in 1986 she was hired as full-time chief flying instructor for the Lindsay Ontario Flying Club. In 1993 she was awarded the Order of Canada.

Of the lengths to which she went to learn to fly, Orr said: "I was always crazy about airplanes. I used to try to fly off the roof of the house in homemade contraptions. I knew when I was fourteen that I wanted to fly. I missed meals, went without new clothes, walked instead of taking the bus and economized in a dozen little ways to make my salary go further. It was a case of doing without, but flying always came first."

See also
Gower, Pauline; Harrison, Helen Marcelle; Milstead, Violet
References
Render, *No Place for a Lady: The Story of Canadian Women Pilots, 1928–1992* (1992)

Pamyatnykh, Tamara

A Russian bomber pilot in World War II, Pamyatnykh was born in September 1919. She learned to fly gliders at the age of 16 and then earned her private pilot's license and flight instructor's certificate from the Uliganovsk aviation school. She joined the military at the start of World War II.

In October 1941 Marina Raskova was asked by the Soviet High Command to recruit 200 women flyers for combat missions. After she broadcast an appeal over Radio Moscow, Raskova received more than 2,000 applications. She also put out personal calls to respected women pilots, one of whom was Pamyatnykh.

After training in the town of Engels in October 1941 Pamyatnykh was assigned to the 586th Fighter Regiment with Olga Yemshokova as squadron leader. Though the 586th also included fighter ace Lily Litviak, Pamyatnykh was given the chance to earn her own fame during a combat mission in which she was assigned to shoot down some German reconnaissance airplanes. The attacking units totaled 42 aircraft in all. After Pamyatnykh ran out of bombs she was shot down but survived the crash.

Once she was retrieved and returned to base Pamyatnykh learned that she had successfully shot down four of the German planes, which had caused the rest of them to turn back. Their mission had been completely thwarted, and for this feat Pamyatnykh earned the Order of the Red Star and was given a gold watch by King George VI of England.

Another time she was shot down by friendly fire, but she survived the war. In 1944 Pamyatnykh married another pilot from the same regiment, and they continued to fly missions until he was shot down by German aircraft, captured, and sent to the Buchenwald concentration camp. The two were reunited after the war and had three children.

See also
Litviak, Lidiia "Lily" Vladimirovna; Raskova, Marina
References
Noggle, *A Dance with Death: Soviet Airwomen in World War II* (1994)

Patterson, Daphne

The first female pilot to earn her commercial rating in Canada, Patterson was also New Brunswick's first female pilot. She was born in Saint John, New Brunswick, in 1905. After earning her bachelor of science degree from McGill University in Montreal Patterson first turned her interest in mechanics to automobile racing.

After achieving the ground speed record for driving between Saint John and Montreal, Patterson decided to look into airspeed records. She joined the Montreal Light Aeroplane Club in 1929 and studied with Tony Spooner, brother of Winnifred Spooner, the first woman to win the King's Cup Race in England. Patterson earned her private pilot's license on August 15, 1929.

She then earned her commercial pilot's license and was the first Canadian woman to reach the highest rating, the public transport license, which she earned on August 9, 1938. Like Violet Milstead and Marion Orr, Patterson soon realized that the only aviation occupation available to women at the brink of World War II was as an instructor. She qualified as an instructor in May 1940, only to be told there were no more openings.

Patterson was in favor of the members of the Canadian Air Force Women's Reserve becoming ferry pilots like the pilots of the Air Transport Auxiliary (ATA) in England, but the Canadian government decided against the idea. By that time Patterson was older than was allowed for ATA recruits. Her age did not disqualify her for the Women's Airforce Service Pilots (WASPS), a ferrying group in the United States under the direction of Jacqueline Cochran, but her lack of U.S. citizenship did.

Since all avenues to wartime aviation were then closed to her, Patterson became a journalist. After the war she retired from aviation completely. Patterson died in 1982.

See also
Cochran, Jacqueline; Milstead, Violet; Orr, Marion Powell
References
Render, *No Place for a Lady: The Story of Canadian Women Pilots, 1928–1992* (1992)

Payette, Julie

An astronaut candidate in the Canadian Space Agency class of 1992, Payette was born on October 20, 1963, in Montreal, Quebec, where she attended primary and secondary school. She received one of six Canadian scholarships to attend the United World International College (International UWC) of the Atlantic in South Wales, Australia, in 1980, and she earned her bachelor's degree in 1982. She then attended McGill University in Montreal as a McGill faculty scholar and graduated with distinction with a bachelor's degree in engineering in 1986.

Between 1986 and 1988 Payette worked as a system engineer for IBM Canada's Scientific and Engineering Division, where she was involved in a high-performance computer architecture project. She received her master's degree in applied science from the University of Toronto in 1990.

In 1991 Payette joined the Communications and Computer Science Department of the IBM Research Laboratory in Zurich, Switzerland, for a one-year visiting scientist appointment. When she returned to Canada, in January 1992, Payette joined the Speech Research Group of Bell-Northern Research in Montreal until her selection as an astronaut by the Canadian Space Agency in June.

After basic training Payette worked as a technical adviser for the Mobile Servicing System (MSS), the Canadian contribution to the International Space Station. In 1993 Payette established the Human-Computer Interaction (HCI) Group at the Canadian Astronaut Program. In addition, she served on the NATO International Research Study Group (RSG-10) on speech processing. In November 1994 the Canadian Council of Professional Engineers awarded her its 1994 distinction for exceptional achievement by a young engineer.

While waiting for training at the Johnson Space Center in Florida Payette studied Russian and contributed to microgravity science experiments aboard various parabolic aircraft (KC-135, T-33, Falcon-20, DC-9), where she logged over 120 hours of reduced-gravity flight time, both as experiment operator and as test subject. In 1995 Payette undertook military jet training at the Canadian Air Force Base in Moose Jaw, Saskatchewan, where she obtained her captaincy and logged 95 hours on the Tutor CT-114 jet aircraft. In April 1996 Payette completed a deep-sea diving-suit training program in Vancouver, British Columbia, and was certified as a one-atmosphere diving-suit operator.

In August 1996 Payette reported to the Johnson Space Center for further astronaut training.

References

Biographical Data Sheets, Lyndon B. Johnson Space Center (1997)

Pellegreno, Ann Holtgren

The woman who completed Amelia Earhart's unfinished flight plan, Pellegreno was born in Chicago in 1938, only a year after Earhart disappeared. She graduated from the University of Michigan in 1959 and took her first flight lesson on August 29, 1960. It was also her first flight in a plane of any kind, though she had spent countless hours as a child gazing at them in the sky.

Together with her husband Pellegreno purchased her first plane in the summer of 1961. The airline mechanic they hired to inspect the plane was Lee Koepke, who on his own time was rebuilding a Lockheed 10 Electra, the sister ship to Earhart's plane. It was Koepke who suggested Pellegreno use his plane to commemorate the thirtieth anniversary of Earhart's disappearance by completing her flight plan.

Koepke was finished rebuilding the plane in July 1966, and Pellegreno began to truly consider the trip. In December Pellegreno flew to Washington, D.C., to arrange the clearances needed to fly into the same airports in the same countries that Earhart visited on her trip. The Airplane Owners and Pilots Association agreed to handle these for her.

Though she set her departure date for May 20, 1967, difficulties with arranging financial backing and completing preparations for the plane delayed takeoff until June 9, when Pellegreno flew to Oakland, California, Earhart's starting point for the trip. Pellegreno had to make an unscheduled stop in Cedar Rapids, Iowa, when her radio failed because of a missing wire. The wire was replaced, and Pellegreno continued the trip.

Pellegreno's navigator on the trip was Bill Polhemus, who, for the sake of historical accuracy, used the same techniques that Fred Noonan did while navigating on Earhart's trip. This involved navigating with a sextant, an instrument that measures the angles and distances between stars and the sun to calculate location. However, because of civil wars in several African countries, Pellegreno could not receive clearances to fly over the exact areas of Earhart's itinerary.

After several new experiences, including riding a camel and catching dysentery twice, Pellegreno reached Howland Island on July 1, 1967. This is the island that Earhart had failed to reach. From the airspace above Howland Pellegreno broadcast a message to a group of international Ninety-Nines who were holding a commemorative service for Earhart at the Smithsonian Institution in Washington, D.C., that day. Pellegreno also dropped a wreath above Howland in honor of Earhart and Noonan.

Pellegreno landed in Honolulu, Hawaii, on July 4, 1967, 30 years to the day from Earhart's planned finish to her trip. Still, Pellegreno had to complete the trip by returning to Oakland, which she reached on July 7. The next day she flew to Newton, Kansas, for a celebration hosted by Muriel Morrissey, Earhart's sister.

July 15 was declared Ann Pellegreno Day by the Michigan State Legislature in honor of her accomplishment. Pellegreno then spent time lecturing and writing about the trip to help defray the $13,000 cost of the flight. In March 1968 Koepke sold the Lockheed plane to Air Canada, who presented it to the National Museum of Science and Technology in Ottawa, which displayed it at the Ottawa International Airport.

In her 1971 book about the flight Pellegreno explained: "We accepted her dream as a challenge, and desired to both commemorate and complete the 1937 endeavor thirty years later. Our flight was a unique synthesis of past, present, and future—a once-in-many-lifetimes adventure."

See also
Earhart, Amelia Mary; Ninety-Nines
References
Pellegreno, *World Flight: The Earhart Trail* (1971)

Peltier, Therese

The first woman to ride as a passenger in an airplane and the first to take the controls and fly solo, Peltier was born in Orleans, France. She was a sculptor by trade, and her works were exhibited from 1900 to 1911 at the Salon de la Société des Artistes Français. Her teacher was the famous French sculptor Leon Delagrange, who also owned a plane.

On July 8, 1908, he took Peltier for a ride in Turin, France. On later flights she operated the controls, and she eventually took her own solo flight. She never, however, attempted to qualify for a license. The first woman to do that was Baroness Raymonde de Laroche, also of France.

See also
Laroche, Baroness Raymonde de
References
Boase, *The Sky's the Limit: Women Pioneers in Aviation* (1979)

Petre, Mary

Petre, who was born sometime around 1890, was one of the first women to fly around the world. She was married to Victor Bruce, a race car driver, and was therefore known more commonly in society and in press reports as the Honor-

able Mrs. Victor Bruce. She had already gained fame as a horsewoman, with several first- and second-place trophies to her name, before she took her around-the-world trip after only 40 solo hours in a plane that she acquired in 1930.

On September 25, 1931, Petre left Heston, near London, and arrived back in Croydon, England, on February 20, 1932. She made three forced landings, near Istanbul, in the Kohimborak Hills of Oman, and near Bangkok. Since radios were nonexistent at the time and navigation equipment was primitive, Petre took ships across the oceans and had the plane shipped from Tokyo to Seattle for the Pacific Ocean crossing and from New York to Le Havre, France, for the Atlantic crossing.

Famed Australian pilot Amy Johnson met Petre in Lympne and flew as her escort to Croydon in celebration of Petre's great accomplishment. On her return home Petre published a short story collection called *The Peregrinations of Penelope* about a young girl adventurer who drives fast cars, rides fast horses, and flies fast planes.

In 1931 renowned British female aviators, including the Duchess of Bedford, gathered for the first British All-Women's Flying Meeting staged at the Sywell Aerodrome. The event helped to foster the idea that women were capable behind the wheel of any new invention, and Bruce was glad to attend.

Then Bruce joined the British Hospitals' Air Pageant Flying Circus and various other air circuses between 1932 and 1933, flying with Pauline Gower, the third woman in England to hold a commercial pilot's license, and her partner, Dorothy Spicer.

Eventually Bruce started her own company, Air Dispatch, which carried freight and passengers and provided air ambulance services. It soon became the fastest air service from Paris to London.

See also
Johnson, Amy
References
Cadogan, *Women with Wings: Female Flyers in Fact and Fiction* (1993)

Powder Puff Derby

See All-Women's Transcontinental Air Race (AWTAR)

Professional Women Controllers (PWC)

Founded in 1978 by Jacquie Smith and Sue Townsend, the Professional Women Controllers (PWC) is an association of air traffic control specialists. Established to encourage women to become air traffic controllers, the group is open to traffic control specialists in good standing with their employers; it is open to both men and women who share the group's vision.

To facilitate that overall goal, PWC assists its members educationally by offering scholarship programs and professionally by providing networking opportunities at national and local conferences. Other goals of the group include fostering a culturally diverse workforce in the air traffic industry and striving for the continued improvement of aviation safety.

In 1997 the PWC joined the National Council for Women in Aviation and Aerospace as a corporate partner to provide support and cooperation to benefit both memberships.

See also
National Council for Women in Aviation and Aerospace (NCWA)
References
Professional Women Controllers, Inc.

Quimby, Harriet

The first American woman to obtain a pilot's license and the first woman to fly the English Channel, Quimby was born in Ovid Township, Michigan, on May 11, 1875. When she was nine years old her family moved to a farm in Arroyo Grande, California, and they moved again later to San Francisco, where Quimby completed her schooling. She became a freelance writer in 1902, contributing to the San Francisco *Dramatic Review* and *The Call-Bulletin and Chronicle*.

In January 1903 Quimby moved to New York, where she made her living as a writer for *Leslie's Weekly*. By 1906 she was their full-time drama critic and part-time travel correspondent, traveling the world and recounting her experiences to the *Weekly*'s readers. One of those experiences was her first air show, held at Belmont Park Racetrack on Long Island in October 1910.

Intrigued by flight, Quimby took flying lessons at the Moisant Aviation School in Hempstead, a flying school operated by John Moisant, the first pilot to take passengers across the English Channel in a plane. His sister, Matilde Moisant, was one of Quimby's best friends and the only other female student at the school in May 1911.

Quimby graduated from the school and obtained her pilot's license on August 1, 1911, the thirty-seventh person and the second woman in the world, after Raymonde de Laroche of France, to obtain one. Quimby's friend Moisant became the second American woman. Together they joined the Moisant International Aviators, a team of exhibition flyers. Quimby's first official air meet was on September 4, 1911, at the Richmond County Fair and involved a moonlit flight over Staten Island, making her the first woman to make a night flight.

Later that month Quimby won $600 in a cross-country race against Helene Dutrieu of France. In October the Moisant International Aviators embarked on a tour of Mexico.

After the Mexican tour and with the backing of the London newspaper *The Daily Mirror*, Quimby set out on April 16, 1912, at 5:30 A.M. to fly the English Channel. Her successful 25-minute flight made her a hero in both Europe and back home in the United States, where she returned to perform in air shows for the next three months.

On July 1, 1912, Quimby was the lead attraction at an air meet at Boston's Squantum Airfield that also included Blanche Stuart Scott, the first woman to solo in a fixed-wing, heavier-than-air machine. Quimby was killed in an accident while flying her new Blériot monoplane around a lighthouse. Her passenger was the organizer of the event, William Willard. Neither wore a safety belt, as they were not yet in common use and most times were not well designed for women's smaller frames. At the height of about 2,000 feet the plane went into a sudden dive, and both Quimby and Willard were killed when they fell from the plane into the shallow water surrounding the lighthouse.

Harriet Quimby, the first American woman to earn a pilot's license, started her plane manually by turning the propeller (ca. 1910)

Quimby's death was witnessed by Scott, who was flying at the time and unable to land as people swarmed across the landing strip to get to Quimby. One of the audience members was Ruth Law, who had taken her first flying lesson that day and would go on to become the first woman to loop-the-loop.

In one of the many articles she wrote to inspire women to careers in aviation, Quimby wrote: "I see no reason why the aeroplane should not open up a fruitful occupation for women. I see no reason why they cannot realize handsome incomes by carrying passengers between adjacent towns, why they cannot derive incomes from parcel delivery, from taking photographs from above, or from conducting schools of flying." It was two months after her death that these words were published and many years before any of Quimby's ideas were realized by women.

See also
Dutrieu, Helene; Laroche, Baroness Raymonde de; Law, Ruth; Moisant, Matilde; Safety Belts/Safety Harnesses; Scott, Blanche Stuart

References
Adams and Kimball, *Heroines of the Sky* (1942); Holden, *Her Mentor Was an Albatross: The Autobiography of Pioneer Pilot Harriet Quimby* (1993); Lomax, *Women of the Air* (1987)

Raiche, Bessica Faith Medlar

The first woman credited with soloing in a plane, Raiche eventually became one of the earliest practicing women physicians in the United States as well. She was born in Beloit, Wisconsin, and earned her medical degree from Tufts Medical School. Raiche then studied music in France, where she watched some of the early exhibitions of Raymonde de Laroche. She came back to America with a newfound interest in aviation and a new husband, François Raiche.

Together the new couple settled in Mineola, New York, and built their own plane from the memory of planes they had seen in France. It was made of bamboo, piano wire, and Chinese silk for stitching, and they built it in the living room of their first home. On September 16, 1910, Raiche flew the plane just a few feet off the ground, qualifying herself as the "First Woman Aviator in America," according to the medal she received from the Aeronautical Society of America. Blanche Stuart Scott had in actuality flown a higher and longer flight two weeks earlier, but because Scott's flight was ruled to have been accidental, Raiche won the medal.

Raiche continued improving her flying, but instead of becoming a record breaker she chose to form the French-American Aeroplane Company with her husband. They made and sold planes based on the model Raiche used in her flying. Combining her music and aviation interests, they pioneered the use of piano wire to reduce the weight of their aircraft.

Raiche's health forced her to quit flying. She and her husband moved to California. Raiche's illness turned her attention to medicine, which she made her second career, becoming a practicing physician in her new state. She died in 1932.

See also
Laroche, Baroness Raymonde de; Scott, Blanche Stuart
References
Adams and Kimball, *Heroines of the Sky* (1942); Lomax, *Women of the Air* (1987)

Rainey, Barbara Allen

The first woman to receive her navy wings and the U.S. Navy's first female pilot to die in an air crash, Rainey was born in Bethesda, Maryland, on August 20, 1948. She graduated from Whittier College and joined the navy, graduating from Naval Officer Candidate School in December 1970.

Rainey worked as a watch commander until 1973 when the services first accepted women into flight training classes. A member of the first class of women allowed to train at the U.S. Navy flight training program at Pensacola, Florida, in 1973, Rainey earned her navy wings on February 22, 1974. A year later she was the first woman to qualify as a navy jet pilot. She then married fellow student John C. Rainey.

In 1977 she transferred to the reserves during her first pregnancy. In October 1981 she returned to active duty as a flight instructor for fellow naval personnel. On July 13, 1982, her current student was practicing touch-and-go landings at Alabama's Middleton Field Naval Base. The student missed an approach and crashed, killing them both and making Rainey the navy's first female pilot to die in an air crash.

Discussing her career, Rainey said: "Everybody goes through a stage of being depressed. The hours are long and the work is hard. You sometimes think, 'What's the use? There's so much to learn. I can never do that.' But all students go through that."

See also
U.S. Navy (USN)
References
Collins, "From Plane Captains to Pilots: Women in Naval Aviation" (1977); Holden and Griffith, *Ladybirds: The Untold Story of Women Pilots in America* (1991)

Rasche, Thea
After World War I the Allies banned all military flying in Germany, but sport flying was so popular that they could not stop it. Rasche, who was born circa 1900, was the first woman to earn her pilot's license during this tense period between the wars. She became a barnstorming stunt pilot, won several records for her efforts, and became a charter member and one of the few international members of the Ninety-Nines.

In 1929 Rasche was the only German and one of two non-U.S. citizens to compete in the first International Women's Air Derby. Rasche competed under anonymous threats of sabotage, whether because of unresolved resentment over the war or for another reason it was never learned. In San Bernardino she was handed a note reading: "Beware of Sabotage." She later found sand in her gas tank, which cut off the fuel to her engine.

Rasche died in 1971. When asked why she flew she was quoted as saying she found "flying more thrilling than love for a man, and far less dangerous."

See also
Ninety-Nines; Women's Air Derby
References
Cadogan, *Women with Wings: Female Flyers in Fact and Fiction* (1993)

Raskova, Marina
Born in 1912, Raskova was one of the most experienced flyers in the USSR at the outbreak of World War II. In 1933 she trained to be a navigator and eventually took a job as an air navigation instructor for the Russian Air Force. In 1937 she was promoted to the Zhukhovski Air Academy and became their first female faculty member.

In September 1938, before the outbreak of the war, Raskova met Valentine Grizodubova, another famous Soviet female pilot, and Polina Osipenko. They flew from Moscow to Komsomolsk-na-Amure with Grizodubova as pilot and Raskova as navigator, established a 6,450-kilometer nonstop distance record for women, and became known as the Winged Sisters for their adventure.

An hour before arrival a snowstorm struck. Ice accumulated on the wings and Grizodubova could not keep the plane at its prescribed flying height. They jettisoned everything they could, and finally Raskova even parachuted out to lighten the load, leaving behind a map with an X marking approximately where they could find her. Grizodubova landed the plane, and Raskova was found in the forest ten days later. For their efforts all three women were honored as Heroes of the Soviet Union. They were the first Soviet women to receive this honor.

For her extraordinary show of courage Raskova was also given the honor of being allowed to attend a prestigious mil-

Marina Raskova (1938)

itary staff college and take flight instruction on light and twin-engine aircraft.

The Nazis invaded Russia in June 1941, and Raskova's national prominence and connection to the air force meant that many other female pilots contacted her about using their aviation skills for their country. Raskova took their offers to Joseph Stalin, who initially spurned them. However, by October of that year Russia had lost so many men and so many aircraft to German bombers that Raskova was asked to recruit more than 200 women. They became the nucleus of the 586th Fighter Regiment.

Raskova died in combat in 1943 and was honored with the first state funeral of the war. Her ashes were interred in the Kremlin wall.

See also
586th Fighter Regiment, 587th Bomber Regiment, and 588th Night Bomber Regiment; Grizodubova, Valentine
References
Moolman, *Women Aloft* (1981); Myles, *Night Witches: The Untold Story of Soviet Women in*

Combat (1981); Noggle, *A Dance with Death: Soviet Airwomen in World War II* (1994)

Rees, Rosemary
A pilot for the British Air Transit Auxiliary (ATA) in World War II, Rees had previously been a professional dancer. Born in London near the turn of the century, Rees was schooled at home by a governess. Her father was a member of Parliament and her mother a caricaturist for the magazine *Vanity Fair*. In 1930, the summer Amy Johnson became the first woman to solo from England to Australia, Rees was making her living dancing in a review that toured England.

In 1932 Rees quit dancing to take a trip around the world with her brother. Upon their return to London, one of his friends who owned an airplane took Rees for her first ride. She started lessons immediately, earning her private pilot's license in 1933. Her mother bought her a Miles Hawk Major plane to celebrate, and Rees used it initially to fly around Europe visiting friends.

In 1938 Rees was in Berlin sharing an extended visit with a cousin who worked for the British embassy. When war between the two countries became imminent, the cousin suggested Rees return home before she and her airplane were grounded for the duration. Back in England the Civil Air Guard was training members of local aero clubs to be instructors. Rees studied for and received her instructor's certificate, but instead of taking a job as an instructor she found one flying. The army was hiring pilots for ten pounds an hour to fly up and down the coast so that their antiaircraft gunners could practice targeting planes.

Soon Pauline Gower heard of Rees, and in 1940 she asked her to be a part of her new experiment. Gower had petitioned for a Women's Section of ferry pilots in the ATA and had been permitted to hire eight female pilots to prove that the women pilots could handle the military planes. Rees and the rest of the group were based at the Hatfield Air Base, where they flew Tiger Moths to troops in Scotland and Wales. Gower asked Rees to become an officer and work in operations, but Rees turned the desk job down, preferring to keep flying instead.

As a member of the ATA Rees was given training on larger and more powerful planes so that she could be as diverse a pilot as necessary. She also had the opportunity of meeting Amy Johnson when the famed flyer joined the next wave of the ATA. In 1941, as the Women's Section expanded, Rees was promoted to second in command at the Hamble Air Base Ferry Pool near Southampton, England.

Her nearest brush with death came on January 5, 1941. It was the anniversary of the first ferry trips made by women of the ATA, and celebrations were scheduled at the main base. Rees was expecting to ride back to the base with Johnson, who took off from Blackpool, England, in cloudy weather. Before Johnson arrived Rees found another plane that needed ferrying back and took it to make sure she returned to base that night. Rees arrived safely. Johnson's engine failed over the Thames River off Herne Bay and crashed into the water. The anniversary party was canceled in her honor.

The Hamble Air Base Ferry Pool closed down in August 1945 as the war seemed to be nearing an end. Reuse's seniority with the ATA allowed her to be transferred back to Hatfield to finish out the war. Hatfield closed, and the ATA was disbanded in March 1946.

Rees returned home and started an air taxi business called Sky Taxi. In 1947 she towed gliders for the annual British Gliding Championships, which had been restarted after the war. When larger airlines began crowding out the smaller businesses Rees decided to cut her losses and close down. She married an old family friend, Phillip du Cros, and took an officer's commission in the Volunteer Air Reserve to keep her flying current.

For a full-time job she returned to the family business of politics, chairing several women's committees at the local government level and serving as chair of Bideford Village, where she and her husband had settled. At the age of 70 she took up horseback riding and dressage.

In her 1983 autobiography Rees discussed the pressure of being part of the experiment that became the ATA: "We, the first eight women, in those early weeks of 1940, carried an appalling burden of responsibility on our shoulders. With the light of publicity and hostility upon us while the war was still in its infancy, we dared not put a foot wrong."

See also
Air Transit Auxiliary (ATA); Gower, Pauline; Johnson, Amy
References
du Cros, *ATA Girl: Memoirs of a Wartime Ferry Pilot* (1983)

Reilly, Molly Beall

One of Canada's most successful female pilots in the postwar era, Reilly was born in Lindsay, Ontario, on February 25, 1922. She graduated from high school in 1940 and began flying lessons at Pat Patterson's Flyers Limited School at Barker Field. Violet Milstead, a future Air Transport Auxiliary (ATA) officer, was one of her instructors until civilian flyers were grounded.

Then Milstead joined the British ATA, organized by Pauline Gower to recruit female pilots to ferry planes from manufacturing plants to military bases and to free up more male pilots for combat flying. Reilly had not completed her studies, so she tried to enlist in the Royal Canadian Air Force (RCAF) to finish her pilot's license requirements. She went down to the recruitment office with her brother, who was also a pilot. He was accepted, but Reilly was turned down because of her sex.

Without her pilot's license the ATA would not accept her either, so in 1941 Reilly signed up with the Women's Division of the RCAF as a photographer. It was the only job she could get that involved flying.

At the war's end Reilly was finally able to finish her flying courses at the Rockcliffe Flying Club. She earned her private pilot's license in 1946 and her commercial license in 1947. That was also the year her name first appeared in aviation articles in Canada. She had entered the Webster Trophy contest and come in three-tenths of a point behind the winner, a male pilot.

Reilly obtained employment in aviation as an instructor with the Leavens Brothers Flying School in Toronto after gaining her instructor's certificate. She was hired by Jack Reilly, her future husband, who also offered her the chance to fly charters. While working for the Leavens Brothers, Reilly had the opportunity to continue her flight training, which made her a more valuable employee. She gained her multiengine and instrument ratings from the Spartan School of Aeronautics, then earned a seaplane rating at Port Alberni in British Columbia.

In 1953 Reilly took a leave of absence to study for her senior commercial license, public transport license, and air transport rating at schools in England, where courses were considered tougher to pass. In 1954 she became the chief flying instructor and charter pilot for Canadian Aircraft Renters. In 1957 she was promoted to the rank of captain when she transferred to another branch of the company, Southern Provincial Airlines, as a full-time charter pilot. Reilly was the first Canadian woman to rise to that rank. While working at Southern Provin-

cial she also became the first woman to fly the Arctic professionally.

In 1959 Reilly took a job with Peter Bawden Drilling in Calgary as the copilot of a DC-3. Her copilot was the same Jack Reilly who gave her her first charter flying job. This time he also proposed marriage. She accepted.

The Reillys moved to Edmonton, Alberta, in 1965 when Molly Reilly was offered the position of chief pilot for Canadian Coachways, making her the first female corporate pilot in the country. In 1973 she was inducted into the Canadian Aviation Hall of Fame. Reilly died in 1980.

See also
Milstead, Violet
References
Render, *No Place for a Lady: The Story of Canadian Women Pilots, 1928–1992* (1992)

Reitsch, Hanna

The woman who would break men's hold on the world of German aviation while collecting nicknames like "The Flying Fräulein" and "Hitler's Test Pilot," Reitsch was born in Hirschberg, Germany, in March 1913. At the age of four her mother found her trying to jump off the first-floor balcony of the family home to experience flight. She received permission from her father, an eye specialist, to take flying lessons by receiving good marks in school. She graduated in 1931 but had to put in one year of study at the Colonial School for Women at Rendsburg before flying lessons. This school prepared young women to care for the home and family, skills Reitsch rarely utilized later in life.

As one of the conditions of the Versailles Treaty Germany had been forbidden to possess engine-powered aircraft after their loss in World War I, so Reitsch's first lessons were in piloting a glider at the School of Gliding at Grunau. She was instructed personally by the school's director, Wolf Hirth. Reitsch was the only woman in the class but was the first student to pass the A test successfully. Nevertheless, she was made to take the test flight again to make sure her success was not just a fluke. Then she passed her B and C tests in the next series of classes before starting her first year of medical studies at the University of Berlin. At the same time that she was a first-year medical student Reitsch studied engine mechanics on her own between lessons at Berlin-Staaken Airfield in flying engine-powered aircraft.

During the summer between her first and second years in medical school Hanna was invited to work as a gliding instructor for her old teacher, Wolf Hirth. She took a contingent of students to the Rhön Soaring Contests in 1933, where they outperformed their teacher; but Reitsch showed such determination in her efforts that she caught the eye of Professor Walter Georgii. He invited her to join an expedition of the International Study Commission for Motionless Flight to study thermal conditions in South America from January to April 1934.

Reitsch made the 3,000-mark contribution required of participants by flying glider stunts for the German film *Rivals of the Air*. For her participation in the study Reitsch became the first woman worldwide to earn the Silver Soaring Medal. Her work on the expedition also gained her a permanent position in the German Institute for Glider Research, a position that allowed her to test-fly new gliders and to break records while testing them. Her first record was the women's long-distance soaring record, which she broke by flying a distance of 100 miles.

After another expedition with the International Study Commission for Motionless Flight, this time to Finland, Reitsch traded in the decoration she was offered in payment for admittance in the Civil Airways Training School in Stettin, where she could learn to fly larger and faster planes. She was the first woman ever admitted to the military-run school, and her entrance caused a sensation.

In May 1935 Reitsch was invited to represent Germany at an international air display at the annual Festivas Lisboa held in Lisbon, Portugal.

On her return Reitsch test-flew a dangerous demonstration of dive brakes, invented by her friend Hans Jacobs, in front of a panel of Luftwaffe generals and so impressed them that in September 1937 she was invited to become a test pilot for their military aircraft.

In May 1937 she became one of the first Germans to cross the Alps by glider, flying at an altitude of 13,000 feet. Also in this year she set the world long-distance record and won the National Soaring contest as the only woman entrant. In July she set a world record for a flight from Magdeburg to Stettin.

Just as gliders were largely perfected by German designing, testing, and redesigning, so too were helicopters, and Reitsch had a hand in test-flying them as well. She flew a private demonstration of the first Focke helicopter for Charles Lindbergh when he visited Germany, and in February 1938 she flew public demonstrations at the International Automobile Exhibition in Bremen, Germany, for which she became the first woman to be honored with the Military Flying Medal.

In August 1938 Reitsch flew a glider display in the International Air Races in Cleveland, Ohio, hoping to interest Americans in the sport of gliding. She spoke to rotary clubs across the United States. Despite the tensions that had been growing between the two nations since Germany began rearming itself, Reitsch loved her visit to her country's future enemy.

Hanna Reitsch, a top Luftwaffe test pilot and Hitler's personal pilot at one time, took part in the Cleveland Air Races in Ohio (1938).

Her career was almost cut short in early 1939 by a three-month bout with scarlet fever followed by muscular rheumatism, but she survived them both. Then war broke out, and Reitsch was requested to test-fly new gliders; the Germans hoped to use them as troop carriers and to land them on oceangoing aircraft carriers. For these test flights she earned the Iron Cross II, which had only once in history been awarded to a woman. It was personally pinned on her by Adolf Hitler on March 28, 1941. She also received the Gold Medal for Military Flying, the second woman ever to do so (the first was a World War I nurse). On a trip to Hirschberg to celebrate this honor Reitsch was also given the Scroll of Honorary Citizenship.

She expanded her test-pilot work by becoming the first person, male or female, to test-fly the first rocket plane, the Messerschmitt 163. It was during one of these tests that Reitsch had her first serious crash, resulting in a skull fracture, compression of the brain, and a broken nose and jawbone, injuries that required five months to heal. For this she was treated by the best plastic surgeon in Germany, and she was awarded the Iron Cross, First Class.

She was test-flying again by November 1943 with the unhappy task of testing glider bombers for the newly desperate Germany's Suicide Group. She helped in the development and design of the gliders, but the idea was made strategically irrelevant when the invasion of Germany began, and the project was scrapped.

Reitsch was injured in an air raid on Berlin but recovered in time to test-fly helicopters for landing during air raids to retrieve the wounded. In April 1945 she was ordered to report to Hitler at his Reich Chancellery in Berlin, a city that was completely surrounded by Russian troops. She flew in with Colonel-General Robert von Greim at the controls. He was hit by artillery fire during the flight, and she had to pilot and land the plane from a standing position above his unconscious body. They entered the Reich Chancellery, under which was housed the bunker where Hitler was in hiding.

Trapped until Hitler allowed them to leave (April 26–28, 1945), Reitsch spent her time calming Joseph Goebbel's children by telling them stories of her flying career. On April 28 a German plane succeeded in landing beside the Chancellery. Hitler ordered Reitsch and von Greim to attack the oncoming Russian invaders by air, a task they knew was impossible with one plane, but it was their chance to escape certain death in the bunker.

When the war ended just weeks later, Reitsch was a prisoner of the Allies, who interrogated her based on rumors that she had flown Hitler to freedom. She remained a prisoner of war for 15 months until her release in August 1946.

It was not until 1949 that the Allied powers allowed Germans to participate in gliding again, and Reitsch began reappearing before the public by giving several lectures on gliding around Germany. Other countries were not so quick to forget her ties to Hitler. She was banned from flying in competitions in England in 1954. In 1958 she was denied a visa to enter a competition in Poland. In April

1959 she was finally allowed to represent Germany on a trip to deliver a replacement glider to a Delhi glider club. She took India's Prime Minister Jawaharlal Nehru gliding and became friends with his daughter Indira Gandhi.

In 1960 Reitsch finally revisited the United States, lecturing to future astronauts on her own experiences as a test pilot. In 1962 she was invited to open a gliding school in Ghana, which she operated personally for three years. Reitsch died on August 22, 1979, of heart failure. She was 67 years old.

Of her beloved gliding she once explained: "Powered flight is certainly a magnificent triumph over nature, but gliding is a victory of the soul in which one gradually becomes one with nature."

References

Lomax, *Flying for the Fatherland* (1988); Reitsch, *Flying Is My Life* (1954); Reitsch, *The Sky My Kingdom* (1955)

Relief Wings, Inc.

Relief Wings was founded on May 27, 1939, by Ruth Nichols, the first licensed woman pilot in New York State and the first to receive a hydroplane license. It was a volunteer aviation organization created to enlist pilots, their private planes, and medical personnel for emergency and disaster relief work. Its slogan was "Humanitarian service by air," following Nichols's wish to serve others through flight.

Relief Wings was run by a largely female board and accepted women at all levels. It was also supported and assisted by women in other aspects of aviation; for example, Olive Ann Mellor Beech donated several planes from her company, Beech Aircraft.

On July 7, 1940, the group staged a "practice" hurricane mobilization at Greenport, Long Island, to demonstrate their capabilities and as a training exercise for members. One hundred planes flew in from six nearby states to participate in the training. Later in the year they simulated a maritime rescue utilizing seaplanes.

In 1942 Nichols offered the services of the group to the Civil Air Patrol as her contribution to winning World War II.

See also
Beech, Olive Ann Mellor; Civil Air Patrol (CAP); Nichols, Ruth Rowland
References
Douglas, *United States Women in Aviation, 1940–1985* (1990); Nichols, *Wings for Life* (1957)

Resnik, Judith Arlene

The second American woman to go into space and the first Jewish astronaut, Resnik was born on April 5, 1949, in Akron, Ohio. She attended Harvey S. Firestone High School, where she was the only female member of the math club, and graduated in 1966 as valedictorian. Despite having the talent to become a classical pianist, Resnik chose to study math and science. She was one of the first women to receive an engineering scholarship to Carnegie-Mellon University.

Resnik received her bachelor's degree in electrical engineering in 1970. That spring she married fellow engineering major Michael Oldak. Resnik then went to work for the RCA Corporation in their missile and surface radar division as well as their service division. While working she began studying for her master's degree at the University of Maryland. In 1974 Resnik became a staff scientist in the Neurophysiology Laboratory at the National Institutes of Health in Maryland. In 1975 she and her husband divorced.

Resnik earned her Ph.D. in electrical engineering at the University of Maryland in 1977. A year later the National

Judith Resnik (1978)

Aeronautics and Space Administration (NASA) admitted women to the astronaut program for the first time. To beef up her résumé Resnik earned a pilot's license. She also took a job as a product developer for Xerox Corporation in Los Angeles where the climate would help her stay in top physical shape for the NASA tests.

Resnik joined Kathryn Sullivan, Shannon Lucid, and three others to become a member of the first class of women astronauts. She and Sally Ride, the first U.S. woman in space, worked together on the design and development of the Remote Manipulator System. Resnik also worked as a commentator for ABC to explain what was happening on board for the fourth shuttle mission.

For her first spaceflight Resnik was one of three mission specialists assigned to STS-41, the maiden voyage of the *Discovery* space shuttle. After two attempts aborted because of safety malfunctions, *Discovery* went into orbit on August 30, 1984. Resnik was in charge of deploying an extendable solar panel outside the shuttle while in orbit. She also worked the IMAX camera, photographing footage later used in the IMAX film *The Dream Is Alive*. Both the satellite deployment and the filming were completed successfully, though the rest of the mission was plagued with technical malfunctions.

Icicles formed on the exterior of the shuttle, which threatened to break off and damage the heat-resistant tiles necessary for the return flight. Resnik used her skills with the remote manipulator arm to chip away at the ice, saving the tiles and possibly their lives. Another malfunction involved an oxygen leak that might have ended the mission early. That problem was solved as well, and Resnik and *Discovery* returned to earth on September 5, 1984.

Resnik was selected for her second mission, the fatal *Challenger* mission, because of her skill with the remote manipulator arm she had helped design. Her responsibility on the mission would be to position a $100 million satellite in space. In preparation for the mission she also helped with the orientation of America's first teacher in space and the first civilian woman in space, Sharon Christa McAuliffe.

After another series of delays due to malfunctions, Resnik and the crew of the *Challenger* space shuttle were finally launched on January 28, 1986, at 11:38 A.M. The failure of the O-rings surrounding the booster rockets caused the shuttle vehicle to explode 72 seconds after takeoff, killing all seven crewmembers on board, including Resnik. She was 36 years old.

Resnik was honored at various memorial services by the presence of many NASA astronauts and speeches by the Ohio governor, Richard Celeste, and the first man to orbit the earth, John Glenn. The Society of Women Engineers named one of their awards, given to a woman who has helped make advancements in space, for Resnik.

Comparing her job as a mission specialist to the public's myth about astronauts, Resnik once said: "Progress in science is as exciting to me as sitting in a rocket is to some people. I feel less like Columbus and more like Galileo."

See also
Challenger Space Shuttle; *Discovery* Space Shuttle; McAuliffe, Sharon Christa; Ride, Sally Kristen

References
Bernstein, Blue, and Gerber, *Judith Resnik: Challenger Astronaut* (1990); Biographical Data Sheets, Lyndon B. Johnson Space Center (1997); Bond, *Heroes in Space: From Gagarin to Challenger* (1987); O'Connor, *Sally Ride and the New Astronauts: Scientists in Space* (1983)

Richey, Helen

Born in McKeesport, Pennsylvania, circa 1910, Richey became the first woman in the United States to pilot an airmail transport aircraft on a regular schedule. Richey's father was a superintendent of schools and financed her flying lessons, which began in 1930. She earned both a private pilot's license and a transport license in that year.

When Frances Marsalis decided to break her own refueling flight endurance record she asked Richey to be her partner. From December 20 to December 30, 1933, the two managed to stay aloft for 9 days, 21 hours, 42 minutes and succeeded in breaking the record.

On August 4, 1934, Richey won $1,000 when she came in first in the first National Air Meet for Women in Dayton, Ohio. Her closest competitor was her friend Marsalis, who was caught in the slipstream of Edna Gardner Whyte's plane. Marsalis lost control of her plane and crashed. Whyte veered to the left at the last minute to avoid a midair collision and appeared to have won the race. But race rules only allowed passing on the right, so Whyte was disqualified and Richey was declared the winner.

On December 31, 1934, Richey won a contest against eight male pilots to become a copilot for Central Airlines, which made Richey the first woman in the United States to pilot an airmail transport aircraft on a regular schedule. She flew passengers and airmail from Washington, D.C., to Detroit, Michigan, and back three times a week. The male pilots did not accept her, however, and refused to admit her to their union. Then they pressured her employers to prohibit her from flying in inclement weather. Richey resigned rather than be treated as less than an equal.

Instead she joined Louise Thaden as an employee of the Air Marking Department of the Bureau of Air Commerce. She and her fellow, mostly female pilots flew from town to town across the United States negotiating fees with local farmers and business owners to post the names of their towns on their tallest buildings to help pilots navigate. But her job did not keep her from attending races. In 1935 the seventh annual Miami All-American Air Maneuvers were open to women for the first time, and Richey took first place in the women's acrobatic competition.

On February 1, 1936, Richey claimed the new speed record for light planes by flying 77 miles per hour. She won $100 for being the first person to break a record in February, a contest held by the National Aeronautical Association to encourage Americans to attempt more aviation records. In May of that year she set a new altitude record. Her new track record did not go unnoticed by America's premier female aviator, Amelia Earhart. In September Richey was invited to serve as Earhart's copilot in the Bendix Air Race from the East Coast to the West Coast. The team came in fifth, first place having gone to Louise Thaden and Blanche Noyes.

In 1940 Richey signed on as the first female flight instructor for the U.S. Army Air Force. In 1942, while the United States debated admitting women to their ferry programs, Jacqueline Cochran recruited fellow American women for the British Air Transit Auxiliary (ATA) organized by Pauline Gower. Richey was one of 25 women pilots who became part of the second unit of women in the ATA. The group was visited by Eleanor Roosevelt and Oveta Culp Hobby on a tour to study the activities of women in wartime Britain.

When Cochran returned to the United States to form the Women's Airforce Service Pilots (WASPS), Richey took command of the U.S. contingent of the ATA. In April 1943 Richey returned to the United States herself and joined the WASPS. She was a member of the fifth class of pilots trained at Avenger Field, Texas. After training, Richey was made B-52 squadron leader at the North American Aircraft plant in Kansas City. Her unit ferried B-52 bombers from the factory to air force bases and training schools for the next 16 months.

The WASPS were disbanded in December 1944. After the war Richey moved to New York City and searched for aviation work. With the many returning male pilots, there were no openings for her. She died on January 7, 1947, of an overdose of pills.

See also

Avenger Field; Cochran, Jacqueline; Gower, Pauline; Hobby, Oveta Culp; Marsalis, Frances Harrell; Noyes, Blanche Wilcox; Roosevelt, Eleanor; Thaden, Louise McPhetridge; Whyte, Edna Marvel Gardner; Women's Airforce Service Pilots (WASPS)

References

Adams and Kimball, *Heroines of the Sky* (1942); Roseberry, *The Challenging Skies: The Colorful Story of Aviation's Most Exciting Years, 1919–1939* (1966)

Ride, Sally Kristen

The first American woman in space and the youngest American astronaut to orbit the earth, Ride was born in Encino, California, in 1951. At 14 she was ranked eighteenth nationally on the junior tennis circuit. She graduated from Westlake School for Girls in 1968, and instead of going on the professional tennis circuit she attended both Swarthmore College, where she became a top-ranked tennis player, and Stanford University, where she earned her doctorate in x-ray physics.

In 1978, while working as a research assistant in x-ray astrophysics at Stanford, Ride became a member of the eighth National Aeronautics and Space Administration (NASA) astronaut class, chosen from a pool of 8,000 applications, 1,544 from women. She had applied to NASA after seeing an ad in her college newspaper calling for astronaut applicants.

Her first duties at NASA, besides training, involved designing and testing the shuttle's Remote Manipulator System in 1981 and acting as capsule communicator (CAPCOM) for the crew of the shuttle *Columbia* in 1982. In that capacity she was the only person at Mission Operations Control, and the first woman in the history of NASA, to talk to the astronauts during their flight.

True to her independent reputation, Ride married fellow astronaut Steve Hawley on July 24, 1982, in her parents' backyard wearing blue jeans. She flew solo to the ceremony, and then flew herself and Hawley to their honeymoon destination.

Ride became the first American woman in space on June 18, 1983, when she served as a mission specialist for STS-7 on board the *Challenger* space shuttle. The mission lasted until June 24 and involved deploying communications satellites for Canada and Indonesia, performing the first satellite deployment and retrieval with the shuttle's robot arm, and conducting materials and pharmaceutical

Sally Kristen Ride (1978)

research. Many professional women, including actress Jane Fonda, were invited to the launch in celebration.

Ride returned for a second shuttle flight on *Challenger* in October 1984, where she was joined by Kathryn Sullivan, America's third woman in space, for mission STS-41G. During this eight-day mission Ride and the crew deployed the earth radiation budget satellite, conducted scientific observations of the earth, and demonstrated the potential for satellite refueling by astronauts.

In 1985 she was inducted into the International Space Hall of Fame with Valentina Tereshkova, Svetlana Savitskaya, and Kathryn Sullivan. In June 1986 Ride began training for her third space shuttle flight. She was also putting the finishing touches on her first book, *To Space and Back*, a children's book describing her experiences in space. Both projects were put on hold, however, by the explosion of the *Challenger* space shuttle on January 28, 1986.

Ride published her book and dedicated it to her friends who had died on *Challenger*. From February to July 1986 she served on the Rogers Commission for the *Challenger* disaster investigation. When her duties there were completed Ride was assigned to NASA headquarters in Washington, D.C., as assistant to the NASA administrator for long-range planning. In this role she created NASA's Office of Exploration and produced a report on the future of the space program entitled "Leadership and America's Future in Space."

Ride retired from NASA in 1987 to become a science fellow at the Center for International Security and Arms Control at Stanford University. In 1989 she joined the faculty at the University of California, San Diego, as a professor of physics. She is also director of the California Space Institute, a research institute of the University of California.

In 1992 Ride's second book, *Voyager: An Adventure to the Edge of the Solar System*, was published. It describes the travels and discoveries of the *Voyager 1* and *2* satellites. In 1997 she released her third book, *The Third Planet: Exploring the Earth from Space*, which explores the earth's environment and the impact on it of human life.

In her first book Ride described her feelings about being an astronaut, even after the *Challenger* disaster: "All adventures—especially into new territory—are scary, and there has always been an element of danger in space flight. I wanted to be an astronaut because I thought it would be a challenging opportunity. It was; it was also an experience that I shall never forget."

See also

Challenger Disaster Investigation; *Challenger* Space Shuttle; Savitskaya, Svetlana; Sullivan, Kathryn; Tereshkova, Valentina Vladimirovna

References

Bond, *Heroes in Space: From Gagarin to Challenger* (1987); Oberg, *Spacefarers of the 80's and 90's: The Next Thousand People in Space* (1985); O'Connor, *Sally Ride and the New Astronauts: Scientists in Space* (1983); Ride with Okie, *To Space and Back* (1986)

Rogers Commission

See *Challenger* Disaster Investigation

Rogers, Edith Nourse

As a congresswoman, Rogers introduced the bill that created a Women's Auxiliary Army Corps, later known as the Women's Airforce Service Pilots (WASPS), in the army and the Women Appointed for Volunteer Emergency Service (WAVES) in the navy.

Rogers was born in 1881. Her interest in government provisions for veterans began in World War I, when she served as a hospital aide overseas. She became a congresswoman when her husband, John J. Rogers, died in office and she succeeded him, winning reelection to the seat for the next 35 years.

On May 28, 1941, Rogers introduced legislation H.R. 4906, which proposed a Women's Auxiliary Army Corps (WAAC). The bill was stalled in Congress until December 1941 after the bombing of Pearl Harbor. It was then debated until the air force showed an interest in using the services of qualified women pilots as part of such a program. The bill was passed on May 15, 1942, nearly a year after it was proposed, on a vote of 249 to 286.

Based on the quick success of the army's WASPS program, Rogers proposed a similar group of militarily sanctioned female pilots in the navy. The WAVES was created by act of Congress in July 1942.

When Rogers died in 1960 at the age of 79 she was in the process of running for reelection yet again. The Women's Army Corps Museum at Fort McClellan in Alabama is named for Rogers in gratitude for her years of service.

See also

Women Appointed for Volunteer Emergency Service (WAVES); Women's Airforce Service Pilots (WASPS)

References

Douglas, *United States Women in Aviation, 1940–1985* (1990); Weatherford, *American Women's History: An A to Z of People, Places, Organizations, Issues, and Events* (1994)

U.S. Representative Edith Nourse Rogers of Massachusetts, chair of the House Veterans' Affairs Committee, marked the completion of 28 years of service in Congress in Washington, D.C. (1953).

Roosevelt, Eleanor

An early supporter of the Women's Airforce Service Pilots (WASPS) and of women in aviation in general, Roosevelt was the first lady of the United States from 1932 to 1945. Roosevelt was born in New York City on October 11, 1884. She was a niece of President Theodore Roosevelt. At the age of 15 she went to boarding school in England. On her return home she did social work in New York before marrying her distant cousin Franklin Delano Roosevelt in 1905. They had six children, one of whom died in infancy.

When Franklin was elected to the presidency in 1932, Eleanor soon became an influential figure in his administration. In April 1933 the president and first lady received Amelia Earhart for dinner to celebrate Earhart's recent solo flight across the Atlantic. After dinner Earhart took the first lady for her first night flight, over the Potomac River.

At Roosevelt's suggestion the Bureau of Air Commerce hired women pilots, including Phoebe Omlie and Blanche Noyes, to negotiate with owners of tall buildings along various air routes to allow place-names to be painted on those buildings as an aid to navigation.

In 1938 Roosevelt presented the International League of Aviators' Harmon Trophy for best woman pilot of the year to Jacqueline Cochran. In September 1939 Roosevelt received a letter from Cochran arguing that with the war in Europe going badly the United States should allow women to fly noncombat missions to free the men for overseas duty. Roosevelt wrote about these ideas in her daily syndicated newspaper column, "My Day," to begin building the public support needed. She also spoke about them frequently with her husband.

Despite Roosevelt's detailed discussions with her husband, he refused to set up such a group in the United States. In 1942 Cochran recruited American women for the British Air Transit Auxiliary. In total she brought 25 women pilots to Britain during 1942.

Roosevelt visited the group with Oveta Culp Hobby on a tour to study the activities of women in wartime Britain. Upon her return home, President Roosevelt changed his mind and invited Cochran to create the Women's Flying Training Detachment (WFTD), a forerunner of the WASPS.

Roosevelt actively involved herself in the formation of another women's military group, the navy's Women Appointed for Volunteer Emergency Service (WAVES). Some congressmen wanted the new group to be a separate entity from the navy, as the WASPS were an auxiliary of the army, but others, including Mrs. Roosevelt, urged for true integration. After long discussions with President Roosevelt, she succeeded in winning him to her side.

Soon after fighting to help create the WASPS and WAVES Roosevelt found herself publicly defending their honor. Some of those who opposed women being involved in the military in even a voluntary manner circulated rumors that the majority of them were prostitutes. These rumors became so rampant that Roosevelt found it necessary to frequently defend the honor of female recruits in the press.

Roosevelt died in New York City on November 7, 1962.

Much of Roosevelt's influence over public opinion came from being the author of "My Day." In the September 1, 1942, installment of her syndicated column she announced her support for the then newly created WASPS by saying: "This is not a time when women should be patient. We are in a war and we need to fight it with all our ability and every weapon possible. Women pilots, in this particular case, are a weapon waiting to be used."

See also
Cochran, Jacqueline; Earhart, Amelia Mary;
Hobby, Oveta Culp; Noyes, Blanche
Wilcox; Omlie, Phoebe Fairgrave; Women
Appointed for Volunteer Emergency Service
(WAVES); Women's Airforce Service Pilots
(WASPS)
References
Van Wagenen Keil, *Those Wonderful Women
in Their Flying Machines* (1979)

Rufus, Maude Squire

Rufus did not learn to fly until her youngest son took her on her first flight. She signed up for lessons the next day and flew all her life, earning the nickname "Flying Grandma." Also known as the Amelia Earhart of Ann Arbor, Rufus was born on November 3, 1880, in Ontario, Canada, the second daughter of the local Methodist preacher and his wife. She spent her childhood traveling with her parents supporting causes such as the Anti-Saloon League.

Rufus earned money for college by teaching elocution and coordinating public speaking events for her pupils. She attended Albion College and studied music and speech, but her mother died before Rufus earned enough credits to graduate. She returned home to care for her father and younger brothers. She was followed by a suitor, Will Carl Rufus, whom she married. Together they entered the ministry of the Methodist church and were sent to the Orient from 1907 to 1917.

On their return to the United States Rufus and her family settled in Ann Arbor, Michigan. Her husband taught astronomy at the University of Michigan. Rufus made extra money by renting rooms to boarding students and conducting the local orchestra. In 1926 they signed up as instructors with the University World Cruise and spent the year teaching and chaperoning students on an around-the-world study tour.

After returning to live near the University of Michigan, Rufus began taking flying lessons in 1936 in a 40-horsepower Aeronica-K airplane. To increase her flight hours Rufus flew from Ann Arbor to Miami to attend the Miami Air Races in both 1939 and 1940, with her son as copilot.

Rufus received her private pilot's license on September 18, 1940. She joined the Ninety-Nines and found herself in the company of such other successful Michigan pilots as Helen Montgomery, founder of the XYZ Soaring Club of Michigan.

On May 1, 1941, at the age of 60, Rufus began a cross-country trip from Michigan to Washington State. Along the way she stopped in at a sectional meeting of the Ninety-Nines in Des Moines, Iowa. She also stopped in Los Angeles and met Gladys O'Donnell, who had come in first in the 1930 Women's Air Derby. When she reached Bellingham, Washington, Rufus took her 91-year-old father on his first airplane ride. The trip proved to be a human interest event that was reported in several newspapers, especially since the entire trip cost only $332.02.

Rufus died in a plane crash in Washington, Pennsylvania, on June 19, 1979, when low-octane gasoline was mistakenly put in her airplane and it crashed on takeoff. In her biography for the *History of the Ninety-Nines*, handed in shortly before her death, she had prophetically written: "I'd rather go like sixty in my ship and end in a crash, than give up my plane."

See also
Montgomery, Helen; Ninety-Nines;
O'Donnell, Gladys
References
History of the Ninety-Nines, Inc. (1979);
Rufus, *Flying Grandma, or Going Like Sixty*
(1942)

Safety Belts/Safety Harnesses

Although seat belts and safety harnesses are now standard equipment in everything from cars to strollers to amusement park rides, at the dawn of aviation they were not widely used, which led to the death of many early aviation pioneers.

Harriet Quimby, the first American woman to obtain a pilot's license and the first woman to fly the English Channel, was the lead attraction at an air meet at Boston's Squantum Airfield on July 1, 1912. She was flying her new Blériot monoplane around a lighthouse with the organizer of the event, William Willard. Neither wore a safety belt. At the height of about 2,000 feet the plane went into a sudden dive, and both Quimby and Willard were killed when they fell from the plane into the shallow water surrounding the lighthouse.

Laura Bromwell, famous for breaking the record for consecutive loop-the-loops by flying 199 on May 21, 1921, was performing in a new plane just two weeks later, on June 5, 1921, lost control of the craft, and crashed. She was not wearing a safety belt because it prevented her from reaching the rudder pedals of the plane, and she died on impact.

Bessie Coleman, the first African American woman to earn a pilot's license, was engaged to lecture around Chicago and to fly stunts for the Negro Welfare League's Field Day on May 1, 1926. The day before the show Coleman went for a test flight of a new plane with William D. Wills, the white pilot who had delivered it to her. Wills flew the plane so that Coleman could study the airfield and decide on an appropriate landing site for the show. At 1,000 feet the plane went into a nosedive, and at 500 feet it flipped upside down. Coleman, who wore no safety belt because it hindered her view over the edge of the cockpit, fell to her death.

However, Ann Walker Welch, a glider pilot in England who became a member of the British Air Transport Auxiliary during World War II, survived a crash from an amphibious Walrus aircraft off the Isle of Wight by *not* wearing her safety belt. She was thrown clear of the fire that immediately engulfed the craft.

See also
Bromwell, Laura; Coleman, Bessie; Quimby, Harriet; Welch, Ann Walker
References
Holden, *Her Mentor Was an Albatross: The Autobiography of Pioneer Pilot Harriet Quimby* (1993); Patterson, *Memoirs of the Late Bessie Coleman, Aviatrix* (1969); Welch, *Happy to Fly: An Autobiography* (1983)

Sage, Letitia

The first British woman to fly in a balloon, Sage was an actress by profession. She answered an advertisement placed by balloon experimenter Vincent Lunardi looking for a woman to fly with him in public. Lunardi was attempting to match the showmanship of his rival, Jean-Pierre Blanchard, whose wife, Marie Madeleine Sophie Armont Blanchard, piloted his balloons in front of paying crowds all across France.

Sage's flight took place over St. George's Fields in London in June 1785. She then published a short piece, "A Letter Describing the General Appearances and Effects of the Expedition with Lunardi's Balloon." She never took another flight but used the publicity to boost her acting opportunities.

See also
Blanchard, Marie Madeleine Sophie Armont
References
May, *Women in Aeronautics* (1962)

Savitskaya, Svetlana

The second woman in space and the first woman to fly twice in space, Savitskaya was born in 1948 and was 34 when she orbited in *Soyuz T-7*, 19 years after Valentina Tereshkova became the first woman in space and one year before the United States sent its first woman into space, Sally Ride.

Savitskaya was born on August 8, 1948, the daughter of the deputy commander of Soviet air defenses, so aviation ran in her family. At age 16 she decided to become a pilot and applied for training at an amateur flying school without her parents' knowledge. She was deemed too young for flight training, so she turned to parachute training in the interim.

Finally gaining her father's support, Savitskaya completed 450 parachute jumps. At the age of 17 she completed a record stratospheric sky dive, jumping from 14,252 meters and falling almost 14 kilometers before opening her parachute at 500 meters.

At 18 Savitskaya enrolled in the Moscow Aviation Institute (MAI) and finally began pilot training. In 1970 at the age of 20 she soloed in a YaK-18 trainer. That same year Savitskaya won the title of Women's World Aerobatics Champion as a member of the Soviet National Aerobatics Team. In 1972 she graduated

Svetlana Savitskaya (1982)

from MAI with both her instructor and test pilot certificates.

Savitskaya's first job was as a trainer for the Central Technical Flying School of the USSR Voluntary Society for the Promotion of the Army, Air Force, and Navy. While there she tried to persuade the other instructors that she would make a good candidate for test pilot school. They finally capitulated, and Savitskaya graduated in 1975 after establishing several new world records in aviation, including being the youngest woman to fly at twice the speed of sound.

Savitskaya's first test pilot position came the following year for the Yakovlev design bureau. In 1980 she was chosen for the Soviet cosmonaut team training. On August 19, 1982, Savitskaya joined Alexander Serebrov and Leonid Popov on *Soyuz T-7* for a weeklong mission to study motion sickness, eye coordination, and the effect of weightlessness on women.

Her next mission was a year later as flight engineer on *Soyuz T-12*, which traveled to the *Salyut* space station. On June 25, 1984, she became the first woman to walk in space when she spent 3 hours, 35 minutes working on repairs to the exterior of the station during the mission.

In 1985 she was inducted into the International Space Hall of Fame with Tereshkova, Sally Ride, and Kathryn Sullivan.

Between spaceflights Savitskaya worked as an engineer and was named as a representative to parliament in 1989. She retired from the cosmonauts in 1993.

Of her place in history, Savitskaya has said: "A hundred years from now, no one will remember it, and if they do, it will sound strange that it was once questioned whether a woman should go into space."

See also
Ride, Sally Kristen; Sullivan, Kathryn; Tereshkova, Valentina Vladimirovna
References
Bond, *Heroes in Space: From Gagarin to Challenger* (1987); O'Connor, *Sally Ride and the New Astronauts: Scientists in Space* (1983)

Schweizer, Virginia

The namesake of the Virginia M. Schweizer Competition Trophy was the first woman in the United States to gain her commercial glider rating. Schweizer began flying gliders at the age of 18. Then, when the United States entered World War II, all nonmilitary flyers were grounded.

After the war Schweizer trained civilians using army surplus gliders. In 1946 she won the Silver C Award for a two-hour flight that also set a distance record of 38 miles. She married and settled near Harris Hill, New York, known as the soaring capital of the country. Together Schweizer and her husband attended conferences around the world to promote the sport of gliding. They also helped organize the National Soaring Museum.

In 1989 Schweizer was honored by the Women Soaring Pilots of America. They named their competition trophy, which goes to the woman with the highest score in the annual soaring championships, for her.

Schweizer credits her love of gliding with her early start in the sport: "I can't explain just how wonderful it is, you have to experience it yourself to understand it but I strongly believe in starting at an early age. If you start when you're young, as I did, and make it a major portion of your life, it is something that stays with you forever, it gets in your blood and you never lose the touch."

References
Holden and Griffith, *Ladybirds II: The Continuing Story of American Women in Aviation* (1993)

Scott, Blanche Stuart

The first woman to solo in a fixed-wing, heavier-than-air machine, Scott was also the first woman to drive a car cross-country, driving from New York to San Francisco. She did both in order to prove that women were as daring and capable as men. Born in Rochester, New York, in 1890, Scott accepted the challenge of the cross-country drive from the Willy's-Overland Company in 1910. This was the first transcontinental automobile trip by a woman. On the heels of that success Scott approached Glenn Curtiss, founder of the Curtiss Exhibition Team, and asked for flying lessons at his school in Hammondsport, New York.

Like many men of his day Curtiss was against women learning to fly, so he placed a block on the plane's throttle, ensuring that it could not leave the ground. After three days of lessons on the ground,

Blanche Scott was not only the first woman to solo in a fixed-wing, heavier-than-air machine, but the first woman to drive a car across the United States (1910).

taxiing back and forth around the small airport at Hammondsport, the block was somehow jolted out of place. On September 2, 1910, Scott flew 40 feet high and landed cleanly, convincing Curtiss to continue the lessons and even to invite Scott into his exhibition troupe.

Scott was not credited by the Aeronautical Society of America with being the first woman to solo, however, because the flight was ruled to have been accidental. That honor went just two weeks later to Bessica Raiche. Whether because of this snub or for other reasons, Scott neglected to obtain a license to fly from the society for the duration of her career.

On October 1, 1910, Scott made her public debut as part of the Curtiss Exhibition Team at an air meet in Chicago, Illinois. She married her publicist after

the summer flying season and declared that she was in retirement. She returned to flying the following year. In June 1912 Scott was flying at an air meet in Boston when she witnessed Harriet Quimby's death. It took three attempts for Scott to finally land her plane after that, but she did finally and continued her own aviation career.

During the next six years she gained the nickname of "Tomboy of the Air" for such daring stunts as flying upside down and under low bridges. Her most famous stunt was named "The Death Dive." Scott would climb to a height of 4,000 feet and nose-dive to 200 feet above the ground before righting the plane and landing to thunderous applause.

In 1916 she was earning as much as $5,000 a week between her salary and her percentage of the ticket sales at the gate. Yet at the age of 27, at the height of her career, Scott retired from flying. She kept her hand in by writing articles about air-mindedness (that is, issues of aviation), which led to an appointment as the head of the educational division of the Maximum Safety Airplane Company in 1929. She died in January 1970.

In explaining her decision to retire to friends and fans, Scott said: "In aviation there seems to be no place for the woman engineer, mechanic or flier. Too often, people paid money to see me risk my neck, more as a freak—a woman freak pilot—than as a skilled flier."

See also
Quimby, Harriet; Raiche, Bessica Faith Medlar
References
Lomax, *Women of the Air* (1987); May, *Women in Aeronautics* (1962); Moolman, *Women Aloft* (1981)

Scott, Sheila Christine Hopkins

The first person to fly a light aircraft solo over the North Pole and the first European woman to fly solo around the equator, Scott was born in 1927 in Worcester, England. She received her first airplane ride as a sixth birthday present, but she sampled other careers—nursing during World War II and acting after the war—before turning to flying. She quit acting in 1959 to pursue aviation, taking lessons first at Elstree Airport and later at Thruxton. By 1960 she had earned her pilot's license and purchased her first plane, a Tiger Moth. She tested the plane that year by making round-trip flights to North America and Africa.

In the summer of 1960 Scott entered the National Air Races, winning her races and the de Havilland Trophy. At the end of the year she signed up at Oxford for commercial pilot's training. She passed all the written and flying exams,

but failed the physical because of her eyesight.

Without a commercial license, Scott had trouble finding work as a pilot until a Cessna dealer hired her to demonstrate their planes at local air races. This job led her to the United States, where she was offered the chance to study for a U.S. commercial license, which she earned quickly. With her U.S. license in hand, Scott petitioned the British Air Ministry for a new physical, which she passed in 1964. Her first big stunt in Europe was to break 15 light aircraft records in 36 hours.

She liked the experience so much that in 1966 she decided to try to become the first European woman to fly solo around the world at the equator. Americans Jerrie Mock and Joan Merriam Smith had already made the 22,000-mile trip, in 29 and 24 days, respectively. Scott stayed closer to the equator, making her route 32,000 miles long, and she completed the trip in 33 days. For this feat she became the first woman awarded the Silver Medal Award of Merit by the Guild of Air Pilots and Air Navigators, which was presented to her at a ceremony chaired by His Royal Highness Prince Philip in November 1966.

In 1967 Scott was hired to promote the opening of a new factory in South Africa by breaking the London–to–Cape Town record. Despite flying over areas involved in the recent Israeli/Arab six-day war, Scott finished the flight, shaving four hours off the record set by Amy Johnson in 1936.

In 1969 Scott entered and won the Top of the Tower Race from London's General Post Office Tower to the Empire State Building in New York. Contestants were given from May 4 through May 12 and were permitted to use any transportation getting from airports to the two towers and back. She set a record for the race, completing it in 26 hours, 54 minutes, 20 seconds.

On January 5, 1970, Scott finished fourth in the England-to-Australia Air Race despite radio and compass failures and an unscheduled stop on an Indonesian island. After the race she flew on to the United States for airplane repairs. She then spent several weeks resting in Fiji, photographing the natives and learning about their diverse cultures. When she returned to England she had completed her second around-the-world trip.

On June 11, 1971, Scott took off from Nairobi, Kenya, in an attempt to be the first person in a light plane to fly across the North Pole. Her flight was supported and sponsored by the Royal Air Force, which studied her sleep patterns, and by the National Aeronautics and Space Administration (NASA), which tracked sulfur dioxide in the atmosphere through which she flew. She made her first refueling stop in London on June 16 and learned that her apartment had been burglarized. Much of the cold-weather gear and video equipment for the trip had been stolen. The thieves had also taken her many race trophies. Despite the loss, she continued the trip, leaving London on June 22 for her second refueling stop in Bodø, Norway. A failed autopilot and jammed landing gear forced her to land in Nord, Greenland. On June 28 she crossed the North Pole with a radio blacked out by the magnetic activity. When she landed in Barrow, Alaska, at the Naval Arctic Research Laboratory, she became the first woman to fly the Arctic Ocean solo. When she returned to England on August 8, 1971, she had flown a total of 34,000 miles, and she had beaten the Darwin-to-London record set in 1934 by Jean Batten.

In 1972, Scott attended Transpo '72 in Washington, D.C., and took the time to meet the many engineers at NASA whose work had benefited from her trip across the Arctic. She was then planning and actively soliciting funding for a flight to Antarctica. While she attended a party at the Goddard Space Center commemorating her Arctic flight, her plane, hangared for repairs, was destroyed by Hurricane Agnes. To pay for its extensive repairs Scott published her first book, *Barefoot in the Sky*.

Finally Scott took the time to earn the driver's license she had been too busy to pursue, only to end up in a car accident that left her nearly blind. By 1974 she had regained most of her sight, but not enough to renew her flying career. She worked instead in broadcasting, writing, and lecturing. She died in 1988.

In *Barefoot in the Sky*, published in 1973, Scott explained her love of flying in this way: "Why did I have to fly to find happiness? I think it is because in the sky I am able to stretch my brain rather than my legs and find motivation to satisfy my insatiable curiosity to experience things myself, to be able to understand them, and to find meaning and a sense of man's superconscious."

See also
Batten, Jean; Johnson, Amy; Mock, Geraldine "Jerrie" Frederitz; National Air Races; Smith, Joan Merriam

References
Briggs, *At the Controls: Women in Aviation* (1991); Scott, *Barefoot in the Sky: An Autobiography* (1973)

Seddon, M. Rhea

A member of the first husband-and-wife astronaut team, Seddon was also among the first group of women astronauts, which included Sally Ride, Shannon Lucid, and Judith Resnik. Seddon was born on November 8, 1947, in Murfreesboro, Tennessee, and graduated from Central High School there in 1965. She received a bachelor of arts degree in physiology from the University of California at Berkeley in 1970 and her M.D. from the University of Tennessee College of Medicine in 1973.

M. Rhea Seddon (1978)

After medical school Seddon completed a surgical internship and three years of a general surgery residency in Memphis with a particular interest in nutrition in surgery patients. Between her internship and residency she served as an emergency department physician at a number of hospitals in Mississippi and Tennessee.

In 1978, the first year that the National Aeronautics and Space Administration (NASA) accepted women in the astronaut program, Seddon applied. She became an astronaut in August 1979. Seddon's first spaceflight was on board the *Discovery* space shuttle for mission STS 51-D from April 12 to April 19, 1985. As a mission specialist Seddon was assigned to operate the robot arm as Judith Resnik had on an earlier mission. Because of technical malfunctions, however, Seddon was not able to repeat Resnik's success, and the errant satellite that *Discovery* had been launched to repair remained out of reach. She did take part in conducting

several medical experiments, activating two Getaway Specials (that is, self-contained experiments sent up by private or public institutions), and filming experiments with toys in space.

Her next spaceflight was again as a mission specialist, this time on the *Columbia* space shuttle from June 5 to 14, 1991. STS-40 was a dedicated space and life sciences mission utilizing Spacelab Life Sciences (SLS-1) for the first time. Seddon and the crew performed experiments that explored how humans, animals, and cells respond to microgravity and readapt to earth gravity on return. They also conducted experiments designed to investigate materials science, plant biology, and cosmic radiation and tests of hardware proposed for the Space Station Freedom Health Maintenance Facility.

For her third spaceflight Seddon was once again aboard the *Columbia* space shuttle, this time as payload commander for the life science research mission. From October 18 to November 1, 1993, Seddon was in charge of Spacelab Life Sciences–2, and her work was recognized by NASA management as the most successful and efficient Spacelab flight to date. The crew performed neurovestibular, cardiovascular, cardiopulmonary, metabolic, and musculoskeletal medical experiments on themselves and 48 rats, expanding our knowledge of human and animal physiology both on earth and in spaceflight.

Between spaceflights Seddon has worked in several other capacities at NASA, including updating the shuttle medical kit and checklist and serving as a launch and landing rescue-helicopter physician. She maintains membership on NASA's Aerospace Medical Advisory Committee. Seddon and her husband, astronaut Robert Gibson, also keep in practice in emergency medicine by serving as emergency department physicians at a number of hospitals in the Houston area in their spare time.

In September 1996 Seddon was sent by NASA to Vanderbilt University Medical School in Nashville, Tennessee, where she assisted in the preparation of cardiovascular experiments designated to fly aboard the *Columbia* space shuttle on the Neurolab Spacelab flight in 1998. In 1997 Seddon served as assistant to the director of flight crew operations for shuttle/*Mir* payloads.

In describing her work, Seddon has said: "I looked out of the T-38 window the other day and asked myself, 'How many people get to have a job like this?'"

See also
Discovery Space Shuttle; Lucid, Shannon W.; Resnik, Judith Arlene; Ride, Sally Kristen
References
Biographical Data Sheets, Lyndon B. Johnson Space Center (1997); Oberg, *Spacefarers of the 80's and 90's: The Next Thousand People in Space* (1985); O'Connor, *Sally Ride and the New Astronauts: Scientists in Space* (1983)

Shakhovskaya, Eugenia Mikhailovna

The first Russian woman military pilot was Princess Shakhovskaya, who flew reconnaissance with the First Field Air Squadron of World War I. She earned her pilot's license on August 16, 1911. Her position among the royalty allowed her to make a personal request to the tsar to be allowed to fly for their country.

Later in life she became the chief executioner for the Kiev secret police.

References
Oakes, *United States Women in Aviation through World War I* (1978)

Sharman, Helen

Britain's first astronaut, Sharman was born in 1964. She was employed as a food technologist from Sheffield, England, and worked for Mars, the candy company, when she applied, along with 13,000 others, for the position.

After a year of training at Star City, Russia, Sharman was a member of the joint Anglo-Soviet Juno mission from the USSR, which made her the third woman, after Valentina Tereshkova and Svetlana Savitskaya, to go into space from Russia. On May 18, 1991, Sharman was a crewmember on *Soyuz TM-12* and was instrumental in manually docking the spacecraft with the *Mir* space station. She also received her ham radio license in order to operate one from *Mir*.

On her return Sharman became one of Britain's Ambassadors of Science, with her contribution being the children's book *The Space Place*, which was published in 1997.

Of her time in space, Sharman said: "I did not want to come back. I was very busy. I could easily have spent another two weeks up in space."

See also
Mir Space Station; Savitskaya, Svetlana; Tereshkova, Valentina Vladimirovna
References
Cadogan, *Women with Wings: Female Flyers in Fact and Fiction* (1993)

Sherlock, Nancy
See Currie, Nancy Jane Sherlock

Skelton-Frankman, Betty

Famous for performing the aerobatic stunt known as the inverted ribbon cut in international air meets, Skelton-Frankman was born on June 28, 1926. She soloed at the age of 12. She graduated from high school in Tampa, Florida, and began working the night shift at Eastern Airlines so that she would be free to take flying lessons by day in Pensacola, Florida. She earned her commercial pilot's license at 18.

At the onset of World War II Skelton-Frankman applied to the Women's Air-

Betty Skelton-Frankman was one of the youngest women to solo at 12 years old and to earn her commercial pilot's license at 18 years old (January 8, 1949).

force Service Pilots (WASPS) but was a year and a half too young to join. She concentrated on learning aerobatic flying and shared her professional air show debut with the U.S. Navy's Blue Angels at a meet in Jacksonville, Florida, in 1946. In 1949 she set the world speed record for powered aircraft.

Thanks to her special trick, the inverted ribbon cut, Skelton-Frankman took the title of International Feminine Aerobatic Championship in 1948, 1949, and 1950. The trick involved flying through a ribbon tied ten feet off the ground between two poles—upside down. It was a showstopper, and Skelton-Frankman was the first woman to master it.

She also made headlines for piloting the smallest plane ever to cross the Irish Sea.

After accomplishing so much, Skelton-Frankman retired from aerobatic flying in October 1951 at the age of 26 because of the expense of the sport. Since the airlines were not hiring women as pilots, she made her living as a flight instructor. She found she could not give up her love of speed, however. Her new hobby, in which she again succeeded at breaking records, was auto racing.

In August 1985 Skelton-Frankman's plane was housed in the Smithsonian Institution's Air and Space Museum. In 1988 she was inducted into the International Aerobatics Hall of Fame.

Regarding her nickname, "The Lady of Firsts," Skelton-Frankman said: "It is not easy to be the best. You must have the courage to bear pain, disappointment, and heartbreak. You must establish your goal, and no matter what deters you along the way, in your every waking moment you must say to yourself, I can do it."

See also
Women's Airforce Service Pilots (WASPS)
References
Holden and Griffith, *Ladybirds II: The Continuing Story of American Women in Aviation* (1993); Russo, *Women and Flight: Portraits of Contemporary Women Pilots* (1997)

Smirnova, Mariya

A Russian bomber pilot in World War II, Smirnova was promoted to squadron commander of the 46th Guards Bomber Regiment after the death of their commander on the unit's first mission.

Smirnova was born in Russia in 1920. When she was 13 she began studies at the teacher's college at Tver. Upon graduation three years later she became an elementary school teacher at a school near an airdrome, where she first saw airplanes up close.

In 1937, with World War II looming, Smirnova signed up for flying lessons. She earned both her pilot's and then her instructor's licenses and began training male cadets for the Russian Air Force.

In October 1941 Marina Raskova, a record-breaking civilian pilot, was asked by the Soviet High Command to recruit 200 women flyers for combat missions. After she broadcast an appeal over Radio Moscow, Raskova received more than 2,000 applications, one of which came from Smirnova.

After undergoing training in the town of Engels, Smirnova was assigned as deputy squadron commander to the 588th Night Bomber Regiment. The group was stationed at the front on May 2, 1942. On June 8, 1942, the 588th flew their first combat mission, during which their squadron commander was shot down. Smirnova took her place.

In January 1943, after eight months of combat flying, they were honored by being renamed the 46th Guards Regiment, the first women's air regiment to receive such an honor. Under Smirnova's direction the women frequently flew 15 to 18 bombing missions a night, for a total of 24,000 combat missions dropping 23,000 tons of bombs. By the end of the war 23 members of the regiment, including Smirnova, were honored as Heroes of the Soviet Union.

After the war Smirnova applied for a job in civilian aviation, but after four years of combat duty her health had deteriorated so that she could not pass the medical exam.

Of her war experiences, Smirnova said: "There is an opinion about women in combat that a woman stops being a woman after bombing, destroying and killing; that she becomes crude and tough. This is not true; we all remained kind, compassionate, and loving. We became even more womanly, more caring of our children, our parents, and the land that has nourished us."

See also
586th Fighter Regiment, 587th Bomber Regiment, and 588th Night Bomber Regiment; Raskova, Marina
References
Noggle, *A Dance with Death: Soviet Airwomen in World War II* (1994)

Smith, Betsy Carroll

The first woman in the United States to earn her F-28 rating, Smith was born in 1952. Her first flying lesson was a gift from her uncle on her sixteenth birthday. She was so hooked that she took an after-school job to finance continued lessons.

After high school Smith attended Parks College of Aeronautics. In 1971, as a member of the college's flying team, Smith won the Top Female Pilot Award at the National Intercollegiate Flying Association's Air Meet. That was also the year Smith won a scholarship from the Beech Aircraft Corporation, whose president, Olive Ann Mellor Beech, was one of the first women to head an aviation company. In 1972 Smith became the first woman to receive a degree from the college.

Smith's first job in aviation was copiloting for a night freight company operating out of the Cleveland Airport in Ohio. When her applications for positions as a corporate pilot kept getting turned down, Smith decided to focus on academia. In 1974 she was hired as a flight and ground school instructor at Parks.

To keep her dream of becoming an airline pilot alive Smith entered Purdue University's Professional Pilot B.S. degree program, where she earned her rating on a Boeing 707. She graduated from the two-year program in 1979 and was hired by Altair Airlines as a copilot. In 1980 she was promoted to captain. When the company expanded their fleet with the new Fokker F-28s and qualified their pilots for them, Smith became the first woman in the United States to earn that rating.

When Altair went out of business in 1982 Smith joined People Express. In 1984 she became the first woman to pilot a Boeing 747 trans-Atlantic flight while with the company. When People Express was purchased by Continental Airlines in 1987 Smith moved back to flying cargo, taking a job as a Boeing 757 captain with United Parcel Service.

Of her early flying career Smith says: "As a teenage pilot I had no intention of flying for an airline, but wanted to pursue something more 'interesting' such as environmental research or perhaps even the space program, as I was an avid science fiction reader and was completely enthralled by the prospect of space exploration. My family has always supported me. I think probably because they are artists they put a very high value on the power of imagination. They always encouraged me to just dream anything."

See also
Beech, Olive Ann Mellor
References
Holden and Griffith, *Ladybirds II: The Continuing Story of American Women in Aviation* (1993)

Smith, Elinor Patricia

The first pilot to successfully maneuver a plane under all four New York City bridges, Smith was born in 1911 to two vaudeville performers. Her family made its home in Freeport, New York, later known as the Hollywood of the East Coast for the proliferation of actors, producers, and other people from the entertainment industry who built homes there.

In 1914 her father, Tom Smith, took the family to Europe, where he was touring as the scarecrow in a stage production of *The Wizard of Oz*. They were in Paris when Archduke Franz Ferdinand was assassinated, triggering the start of World War I. They escaped on the last ship to leave France before war was declared.

Her first plane ride, at the age of six, came as payment for helping her mother cook and serve for a summer's worth of dinner parties. She, her younger brother Joe, and her father took a $5 ride with Louis Gaubert, one of France's leading flyers of the day, who was spending his summer barnstorming in the United States. The Smith children spent the summer of 1917 begging rides with Gaubert, and once he let Smith help steer. On landing he told Smith's father that "she has the touch." Her father began hiring pilots to fly him to his performance dates, and it was with these men, at the age of ten, that Smith began taking informal flying lessons—along with the French, piano, and tap lessons provided by her mother.

She soloed at 15, and at the age of 16 Smith became the youngest pilot ever to receive a Fédération Aéronautique Internationale (FAI) license. Her license was signed by none other than Orville Wright. On the same day she received it she broke the world's light-plane altitude record by flying her father's Waco 9 biplane to a height of 11,874 feet. At 17 she became the first and only pilot ever to successfully maneuver a plane under all four New York City bridges, a stunt that resulted in a ten-day grounding by the mayor of New York and a storm of publicity. Soon she was hired by the local Waco plane distributor to demonstrate and deliver new purchases to their clients in the Northeast. She was even paid a wage equal to that of the male pilots who worked for the company.

She met Amelia Earhart as her guest at the Chicago Air Show in 1928. She was so inspired by the meeting that when she returned home she accepted the job of setting a solo endurance record for the Brunner Winkle Aircraft Corporation's newest Bird biplane. Viola Gentry had set the world's solo endurance record for women at 8 hours, 6 minutes in December of that year. Bobbi Trout increased it to 12 hours in the beginning of January 1929. On January 30, 1929, Smith beat them both, managing 13 hours, 16 minutes, 37 seconds in the air. Her record was quickly broken by Louise Thaden, however, so in April she found herself defending it. On April 24, 1929, she increased the world's solo endurance record for women to 26 hours, 23 minutes, 16 seconds.

Smith was hired by the Bellanca Company to take their new Pacemaker plane on a cross-country demonstration tour, culminating in an appearance at the first-ever Cleveland Air Races. There she was the pilot for the first mass parachute drop when seven parachutists jumped from her plane.

Smith was invited by Bobbi Trout to share the chores in trying for the first midflight refueling endurance record for women. In November 1929 they managed to stay in the air for 42 $\frac{1}{2}$ hours, landing only because their refueling plane had mechanical problems and could not return with a fourth load of fuel. The difficulties of the flight kept her from deciding to defend that record in the future. Instead, she took another offer from the Bellanca Company, this time to test their new high-altitude plane. Her experience and ability to attract press attention and the fact that she weighed less than most male test pilots of the day combined to make her an attractive candidate for the position.

On March 10, 1930, Smith spent 45 minutes aloft at an altitude above 25,000 feet, creating a new high-altitude record for women. Her fame and her family ties to the entertainment business combined in 1930 when NBC offered her a thrice-weekly aviation spot sponsored by the Daggett and Ramsdell cosmetics company. She broadcast on site from the airports at which she worked, interviewing her fellow aviators about their newest accomplishments.

She also began contributing articles to such magazines of the day as *Liberty* and *Vanity Fair*. She eventually became *Liberty*'s aviation editor. This finally gave her a stable income that allowed her to support and therefore further her aviation career. Smith took and passed the written and flight tests for her transport license in 1930, becoming the youngest woman to qualify for flying the widest variety of aircraft for both personal and professional reasons. However, her broadcasting career did also get in the way of her aviation goals. She was unable to compete in the Cleveland Air Races of 1930 because of a conflict in covering the event for NBC on the radio.

Smith was still only 19 in 1930 when she was voted the Best Woman Pilot in the United States, and her childhood hero, Jimmy Doolittle, was voted Best Male Pilot. Having reached the pinnacle of her dreams, Smith had no reservations about retiring.

Smith married and raised four children before returning to the aviation world in 1956. The U.S. Air Force invited her to speak to aviators and then invited her to participate in war games, training young flyers to carry paratroopers in C-119 jets. Her years of dropping parachuters in aviation shows came in handy for these maneuvers.

Of her time in the air, Smith said: "To some young women with dreams of a wider world, there seemed to be two paths to follow; one led to Hollywood, the other to a career in the sky. For me there was only one path: I knew from the age of six that I wanted to fly."

See also
Earhart, Amelia Mary; Gentry, Viola; Thaden, Louise McPhetridge; Trout, Evelyn "Bobbi"

References
Adams and Kimball, *Heroines of the Sky* (1942); Smith, *Aviatrix* (1981)

Smith, Joan Merriam

In 1964, at the same time that Geraldine Mock was doing her around-the-world flight, Smith flew solo around the world at the equator. It was the first time anyone had tried to fly around the world since Amelia Earhart's disappearance in 1937. Following Earhart's intended route, Smith completed the trip in 23 days.

In an article for the *Saturday Evening Post* Smith described the genesis of her dream: "When I was in high school, I would tell my friends and classmates that someday I was going to fly around the world just like Amelia Earhart. Everybody just laughed. They knew I was a baseball-playing tomboy, and this was a tomboy fantasy. But I knew that since Amelia disappeared in 1937, no other woman had attempted to fly around the world. This only heightened my ambition to be the first."

See also
Earhart, Amelia Mary; Mock, Geraldine "Jerrie" Frederitz
References
Cadogan, *Women with Wings: Female Flyers in Fact and Fiction* (1993); Merriam, "I Flew around the World Alone" (1964)

Smith, Margaret Chase

Considered the champion of legislation allowing women to serve in the military, Senator Chase was born on December 14, 1897, in Skowhegan, Maine. She was

Pilot Margaret Chase Smith, who succeeded her late husband, Clyde Smith, to the House of Representatives, was responsible for federal legislation admitting women to military service (June 10, 1940).

the first woman to serve in both the U.S. House of Representatives and in the Senate and the first to have her name placed into nomination for the presidency by a major political party.

Smith graduated from Skowhegan High School in 1916 and took a job teaching at a local country school. After a period working as an assistant to a phone company manager and as the office manager of a woolen mill, Smith met and married Clyde H. Smith in 1930. She entered politics when he ran for Congress, and she served as his executive secretary.

When he died in 1941 she won his congressional seat and kept it until 1949, when she won a seat in the Senate. Those were the years she was active in advancing pension benefits and recognition for women who had served in the Women's Airforce Service Pilots (WASPS) and Women Appointed for Volunteer Emergency Service (WAVES) during World War II.

In 1949 Smith became the first female Republican member of the Senate and the first woman elected to the Senate without having been appointed to fill a vacancy. In 1964 Smith ran for the presidential nomination of the Republican Party, coming in fifth in the New Hampshire primary election. She remained in the Senate until her retirement in 1972. She then spent her time lecturing at colleges.

Smith suffered a stroke and died on May 29, 1995, at her home in Skowhegan, Maine. Her stand on women in politics could be said to encompass women in all walks of life: "Women are people. They should expect office only on the basis of personal qualifications."

See also
Women Appointed for Volunteer Emergency Service (WAVES); Women's Airforce Service Pilots (WASPS)

References
Ebbert and Hall, *Crossed Currents: Navy Women from WWI to Tailhook* (1993); "The Lady from Maine Is Recognized: Margaret Chase Smith, Four-Term Senator from Maine Dead at 97" (1995)

Snook, Anita "Neta"

Most famous for teaching Amelia Earhart to fly, Snook was also the first woman to operate her own aviation business. She was born on February 14, 1896, in Mount Carroll, Illinois. As a child she was fascinated with the then-new invention, the automobile. Her father purchased one when she was nine, and together they learned how to maintain and repair the vehicle, a skill that would come in handy later in life. She was tutored at home in her other studies as well, until she attended the Frances Shimer Academy for music and dance. Then she attended Iowa State College, where she studied mechanical drawing and the repair of tractors and other farm machinery.

After two years of college Snook signed up for flying lessons from the Davenport Flying School in Davenport, Iowa, in June 1917. Before the lessons could begin the students had to successfully build their own plane. They soon finished the task, and on July 21, 1917, at the age of 21, Snook took her first flight. Unfortunately, the president of the school died in a plane crash that September, and the school closed.

Snook moved to Williamsburg, Virginia, in October 1917 to attend the Curtiss-Wright School where Eddie Stinson, brother of famous female pilots Katherine and Marjorie Stinson, was an instructor. Tuition there was higher than at the Davenport Flying School, so Snook did odd jobs for the instructors to earn extra flight time.

When the United States entered World War I all Curtiss School planes were grounded from flying in the area for fear that spies would sign on as students and take pictures of the local military bases from the planes. Snook and the school relocated to Miami, Florida, but before she could solo and qualify for her license the government banned all civilian flying across the country.

Snook took a job at the Willys Morrow factory in Elmira, New York. There she used what she had learned in ground school to inspect aircraft engines that were then sent to the British Air Ministry.

When the war ended in November 1918 Snook worked part time in a photography store to pay for the rest of her flight lessons. She experimented with building planes and soon knew all sides of the aviation business. Snook purchased a wrecked Canadian training plane, repaired it, and finally soloed. She received her private pilot's license on July 18, 1919. It did not permit her to fly passengers but, like many pilots of her day, she did. Snook spent the summer as a barnstormer, charging passengers $15 for 15 minutes of airtime. She also earned money flying demonstrations at local county fairs, beginning with the Mount Carroll, Illinois, fair, which paid Snook $1,000 for making two flights a day during the three-day fair.

In 1920 Snook moved to California and took a job at the Kinner Field Airport in Los Angeles. In exchange for being allowed to use the field to operate her own commercial flying business, offering flight instruction, passenger service, and aerial advertising, Snook flew test flights of other designers' experimental planes, including the Kinner Airster, designed by Bert Kinner, the owner of the field.

On January 3, 1921, Snook stepped into the history books when Earhart took her first lesson. Earhart's parents had been against their daughter learning to fly, but they gave permission on one condition: that Earhart find a female teacher.

On February 22, 1921, Snook entered a speed race at the first air meet organized by the Aero Club of California, which took place at the Beverly Hills Speedway. She came in fifth. On April 1, 1921, she attended a fly-in at the L. C. Brand Aerodrome in Glendale, California, where she met the first woman to qualify for a hydroplane license and the founder of Relief Wings, Ruth Rowland Nichols. Nichols was later instrumental in starting the Ninety-Nines with Earhart.

Snook's first crash was in the Kinner Airster as she was instructing Earhart on July 17, 1921. When the plane was repaired, Earhart bought it.

In December 1921 Snook was asked to use her previous knowledge of airplane building to assist in setting up the wing department at the Douglas Aircraft Company. In the spring of that year she married Bill Southern. After the birth of their first child, Snook sold her business and retired from flying. She used her profits to purchase farmland in the Santa Clara Valley.

Snook became a popular lecturer at schools and pilots' associations, speaking about her own career as well as about Earhart once the latter was lost at sea in 1937. She took her next flight as a passenger in a commercial plane in 1977 at the age of 81 and her last flight at the age of 95.

In her 1974 autobiography, *I Taught Amelia to Fly*, Snook traced her own love of flying to an experience she had at the age of four. Her family doctor often took his children and Snook on car rides over the hilly countryside. Snook recalled: "He'd race to the top of each and coast down the other side. We called it flying. It was a roller coaster sensation before we knew about roller coasters. I think that triggered my first interest in mechanical locomotion, as well as a desire to fly."

See also

SPARS

References
Holden and Griffith, *Ladybirds II: The Continuing Story of American Women in Aviation* (1993); Lovell, *The Sound of Wings: The Life of Amelia Earhart* (1989); Southern, *I Taught Amelia to Fly* (1974)

SPARS

The first women to serve in the Coast Guard did so as SPARS in World War II. The abbreviation comes from the Coast Guard motto: "Semper paratus—Always ready."

The equivalent to Women's Auxiliary Army Corps (WAACS), Women Appointed for Volunteer Emergency Service (WAVES), and Women's Airforce Service Pilots (WASPS), SPARS were the smallest women's military unit of the war.

The SPARS were created on November 23, 1942. To head the group, the WAVE commander, Mildred McAfee, suggested Captain Dorothy Stratton, who had trained as a WAVE. By special request of the commandant of the Coast Guard, Stratton resigned from the WAVES and accepted the post. Eleven other WAVES transferred to the SPARS upon graduation from officer training and formed the nucleus of the group.

Unlike members of the other branches of the military, SPARS were not required to have high school diplomas. Equivalent business experience could serve as well. Once accepted, the women trained in Palm Beach, Florida, and were then dispersed to specialized schools based on their abilities. Female officer candidates were permitted to train side by side with male officer candidates at the Coast Guard Academy in New London, Connecticut, which was one of the earliest coeducational opportunities in the U.S. military.

See also
McAfee, Mildred; Women Appointed for Volunteer Emergency Service (WAVES); Women's Airforce Service Pilots (WASPS)

References
Weatherford, *American Women's History: An A to Z of People, Places, Organizations, Issues, and Events* (1994)

Spicer, Dorothy

The first woman to hold all four ground engineer's licenses, Spicer was in the air taxi business with Pauline Gower in the years before World War II. Spicer, who was born circa 1910, learned to fly at Stag Lane, taking classes with Gower and Amy Johnson. She earned her flight school tuition working as a salesgirl in a department store in London, and she received her pilot's license in 1930. She spent the next year working six months at the Saunders-Roe Company on the Isle of Wight to learn aircraft construction and six more with the Napier Engineering Company in London to study engines.

She and Gower wanted to run their own joyriding business, and approached Johnson about joining their efforts. Johnson chose to focus on record-breaking flights, so in 1931 Spicer and Gower purchased their first plane and opened their business. They began by offering flights to tourists in and around Gower's hometown of Kent, England.

At the end of that first summer they were invited to attend the first British All-Women's Flying Meeting held at the Sywell Aerodrome in Northhampton, sponsored by the Duchess of Bedford.

Because of the weather, the team closed down their joyriding business for the winter. They did, however, fly passengers upon appointment around England during the winter to keep the plane in operation and for the extra money.

Spicer and Gower joined various air circuses in 1932 and 1933 for the chance to gain flying experience faster and for the larger crowds that such events drew. They ended up flying with the likes of Mary Petre and the Honorable Mrs. Victor Bruce and learning much about the business of running air meets.

In the winter of 1933 Spicer earned her engineer's B license after six months of studying at Spartan Aircraft. In 1934 and 1935 she and Gower were on their own again. They formed the Air Trips Ltd. company, giving joyrides out of a field near Hunstanton, England, which provided a steady stream of tourists as customers. But Spicer also made time to continue studying engineering. By June 1935 she had become the first woman to obtain all four engineering qualifications.

In the summer of 1936 the women joined Tom Campbell Black's Air Display, where Gower's plane was hit on takeoff by another plane performing a landing. She was hospitalized for a short time, and the experience ended her enthusiasm for air circuses.

The team split up, with Gower going off in 1938 to create the Women's Section of the British Air Transport Auxiliary (ATA). Spicer continued to run the air garage alone.

She married Dick Pierce, who was with the Civil Aviation Department of the Air Ministry. They died together in a crash in South America shortly after the war.

See also
Air Transport Auxiliary (ATA); Gower, Pauline; Johnson, Amy; Petre, Mary
References
Curtis, *The Forgotten Pilots: A Story of the Air Transport Auxiliary, 1939–45* (1971); Gower, with prologue by Spicer, *Women with Wings* (1938)

Stefanyshyn-Piper, Heidemarie

A naval diver and an astronaut candidate in the National Aeronautics and Space Administration (NASA) class of 1996, Stefanyshyn-Piper was born on February 7, 1963, in St. Paul, Minnesota. She graduated from Derham Hall High School there in 1980 and received a bachelor of science degree in mechanical engineering from the prestigious Massachusetts Institute of Technology (MIT) in 1984 and a master of science degree in mechanical engineering there in 1985.

Stefanyshyn-Piper then joined the U.S. Navy Reserve Officers' Training Corps (ROTC) Program at MIT in June 1985. She completed training at the Naval Diving and Salvage Training Center in Panama City, Florida, as a navy basic diving officer and salvage officer. Stefanyshyn-Piper completed several tours of duty as an engineering duty officer in ship maintenance and repair.

In September 1994 Stefanyshyn-Piper reported to the Naval Sea Systems Command as underwater ship husbandry operations officer for the supervisor of salvage and diving. In that capacity she advised fleet diving activities in the repair of naval vessels while at sea. Additionally she is a qualified and experienced salvage officer and has been involved in major salvage projects, including the development of a salvage plan for the Peruvian Navy salvage of the Peruvian submarine *Pacocha* and the de-stranding of the tanker *Exxon Houston*, off the coast of Barber's Point on the island of Oahu, Hawaii.

In 1996 she applied for and was chosen as an astronaut candidate by NASA and began two years of training, after which she will qualify as a mission specialist on a future space shuttle flight crew.

References
Biographical Data Sheets, Lyndon B. Johnson Space Center (1997)

Stephens College

The first college to offer a comprehensive program of classes in "air-mindedness" for women was Stephens College in Columbia, Missouri. Founded as a women's academy on August 24, 1833, it was christened Stephens College in 1870. Under the leadership of James Madison Wood from 1912 to 1947, Stephens became one of the first institutions to provide women with an educational program designed specifically to meet their needs.

The college began offering the aviation studies program in 1944. The program was developed in cooperation with the Army Air Force, the Civil Aeronautics Administration (CAA), and 12 different airlines hoping to train future employees. Classes included scheduling reservations, drafting aircraft designs, blueprint reading, and aircraft mechanics. Parental permission was required to participate in the aviation studies program.

Many graduates of Stephens went on to join the Women's Airforce Service Pilots (WASPS) in World War II and to work in the aviation industry in the postwar years. By the 1950s more than 1,000 women had graduated from the aviation courses, which were terminated when funding ran out in 1959.

Recruitment literature of the 1950s explained the classes simply by saying: "The purpose of aviation studies at Stephens is to develop attitudes based on the realities of the Air Age since students will be participants in a society using airplanes as the dominating force for world unity."

See also
Civil Aeronautics Administration; Women's Airforce Service Pilots (WASPS)
References
Douglas, *United States Women in Aviation, 1940–1985* (1990)

Still, Susan Leigh

A navy test pilot and one of the first female space shuttle pilots, Still was born on October 24, 1961, in Augusta, Georgia. Her family moved to Natick, Massachusetts, where she graduated from Wal-

Susan L. Still (1997)

nut Hill High School in 1979. She attended Embry-Riddle University, where she received a bachelor of science degree in aeronautical engineering in 1982. After graduation Still worked as a wind tunnel project officer for Lockheed Corporation in Marietta, Georgia, while working on her master of science degree in aerospace engineering, which she earned from the Georgia Institute of Technology in 1985.

Still joined the U.S. Navy in 1985. She was a distinguished naval graduate of Aviation Officer Candidate School. After becoming a distinguished graduate of the U.S. Naval Test Pilot School, Class 103, Still was designated a naval aviator in 1987. She was selected to be a flight instructor in the TA-4J Skyhawk. She later flew EA-6A Electric Intruders for Tactical Electronic Warfare Squadron 33 in Key West, Florida. After completing test pilot school she reported to Fighter Squadron 101 in Virginia Beach, Virginia, for F-14 Tomcat training. In the navy Still logged over 2,000 flight hours in more than 30 different aircraft.

In 1995 Still applied to and was accepted into the astronaut program at the National Aeronautics and Space Administration (NASA).

On her first flight, from April 4 to April 8, 1997, she piloted the *Columbia* space shuttle on mission STS-83, which was cut short because of problems with one of the shuttle's three fuel cell power-generation units.

Her second flight was longer. From July 1 to July 17, 1997, Still piloted the shuttle for mission STS-94, a reflight of the Microgravity Science Laboratory (MSL-1) Spacelab mission. It focused on materials and combustion science research in microgravity.

Regarding her ability to choose aviation as a career, Still has said: "All the women in my life were nurses, hairdressers or secretaries, and that's why I thought my father would not support my being a pilot. I can remember asking him, 'What would you think if I told you I wanted to be a pilot when I grow up?' expecting him to say no or disagree. He said, 'I think that would be fantastic.' Had he not said those words, I don't know what would have happened to me."

See also

Columbia Space Shuttle; National Aeronautics and Space Administration (NASA); U.S. Navy (USN)

References

Biographical Data Sheets, Lyndon B. Johnson Space Center (1997); Russo, *Women and Flight: Portraits of Contemporary Women Pilots* (1997)

Stinson, Katherine

The first woman to fly the mail, Stinson was also the first woman to own a flying school anywhere in the world and the fourth licensed female pilot in the United States. She was born in Alabama on Feb-ruary 14, 1891, and first went aloft in a balloon rather than an airplane. At the age of 16 she won a balloon trip in a raffle and enjoyed it. After reading about the grand salaries commanded by the stunt pilots of her day, Stinson decided to become one to help finance her music studies.

Stinson took flying lessons from a school run by Swedish pilot Max Lillie. During these lessons the two of them became infamous for being arrested for landing their plane in the middle of a public park filled with picnickers. Then Stinson's first solo flight ended in an emergency landing because of engine failure. Whether because she was intimidated by these events or because she was still so young, Stinson waited a year between receiving her license on July 12, 1912, and formally entering the aviation exhibition business.

In April 1913 Katherine and her mother entered the business with a bang. They created the Stinson Aviation Company to rent and sell planes. In May they acquired their first plane, a Wright B model that Lillie modified for Stinson's stunt-flying needs. She performed in air meets in Cincinnati, Ohio, and Columbus, Indiana. In September 1913, while Stinson was performing at a fairground in Helena, Montana, she also carried mail from the fairgrounds to the center of town on each of her four days there, thus becoming the first woman airmail pilot.

In 1915 the Stinson Aviation Company moved to a new operating site in San Antonio, Texas, where they were able to expand into the training business and employ two other family members. Katherine's sister, Marjorie Stinson, had since earned a license and became their chief instructor. Her brother, Eddie Stinson, joined as a mechanic and designer. He later became famous for designing the Stinson Detroiter, which was flown by such pilots as Ruth Elder.

Stinson became famous herself for the "dippy twist" loop, a variation of Ruth Law's loop-the-loop. In the "dippy twist" loop Stinson would hit the top of the vertical bank and do a wingover before continuing the loop. When a male pilot perfected night loop-the-loops, Stinson was not far behind in performing them. In December 1915 she traced the letters C-A-L in the sky, using magnesium flares, during her nighttime loop-the-loops. In June 1916 she performed as a guest of the Canadian government in return for the training her company had provided their military.

In 1917 Stinson toured the Orient, becoming the first woman to fly in either China or Japan, and performed for crowds as large as 25,000. She was such a popular figure among the children there that they formed youth clubs in her name and inundated her with fan mail, calling her the "Air Queen."

Stinson returned to the United States later that year, at the start of World War I. Like the other aviators of her day, Stinson volunteered for army flying service, but she was turned down because of her sex. Still determined to aid the war effort through flying, she undertook a flying tour to raise funds for the Red Cross. On June 24, 1917, she flew from Albany, New York, to Washington, D.C., on a fund drive that also served as a test run for her next challenge. Later that year, on December 11, 1917, Stinson broke Ruth Law's nonstop cross-country flight record, flying 610 miles between San Diego and San Francisco.

The Stinson Flying School aided the war effort by training Canadian pilots, as there was not yet any flying instruction available in Canada. These pilots were then able to join the Royal Air Force in England. Early in 1918 civilian flying was banned because of the war, so the Stinsons closed their school. Stinson went to Europe to drive ambulances for the Allies and had a chance to fly for the Red Cross.

In 1918 Stinson returned to North America, performing in stunt shows for the troops in Canada as well as flying another airmail route. The town of Edmonton declared Katherine Stinson Day when she arrived with their first load of mail from Calgary. A few weeks later Stinson applied to the U.S. Postal Service for a job as an airmail pilot. She had to fight for the position, but it was eventually granted. She flew from New York to Washington once and promptly quit. Whether she quit because the new planes operated with only one rudder (she had learned with two), because her flight had been treated as a race, or even because the Postal Service had assigned her an escort, she never said.

Late in the year she caught influenza during the flu pandemic. It turned into tuberculosis, which so damaged her health that she retired from flying completely at the age of 25 and became an award-winning architect. In 1928 Stinson married Judge Michael Otero Jr., who had served as an airman in World War I.

In 1969 Stinson received the Elder Statesman of Aviation Award from the National Aeronautic Association of the United States. She died in 1977.

When people asked her if she was afraid while flying, Stinson was fond of saying: "Fear, as I understand it, is simply due to lack of confidence or lack of knowledge—which is the same thing."

See also
Elder, Ruth; Law, Ruth; Stinson, Marjorie
References
Adams and Kimball, *Heroines of the Sky* (1942); Lomax, *Women of the Air* (1987); Moolman, *Women Aloft* (1981); Underwood, *The Stinsons: A Pictorial History* (1986)

Stinson, Marjorie

Known as "The Flying Schoolmarm," Marjorie Stinson was born in Alabama in 1896. She earned her license on August

Marjorie Stinson (ca. 1914–1918).

12, 1914, at age 18, making her the youngest licensed female pilot in the United States at that time. She was the ninth U.S. woman to win a license. Like her older sister, Katherine Stinson, Marjorie began as a stunt pilot with a debut at that year's Fall Fair in Brownwood, Texas.

In April 1913 her mother and sister had created the Stinson Aviation Company to rent and sell planes. In 1915 the company moved to a new operating site in San Antonio, Texas, where they were able to expand into the training business and employ Stinson as their chief instructor. Her brother, Eddie Stinson, joined as a mechanic and designer; he later became famous for designing the Stinson Detroiter, flown by Ruth Elder on her unsuccessful attempt to become the first woman to fly the Atlantic.

The Stinson Flying School aided the war effort by training Canadian pilots, as there was not yet any flying instruction available in Canada. These pilots were then able to join the Royal Air Force in England. Their first class graduated in November 1915. Before she was 22 Stinson had trained over 100 male pilots. As the war escalated civilian flying was banned, so the Stinsons closed their school and Katherine became an ambulance driver in Europe.

After their school closed Marjorie barnstormed county fairs, street circuses, and air meets until 1928. She quit flying in 1930 and went to work as a draftsperson for the Aeronautical Division of the U.S. Navy. Later she became a founding member of the Early Birds, a fraternity for "pilots who flew during the first decade of practical flight."

In 1968 Stinson received the Elder Statesman of Aviation Award from the National Aeronautic Association of the United States. She died in 1975 at age 79. Her ashes were scattered over Stinson Field in Texas from a 1931 Curtiss Pusher.

See also
Early Birds; Elder, Ruth; Law, Ruth; Stinson, Katherine
References
Lomax, *Women of the Air* (1987); Moolman, *Women Aloft* (1981); Underwood, *The Stinsons: A Pictorial History* (1986)

Sullivan, Kathryn

A member of the first National Aeronautics and Space Administration (NASA) group of female astronauts, at 26 Sullivan was also the youngest chosen. She became the first American woman to walk in space. Sullivan was born on October 3, 1951, in Paterson, New Jersey, but grew up in Woodland Hills, California. She graduated from Taft High School there in 1969 and received her bachelor of science degree in earth science from the University of California at Santa Cruz in 1973.

For her Ph.D. studies in geology Sullivan attended the Dalhousie University in Halifax, Nova Scotia, receiving her degree in 1978. In January of that year she applied to and was accepted as an astronaut candidate by the NASA space program.

From October 5 to October 13, 1984, Sullivan joined America's first woman in space, Sally Ride, for STS-41G, the thirteenth mission of the *Challenger* space shuttle. It was the first mission to have two female astronauts. As a mission specialist Sullivan became the third American woman in space and the first American woman to spacewalk. On October 11, 1984, she and Mission Specialist David Leestma tested a new satellite refueling technique outside the safety of the space shuttle. For this first, Sullivan was inducted into the International Space Hall of Fame along with Valentina Tereshkova, Sally Ride, and Svetlana Savitskaya in 1985. She was also appointed to President Ronald Reagan's National Commission on Space, which was entrusted with planning the next 25 years of civilian space activities.

Sullivan returned to space from April 24 to April 29, 1990, aboard the *Discovery* space shuttle for STS-31. As a mission specialist one of her duties was to help deploy the Hubble space telescope. Sullivan also helped operate the IMAX camera on this mission and performed a number of experiments involving protein crystal growth and polymer membrane processing.

For Sullivan's third mission, from May 24 to April 2, 1992, she served as payload commander in charge of the Atmospheric Laboratory for Applications and Science (ATLAS-1). The experiments aboard mission STS-45 included measuring atmospheric chemical and physical properties to increase our knowledge of our climate.

In 1992 Sullivan retired from NASA to become the chief scientist for the National Oceanic and Atmospheric Administration.

Before NASA chose which of the first class of female astronauts would actually become the first to go into space, Sullivan said: "I wouldn't mind being the first woman in space, but I think it might be even better to be the second one. Then I would be less famous and could return to the scientific work more quickly."

See also
Ride, Sally Kristen; Savitskaya, Svetlana; Tereshkova, Valentina Vladimirovna

References
Biographical Data Sheets, Lyndon B. Johnson Space Center (1997); Bond, *Heroes in Space: From Gagarin to Challenger* (1987); O'Connor, *Sally Ride and the New Astronauts: Scientists in Space* (1983)

Tailhook Sexual Harassment Scandal

The Tailhook sexual harassment scandal of 1991 brought down a navy admiral and brought to the attention of the U.S. public the rampant sexual harassment that female military personnel had been suffering for years.

Tailhook was the name for a convention organized by U.S. Navy and Marine Corps pilots. (A tailhook on an airplane is the hook that drops down and catches the arresting wires of an aircraft carrier, braking the plane before it can roll off the other end of the ship.)

In 1956 Tailhook members began meeting once a year in Mexico. In 1963 they began meeting in Las Vegas, Nevada, but were thrown out of a succession of hotels for causing excessive property damage, including throwing pianos off hotel roofs and tossing people from broken room windows into the pool.

To make the event more formal the navy began offering seminars for aviators in the mornings. These gave new recruits the chance to meet and talk with senior officials of the military. Individual squadrons or companies that catered to pilots would rent suites in the hotel and sponsor information sessions about their work as well.

When women were first trained as military pilots they too began attending Tailhook conventions for the chance to meet their superiors. In 1991, 83 women, some of them guests of the Hilton Hotel, many of them female pilots attending the convention, finally initiated a lawsuit against the navy for allowing the harassment to go on unchecked. This harassment was revealed to include "The Gauntlet," a line of male aviators through which women had to pass while having their clothing ripped off and their bodies groped. The most serious assault was

against a minor, who had been stripped naked and left in a corner, crying.

Lt. Paula Coughlin ran the Gauntlet while trying to meet up with another admiral's aide on the night of September 7, 1991. She reported the harassment to her superior, Rear Admiral Jack Snyder, the next morning, but he ignored it. She then took her complaint to the Bureau of Personnel. Nothing was done until a letter from the president of the Tailhook Association describing the severity of the Gauntlet and requesting restraint for next year's convention was leaked to the press in October of that year.

This reached the attention of the assistant secretary of the navy, Barbara Pope, who insisted that the navy conduct a full investigation. The nation's highest-ranking civilian female, Pope was the first female assistant secretary of the navy.

During the investigation into Coughlin's allegations she was invited to meet with President George Bush, a former naval aviator, at the White House on June 26, 1992. Even with his pressing the navy, eventually only two of the men who had participated in the Gauntlet were brought to trial, and each was found not guilty based on lack of evidence.

In the aftermath of the Tailhook scandal Coughlin was transferred from the Pax River Base and subjected to fierce attacks on her character. On February 7, 1994, Coughlin resigned from the navy. In her letter she stated that both the attack at Tailhook and the subsequent attacks on her character rendered her unable to serve effectively in the military.

On October 28, 1994, Coughlin won a civil lawsuit against the Hilton Hotel and was awarded $1.7 million in compensatory damages and $5 million in punitive damages.

See also

Coughlin, Paula; Hultgreen, Kara; U.S. Marine Corps (USMC); U.S. Navy (USN)

References

Vistica, *Fall from Glory: The Men Who Sank the U.S. Navy* (1995); Zimmerman, *Tailspin: Women at War in the Wake of Tailhook* (1995)

Tereshkova, Valentina Vladimirovna

The first woman in space, Tereshkova went up in the Soviet space capsule *Vostok 6*, 20 years before Sally Ride flew on the *Challenger*. Tereshkova was born in Maslennikovo, Russia, on March 6, 1937. Her father died in World War II, and Tereshkova and her two siblings were raised by their mother in Yaroslav, Russia. Tereshkova graduated from Girls High School No. 32 there in 1953.

The family's finances did not allow Tereshkova to attend college. Instead, she took correspondence classes in technology while working during the day in a textile factory. In 1958 she joined the Yaroslav Air Sports Club for recreation and took up parachuting as a sport, making her first jump on May 21, 1959. Tereshkova completed 126 jumps before she was 26.

In 1960 Tereshkova completed her degree in textile engineering. On August 6, 1961, the Soviet Union launched its second manned spaceflight, and Tereshkova took that opportunity to write to the Supreme Soviet and ask about the possibility that women might train as cosmonauts.

In fact the Supreme Soviet was at that time considering women and had decided that parachuting was a good background for women who wanted to be cosmonauts. Officials from the USSR Voluntary Society for the Promotion of the Army, Air Force, and Navy spread across the country to interview female parachutists. One came to Yaroslav to meet Tereshkova, who was then invited to undergo the same tests that Yuri Gagarin, the first man in space, had passed. Tereshkova passed the tests and joined the Soviet space team, along with three other female candidates, on March 2, 1962. She moved to Star City, Russia, to begin training. She was then made a junior lieutenant in the Soviet Air Force.

On June 16, 1963, Tereshkova became the first woman in space. Scientists studied the effects of space travel and G-forces on her anatomy as she orbited for 70 hours, 50 minutes with fellow cosmonaut Valery F. Bykovsky. When she returned to earth she was given a victory parade in Red Square and celebrated at a state dinner at the Kremlin.

Tereshkova's flight made her an instant celebrity in the Soviet Union, and that is exactly how the Soviet Space Agency employed her. It was 19 years before they assigned another woman, Svetlana Savitskaya, to a space mission. Tereshkova spent the rest of her career giving public speeches around the world about Soviet space technology; serving as deputy editor of the *Aviatisiya I Kosmonavtika*, an aviation journal; and teaching at the Yuri Gagarin Training Center for Cosmonauts.

When she married fellow cosmonaut Andrian Nikolayev on November 3, 1963, she was given away at the ceremony by Soviet Premier Nikita Khrushchev. In June 1964 she gave birth to a daughter, Yelena Nikolayev. It was also the year she received the Gold Space Medal from the Fédération Aéronautique Internationale.

Tereshkova was a member of the World Peace Council in 1966 and then spent time in politics as a member of the Yaroslavl Supreme Soviet in 1967. In 1968 she was elected president of the Soviet Women's Committee.

On May 31, 1969, Tereshkova graduated from the Zhukovsky Air Force Engineering Academy as an aerospace engineer. Her job as a cosmonaut had finally funded the education she had missed earlier in life. Tereshkova was elected to the presidium of the Supreme Soviet in 1974.

In 1985 she was inducted into the International Space Hall of Fame. Other honors bestowed upon her included being designated the Soviet representative to the UN Conference for International Women's Year in Mexico City in 1975, reaching the rank of deputy to the Supreme Soviet, and being voted president of the Soviet-Algerian Friendship Society.

In her speech accepting the presidency of the Soviet Women's Committee she discussed her goals: "The Soviet women have done me a great honor. I am proud of their trust and shall do everything in my power to strengthen the solidarity of the Soviet women and the women of the entire planet and their determination to work for peace, for the happiness of our children."

See also
Ride, Sally Kristen; Savitskaya, Svetlana
References
Bond, *Heroes in Space: From Gagarin to Challenger* (1987); Oberg, *Spacefarers of the 80's and 90's: The Next Thousand People in Space* (1985); Tereshkova, *It Is I, Sea Gull* (1975)

Thaden, Louise McPhetridge

The winner of the first Women's Air Derby and the only woman to hold three aviation records simultaneously (for altitude, endurance, and speed), Thaden was born in Bentonville, Arkansas, in 1905. At the age of 15 she entered the University of Arkansas and majored in journalism. Restless, she quit school after two years to take a job in Wichita, Kansas, selling building materials. While there she went to an airfield and fell in love with planes but feared the expense would never allow her to pursue this love. She returned to college and took a premed major.

In the fall of 1926 she was hired by Walter Beech as the assistant to the West Coast distributor of Travel Air airplanes in San Francisco. Thaden worked as a secretary by day and took flying lessons at night, winning her private pilot's license in 1927. With a plane borrowed from Travel Air she logged the hours needed for her transport license.

On December 7, 1928, Thaden set a new altitude record of 20,200 feet, beating Lady Sophie Heath's record of 16,438 feet. On March 16, 1929, she set a new flight endurance record of 22 hours, 3 minutes, 28 seconds in the air and became the fourth woman to receive a transport license in the United States. She met Herbert Thaden, an ex–army pilot, at the local airport and married him in Reno, Nevada, that year.

Thaden entered the first Women's Air Derby, an air race that began in Santa Monica, California, on August 18, 1929, and ended 2,800 miles away at the Municipal Airport in Cleveland, Ohio, on August 26, 1929. The first derby drew 20 contestants, including Thea Rasche of Germany; Jessie Miller of Australia; and Amelia Earhart, Phoebe Omlie, Ruth Nichols, Marvel Crosson, Pancho Barnes, Bobbi Trout, and Mae Haizlip of the United States. All contestants were required to carry a three-day supply of food and water and a parachute in case of emergency.

The only fatality in the first derby was Marvel Crosson, who experienced engine trouble and bailed out too low, as the use of parachutes was not yet perfected. Four others, including Pancho Barnes, were troubled by mechanical difficulties or accidents, leaving 15 women who completed the race. Louise Thaden came in first, Gladys O'Donnell second, and Amelia Earhart third. Thaden dedicated her Symbol of Flight Trophy to Crosson and sent it to Crosson's mother.

The women who met at that race, including Thaden, formed the nucleus of the first women's pilot organization, the Ninety-Nines. When her husband's job transferred him to Pittsburgh, Pennsylvania, Thaden went with him. Though she managed to continue to meet her obligation as national chairman of the Ninety-Nines she had no time or money for entering new air meets. Instead she took a job as the director of the Women's Division of the Penn School of Aviation. After a few months Thaden was offered the position of director of public relations for the Pittsburgh Aviation Industries Corporation.

Thaden had her first child in July 1930 in Pittsburgh. She was back behind the controls of a plane a week later. In 1931 the Thaden family moved to New Jersey and then in 1932 to Baltimore, Maryland.

There Thaden was invited by Frances Harrell Marsalis, an employee of the Curtiss Exhibition Team, to take part in a publicity stunt for the company. Thaden and Marsalis attempted to beat the current refueling endurance flight record, which had been set at 123 hours by Bobbi Trout. The event was being organized by Viola Gentry, the pilot who set the first women's endurance record sanctioned by the Fédération Aéronautique Internationale. They took to the air on August 14, 1932. Marsalis was struck by a mild attack of appendicitis while in flight but refused to land and lose the record. She spent a day packed in ice while Thaden flew and was able to fly again on their last day aloft.

Despite the appendicitis, a fierce storm, and a faulty oil gauge, Thaden and Marsalis spent 73 more hours in flight than Trout did. For this feat they were celebrated at a dinner held at the White House with President Herbert Hoover.

In 1933 Thaden had her second child. In 1935 she joined Phoebe Omlie in the Bureau of Air Commerce's campaign for air marking. The Air Marking Division negotiated with farmers and small towns to have the town's name painted on top of the highest buildings and barns for flyers to use in navigation instead of following railroad tracks. Thaden was assigned the western part of the United States because she had worked in San Francisco.

On July 12, 1936, Thaden borrowed a 90-horsepower plane and set a new speed record of 109 miles per hour for planes of that class. On September 4, 1936, she and copilot Blanche Noyes became the first female team to win the Bendix Transcontinental Air Race against male competition. Laura Ingalls was second to arrive, and Amelia Earhart and Helen Richey placed fifth that year. Thaden's and Noyes's plane was once again a loaner from Thaden's former employer at Travel Air, Walter Beech. He and his wife, Olive Ann Mellor Beech, had formed their own company and thought the race would be a good way to advertise it. After the race, Thaden joined the Beech Aircraft Company as a demonstrator of biplanes.

For her aviation efforts Thaden won the 1936 Harmon Trophy for Outstanding Aviator. In 1937 she ceased flying full time as a career in order to concentrate on her growing children. During World War II she volunteered to train pilots for the Civil Air Patrol (CAP), and after the war she flew search-and-rescue missions for them. Thaden also volunteered with Ruth Nichols's Relief Wings and officiated at several major air races.

She continued in aviation by working with her husband at the Thaden Engineering Company, founded in Roanoke, Virginia, which manufactured and tested flight equipment for the navy. Upon her husband's death in 1969 Thaden took over his duties as well, until she died of a heart attack on November 9, 1979.

In her autobiography Thaden described the early years of aviation: "There was a time, long ago, when we flew along a fringe of dreams not yet born. We knew the ecstasy of discovery. Adventure was a part of every flight, spine-tingling, inspiring. Only the unbounded sky and the ever far horizon presented by an infant aviation industry limited individual challenges."

See also
Beech, Olive Ann Mellor; Bureau of Air Commerce; Gentry, Viola; Heath, Lady Sophie Mary; Marsalis, Frances Harrell; Nichols, Ruth Rowland; Ninety-Nines; Omlie, Phoebe Fairgrave; Relief Wings, Inc.; Trout, Evelyn "Bobbi"
References
Adams and Kimball, *Heroines of the Sky* (1942); Thaden, *High, Wide, and Frightened* (1973)

Thible, Elisabeth

The "world's first female aeronaut," Thible was the first woman to ascend in an untethered fire balloon (also known as a hydrogen air balloon). She made the ascent on June 4, 1784, watched by a crowd that included the King of Sweden, who preferred to remain on the ground.

The flight, which took place just outside of Lyon, France, was arranged by the French painter Fleurant, who was the copilot. The two ascended in a balloon designed by the Montgolfier brothers in 1783.

On Thible's flight the balloon rose to the height of a mile above ground, where the temperature dropped to 43 degrees Fahrenheit. Thible and her pilot stayed airborne for just over half an hour, land-

ing eight miles from Lyon. Upon landing Thible sang an aria as a present to her copilot as thanks for the trip.

References
Holden and Griffith, *Ladybirds II: The Continuing Story of American Women in Aviation* (1993); May, *Women in Aeronautics* (1962)

Thornton, Kathryn C.

One of the few American women to have performed a spacewalk, Thornton was born on August 17, 1952, in Montgomery, Alabama. She graduated from Sidney Lanier High School there in 1970 and received a bachelor of science degree in physics from Auburn University in 1974. She went to the University of Virginia for a master of science degree in physics in 1977 and a doctorate of philosophy in physics in 1979.

Thornton was then awarded a one-year NATO Postdoctoral Fellowship to continue her research at the Max Planck Institute for Nuclear Physics in Heidelberg, West Germany. When she returned to the United States Thornton worked as a physicist at the U.S. Army Foreign Science and Technology Center in Charlottesville, Virginia, until she applied and was accepted for astronaut training by the National Aeronautics and Space Administration (NASA) in May 1984.

Thornton's first flight was as a mission specialist on the crew of the *Discovery* space shuttle for STS-33. From November 22 to November 27, 1989, she was in charge of the Department of Defense payloads and the other secondary payloads.

For her second flight, from May 7 to May 16, 1992, Thornton served on the crew of STS-49. It was the maiden flight of the new *Endeavor* space shuttle, considered a symbol of NASA's return to full operations after the explosion of the *Challenger* space shuttle in 1986. Thorn-

Kathryn C. Thornton (1984)

ton made her first spacewalk on this mission, where she demonstrated and evaluated numerous extravehicular tasks to be used for the future assembly of the space station *Freedom*. Other duties included retrieving, repairing, and redeploying the International Telecommunications Satellite (INTELSAT).

Thornton took her second and third spacewalks on her third flight, as a mission specialist aboard the *Endeavor* space shuttle. This mission, STS-61, was designed to service and repair the Hubble space telescope. From December 2 to December 13, 1993, the crew of *Endeavor* captured and restored the Hubble to full capacity. Despite problems with her spacesuit, Thornton and fellow spacewalker Tom Akers replaced the telescope's two solar arrays, which provide power to the telescope, during their first spacewalk of the mission. On the second one, they replaced the Hubble's High Speed Photometer with a Corrective Optics Space Telescope Axial Replacement system. The unit corrected the spherical aberration of the main mirror for all instruments on board the Hubble.

Thornton was promoted to payload commander for the second U.S. microgravity laboratory mission from October 20 to November 5, 1995. Mission STS-73 took place on board the *Columbia* space shuttle and focused on materials science, biotechnology, combustion science, the physics of fluids, and numerous scientific experiments housed in the pressurized Spacelab module.

Between spaceflights Thornton's technical assignments have included working with flight software verification in the Shuttle Avionics Integration Laboratory and serving as a team member of the Vehicle Integration Test Team and as a spacecraft communicator (CAPCOM).

In August 1996 Thornton left NASA to join the faculty of her alma mater, the University of Virginia.

See also
Challenger Space Shuttle; *Endeavor* Space Shuttle
References
Biographical Data Sheets, Lyndon B. Johnson Space Center (1996)

Tiburzi, Bonnie Linda

The first American female pilot to be hired as a pilot for a major airline, Tiburzi was born on August 31, 1948, and grew up in Connecticut. Her father was an airline pilot who retired and began his own small commuter airline between Danbury and New York City. The whole family worked in the business, so Tiburzi's first job in aviation was selling tickets and servicing planes for her father's airline at the age of 14.

The business failed, however, before Tiburzi was old enough to formally take lessons from her father and solo. The family moved to Florida, where Tiburzi attended high school in Pompano Beach, graduating in 1967. Her high school guidance counselor had told her she could not grow up to be an airline pilot as

Bonnie Linda Tiburzi, at the age of 24, became the first female pilot of a major passenger airline, American Airlines (June 4, 1973).

the airlines were not hiring women at that time. Since there was no other career Tiburzi felt like pursuing, she spent a year in Europe working as an au pair and even filming some commercials to earn some money and see the world.

In December 1968 Tiburzi returned to Florida and began taking flying lessons. It took Tiburzi eight months to amass the 40 hours she needed to obtain her private pilot's license. The 200 hours required for the commercial pilot's license were harder. Tiburzi ferried planes on return flights all over Florida for Pompano Aviation, a small local charter company.

In 1970 Tiburzi went back to Europe and was hired by Publi-Air in Brussels. Her job was to sell U.S. companies on using Publi-Air for their business travel. She was given the opportunity to copilot the flights she arranged, which saved the company a salary and allowed Tiburzi to accumulate flight time. Through a similar barter system she also arranged free time in a flight simulator by offering English lessons to the owner's wife.

In 1971 Tiburzi returned to Florida, passed her commercial pilot's license test in February, and gained her instructor's permit a month later. She then worked as a ferry pilot and flight instructor for local aviation companies, delivering and collecting planes from servicing stations and then taking students up in them for lessons. She continued bartering for flight time and lessons on larger and larger aircraft to make herself fully qualified for the major airlines.

Tiburzi applied to all the major airlines in the United States for a position as pilot. In February 1973 American Airlines called her in for an interview. There were 15,000 applicants for the 214 positions available. At the age of 24, Tiburzi was both the youngest and the first woman ever hired by a major airline.

Tiburzi began training on March 30, 1973, and earned her wings with American Airlines on June 4, 1973. She was posted first, as was policy for all new pilots, as a flight engineer on a Boeing 727 based in New York City. Her responsibilities included checking all the mechanical systems of the plane before all flights, and she had to be capable of flying the plane in an emergency.

Tiburzi passed her first year's probation only to be furloughed in December when the airline found themselves overstaffed. Last hired, first fired was the policy, and Tiburzi and her class were the last hired that year. While she was on furlough she married a fellow American Airlines pilot and old family friend on April 20, 1974. While waiting to be recalled to American, Tiburzi took a job as a flight operations engineer for the CF-6 engines built by General Electric. Then she worked as a flight instructor at various airports.

In May 1976 American recalled Tiburzi and the other members of her furloughed group to full-time work. Tiburzi was first based out of Boston, and in January 1979 she received a transfer back to New York. On July 27, 1979, Tiburzi was made a copilot.

In her 1984 autobiography Tiburzi summed up the romance of modern flying when she wrote: "Many famous flyers have written about the joy and the wonder of flight in days long gone. Charles and Anne Lindbergh, Antoine de Saint-Exupéry, Amelia Earhart—these people lived, breathed and spoke the language of flying and knew the blessed immensity of the sky before it was mapped by jet trails. Nothing can match what they experienced. But don't let anybody kid you. Flying is still magic. Flying jets is exhilarating. It may not be as much of a thrill in the passenger seat, but up front, where the action is, the airplane is a marvelous man-made bird

soaring through an element that man started to explore only this century."

References

Briggs, *At the Controls: Women in Aviation* (1991); Tiburzi, *Takeoff! The Story of America's First Woman Pilot for a Major Airline* (1984); Yount, *American Profiles: Women Aviators* (1995)

Tier, Nancy Hopkins

An early pioneer of aviation, Tier was born in 1909 and earned her pilot's license in 1930; it was signed by Orville Wright. She was also a charter member of the Ninety-Nines. In 1930 Tier started her career as a sales representative for the Viking Flying Boat Company, whose airplanes she flew in competitions around the country for the sake of publicity. Her first big job for the company was flying the 5,000-mile Ford Reliability Tour, which was followed closely by the 2,000-mile Women's Dixie Derby.

In 1931 Tier was named the Connecticut Speed Champion of the Year. She continued breaking racing records until the outbreak of World War II, when she joined the Civil Air Patrol (CAP). In her 18-year career with the group Tier had the distinction of becoming the first female wing commander and the first female major. Eventually she became a member of the CAP's National Advisory Staff.

In 1969 Tier joined the official board organized by the Ninety-Nines to create the International Women's Air and Space Museum (IWASM) in Dayton, Ohio. In 1976 Tier was named New England's Woman of the Year, and in 1981 she was honored by the Civil Air Patrol for her outstanding service. She became the IWASM's first president when it opened in March 1986.

See also
Civil Air Patrol (CAP); International Women's Air and Space Museum; Ninety-Nines

References
Holden and Griffith, *Ladybirds II: The Continuing Story of American Women in Aviation* (1993)

Todd, E. Lillian

The first woman to design a plane, Todd began working when the Wright Brothers and Glen Curtiss were the only competition. In December 1906 Todd presented her first plane at the Aero Club of America's yearly exhibition. It included fans that directed air to the two propellers and pneumatic wheels to cushion the landings. No engine had been found that would fit into the aerodynamic design of her plane, so it functioned more as a glider.

No investors could be found for the project, so Todd earned money teaching young men to design and build models.

References
Adams and Kimball, *Heroines of the Sky* (1942); Oakes, *United States Women in Aviation through World War I* (1978)

Tonkin, Lois Coots

The first woman to earn a meteorology scholarship from the Civil Aeronautics Authority, Tonkin was one of the first female meteorologists in the United States. Born in West Virginia, Tonkin studied for her medical license at Marietta College in Ohio.

After taking her first plane ride with another student, Tonkin promptly quit medicine and signed up for the college's Civilian Pilot Training Program. She earned her pilot's licenses and instructor's permit and followed her trainer, Lenore Harper McElroy, to a flight instructor's post at Detroit's Hartung Field. Her classes included meteorology and navigation.

In 1940, when the country was facing a manpower shortage because of the impending war, five universities opened up eight-month programs leading to meteorology degrees to female candidates. These women had to meet the previous male requirements, which were a private pilot's license and a four-year college degree that included a year each of calculus and physics. When Tonkin's former physics teacher informed her of the opportunity, Tonkin signed up for the eight-month program at New York State University. She was the only woman in a class of 200 military men.

After completing the course Tonkin was offered a job at the government weather bureau in Washington, D.C. Her duties included plotting and charting weather maps, studying cloud formations, and helping to recruit other women for the department. This required a six-week recruiting tour of the Midwest, where Tonkin spoke at many colleges encouraging women to enter the field of meteorology. She then became the assistant chief of the training division. While in Washington, D.C., she met and married another meteorologist, Lieutenant Henry Tonkin, who spent the war forecasting weather in England. Lois transferred to the Detroit Airport in 1943.

Regarding her position as the first woman meteorologist in the bureau, Tonkin said: "Once the initial prejudice against women ran its course, nary a complaint was heard from any of our male associates. As a matter of fact, they were soon asking for more women to do the same type of the work."

References
Knapp, *New Wings for Women* (1946)

Tribe, Mary Du Caurroy

See du Caurroy, Mary Tribe, Duchess of Bedford

Trout, Evelyn "Bobbi"

A record-setting pilot and accomplished airplane mechanic in the early days of aviation, Trout was born in Greenup, Illinois, on January 7, 1906. During her high school years her parents' marital problems meant that Bobbi and her brother lived with a variety of relatives in various cities before finally settling in Los Angeles with their father in the spring of 1920. Their mother rejoined them in 1921. Bobbi then ran a service station in partnership with her mother. One of her customers owned his own airplane and took Trout for her first ride on December 27, 1922.

She graduated from Roosevelt High School in Los Angeles, California, in 1926 and began studying architecture at the University of Southern California. There she gained her nickname "Bobbi" from the new haircut of the day, the bob. Family troubles forced her to leave college to work in the service station full time. But slowly she saved enough money to take her beloved flight lessons.

Trout studied flying at the Budett Air Lines School of Aviation in Los Angeles. On March 15, 1928, she survived her first crash. Trout bought a safer plane and continued her lessons, soloing and earning her pilot's license on April 30, 1928. To support her flying Trout earned money by renting her plane to be part of a display at the May Company Department Store.

This led to a job demonstrating Golden Eagle monoplanes to potential customers across the country for the R. O. Bone Company. She was also required to serve as her own mechanic, maintaining everything from the engine to the fabric covering the wings. On December 14, 1928, she won first place with one of their planes in an air race at the dedication of the Los Angeles Metropolitan Airport (now Van Nuys Airport).

On January 2, 1929, Trout used the Golden Eagle to break the women's solo endurance record recently set at 8 hours by Viola Gentry. Trout managed 12 hours, 11 minutes and gained her first record. Elinor Smith beat it by one hour on January 31, so Trout went back up on February 10, 1929; she regained her record by staying in the air for 17 hours, 24 minutes. That flight also gained her records for the first all-night flight for a woman, the most miles covered by a 60-horsepower engine, and the heaviest fuel takeoff to date.

At the opening of the Glendale Grand Central Airport on February 22, 1929, Trout took third place in the women's pylon races, with Pancho Barnes taking first. On June 16 she broke the women's altitude record by flying at a height of 15,200 feet.

Trout visited Barnes at her California home before the start of the first Women's Air Derby on August 18, 1929, where the two women would again compete. Neither did well at the race because of technical malfunctions and possible sabotage. Trout's motor stalled, and she was forced down in northern Mexico on the second day of the race. Investigators discovered that an altitude adjustment on her engine had been tampered with before the race. After repairs she returned to the race, but two days later her engine stalled again, and this delay cost her the race.

This first derby gathered together many of the working female pilots of the time, and one outcome of that was the creation of the Ninety-Nines. Trout was a charter member of this first organization for women "dedicated to the improvement of women's opportunities in aviation."

Trout's next successful record attempt was again for endurance. But to stay up long enough to beat her own and others' previous times required midair refueling and a copilot. Trout chose her former competitor, Elinor Smith. After several practice runs they took off on November 27, 1929. They stayed airborne for 42 hours, 3.5 minutes. The flight not only set an endurance record but was also the first refueling endurance record ever attempted by a female team.

Trout's next first-place trophy came from winning the Women's Air Race at the opening of the Burbank Airport in May 1930. And on January 4, 1931, she challenged her own refueling endurance record with copilot Edna May Cooper. This time they stayed aloft for 172 hours, 50 minutes.

In May 1931 Trout began earning side money as an aviation editor, and in July she hired on as a flight instructor for the Cycloplane Company Ltd. in Los Angeles. Many of her students were female, and many of those went on to join the Women's Airforce Service Pilots (WASPS) during World War II.

Trout joined one of several emergency aid groups, the Women's Air Reserve (WAR), which was founded by her friend Pancho Barnes in October 1931. The members studied first aid and practiced to be available during state emergencies to pilot doctors and supplies to disaster sites. Due to Barnes's interest in all things military, the group wore uniforms, practiced marching, and were assigned military titles. Trout reached the rank of captain during her time in WAR.

On August 31, 1934, five pilots, including Barnes and Trout, made a cross-country flight from Los Angeles to New York to attract new members to WAR. They spent two months on the East Coast visiting government officials and returned to Los Angeles in October. As a member of WAR, Trout was one of five given honorary aero policewoman badges by the Los Angeles Police Department to fly air support over the city if necessary. The city was never in need of air support, but the badge allowed Trout to do target practice at the Police Academy.

Trout spent most of 1932 collecting advertisers for a planned flight that would make her the first woman to fly from Los Angeles to Honolulu. She was not able to attract enough funding, and Amelia Earhart became the first woman to make the flight, in 1935.

In 1938 Trout started the Aero Reclaiming Company, a rivet-separating business, and with customers like Douglas Aircraft she managed to make good money and discovered a knack for inventing. In 1943 she sold the business to her partner in order to join the Civil Air Patrol (CAP) and help train male flyers for World War II. Trout found she missed business, however, and entered into a partnership to run the Deburring Service, which smoothed out metal parts for use on airplanes. Then she invented and manufactured a plastic container for eggs to replace the flimsier cardboard ones.

Trout and her partner in CAP, Pat Lewis, started a research-and-development company where they worked on streamlining remote-control rearview mirrors for cars. She later opened a real estate and mutual funds office in Palm Springs, California. She retired in 1976. She spent much of her time lecturing about the early days of aviation and videotaping interviews with other pioneers for museums and historians. In 1976 Trout was named Woman of the Year by the OX5 Aviation Pioneers, a group named for the Curtiss OX5 engine that powered early planes.

In 1979 Trout dropped the flag for the contestants in the fiftieth anniversary race of the Women's Air Derby. She took her last flight on February 11, 1984, to celebrate the fifty-fifth anniversary of being the first woman to fly all night.

On January 18, 1996, Trout was the first woman to receive the Howard Hughes Memorial Award from the Aero Club of Southern California. In celebration of the award and of her ninetieth birthday, she was taken on a helicopter ride over Los Angeles by the police department in memory of her service to them in World War II.

References
Holden and Griffith, *Ladybirds II: The Continuing Story of American Women in Aviation* (1993); Veca and Mazzio, *Just Plane Crazy: Biography of Bobbi Trout* (1987)

U.S. Air Force (USAF)

The U.S. Air Force first allowed female pilots in flight training in 1976 and graduated their first class in 1977. The first female officer's candidates graduated the U.S. Air Force Academy on May 28, 1980, with Lieutenant Kathleen Conly the highest-ranked woman, coming in eighth in her class.

In 1993 First Lieutenant Jeanne Flynn was the first woman selected for combat pilot training, which she completed on February 10, 1994.

On May 1, 1996, the fraternization rules were upgraded to state that it was against air force policy to have any kind of relationship (whether platonic or sexual) with any enlisted person inside or outside one's chain of command. Until then a relationship with an enlisted person outside one's chain of command was acceptable. This new policy was crucial to the case of Lieutenant Kelly Flinn, the first female B-52 pilot, who, on November 24, 1996, was accused of adultery, fraternization, and conduct unbecoming an officer for having entered into an affair with the husband of an enlisted woman on her base.

Rather than face a prison term Flinn resigned from the air force on May 28, 1997. Her case caused such turmoil within the highest ranks of the air force that the first female secretary of the air force, Dr. Sheila Widnall, resigned as well.

See also
Flinn, Kelly; Widnall, Sheila E.
References
Boyne, *Beyond the Wild Blue: A History of the U.S. Air Force, 1947–1997* (1997); Ebbert and Hall, *Crossed Currents: Navy Women from WWI to Tailhook* (1993); Holm, *Women in the Military: An Unfinished Revolution* (1982)

U.S. Army

In 1915 Tiny Broadwick, the first woman to make a parachute jump from a plane, became both the first woman and the first person to demonstrate parachutes to the U.S. Army.

At the outbreak of World War I female barnstorming pilots like Alys McKey Bryant, Katherine Stinson, and Ruth Law applied to the Army Air Service as pilots but were rejected on the basis of gender. Many of these women were still able to use their aviation skills to contribute to the war effort by flying fundraising drives for the Red Cross.

At the start of World War II the army was willing to accept female pilots as instructors. In 1940 Helen Richey signed on as the first woman pilot instructor for the U.S. Army Air Force. The only other way women were allowed to fly was as flying nurses. In 1942 Ellen Church entered the Air Evacuation Service of the Army Nurse Corps and became an instructor in flight nursing at the Army Air Force School of Aviation.

In 1938 Teddy Kenyon, a female test pilot for the Sperry Instrument Company, was one of the first women to fly before military officials when she demonstrated the automatic pilot device for the army.

The first group of militarily sanctioned female pilots in the United States was the Women's Auxiliary Ferrying Squadron (WAFS)/Women's Airforce Service Pilots (WASPS) of World War II. These groups were brought about by the energetic and enthusiastic work of two dedicated female pilots, Jacqueline Cochran and Nancy Harkness Love. The program began under Love's direction as the Women's Auxiliary Ferrying Squadron (WAFS) on Thursday, September 10, 1942. Licensed female pilots with two letters of recommendation, high school degrees, and 500 hours of logged flying time were recruited.

Meanwhile Cochran became director of the Women's Flying Training Detachment (WFTD), a group organized to train novice women pilots to fulfill the WAFS' requirements. In July 1943 the Pentagon combined the WAFS and WFTD and renamed them Women's Airforce Service Pilots (WASPS). To support their efforts, Walt Disney created Fifinella, a female gremlin mascot for the group.

On December 20, 1944, when the war in Europe seemed to be going well for the Allies, the WASP program was deactivated. In the end, there were 1,074 female pilots in the WASP program and 38 fatalities.

Women were not heard of much in the army again until 1974, the first year the army accepted women to flight school. In the first class to mix male and female students, the army trained its first female pilot. The only woman among 24 men, Sally Murphy received her wings on June 4, 1974.

In 1975 Rose Loper became the first woman to graduate with honors from the U.S. Army Flight School, and in November 1979 Marcella Hayes became the first African American woman to graduate from the U.S. Army Aviation School.

See also
Broadwick, Georgia "Tiny"; Bryant, Alys McKey; Church, Ellen; Kenyon, Cecil "Teddy"; Law, Ruth; Stinson, Katherine
References
Boyne, *Beyond the Wild Blue: A History of the U.S. Air Force, 1947–1997* (1997); Ebbert and Hall, *Crossed Currents: Navy Women from WWI to Tailhook* (1993); Holm, *Women in the Military: An Unfinished Revolution* (1982)

U.S. Coast Guard (USCG)

Considering their motto, "Semper paratus—Always ready," it makes sense that the U.S. Coast Guard (USCG) provided women one of the earliest coeducational opportunities in the military. The SPARS of World War II were the first women to serve in the USCG. They were the smallest military group of women, and it was not considered worth the expense to create a new academy for them. Therefore female officer candidates trained side by side with male officer candidates at the Coast Guard Academy in New London, Connecticut.

The SPARS were created on November 23, 1942. To head the group, the commander of the Women Appointed for Volunteer Emergency Service (WAVES), Mildred McAfee, suggested Captain Dorothy Stratton, who had trained as a WAVE. By special request of the commandant of the Coast Guard Stratton resigned from the WAVES and accepted the post. Eleven other WAVES transferred to the SPARS upon graduation from officer training, forming the nucleus of the group.

Women appeared in the Coast Guard again in July 1976, when they were admitted to the Coast Guard Academy when there was no war threatening. It was the first military academy to open its doors to women.

In April 1979 the first woman was assigned command of a USCG cutter.

See also
McAfee, Mildred; SPARS; Women Appointed for Volunteer Emergency Service (WAVES)
References
Ebbert and Hall, *Crossed Currents: Navy Women from WWI to Tailhook* (1993); Holm, *Women in the Military: An Unfinished Revolution* (1982)

U.S. Marine Corps (USMC)

The first female aviator in the U.S. Marine Corps was Sarah Deal. Deal had trained as an air traffic controller, since women were banned from combat flying. In April 1993 the secretary of defense lifted that ban, and Deal immediately applied to flight school. On September 26, 1995, Deal, then a first lieutenant, completed her final flight hour at Marine Helicopter Training Squadron 302 and earned her wings.

See also
Deal, Sarah
References
Ebbert and Hall, *Crossed Currents: Navy Women from WWI to Tailhook* (1993); Holm, *Women in the Military: An Unfinished Revolution* (1982)

U.S. Marine Corps Women's Reserve (MCWR)

Established in February 1943, the U.S. Marine Corps Women's Reserve (MCWR) was a sister program to the army's Women's Airforce Service Pilots (WASPS) and the navy's Women Appointed for Volunteer Emergency Service (WAVES). They provided female recruits for noncombat roles in the Marines to free up the men for combat duty.

The first director of the MCWR was Major Ruth Streeter.

See also
Women Appointed for Volunteer Emergency Service (WAVES); Women's Airforce Service Pilots (WASPS)

References
Ebbert and Hall, *Crossed Currents: Navy Women from WWI to Tailhook* (1993); Holm, *Women in the Military: An Unfinished Revolution* (1982)

U.S. Navy (USN)

The first women to serve in the U.S. Navy (USN) did so in World War I, but not yet as pilots. In 1916 Secretary of the Navy Josephus Daniels needed more recruits to work in the clerical departments. He checked with the navy's legal advisers and learned that there was no law barring women from enlisting. On March 19, 1917, the navy first authorized the recruitment of women. By the end of World War I there were 11,275 female yeomen in the USN. As the war progressed their jobs had expanded to include fingerprint experts, camouflage designers, translators, and draftsmen.

At the start of World War II Congresswoman Edith Nourse Rogers proposed a new group of militarily sanctioned female pilots in the navy. To support her idea Rogers offered a proposal created by Captain Joy Bright Hancock from the Bureau of Aeronautics outlining the ways women could help. The Women Appointed for Volunteer Emergency Service (WAVES) was created by act of Congress on July 30, 1942.

A debate quickly ensued as to whether WAVES would be an auxiliary branch of the navy or whether they should be integrated as true military personnel. First Lady Eleanor Roosevelt was for true integration, and after long discussions with President Roosevelt she succeeded in winning him to her side. Mildred McAfee was appointed the WAVES' first director, with Hancock as women's representative to the chief of the Bureau of Aeronautics, which put her in charge of all WAVES assigned to that organization.

Originally recruited to again fill clerical voids in the navy, the WAVES were never intended to fly aircraft. However, they soon proved their usefulness in naval aviation positions involving air traffic control, engineering, celestial navigation, and both gunnery and flight instruction. Two thousand women were assigned to naval aviation duties during the course of the war.

Though McAfee petitioned from the very beginning to include black women in the ranks of the WAVES, it was not until December 22, 1944, that the first two black female WAVES, Harriet Ida Pickens and Frances Wills, graduated from training.

After the Japanese surrendered, demobilization was mandated by law so that soldiers could return to their prewar occupations. The WAVES had been so well integrated into the navy that, rather than discharge them all, the navy simply discontinued the training of new female recruits. There were 5,500 WAVES who stayed with the navy, 2,000 of whom joined the reserves.

The first female navy pilots were noncombat pilots, and they began training nearly 30 years later, in 1974. They were Judith Neuffer, Barbara Allen Rainey, Rosemary Conaster Mariner, Jane Skiles O'Dea, Anna Scott Fuquoa, and Jo Ellen Drag Oslund. On February 22 of that year the navy became the first service to graduate a female pilot, Rainey. In 1979 the Naval Flight Officer program was opened to women, as was the jet-training program in 1981.

In 1982 Lieutenant Colleen Nevius was the first woman selected for Naval Test Pilot School. In 1988 the first navy woman selected as an astronaut by the National Aeronautics and Space Administration (NASA) was Lieutenant Commander Kathyrn Sullivan, U.S. Navy Reserves, though she was a nonaviator.

In 1989 the first woman executive director of an aircraft squadron was Com-

mander Rosemary Mariner, who headed Tactical Electronic Warfare Squadron (VAQ) 34. She became the first woman commanding officer of an aircraft squadron in 1990.

The first woman to fly solo in a navy training plane was Ensign Gale Ann Gordon, a member of the Medical Services Corps, who took the flight in order to become an aviation experimental psychologist.

On May 22, 1993, Lieutenant Commander Kathryn P. Hire flew her first mission as a tactical crewmember on maritime patrol during bombing practice. She became the first woman in the navy to be assigned to a combat unit. The first aircraft carriers to go to sea with women combat pilots assigned to them were the *Abraham Lincoln* and the *Dwight David Eisenhower*, in 1993.

On July 2, 1997, the secretary of the navy released a report announcing that they neither discriminated against nor gave preferential treatment to the first group of women aviators to fly combat planes. This was in answer to accusations over the death of Lieutenant Kara Hultgreen, the navy's first female F-14 Tomcat pilot, who died attempting a carrier landing in 1994.

See also
Hancock, Joy Bright; Hultgreen, Kara; Mariner, Rosemary Conaster; Neuffer, Judith Ann; Nevius, Colleen; Rainey, Barbara Allen; Rogers, Edith Nourse; Roosevelt, Eleanor; Women Appointed for Volunteer Emergency Service (WAVES)

References
Douglas, *United States Women in Aviation, 1940–1985* (1990); Ebbert and Hall, *Crossed Currents: Navy Women from WWI to Tailhook* (1993); Holm, *Women in the Military: An Unfinished Revolution* (1982); Perry, "Navy Not Biased against Women, Report Finds" (1997)

U.S. Space Academy
See U.S. Space Camp

U.S. Space Camp

The U.S. Space Camp was founded in 1982 to expose young people to practical applications of science and math. Initially attended largely by boys, female participation at Space Camps rose more than 30 percent when Sally Ride became America's first female astronaut.

The inspiration for Space Camp came from rocket scientist Wernher von Braun and was implemented by his assistant, Edward O. Buckbee. Modeled after traditional sports and band camps, Space Camp offers students a hands-on chance to learn the science and history of the space program in its six-day courses. The students work on simulators and listen to lectures from America's preeminent astronauts.

Famous women in aviation who have been involved with Space Camp include space shuttle astronaut Jan Davis, a native of Huntsville, Alabama, where the first Space Camp took place, who speaks to the attendees frequently; and Kelly Flinn, America's first female B-52 bomber pilot, who attended Space Camp twice while in high school.

The first Space Camp was located at the U.S. Space and Rocket Center at the Marshall Space Flight Center in Huntsville, Alabama. Further sites opened in Florida near the Kennedy Space Center in 1988, in Japan in 1990, in Belgium in 1991, in Canada in 1994, and in California in 1996.

Thad Mauldin, executive director of the U.S. Space and Rocket Center, explains the program this way: "Young people are excited about space travel and use their experiences in our programs as a motivation toward higher scholastic achievement."

See also
Flinn, Kelly; Davis, N. Jan; Ride, Sally Kristen

Van Meter, Victoria

The youngest girl to fly across country and the youngest pilot to fly it east to west, Van Meter was born on March 13, 1982, in Meadville, Pennsylvania. She wanted to be an astronaut when she grew up so she took her first flying lesson in 1992 at the age of ten. Deciding she wanted to earn a pilot's license, Van Meter took ground school classes after school instead of playing on the school's basketball team. She passed ground school on her second try but could not receive a license until she was 16. However, until then she could fly a plane herself if there was an instructor in the copilot seat.

Her first long-distance flight was the 400-mile trip from Meadville to Winston-Salem, North Carolina, to attend her sister's graduation from the School of Arts in June 1993. She spent the summer planning her next long-distance flight, a cross-country trip. At 7:21 A.M. on September 19, 1993, she took off from Augusta, Maine.

Vicki Van Meter (June 5, 1994)

After overnight stops in Columbus, Ohio; Oklahoma City, Oklahoma; and Phoenix, Arizona, Van Meter landed in San Diego, California, becoming the youngest girl ever to fly across country. There she was greeted by celebrities and local dignitaries including Bobbi Trout, holder of the 1932 women's flight endurance record. She was also interviewed by Bryant Gumbel on the *Today Show* and appeared on *The Tonight Show* with Jay Leno.

Van Meter was invited by the National Aeronautics and Space Administration (NASA) to tour the Johnson Space Center on her way home. Astronaut Tamara Jernigan led the tour and allowed Van Meter to use the shuttle simulation equipment. Van Meter was also invited to attend a week at the U.S. Space Camp in Huntsville, Alabama, and her entire sixth-grade class spent a week in Washington and met Vice President Al Gore and his family, since President Clinton was out of town. She also met Senator John Glenn, who in 1962 was the first American to orbit the earth.

Her second record-breaking long-distance trip began on June 4, 1994, again from Augusta, Maine. She was heading across the Atlantic Ocean. After stops in Goose Bay, Canada; Narsarsuak,

Greenland; and Reykjavik, Iceland, she landed in Glasgow, Scotland, at 6:30 P.M. on June 7, 1994.

About the scope of her accomplishments, Van Meter has said: "Every accomplishment, great or small, starts out with the right decision. That decision is, I'll try."

See also
Jernigan, Tamara E.; Trout, Evelyn "Bobbi"; U.S. Space Camp
References
Russo, *Women and Flight: Portraits of Contemporary Women Pilots* (1997); Van Meter with Gutman, *Taking Flight: My Story* (1995)

Vollick, Eileen

The first Canadian woman to earn her pilot's license and the first to be trained on a ski plane, Vollick was born in 1908. Born and raised in Hamilton, Ontario, Vollick was working as a textile analyst near the Hamilton Airport while it was under construction. She took flying lessons from J. V. Elliot's Flying Service, which was located at the airport, but only after Elliot had her request for lessons approved by the Department of National Defence.

Then Elliot assigned her his toughest instructor, Earl Jellison, who in an attempt to dissuade Vollick from taking lessons broke the school rules and tried to get her airsick with aerobatics on her test ride. Vollick was undeterred. She received her license on March 13, 1928.

Vollick found more work in traveling the country giving speeches than in aviation, but she was determined to ply her trade in her home country. To that end she turned down employment by a few U.S. aircraft companies in order to study aerobatic flying and skydiving. During this training, in the summer of 1928, Vollick became the first Canadian woman to parachute into water safely.

When employment still eluded her Vollick stuck to flying as a hobby. She died in Canada in 1966.

In 1975 Vollick was awarded the Amelia Earhart Medallion posthumously in honor of her pioneering efforts in aviation.

See also
Earhart, Amelia Mary
References
Render, *No Place for a Lady: The Story of Canadian Women Pilots, 1928–1992* (1992)

Von Etzdorf, Marga

Because she was born into the aristocracy of pre–World War I Germany, in 1907, Etzdorf had many opportunities not available to most women of her time. She earned her pilot's license at the age of 20 and became a copilot with the fledgling Lufthansa Airline. Though the commercial routes she flew took her as far away as Switzerland, Etzdorf yearned for larger aviation challenges.

In 1930 she bought her own plane and studied aerobatics. Being wealthy, she did not need to fly exhibitions for her living, so she simply enjoyed the fun of flying. Her first excursion took her from Berlin through the Balkans and into Istanbul, Turkey.

In 1931 she made a solo flight from Berlin to Tokyo, Japan, in 11 days. She lectured about this trip and women's future in aviation around Europe and Asia. In 1933, however, her career came to an end as she attempted to fly from Germany to Australia. Bad weather forced her to crash-land in Syria. She survived the crash, but her plane was irreparably damaged. That failure was too hard to accept for a woman who came from a well-respected German military family, and she shot herself at her family's estate. Her fame was so great, however, that the prime minister ordered a state funeral in her honor.

References
Moolman, *Women Aloft* (1981)

Voss, Janice

A veteran of four space shuttle flights, Voss was born on October 8, 1956, in South Bend, Indiana. Her family moved to Wilbraham, Massachusetts, where she graduated from Minnechaug Regional High School in 1972. From 1973 to 1975 Voss took correspondence courses at the University of Oklahoma that built on her engineering degree while pursuing her bachelor of science degree in engineering science from Purdue University, which she earned in 1975. During her college years she worked at the National Aeronautics and Space Administration (NASA) Johnson Space Center doing computer simulations in the Engineering and Development Directorate.

Voss then entered the Massachusetts Institute of Technology (MIT) to work toward a master of science degree in electrical engineering, which she received in 1977. Then she returned to the Johnson Space Center working as a crew trainer, teaching entry guidance and navigation, until 1978.

Voss received her doctorate in aeronautics and astronautics from MIT in 1987 and took a job with the Orbital Sciences Corporation. Her responsibilities there included mission integration and flight operations support for an upper stage called the Transfer Orbit Stage (TOS).

In 1990 Voss applied to and was selected for astronaut training by NASA. Her first shuttle mission was STS-57, which orbited the earth from June 21 to July 1, 1993. Voss was in charge of the Liquid Encapsulated Melt Zone experiment, which used a process called floating zone crystal growth. Also, with fellow astronauts Ron Grabe and Brian Duffy, Voss participated in the Neutral Body

Astronaut Janice Voss on the space shuttle Columbia *(July 17, 1997).*

Position study. This involved still and video photography of the crewmembers in relaxed positions taken throughout the mission, photos that will help doctors on earth understand the body's basic posture changes while in microgravity.

For her second flight, from February 3 to February 11, 1995, Voss was a mission specialist on mission STS-63. Mission highlights included a rendezvous with the Russian space station *Mir*, the deployment and retrieval of *Spartan 204*, and the third flight of Spacehab.

Voss was promoted to payload commander on STS-83, the Microgravity Science Laboratory (MSL-1) Spacelab mission. The mission only lasted from April 4 to April 8, 1997, because of prob-lems with one of the shuttle's three fuel cell power-generation units, so the crew and its payload returned to space together from July 1 to July 17, 1997. The STS-94 MSL-1 Spacelab mission focused on materials and combustion science research in microgravity.

Between spaceflights Voss's technical assignments have included working on Spacelab/Spacehab issues for the Astronaut Office Mission Development Branch and robotics issues for the EVA/Robotics Branch.

References
Biographical Data Sheets, Lyndon B. Johnson Space Center (1997)

Wagstaff, Peggy Combs

The first woman to win the U.S. National Aerobatic Championship and the first person of either sex to win three years in a row, Wagstaff was born Patricia Combs in St. Louis, Missouri, on September 11, 1951. Her father was an air force pilot, so the family lived in several cities around the world and Wagstaff attended a myriad of different schools in her childhood. She graduated from high school in San Mateo, California, in 1969.

Wagstaff's parents then sent her to secretarial college in Tokyo, a city they had lived in during her childhood, hoping to keep her out of the antiwar turmoil of the United States in the late 1960s. After a string of odd jobs around the country ranging from barmaid to emergency medical technician and a short-lived marriage to an Australian abalone fisherman, Wagstaff learned to fly in 1979. She took her lessons with Bob Wagstaff, who soon became her second husband.

On September 10, 1980, Wagstaff received her private pilot's license. In August 1981 she earned her seaplane license, and in June 1982 Wagstaff began aerobatic flying. In November 1982 she earned her instrument rating. She earned flying hours toward her commercial license, multi-engine rating, and instructor's certificate by flying as a safety pilot for her husband. In the winter of 1982 she began teaching flying to students at Jack Nielsen's flight school at Merrill Field, Alaska.

Her first aerobatic performance in an air show was at Gulkana, Alaska, in May 1984. She earned $300 for performing a routine in an 1118 Echo airplane under her first married name, Patty Beck. In July of that year she formed her own company, selling her services as a performer to an assortment of air shows across Alaska. In July she competed at her first meet at Fond du Lac, Wisconsin, and she and Wagstaff married.

To improve her aerobatic techniques Wagstaff studied with famed pilot Clint McHenry in Pompano, Florida, over the winter. In 1985 she studied under Betty Stewart, whom Wagstaff credited with helping her win the first-place Foreign Pilot Award at the Canadian National Aerobatic Championships that year and a place on the U.S. Women's Aerobatic Team. In 1986 Wagstaff was one of five women representing the United States at the World Aerobatic Championship Games in South Cerney, England. There Wagstaff placed seventh in the world in the women's competition.

On December 26, 1986, Wagstaff renamed her corporation to reflect her second married name. She continued to fly in air shows and national competitions, making the U.S. Women's Aerobatic Team in both 1986 and 1987. In 1987 Wagstaff won the first place in the Gold Cup Regional Contest of the International Aerobatic Competition held in Taft, California, and in 1988 she and the team won the World Aerobatic Championship in Red Deer, Canada. With this trophy behind her, Wagstaff spent 1989 performing in air shows in Washington State, Arizona, California, and Florida. That year a reader poll conducted by *General Aviation News* and *Flyer* named

Wagstaff the Favorite Female Air Show Pilot of the Year. The *Western Flyer* magazine's Reader's Choice Award for Favorite Female Performer also went to Wagstaff in 1989.

At the 1990 U.S. Nationals Wagstaff not only led the women's team but won the Betty Skelton First Lady of Aerobatics trophy for her performance. It was an award she would win again three more times in her career. Then in 1991 Wagstaff became the first woman to win the U.S. National Aerobatic Championship. She went on to win the title in 1992 and 1993 as well.

In 1991 Wagstaff and two other American pilots were invited to train for two weeks at the Soviet Team Training Camp in Borki, Russia. In 1992 she began flying stunts in movies like *Forever Young* and *Drop Zone* and on television on such shows as *Lois and Clark* both to make money and to get the experience. In 1994 one of her airplanes was included as part of the Pioneers of Flight collection at the Smithsonian Institution, a collection that includes planes flown by Amelia Earhart and Betty Skelton. That year she also won the National Air and Space Museum Award for Current Aviation Achievement.

In 1995 Wagstaff won the top award from the International Council of Air Shows, the Sword of Excellence. In 1996 Wagstaff flew her last international competition, the World Aerobatic Championship held in Oklahoma City, Oklahoma. She had decided to concentrate on air show performing rather than winning any more titles in competition.

In her 1997 autobiography, Wagstaff described her love of flying this way: "This is where I belong and where I feel alive, even joyous. Each time I fly aerobatics, I feel more at home in my machine and in the air. I believe in the elements: air, earth, water and fire. I believe that people are basically elemental, drawn instinctively and specifically to one or two of them, like the animals that we are. Air and fire are seductive to me. I feel them. Air and fire—my equation for the airplane."

See also
Earhart, Amelia Mary; Skelton-Frankman, Betty
References
Wagstaff, *Fire and Air: A Life on the Edge* (1997)

Walker, Ann
See Welch, Ann Walker

Walton, Nancy Bird
See Bird, Nancy De Low

Warren, Violet
See Milstead, Violet

Weber, Mary Ellen
A silver medalist in the U.S. National Skydiving Championships and veteran of one shuttle flight, Weber was born on August 24, 1962, in Cleveland, Ohio. She graduated from Bedford High School in 1980. Weber began skydiving in 1983 while studying at Purdue University, where she received her bachelor of science degree in chemical engineering in 1984. During this time Weber held engineering internships at Ohio Edison, Delco Electronics, and 3M companies.

For her doctoral studies Weber attended the University of California at Berkeley, from which she received a Ph.D. in physical chemistry in 1988. She was hired by Texas Instruments to research new techniques in microelectronics manufacturing. She developed a world-class high-density plasma reactor. In 1991 Weber received a silver medal in the U.S. National Skydiving Championships 20-Way Freefall Formation event.

In 1992 Weber applied to and was selected for astronaut training by the National Aeronautics and Space Administration (NASA). Her first spaceflight was as a mission specialist on board the *Discovery* space shuttle for STS-70. From July 13 to July 22, 1995, Weber deployed the sixth NASA Tracking and Data Relay Satellite, performed a myriad of biotechnology experiments, and served as flight crew medical officer. She was trained to be a contingency spacewalk crewmember, but the need for those services did not arise.

Between shuttle flight training Weber continued to skydive, again taking the silver medal in the U.S. National Skydiving Championships 20-Way Freefall Formation event in 1995. In 1996 she participated in the world's largest freefall formation, a 297-way.

On the ground Weber's technical assignments at NASA have included assisting in the processing and launch of shuttles at the Kennedy Space Center and in payload and robotics development. On the administrative side she was chair of the Source Evaluation Board for procurement of a biotechnology contract and member of the Station Research Facilities Assessment Review Team. In 1997 Weber was assigned to Legislative Affairs at NASA headquarters as a liaison to Congress.

On her goals as an astronaut, Weber has said: "Being an effective crew member and making the mission successful, that's what I'm striving for."

See also
Discovery Space Shuttle
References
Biographical Data Sheets, Lyndon B. Johnson Space Center (1997); Russo, *Women and Flight: Portraits of Contemporary Women Pilots* (1997)

Welch, Ann Walker

The founder of the Surrey Gliding Club and a member of the British Air Transport Auxiliary (ATA) during World War II, Welch was born Ann Walker in 1917 in London, England. In 1924 the family moved to Kent, England, where Welch saw her first airplanes as they passed through the clear sky overhead. She began making models of them from kits and from scratch when she could get no more kits. She also avidly followed the exploits of early British flyers like Lady Mary Bailey and Amy Johnson.

When she was 15 Welch bought a bicycle to enable her to ride to the Croydon Airport, where many of the famous flights began and ended. Here she took her first flight. Her family tried to dissuade her from a career in aviation by offering to pay for painting lessons. When these failed to capture Welch's interest her father gave in and financed the lessons she needed to apply for her private pilot's license. She took these lessons at the Barnstaple Aerodrome near Devon, England, soloed on September 5, 1934, and qualified for her license on October 8.

In August 1937 Welch was introduced to gliding through a two-week course, at the end of which she received her gliding license. She began instructing other students soon after and then purchased her first glider for 50 pounds. In 1938, with financial backing from Graham Douglas, another avid glider pilot, Welch founded the Surrey Gliding Club. She was finally in the business of aviation. In 1939, with the club flourishing and World War II on the horizon, Welch married Douglas.

All civilian flying was prohibited during the war, so the club closed for the duration. Welch's husband joined the Royal Air Force and she volunteered at a variety of jobs, including checking out new ambulance drivers. When Pauline Gower formed the Women's Section of the ATA, Welch applied.

On November 11, 1940, Welch reported to the Hatfield Aerodrome for a flight test and passed. She reported for full-time duty on December 1. Her job as a junior officer of the ATA involved ferrying military planes from manufacturing sites to military bases so that male pilots could be free to fly combat missions. In the spring of 1941, as new pilots were recruited to the ATA, Welch and the first group were promoted to flying larger military planes. One of these, the Walrus, was an amphibious aircraft. Welch survived a crash in a Walrus off the Isle of Wight by not wearing her safety belt: She was thrown clear of the immediate fire that engulfed the craft and returned to her base to continue flying.

At the end of the summer of 1942 Welch's husband was relieved of combat flying and made an instructor. With his future safety ensured, Welch retired from the ATA to begin a family. After the war she and her husband returned to running gliding clubs once new gliders could be manufactured and purchased. Those they had stored before the war had either been requisitioned for parts during the war or had been destroyed by rot during storage. The Surrey Gliding Club and others worked out a barter system with the government to acquire confiscated German gliders in return for running tests on them to learn more about German engineering. In addition, in order to obtain the new gliders developed and manufactured after the war, they traded the services of themselves and their member pilots as glider test pilots.

In 1948 the first Wasserkuppe International contests for gliders since the war began were held in Switzerland. Each competing country could send only one team of six pilots. Britain's team that year was all male, but they hired Welch as their team manager. Sadly, two of their pilots were killed in accidents, and the British team returned home in mourning. Welch continued managing the team for the next 20 years, becoming its director in 1965.

In 1955 the group running the British National Championships retired, and the job of hosting and organizing the annual event fell to Welch and the Surrey Gliding Club. In 1961 Welch took a break from organizing and earned her gold glider badge for a flight of 500 kilometers. This feat also earned her the Women's British National Goal Flight record.

In 1962 the World Gliding Championships were awarded by the Fédération Aéronautique Internationale (FAI) to England, and Welch was given the job of organizing them. Two years later she gave up this post to work instead as the British delegate to the FAI International Gliding Committee, deciding worldwide rules for competition. In 1974 Welch was awarded the top gliding award, the Lilienthal Medal, for her pioneering work with gliding as a sport. This included her writing about the sport in such books as *Pilots' Weather* and *New Soaring Pilot*.

In 1976 Welch was elected chair of the International Jury for the World Gliding Championships, and in 1981 she was awarded the FAI Gold Air Medal for her distinguished career in aviation.

In her 1983 autobiography Welch wrote of her love for flying and described her career by saying: "My flying has never been dramatic or ambitious; no fighter pilot stuff or long pioneering flights to Australia. It has just been fun, sometimes a little frightening, but I would not have missed any of it. I think it is only rarely that an isolated happening determines a whole future, it is probably more of a trigger mechanism. For me it was an unexpected five-minute flight that somehow collected together all the loose ends of interests and ideas which had until that moment no particular direction."

See also
Air Transit Auxiliary (ATA); Bailey, Lady Mary; Gower, Pauline; Johnson, Amy; Safety Belts/Safety Harnesses
References
Welch, *Happy to Fly: An Autobiography* (1983)

Wells, Fay Gillis

The first air saleswoman hired by the Curtiss-Wright Corporation and a charter member of the Ninety-Nines, Wells was born on October 15, 1908, in Minneapolis, Minnesota. Her father was a foreign correspondent, so the family moved frequently. Wells attended Michigan State Farming University, but when she took her first flying lesson on August 6, 1929, it was clear flying would be her career.

She soloed on September 1, 1929. The next day, Wells was invited to copilot the test flight of an experimental airplane. Midair, the vibrations of the aerobatics loosened the engine, and the plane plummeted toward earth. Wells parachuted to safety, and on October 5, 1929, ten days before her twenty-first birthday, Wells earned her pilot's license at the Curtiss Flying School on Long Island.

Curtiss then hired Fay to demonstrate and sell Curtiss-Wright aircraft across the country. In this capacity Wells had the chance to attend air meets and aviation clubs around the country and to meet many famous female aviators of the day. She also added up hours to apply for and receive her commercial pilot's license in 1930.

To make extra money, and because journalism was in essence the family business, Wells followed her father on a job transfer to Russia, where she freelanced for the *New York Herald Tribune* and many aviation magazines from 1930 to 1934. She also lectured on the art of parachuting. Wells became the first woman to pilot a Soviet civil aircraft and the first foreigner to own a glider in the Soviet Union.

While there she was able to assist Wiley Post by arranging the landing fields and fuel storage logistics for the critical Russian leg of Post's 1933 record solo flight around the world. He invited her to accompany him, but she declined in order to elope with pioneer journalist and pilot Linton Wells. The marriage offered Wells two immediate benefits: She became part of the only husband-and-wife team of foreign correspondents to have front-page byline articles side by side, and she avoided perishing when Post crashed on August 15, 1935, in Alaska. Famed humorist Will Rogers had taken her place on the doomed flight.

Wells and her husband went to Africa in 1935 to cover the Italo-Ethiopian War for the *New York Herald*. At one point she was accused of being a spy by the British and arrested for a short time. In 1939 she founded the Overseas Press Club.

On April 7, 1940, Wells proposed that the Ninety-Nines found the Amelia Earhart Memorial Scholarship Fund to help deserving members of the Ninety-Nines to further their accomplishments. She also wrote a history book celebrating the fifteenth anniversary of the Ninety-Nines that year.

In 1963 Wells was awarded the Lady Hay Drummond-Hay Award trophy for Outstanding Achievement in Aeronautics. That was also the year she succeeded in her push to get the U.S. Post Office to issue stamps honoring women in aviation.

In 1967 Wells chaired the first international convention of the Ninety-Nines, which was held in Washington, D.C., during International Tourist Year as proclaimed by the United Nations. In 1975 she was named Most Valuable Pilot by the Washington, D.C., chapter of the Ninety-Nines.

In 1972 Wells was one of only three women selected to accompany President Richard Nixon on his historic visit to the People's Republic of China. Through her efforts in the White House, many more women served in government.

Wells served as chair of the Ninety-Nines International Bicentennial Celebration and helped to create the International Forest of Friendship in Earhart's birthplace, Atchison, Kansas. At the First

World Aviation Education and Safety Congress in Delhi, India, in 1986 Wells was a key speaker, among other world aviation leaders. While on a National Aeronautics and Space Administration (NASA) committee working to choose the first journalist to fly in a space shuttle Wells said: "If I were younger, I would probably become an astronaut."

See also
Ninety-Nines
References
Holden and Griffith, *Ladybirds II: The Continuing Story of American Women in Aviation* (1993)

Whirly-Girls

The first organization dedicated to promoting interest among women in rotary aircraft, the Whirly-Girls were founded by Jean Ross Howard, one of the first women in the United States to earn her helicopter pilot's license, on April 28, 1955. At the time there were only 12 other women helicopter pilots in France, West Germany, and the United States. The Whirly-Girls did not elect formal officers, but Howard served as executive secretary.

The Whirly-Girls are actively involved in promoting helicopter aviation, encouraging safety through professionalism within the helicopter-flying world, and assisting the advancement of women in helicopter aviation. The Whirly-Girls offer two annual $5,000 flight scholarships to help women earn their helicopter licenses and serve as standby reserves for national emergencies. One is in memory of Gini Richardson, Whirly-Girl number 64, who died of cancer in 1990. In 1966 the Doris Mullen Memorial Flight Scholarship was established in memory of Doris Mullen, Whirly-Girl number 84, who died in an airplane accident that year and who personified the high standards and ideals of women in aviation.

The Whirly-Girls also encourage the establishment of hospital heliports. The Judy Short Memorial Hospital Heliport Certificate is given in recognition of a hospital establishing a heliport for the life-saving helicopter in emergency medical service. Judy Short, Whirly-Girl number 29, was instrumental in establishing the first hospital heliport in Kentucky.

The Whirly-Girls have also participated in the World Helicopter Championships from their inception in 1971. In 1973 the U.S. branch of the Whirly-Girls entered an all-woman team in the competition.

In 1991 Howard said of the group: "From the beginning, our instant rapport was amazing."

See also
Howard-Phelan, Jean Ross
References
Douglas, *United States Women in Aviation, 1940–1985* (1990); Holden and Griffith, *Ladybirds: The Untold Story of Women Pilots in America* (1991)

Whitsitt, Wanda

The founder of Lifeline Pilots, a group dedicated to flying patients and supplies to hospitals, Whitsitt did not take her first plane ride until she was married and the mother of four. In 1979 she and her husband took their first test ride and decided to take lessons as a hobby. That same year she earned her private pilot's license, immediately followed by her commercial license and instructor's certificate.

She founded Lifeline Pilots in the state of Illinois as a way to use her new skills for the benefit of others besides herself. The group concentrates on transporting organs, blood donations, and patients to and from hospitals. When time permits they also deliver medical personnel and supplies to disaster areas, as Ruth Nichols's Relief Wings did before World War II. The group operates on private donations from supporters, and the volunteers offer the use of their personal planes for free.

In 1986 Whitsitt was inducted into the Illinois Aviation Hall of Fame for her work with Lifeline. In 1992 the National Aeronautic Association awarded her their Certificate of Honor for her efforts.

In discussing the reason she so enjoys working with Lifeline, Whitsitt said: "Today we are often caught up in negative messages. They are all over the media. Flying provides a positive influence and I have met and been encouraged by many generous and compassionate people. I have had the opportunity to know and work with some of the finest people I have ever met."

See also
Nichols, Ruth Rowland; Relief Wings, Inc.
References
Holden and Griffith, *Ladybirds II: The Continuing Story of American Women in Aviation* (1993)

Whitson, Peggy

An astronaut candidate in the National Aeronautics and Space Administration (NASA) class of 1996 and project scientist of the Shuttle-*Mir* Program, Whitson was born on February 9, 1960, in Mount Ayr, Iowa. She graduated from the Community High School there in 1978. As a State of Iowa Scholar she attended Iowa Wesleyan College and received a bachelor of science degree in biology and chemistry, graduating summa cum laude in 1981. That summer she earned her pilot's license.

Her doctorate in biochemistry came from Rice University in 1985. As a Robert A. Welch Postdoctoral Fellow, Whitson continued at Rice until October 1986, when she became a National Research Council resident research associate at NASA's Johnson Space Center in Houston, Texas.

In April 1988 Whitson served as the supervisor for the Biochemistry Research Group at KRUG International, a medical sciences contractor at NASA–Johnson Space Center (JSC). In 1991, Whitson became an adjunct assistant professor in the Department of Internal Medicine and the Department of Human Biological Chemistry and Genetics at the University of Texas Medical Branch in Galveston, Texas.

From 1991 to 1992 Whitson was the payload element developer for the Bone Cell Research Experiment that rode STS-47, and she was a member of the US-USSR Joint Working Group in Space Medicine and Biology. In 1992 she was named the project scientist for the Phase 1A Program of the Shuttle-*Mir* Program. From 1993 to 1996 Whitson held the additional responsibilities of the deputy division chief of the Medical Sciences Division at NASA-JSC. In 1995 she became cochair of the U.S.-Russian Mission Science Working Group and was awarded the American Astronautical Society Randolph Lovelace II Award.

In 1996 Whitson shared in the Group Achievement Award for the Shuttle-*Mir* Program. She applied to and was accepted by NASA for training as a mission specialist on a space shuttle flight crew. "I've always wanted to go to Mars and make new discoveries there."

References
Beatty, "Meet the Astronauts of the 21st Century" (1997); Biographical Data Sheets, Lyndon B. Johnson Space Center (1997)

Whyte, Edna Marvel Gardner

A former president of the Ninety-Nines and a navy nurse, Whyte trained military pilots when she herself was denied the chance to fly for the navy. She was born on November 3, 1902, in Minnesota but her family moved to Oregon when she was three. Her father died when she was eight, and Whyte was shuttled from relative to relative until she graduated from New Salem High School in Wisconsin in 1921.

Whyte became a registered nurse, holding her first position at the University Hospital in Madison, Wisconsin. Tiring of it soon enough, she moved to Seattle, Washington, in 1926. There she took her first airplane ride in the winter of 1927, and she instantly signed up for her own flying lessons. In 1929 Whyte joined the U.S. Naval Nurse Corps and was assigned to the Great Lakes Naval Hospital in Illinois. She continued her flying lessons at the Waukegan Flying Club, soloing on January 1, 1931.

On May 14, 1931, she had finished the flying hours and passed the written test to earn her private pilot's license. To celebrate she joined the Ninety-Nines, purchased a Travel Air for $600, and attended the National Air Races in Cleveland in August of that year. Her new plane was not fast enough to enter the race, so she offered to fly for a male parachutist for his contests, agreeing to split the prize money. At the end of the week, however, the parachutist disappeared without paying Whyte a dime.

In May 1932 the opportunity arose for Whyte and her former flight instructor to invest in a small airfield in New Bedford, Massachusetts. She was chosen as copilot for a medical flight across the Atlantic to Italy commemorating Florence Nightingale's birth but could not receive leave from the navy to make the flight. It turned out to be a lucky loss for Whyte, as the pilot who took her place perished with the crew when the plane crashed over the Azores Mountains.

Whyte received her transport license in December 1932. She was the first female pilot in Rhode Island to do so. In June 1933 she won fifth place in the All-Women's Air Race at Floyd Bennett Field. In September she took first-place prizes in four different contests at the Legion Air Meet in Springfield, Massachusetts, and she won the $500 first prize in an all-women's race at Roosevelt Field in October, beating such well-known pilots as Jacqueline Cochran.

In 1934 Whyte was transferred to a naval hospital in Washington, D.C., leaving her partner behind to run their airfield. That year she won the first-place prize, $300, in a pylon race in Maryland, sponsored by the Curtiss-Wright Company, against all-male competition. The next year women were barred from the competition.

Whyte won first place in the Third Annual Annette Gipson Race in Long Island in June 1934, beating female pilots like Frances Marsalis and Helen MacCloskey. Whyte met Marsalis again at the Women's National Air Meet in Dayton, Ohio, in August, when they competed in the 50-Mile Free-for-All. Whyte's and Marsalis's planes nearly collided midair. Marsalis lost control of her plane and crashed. Whyte veered to the left at the last minute and came in first but was disqualified because race rules only allowed passing on the right. Helen Richey was declared the winner.

In 1935 the seventh annual Miami All-American Air Maneuvers were open to women for the first time. Whyte took second place in the Women's Acrobatic competition, once again behind Richey. However, she won the women's speed race that she entered the next day for a prize of $250—just enough to pay for the repairs her airplane needed before she could fly it home. In 1935 she also married Ray Kidd, a writer for the U.S. Information Service, and resigned from the navy to become a full-time flight instructor.

On March 1, 1936, while her husband was stationed overseas, Whyte moved to New Orleans to work as a flight instructor out of the Shushan Airport on the shore of Lake Pontchartrain. There, in

1937, she shared dinner with Amelia Earhart just before the legendary pilot's ill-fated around-the-world flight.

At Shushan Whyte was so popular with students that she opened her own flight school, the Southern Aviation School, with her husband as business manager and herself as chief instructor. This caused intense competition with her previous boss, so she and Kidd relocated to the Wedell-Williams Airport. They took a lease on the property and called their new business the New Orleans Air College. All this instructing added so many hours to Whyte's flight log that in 1938 she was first in a *Look Magazine* list of American female pilots ranked by hours flown.

Whyte continued to fly races to keep herself in the news and to make her flying school attractive to customers. In 1939 and 1940 she won first-place trophies at the Miami All-American Air Maneuvers again. But the racing circuit cut back as World War II approached, so Whyte turned her attention to her school and to training pilots for the military.

After divorcing her husband in 1940 for infidelity, Whyte ran the school alone. She expanded the business to include flying charters. Later that year the navy bought out her lease on the airport at twice what she paid. After selling her equipment, and her trainer planes as well, Whyte relocated to Texas in 1941 to earn her instrument rating.

When the Japanese bombing of Pearl Harbor drew the United States into World War II, Whyte spent three years training pilots for military duty at the Spartan School of Aeronautics in Tulsa, Oklahoma. Then she joined the Army Nurse Corps and spent two years overseas.

When the war was over in 1946 Whyte returned to the United States and became a flight instructor at Meacham Field in Fort Worth, Texas. She earned extra money ferrying airplanes from factories to dealers nearby. In August she married former marine and fellow instructor George Murphy Whyte. With the war over, air races began again. In the first postwar race Whyte flew, the 1947 Halle Trophy Race in Cleveland, Ohio, she came in third.

In the early 1950s Whyte and her husband moved to Aberdeen, Mississippi, where they taught at the Columbus Air Force Base. From 1955 to 1957 Whyte served as president of the Ninety-Nines and became the tenth woman in the United States to obtain her helicopter rating. In 1957 Whyte and her mother, who had once tried to talk Whyte out of flying lessons, flew the Dallas Doll Derby and came in first. In 1960 Whyte won the International Air Race, and in 1967 she won second place in the stock plane class and was voted outstanding competitor and best sport at the Cleveland Air Races. It was also in 1967 that she divorced her second husband.

Whyte moved to Roanoke, Texas, in 1969 and opened a private airport and flying school on a 22-acre lot she purchased. She built the property into a full-fledged airport, calling the venture Aero Valley Airport, complete with ground school, Federal Aviation Administration (FAA) testing, hangars to rent to local private plane owners, and a home, all while she was in her late seventies. By this time she had also been awarded the Charles Lindbergh Lifetime Achievement Award in Aviation. She died on February 15, 1993.

In her 1991 autobiography Whyte summed up her life as a woman in this way: "People have said that I am a liberated woman, born too soon. I was born too soon to be accepted as a military pilot, although I was qualified to teach male pilots. I was born too soon to be chosen as an airline pilot, yet I trained hundreds of pilots who now fly for various airlines. I wasn't born too soon. I was very much a woman of my time, an independent woman of the 1930's."

References
Holden and Griffith, *Ladybirds II: The Continuing Story of American Women in Aviation* (1993); Whyte with Cooper, *Rising above It: An Autobiography* (1991)

Widnall, Sheila E.

The first woman to serve as secretary of the U.S. Air Force (USAF), Widnall was born in Tacoma, Washington, in 1938. She received a bachelor of science degree in aeronautics and astronautics in 1960, a master's in 1961, and her doctorate in 1964, all in the same field and all from the Massachusetts Institute of Technology (MIT).

After she earned her doctorate Widnall joined the faculty of MIT as an assistant professor in 1964. In 1970 she was promoted to associate professor and attained her full professorship in 1974. Widnall became the head of the fluid mechanics division in 1975 and director of the Fluid Dynamics Research Laboratory in 1979. She was made associate provost in January 1992.

While with MIT Widnall's expertise made her a valuable member of the USAF Academy Board of Visitors and of advisory committees to Military Airlift Command and Wright-Patterson Air Force Base in Ohio, as well as of many boards, panels, and committees in academia and industry. But it was her work with the USAF that resulted in her being offered the position of secretary of the air force, a job she began on August 6, 1993.

As secretary of the air force Widnall was responsible for overseeing the recruiting, training, and equipping of the air force, the air national guard, and the air reserve. To do that job, she was in charge of justifying and allocating an annual budget of approximately $62 billion.

In 1993 the National Academy of Engineering awarded Widnall their Distinguished Service Award. In 1995 she earned the W. Stuart Symington Award and the Maxwell A. Kriendler Memorial Award from the Air Force Association and the Boston USO Military Service Award. In 1996 Widnall was elected to the Women in Aviation Pioneer Hall of Fame.

On November 24, 1996, Lieutenant Kelly Flinn, the first woman to pilot a B-52 bomber for the U.S. Air Force, was accused of adultery, fraternization, and conduct unbecoming an officer for having entered into an affair with the husband of an enlisted woman on her base. Flinn's case caused such turmoil within the highest ranks of the air force that Widnall resigned as well, on October 31, 1997.

References
www.womweb.com/widnall.html

Wilihite, Nelle Zabel

The first licensed female pilot in South Dakota and one of the earliest deaf pilots, Wilihite, who was born circa 1900, lost her hearing after developing the measles as a child but still earned her pilot's license on January 13, 1928.

Wilihite made her living on the air meet circuit, performing tricks like bombing the crowd with flour and popping balloons in midair with her plane, which required precision and skill.

During World War II Wilihite used her aviation experience to help the Allied war effort by offering her services as a ground school instructor and later as a propeller inspector. She died in 1991.

References
Holden and Griffith, *Ladybirds: The Untold Story of Women Pilots in America* (1991)

References
Biographical Data Sheets, Lyndon B. Johnson Space Center (1997)

Wilson, Stephanie

An astronaut candidate in the National Aeronautics and Space Administration (NASA) class of 1996, Wilson was born on September 27, 1966, in Boston, Massachusetts. She graduated from Taconic High School in Pittsfield, Massachusetts, in 1984 and received a bachelor of science degree in engineering science from Harvard University in 1988.

From 1988 to 1990 Wilson worked for the Martin Marietta Astronautics Group in Denver, Colorado, as a loads and dynamics engineer for *Titan IV.* Her responsibilities included performing coupled-loads analyses for the launch vehicle and payloads of the space shuttles during flight events. In 1990 she quit to attend graduate school at the University of Texas, where her research focused on the control and modeling of large, flexible space structures.

Wilson earned her master of science degree in aerospace engineering in 1992 and was hired by the Jet Propulsion Laboratory in Pasadena, California. As a member of the attitude and articulation control subsystem group for the *Galileo* spacecraft Wilson was responsible for assessing attitude controller performance, science platform pointing accuracy, antenna pointing accuracy, and spin rate accuracy. Wilson also supported the Interferometry Technology Program as a member of the Integrated Modeling Team, which was responsible for finite element modeling, controller design, and software development.

In April 1996 Wilson began two years of training and evaluation at NASA with the goal of becoming a mission specialist on a future space shuttle flight crew.

Women Appointed for Volunteer Emergency Service (WAVES)

Based on the quick success of the U.S. Army's Women's Airforce Service Pilots (WASPS) program, Congresswoman Edith Nourse Rogers proposed a similar group of militarily sanctioned female pilots in the navy. To support her idea Rogers offered a proposal created by Captain Joy Bright Hancock from the Bureau of Aeronautics outlining the ways women could help.

Professor Elizabeth Reynard of Barnard College came up with the acronym, WAVES, and described the process in this way: "I realized that there were two letters that had to be in it: W for women and V for volunteer, because the Navy wanted to make it clear that this was a voluntary service and not a drafted service. So I played with those two letters and the idea of the sea and finally came up with WAVES. I figured the word Emergency could comfort the older admirals because it implied that we were only a temporary crisis and wouldn't be around for keeps."

The Women Appointed for Volunteer Emergency Service (WAVES) was created by act of Congress on July 30, 1942. The "Appointed" was later changed to "Accepted" when they realized "Appointed" was a word used only in reference to officers.

A debate quickly ensued as to whether WAVES would be an auxiliary branch of the navy, as the WASPS were an auxiliary of the army, or whether they should be integrated into the navy as true military personnel. First Lady Eleanor Roosevelt was for true integration, and after long discussions with President Roosevelt she succeeded in winning him to her side.

The WAVES' first director, Mildred McAfee, was chosen not from the ranks of female flyers but from academia. Her preceding position had been as president of Wellesley College for Women. Hancock was appointed women's representative to the chief of the Bureau of Aeronautics, putting her in charge of all WAVES assigned to that organization. Because of McAfee's background in academia, her recruits took their training at colleges across the country instead of at naval bases. WAVE officer candidates were first trained at Smith College in Northhampton, Massachusetts, then at Mount Holyoke College in South Hadley, Massachusetts.

Originally recruited to fill clerical voids in the navy, the WAVES were never intended to fly aircraft. However, they soon proved their usefulness in naval aviation positions involving air traffic control, engineering, celestial navigation, and both gunnery and flight instruction. During the course of the war 2,000 women were assigned to naval aviation duties.

Having been integrated into the navy as military personnel, WAVES were able to receive pay and training equal to that of their male counterparts, though they took their training in single-sex classes. Officers in the WAVES trained at the Naval Reserve Midshipmen's School of Smith College in Northhampton, Massachusetts. Enlisted women trained at Hunter College in New York City.

Minor adjustments to living quarters on the bases had to be handled before the WAVES could be sent to their assignments. Frequently there was not time for these renovations, so the women bunked in local motels, and the military paid the rent. On bases where there was no time to install new rest room facilities women shared with men. A peg would be installed outside the rest room to hold the occupant's hat. If a man's hat hung there, only other men would enter. If a woman's uniform hat hung there, only women would enter.

In September 1944 WAVES were allowed to be assigned to overseas bases within the American territories, which included Alaska and Hawaii, not yet states, the West Indies, and Panama.

Though McAfee petitioned from the very beginning to include black women in the ranks of the WAVES, it was not until December 22, 1944, that the first two black women, Harriet Ida Pickens and Frances Wills, graduated from Northhampton.

By July 1945, a month before the war ended, 86,000 women were enlisted in the WAVES. They had released 50,500 men for duty overseas and comprised 55 percent of the uniformed personnel in the Navy Department in Washington, D.C.

After the Japanese surrendered demobilization was mandated by law so that soldiers could return to their prewar occupations. The WAVES had been so well integrated into the navy that, rather than discharge them all, the navy simply discontinued the training of new female recruits. There were 5,500 WAVES who stayed with the navy, 2,000 of whom joined the reserves.

McAfee returned to her job as president of Wellesley College and was succeeded first by Captain Jean Palmer and then by Hancock, who oversaw the integration of WAVES into the regular navy for postwar work.

Hancock said of the WAVES' ability to serve well: "Where they were given responsibility somewhat in accordance with their ability they left no stone unturned to learn the job quickly and carry it out efficiently. Never have I encountered a finer 'can do' attitude. And how it delighted my heart, when on my regular visits to the activities, to listen to the commanding officer relating with great pride what his WAVES were doing and how well they were doing it."

See also
Hancock, Joy Bright; McAfee, Mildred; Rogers, Edith Nourse; Roosevelt, Eleanor; Women's Airforce Service Pilots (WASPS)
References
Douglas, *United States Women in Aviation, 1940–1985* (1990); Hancock, *Lady in the Navy: A Personal Reminiscence* (1972); Van Wagenen Keil, *Those Wonderful Women in Their Flying Machines* (1979); Zimmerman, *Tailspin: Women at War in the Wake of Tailhook* (1995)

Women Apprentice Mechanics (WAMS)

In response to World War II the Departments of War and of the Navy joined commercial airlines to develop a program to provide female replacement mechanics for male mechanics sent to war. Although many early female flyers like Amy Johnson were certified as ground mechanics, this program represented the first concerted effort to train women as mechanics by either group.

Transcontinental, Western, and Pan American airlines were among the first to participate, with Pan American boasting of an all-female mechanic crew at New York's famous La Guardia Field.

See also
Johnson, Amy
References
Douglas, *United States Women in Aviation, 1940–1985* (1990)

Women Flyers of America

The Women Flyers of America (WFA) was a national flying club founded in April 1940 by Opal Kunz and Chelle Janis. First opened to New Yorkers, interest in the club was so high that the WFA was opened to women nationwide.

To join the Ninety-Nines women had to already be pilots, but the WFA was open to any woman with an interest in flying and the $5 membership fee.

Founded to help lower-income women learn to fly, the clubs offered ground school classes at affordable prices. Once a group of members passed these classes, the club negotiated with local flying schools to provide flying lessons at minimal fees, sometimes 20 percent less than advertised fees.

Vita Roth took over the club in August 1940, and immediately began lobbying Washington to provide more training opportunities for women in case of war. The WFA also expanded its own training programs to include meteorology, air traffic control, and parachute-rigging classes. In the early 1950s the WFA began an All-Women's Aircraft and Engine Mechanics class at New Jersey's Teterboro School of Aeronautics.

The club was in operation for 14 years, disbanding in 1954 as the postwar interest in flying among civilian women dwindled.

See also
Ninety-Nines
References
Douglas, *United States Women in Aviation, 1940–1985* (1990)

Women in Military Service for America Memorial

The Women in Military Service for America Memorial was unveiled on Saturday, October 18, 1997, at the end of four days of celebration. It stands at the entrance to Arlington National Cemetery and cost $21.5 million from inception to creation. A fountain and reflecting pool front an exhibition hall housing educational displays about the more than two million women whose contributions to the various branches of the U.S. military date from the days of the American Revolution.

The unveiling ceremonies were attended by retired military women whose service to their country dated back to World War I. They also drew such distinguished military veterans as Colin Powell and John M. Shalikashvilli, both retired chairmen of the Joint Chiefs of Staff.

At the unveiling, then–Vice President Gore said: "This memorial has been forged by the countless acts of bravery and sacrifice of generations of America's servicewomen, by their centuries of patriotism and patience, their blood and valor, their pain and perseverance."

References
Abu-Nasr, "Servicewomen Rejoice at Recognition" (1997); Richter and Gray, "For Women in Uniform, a Place of Honor" (1997)

Women's Air Derby
Organized as the opening attraction of the National Air Races in Cleveland, Ohio, the Women's Air Derby began in 1929. It was the first cross-country competition exclusively for women.

For a grand prize the first year of $2,500, women with a pilot's license and 100 hours of solo flying time competed for the best cross-country time. The race began in Santa Monica, California, on August 18, 1929, and ended 2,800 miles away at the Municipal Airport in Cleveland, Ohio, on August 26, 1929.

The first Derby drew 20 contestants, including Thea Rasche of Germany, Jessie Miller of Australia, and Amelia Earhart, Phoebe Omlie, Ruth Nichols, Bobbi Trout, and Mae Haizlip of the United States. All contestants were required to carry a three-day supply of food and water and a parachute in case of emergency. The only fatality in the first year's race was Marvel Crosson, who experienced engine trouble and bailed out too low, as the use of parachutes was not yet perfected. Four others, including Pancho Barnes, were troubled by mechanical difficulties or accidents, leaving 15 women who completed the race. Louise Thaden came in first, with a flight time of 19 hours, 35 minutes, 4 seconds; Gladys O'Donnell was second and Amelia Earhart third. Thaden dedicated her Symbol of Flight Trophy to Crosson and sent it to Crosson's mother.

After winning the first competition, Louise Thaden explained her reason for entering: "The successful completion of the derby was of more import than life or death. . . . We women of the Derby were out to prove that flying was safe."

See also
Crosson, Marvel; Earhart, Amelia Mary; Haizlip, Mae (Mary); Nichols, Ruth Rowland; O'Donnell, Gladys; Omlie, Phoebe Fairgrave; Rasche, Thea; Thaden, Louise McPhetridge; Trout, Evelyn "Bobbi"
References
Holden and Griffith, *Ladybirds II: The Continuing Story of American Women in Aviation* (1993)

Women's Air Reserve
One of several emergency aid groups, the Women's Air Reserve (WAR) was founded on October 1, 1931, by Pancho Barnes, who became general and commanding officer, and Lavelle Sweeley, as squadron commander and second-in-command. The group's objective was to "build and maintain an organization insofar as may be practical along the tenor of the United States Army."

The group studied radio communications, aircraft mechanics, and first aid to be prepared to help in times of national disaster. They ran practice rescues and operated the first aid department at the 1933 National Air Races. They had the full support of the Army Air Corps, who donated the use of the Officer's Clubhouse in Long Beach, California, as WAR headquarters for meetings and classes. Members included the actress Bebe Daniels Lyons and record-breaking pilots Louise Thaden, Blanche Noyes, and Bobbi Trout.

On August 31, 1934, WAR sponsored a cross-country trip to help promote membership and to underscore Phoebe Omlie's petition for equal pilot licensing standards for men and women. They made stops in Kingman, Arizona; Washington, D.C.; and Philadelphia, Pennsylvania. In New York City the members were almost banned from a cocktail party in their honor. They arrived in full dress uniform, only to be told that women were not allowed to appear in public in masculine attire.

WAR disbanded in 1941, the victim of financing problems, new opportunities for women pilots in the Women's Airforce Service Pilots (WASPS), and the approaching World War II.

See also
Air Transport Auxiliary (ATA); Barnes, Florence Lowe "Pancho"; Noyes, Blanche Wilcox; Omlie, Phoebe Fairgrave; Thaden, Louise McPhetridge; Trout, Evelyn "Bobbi"; Women's Airforce Service Pilots (WASPS)
References
Schultz, *Pancho: The Biography of Florence Lowe Barnes* (1996)

Women's Airforce Service Pilots (WASPS)

The energetic and enthusiastic work of two dedicated female pilots, Jacqueline Cochran and Nancy Harkness Love, resulted in the formation of the Women's Airforce Service Pilots (WASPS), the first group of militarily sanctioned female pilots in the United States.

In September 1939 Cochran wrote a letter to Eleanor Roosevelt declaring that with World War II going badly in Eu-

rope the United States should begin allowing women to fly noncombat missions to free the men for overseas duty. She received a polite and supportive response from the first lady but knew that the decision would not be up to her.

In May 1940 a similar letter was sent to the Army Air Corps (AAC) Plans Division by Love. Her letter also met with inaction.

In 1941 Cochran met with General H. H. "Hap" Arnold, chief of the U.S. Army Air Corps, and again put forth her idea. Something similar was already under way in England, the Air Transport Auxiliary (ATA), and they were taking volunteers from all countries. Arnold recommended that Cochran work with them to help show the U.S. military that women ferrying pilots were a good idea. Cochran agreed to ferry a bomber plane for the ATA from its manufacture site in North America to its base in England. Though she successfully completed the mission, the U.S. government was still not convinced that their military could benefit from such a group. Cochran put her efforts toward recruiting American female pilots for the British ATA.

On May 28, 1941, Congresswoman Edith Nourse Rogers proposed to Congress the legislation that would establish a Women's Auxiliary Army Corps (WAAC). The bill was stalled in Congress until December 1941. After the bombing of Pearl Harbor the bill was debated until the air force showed an interest in using the services of qualified women pilots. The bill was passed on May 15, 1942, nearly a year after it was proposed.

Then Love, who had moved to Washington, D.C., when her husband was called to military duty, met with his superiors at the Air Transport Command (ATC) to reintroduce the concept of women ferry pilots. The new commander, Brigadier General Harold L. George, liked the idea and asked Love to draft a proposal.

Women's Airforce Service Pilots (WASPS) were the first female pilots officially sanctioned to serve in the U.S. military forces. These four pilots graduated from the four-engine school at Lockbourne Field, Ohio (1944).

On Thursday, September 10, 1942, Love's proposal was announced in the newspapers. Women who met the requirements were asked to apply to what was then called the Women's Auxiliary Ferrying Squadron (WAFS). Love was named director of the group. Requirements for applicants included two letters of recommendation, a high school diploma, and 500 hours of logged flying time. Although male pilots could be accepted to the ATC between the ages of 19 and 45, female applicants to the WAFS had to be between 21 and 35.

When Cochran returned from her recruitment efforts for the British ATA she was astounded to learn that an American group had been created without her. General Arnold made her the director of

the Women's Flying Training Detachment (WFTD), a group organized to train novice women pilots to fulfill the WAFS' requirements. To join Cochran's group of novices women were given the army's rigorous Form 64 physical exam.

In July 1943 the Pentagon combined the WAFS and WFTDs and renamed them all Women's Airforce Service Pilots (WASPS). To support their efforts Walt Disney created Fifinella, a female gremlin mascot for the group.

After the merger Cochran was promoted to director of women pilots. She went about securing even more varied flying tasks for the women in her command. Through her efforts the WASPS flew larger aircraft and not only ferried these aircraft to bases around the country but also towed targets for bombers. They also flew as check pilots on planes reported faulty by male pilots, which led to some of the few fatalities associated with the WASP program.

In February 1944 this expanded work led to a bill known as H.R. 4219, legislation presented in Congress to militarize the WASPS. Militarization would provide the WASPS all the benefits of soldiers, from free uniforms to postwar pensions. This drew angry letter-writing campaigns from male pilots who had failed to pass military tests and physicals. They wanted the duties of the WASPS to be handed to them, even though the WASPS were better qualified. These complaints were considered by the House Committee of Military Affairs in March 1944, along with testimony by only one witness, General Arnold. His positive portrayal of the WASP program was countered by the arguments that training too many pilots would create a postwar employment problem and that the program had always been just an experiment. In the end the vote was 169 to 188 against militarization. H.R. 4219 was killed in Congress on June 21, 1944.

At this time the WASP program was also cut, allowing those already in service to continue through the end of the war but denying any further training to women for the purposes of entering the WASPS. A new class of trainees already en route to Avenger Field had to be sent home when they arrived.

As the war in Europe seemed to be going well for the Allies, the WASP program was deactivated on December 20, 1944. In the end there were 1,074 female pilots in the WASP program and 38 fatalities.

In 1953 the military recalled interested former WASPS to their old posts to provide support during the Korean War.

In September 1976 the U.S. Senate finally voted to make the WASPS official veterans of World War II, but only after yet another fight by the WASPS' alumnae group known as the Order of Fifinella.

Jacqueline Cochran greeted her first group of recruits with the promise: "If things don't run smoothly at first just remember that you will have the honor and distinction of being the first women to be trained by the Army Air Forces. You are very badly needed."

In their deactivation letters, General Arnold wrote to the WASPS: "When we needed you, you came through and have served most commendably under very difficult circumstances."

Perhaps the feel of being a WASP was best expressed by Cornelia Fort, who died on duty with the WASPS. Before she died she wrote: "As long as our planes fly overhead the skies of America are free and that's what all of us everywhere are fighting for. And that we, in a very small way, are being allowed to help keep that sky free is the most beautiful thing I have ever known. I, for one, am profoundly grateful that my one talent, my only knowledge, flying, happens to be of use to my country when it is needed. That's all the luck I ever hope to have."

See also
Air Transport Auxiliary (ATA); Cochran, Jacqueline; Fifinella; Fort, Cornelia; Love, Nancy Harkness; Order of Fifinella; Rogers, Edith Nourse; Roosevelt, Eleanor

References
Douglas, *United States Women in Aviation, 1940–1985* (1990); Noggle, *For God, Country, and the Thrill of It: Women Airforce Service Pilots in World War II* (1990); Van Wagenen Keil, *Those Wonderful Women in Their Flying Machines* (1979)

Women's Auxiliary Air Force (WAAF)
See Women's Royal Air Force (WRAF)

Women's Auxiliary Army Corps (WAAC)

See Women's Airforce Service Pilots (WASPS)

Women's Auxiliary Ferrying Squadron (WAFS)

See Women's Airforce Service Pilots (WASPS)

Women's Flying Training Detachment (WFTD)

See Women's Airforce Service Pilots (WASPS)

Women's Royal Air Force (WRAF)

England initiated their Royal Air Force and their Women's Royal Air Force (WRAF) at approximately the same time, in April 1918. Two years into World War I it was evident that an air corps was needed. It was also evident that with the extreme loss of men in trench warfare, women would be needed in support positions to free up as many men as possible for combat assignments.

The first members of the WRAF were taken from the ranks of the Women's Legion Motor Drivers and the Women's Royal Naval Service, where they had been serving as drivers, doctors, clerks, and cooks. In the WRAF they began to be trained as aircraft and radio mechanics, plotters, welders, radar operators, and electricians. They continued in these functions for most of World War I.

When the war was over in 1918 the English government did not immediately deactivate the WRAF. England was supporting an army of occupation in Germany to keep down further revolts while at the same time trying to discharge men who wanted to return home after four years of combat. Therefore women began to be assigned to bases in other countries, which had been unthinkable during the war.

This deployment lasted until all the peace treaties had been signed. On April 1, 1920, the last members of the WRAF returned to their civilian lives.

The WRAF was revived in 1939 at the start of World War II but was renamed the Women's Auxiliary Air Force (WAAF). Under that new name ex-WRAF women were asked to return to service and new women were again recruited to free men for combat. Their new director was Air Chief Commandant Dame Katherine Jane Trefusis-Fobes, who kept the post through 1943.

As Germany advanced through Europe refugees from fallen countries clamored to join the fight against Hitler. The WRAF was soon accepting recruits from Poland, Czechoslovakia, and Holland. It was one of the first times that women from all social classes in English society lived and worked together.

Major losses in the field of battle led to the adoption of the Registration for Employment Order of April 19, 1941, which made England one of the first countries to require women to register for war service, either as factory workers or in the military. Also in 1941 women with the WRAF were first allowed to fly as passengers in military aircraft. Those who wanted to pilot planes to aid the war effort were denied the opportunity until Pauline Gower formed the Women's Division of the Air Transport Auxiliary (ATA) in 1940. But WRAF/WAAF members who wanted to join the ATA had to request discharges from the military, for the ATA was a civilian organization. By 1943, however, the pool of pilots was so low that the military reversed their position and actively recruited WRAF women to transfer to the ATA. After their first announcement, 1,400 WRAF women applied for 30 available positions.

The WRAF/WAAF was demobilized in June 1945, but Parliament decided to allow a certain number of women to be retained on a permanent basis in peacetime. The details of such a plan were worked out by 1949, and the service went back to its World War I name, WRAF.

In 1961 WRAF women were integrated into units with male RAF pilots for the first time. In 1968 they achieved pay parity. In 1989 they were finally allowed to train as pilots and navigators alongside the men of the RAF.

See also
Air Transport Auxiliary (ATA); Gower; Pauline
References
Escott, *Women in Air Force Blue: The Story of Women in the Royal Air Force from 1918 to the Present Day* (1989)

Wood, Ann

One of the original 24 women pilots handpicked by Jacqueline Cochran to join the Air Transport Auxiliary (ATA) in England during World War II, Wood stayed active in the aviation industry throughout her life.

After the war jobs as pilots were scarce for women without connections to the military or aviation company executives. Wood worked for the U.S. embassy in London assisting America's first civil air attaché.

In the 1950s she joined Northeast Airlines as director of public relations at their base in Boston. In the 1960s she was a project officer for the Massachusetts Mass Transportation Demonstration Project. In 1966 Wood joined Pam American World Airways, again in the public relations department. She rose to the rank of staff vice president before moving to Air New England as assistant to the president.

See also
Air Transport Auxiliary (ATA); Cochran, Jacqueline
References
Douglas, *United States Women in Aviation, 1940–1985* (1990)

Wright, Katherine

Though she never flew an airplane, the experiments of Orville and Wilbur Wright would not have been possible without the financial and moral support of their sister, Katherine B. Wright. Born on August 19, 1874, in Dayton, Ohio, Wright was the seventh child of Bishop Milton and Susan Koerner Wright. At 14 she was in charge of the house and assisted in the family bicycle shop after her mother's early death from tuberculosis in 1889.

Wright graduated from Oberlin College, the first college to admit women, in 1898. She became a teacher of Latin and English at Steele High School and gave two-thirds of her salary to her brothers to fund their experiments. They had moved on from bicycles to studying the possibility of flight. Wright kept the bicycle shop running with the help of another brother, and that money too went to help Wilbur and Orville.

Wright eventually took a year's sabbatical from teaching to be social secretary and manager of her brothers' careers. She flew with them on demonstration flights in England, France, and Italy, making her first flight in February 1909 in Pau, France. Wright's presence in the plane helped calm the crowd.

When Wilbur died of typhoid in 1912 Katherine became more heavily involved in the business to assist Orville. She toured Europe with him again, as well as the United States; he demonstrated their airplanes and they took orders. Katherine also handled the legal business of guarding their government patents.

She married Henry Haskell in 1926 and moved to Kansas City. This caused a rift in her relationship with her brother Orville, a rift that she was never able to heal. Three years later she caught pneumonia and died on March 3, 1929. A fountain was erected in her honor at Oberlin College, where she had served as head of the alumni group and on the Board of Trustees.

Wilbur Wright once said of his sister: "If ever the world thinks of us in connection with aviation it must remember our sister."

References

International Women's Air and Space Museum Quarterly; Jakab, *Visions of a Flying Machine: The Wright Brothers and the Process of Invention* (1990); www.infinet.com/~iwasm

Yeager, Jeana

The first woman to make an around-the-world flight on one tank of gas, Yeager did not begin flying lessons until she was 26 years old. She was born in Fort Worth, Texas, in 1952, and her childhood was filled with horses and high school sports.

After a short marriage Yeager worked as a draftsperson, did seismic mapping for an offshore oil-drilling company, and eventually worked on Project Private Enterprise, a company with the goal of putting someone into space using private funds. She had been hired to do the aeronautical drafting but learned much more about rockets while there.

Yeager earned her pilot's license in 1978 at a flight school in Santa Rosa, California. In 1980 she met Dick Rutan, and the two began competing for speed and distance records in experimental aircraft. Eventually they discussed those records not yet held by either pilot and decided upon the *Voyager* project, which would be the first around-the-world flight on one tank of gas. Yeager would design the necessary aircraft and would copilot with Rutan. Together they formed a corporation to support the project and raise the $2 million needed to fund it.

It took six years to build and test the aircraft. *Voyager*'s historic flight took place from December 14 to December 23, 1986, and lasted 9 days, 13 minutes,

44 seconds. The flight covered 26,358 miles. In May 1987 Yeager became the first woman to receive the Collier Trophy, aviation's most prestigious award, for her pioneering effort. In April 1992 she was also honored with the Crystal Eagle Award of the Aero Association of Northern California.

When discussing her *Voyager* experience at lectures and speeches, Yeager has said: "It was exciting watching it all come together, exploring your own self and finding out, yeah, I can do this; I'm capable." Yeager holds five world records in speed and distance.

References

Holden and Griffith, *Ladybirds: The Untold Story of Women Pilots in America* (1991); Yeager, *Voyager* (1987); Yount, *American Profiles: Women Aviators* (1995)

Bibliography

Organizational Sources

Amelia Earhart Birthplace Museum. (913) 367-4217.

Aviation Hall of Fame. Publicity Department. Teterboro, New Jersey (201) 288-6344.

Biographical Data Sheets, 1996, 1997. Lyndon B. Johnson Space Center, Houston, Texas. Also available on the World Wide Web at www.jsc.nasa.gov/Bios/.

International Women's Air and Space Museum. 26 North Main Street, Centerville, Ohio 45459-4619. (937) 433-6766.

National Council for Women in Aviation. P.O. Box 716, Lemont, Illinois 60439-0716. (800) 727-6292.

Professional Women Controllers, Inc. P.O. Box 44085, Oklahoma City, Oklahoma 73144. (800) 232-9792.

Print Sources

Abu-Nasr, Donna. "Servicewomen Rejoice at Recognition." Associated Press, October 19, 1997.

Adams, Jean, and Margaret Kimball. *Heroines of the Sky.* Garden City, N.Y.: Doubleday, Doran, and Co., 1942.

Anzovin, Steven, ed. *The Reference Shelf: Our Future in Space.* New York: H. W. Wilson Co., 1991.

"Army's First Female Pilot Wins Helicopter Wings." *Army Magazine*, July 24, 1974, p. 43.

Auriol, Jacqueline. *I Live to Fly.* New York: E. P. Dutton and Co., 1970.

Batten, Jean. *My Life.* London: George G. Harrap and Co., 1938.

Beatty, Kelly. "Meet the Astronauts of the 21st Century." *Parade Magazine*, June 29, 1997, pp. 4–6.

Beauchamp, Cari. *Without Lying Down: Frances Marion and the Powerful Women of Early Hollywood.* New York: Scribner, 1997.

Begley, Sharon. "Down to Earth." *Newsweek*, October 7, 1996, p. 6.

Bernstein, Joanne E., Rose Blue, and Alan Jay Gerber. *Judith Resnick: Challenger Astronaut.* New York: Lodestar Books, 1990.

Biel, Timothy Levi. *World Disaster Series: The Challenger.* San Diego, Calif.: Lucent Books, 1991.

Bird, Nancy. *Born to Fly.* London: Angus and Robertson, 1961.

Boase, Wendy. *The Sky's the Limit: Women Pioneers in Aviation.* New York: Macmillan, 1979.

Bond, Peter. *Heroes in Space: From Gagarin to Challenger.* Oxford: Basil Blackwell, 1987.

Boyne, Walter J. *Beyond the Wild Blue: A History of the U.S. Air Force, 1947–1997.* New York: St. Martin's Press, 1997.

Bragg, Janet Harmon, and Marjorie M. Kriz. *Soaring above Setbacks: The Autobiography of Janet Harmon Bragg.* Washington, D.C.: Smithsonian Institution Press, 1996.

Briggs, Carole S. *At the Controls: Women in Aviation.* Minneapolis, Minn.: Lerner Publications Co., 1991.

———. *Women in Space: Reaching the Last Frontier.* Minneapolis, Minn.: Lerner Publications Co., 1988.

Bibliography

Bruno, Harry. *Wings over America: The Inside Story of American Aviation.* New York: Robert McBride and Co., 1942.

Cadogan, Mary. *Women with Wings: Female Flyers in Fact and Fiction.* Chicago: Academy Chicago Publishers, 1993.

Caidin, Martin. *Barnstorming: The Great Years of Stunt Flying.* New York: Duell, Sloan, and Pearce, 1965.

Callender, Ealena. "Why Did They Take Off? Asks Lancaster Pilot, 13." *Los Angeles Times,* April 12, 1996.

Cassutt, Michael. *Who's Who in Space.* Boston: G. K. Hall and Co., 1987.

Christman, Timothy. "Navy's First Female Test Pilot." *Naval Aviators News,* November/December 1985, pp. 24–26.

Cobb, Jerrie, and Jane Rieker. *Woman into Space: The Jerrie Cobb Story.* Englewood Cliffs, N.J.: Prentice-Hall, 1963.

Cochran, Jacqueline, and Maryann Bucknum. *Jackie Cochran: An Autobiography.* Toronto and New York: Bantam Books, 1987.

Cochran, Jacqueline, with Floyd Odlum. *The Stars at Noon.* London: Robert Hale, 1954.

Cole, Jean Hascall. *Women Pilots of World War II.* Salt Lake City: University of Utah Press, 1992.

Cole, Michael D. *Challenger: America's Space Tragedy.* Springfield, Ill.: Enslow Publishers, 1995.

Collins, Helen F. "From Plane Captains to Pilots: Women in Naval Aviation." *Naval Aviation News,* July 8, 1977, pp. 8–18.

Corrigan, Grace. *A Journal for Christa: Christa McAuliffe, Teacher in Space.* Lincoln and London: University of Nebraska Press, 1993.

Current Biography Cumulated Index 1940–1995. New York: H. W. Wilson Co., 1996.

Current Biography Yearbook, 1940–1985. New York: H. W. Wilson Co., 1993.

Curtis, Lettice. *The Forgotten Pilots: A Story of the Air Transport Auxiliary, 1939–45.* Henley-on-Thames, Oxfordshire, Eng.: G. T. Foulis and Co., 1971.

Douglas, Deborah G. *United States Women in Aviation, 1940–1985.* Washington, D.C.: Smithsonian Institution Press, 1990.

du Cros, Rosemary Rees. *ATA Girl: Memoirs of a Wartime Ferry Pilot.* London: Frederick Muller Limited, 1983.

Earhart, Amelia. *20 Hrs. 40 Min.* New York: Putnam, 1928. Reprint, New York: Arno Press, 1980.

Easterling, Jerry. "The Woman Pilots a Helicopter." *Oregon Territory,* August 21, 1977.

Ebbert, Jean, and Marie-Beth Hall. *Crossed Currents: Navy Women from WWI to Tailhook.* Washington, D.C.: Brassey, 1993.

Edwards, Anne. *The DeMilles: An American Family.* New York: Harry N. Abrams, 1988.

Eisenhower, Julie Nixon. *Special People.* New York: Simon and Schuster, 1977.

Escott, Beryl E. *Women in Air Force Blue: The Story of Women in the Royal Air Force from 1918 to the Present Day.* Northhamptonshire, Eng.: Patrick Stephens, 1989.

Ferrante. *Chronology of the United States Marine Corps.* 1995.

Flinn, Kelly. *Proud to Be: My Life, the Air Force, the Controversy.* New York: Random House, 1997.

Gower, Pauline. *Women with Wings.* London: John Long, 1938.

Grey, Elizabeth. *Winged Victory: The Story of Amy Johnson.* Boston: Houghton Mifflin, 1966.

Gunston, Bill, ed. *Chronicle of Aviation.* London: Chronicle Communications, 1992.

Hancock, Joy Bright. *Lady in the Navy: A Personal Reminiscence.* Annapolis, Md.: Naval Institute Press, 1972.

Hardesty, Von, and Dominick Pisano. *Black Wings: The American Black in Aviation.* Washington, D.C.: National Air and Space Museum, Smithsonian Institution Press, 1983.

Harris, Grace. *West to Sunrise.* Ames: Iowa State University Press, 1980.

Harris, Sherwood. *The First to Fly: Aviation's Pioneer Days.* New York: Simon and Schuster, 1970.

Harrison, James P. *Mastering the Sky: A History of Aviation from Ancient Times to the Present.* New York: Sarpedon, 1996.

Hart, Marion Rice. *I Fly as I Please.* New York: Vanguard Press, 1953.

Heath, Lady Sophie, and Stella Wolfe Murray. *Woman and Flying.* London: John Long, 1929.

Herrmann, Dorothy. *Anne Morrow Lindbergh: A Gift for Life.* New York: Ticknor and Fields, 1992.

Hine, Darlene Clark, Elsa Barkley Brown, and Rosalyn Terborg-Penn, eds. *Black Women in America: An Historical Encyclopedia. Volume A-L.* Bloomington, Ind., and Indianapolis, Ind.: Carlson Publishing, 1993.

History of the Ninety-Nines, Inc. Oklahoma City, Okla.: The Ninety-Nines Inc., 1979.

Hohler, Robert T. *I Touch the Future: The Story of Christa McAuliffe.* New York: Random House, 1986.

Holden, Henry M. *Her Mentor Was an Albatross: The Autobiography of Pioneer Pilot Harriet*

Quimby. Mt. Freedom, N.J.: Black Hawk Publishing Co., 1993.

Holden, Henry M., and Lori Griffith. *Ladybirds: The Untold Story of Women Pilots in America*. Mt. Freedom, N.J.: Black Hawk Publishing Co., 1991.

———. *Ladybirds II: The Continuing Story of American Women in Aviation*. Mt. Freedom, N.J.: Black Hawk Publishing Co., 1993.

Holm, Jeanne. *Women in the Military: An Unfinished Revolution*. Novato, Calif.: Presidio Press, 1982.

Jakab, Peter L. *Visions of a Flying Machine: The Wright Brothers and the Process of Invention*. Washington, D.C.: Smithsonian Institution Press, 1990.

Johnson, Amy. *Skyroads of the World*. 1939.

Kinert, Reed. *American Racing Planes and Historic Air Races*. New York: Wilcox and Follett Co., 1952.

King, Alison. *Golden Wings: The Story of Some of the Women Ferry Pilots of the Air Transport Auxiliary*. London: C. Arthur Pearson, 1956.

Knapp, Sally. *New Wings for Women*. New York: Thomas Y. Crowell Co., 1946.

"The Lady from Maine Is Recognized: Margaret Chase Smith, Four-Term Senator from Maine Dead at 97." Associated Press, May 29, 1995.

Letson, Dawn, ed. *Oral History of Leoti Deaton, WASP Chief Establishment Officer*. Denton, Texas: Texas Women's University Special Collections, 1995.

Leuthner, Stuart, and Oliver Jensen. *High Honor: Recollections by Men and Women of World War II Aviation*. Washington, D.C.: Smithsonian Institution Press, 1989.

Lomax, Judy. *Flying for the Fatherland*. London: John Murray Publishers, 1988.

———. *Women of the Air*. New York: Dodd, Mead, 1987.

Lovell, Mary S. *The Sound of Wings: The Life of Amelia Earhart*. New York: St. Martin's Press, 1989.

———. *Straight on till Morning: The Biography of Beryl Markham*. New York: St. Martin's Press, 1987.

Magill, Franklin, ed. *Great Lives from History*. American Series, vol. 3. Pasadena: Salem Press, 1987.

Markham, Beryl. *The Splendid Outcast*. San Francisco: North Point Press, 1987.

———. *West with the Night*. San Francisco: North Point Press, 1983.

May, Charles Paul. *Women in Aeronautics*. New York: Nelson Publishing, 1962.

McCullough, Joan. *First of All: Significant "Firsts" by American Women*. New York: Holt, Rinehart, and Winston, 1980.

Mellinger, George. "Lidiia Litviak." *The Aero Historian: The Newsletter of the Twin City Aero Historians* 31, nos. 1–2 (January/February 1997).

Melwani, Lavinia. "Sky's Not the Limit." *Hinduism Today International*, April 1997. World Wide Web address hinduismtoday.kauai.Hi.US/April97.html.

Merriam, Joan. "I Flew around the World Alone." *Saturday Evening Post*, July 25–August 1, 1964, pp. 77–83.

"Mildred McAfee Horton Dies; First Head of WAVES Was 94." *New York Times*, September 4, 1994.

Miller, Francis Trevelyan. *The World in the Air: The Story of Flying in Pictures*. Volume 2. New York: G. P. Putnam's Sons, 1930.

Milton, Joyce. *Loss of Eden: A Biography of Charles and Anne Morrow Lindbergh*. New York: HarperCollins Publishers, 1993.

Mock, Jerrie. *Three-Eight Charlie*. Philadelphia: J. B. Lippincott Co., 1970.

Moolman, Valerie. *Women Aloft*. Alexandria, Va.: Time-Life Books, 1981.

Morris, Dan, and Inez Morris. *Who Was Who in American Politics*. New York: Hawthorn Books, 1974.

Myles, Bruce. *Night Witches: The Untold Story of Soviet Women in Combat*. Novato, Calif.: Presidio Press, 1981.

Nagy, Barbara. "Linda Finch: A Woman Amelia Earhart Would Admire." Web posted, February 9, 1997.

Nichols, Ruth. *Wings for Life*. Philadelphia: Lippincott, 1957.

Noggle, Anne. *A Dance with Death: Soviet Airwomen in World War II*. College Station: Texas A&M University Press, 1994.

———. *For God, Country, and the Thrill of It: Women Airforce Service Pilots in World War II*. College Station: Texas A&M University Press, 1990.

Oakes, Claudia M. *United States Women in Aviation through World War I*. Washington, D.C.: Smithsonian Institution Press, 1978.

———. *United States Women in Aviation: 1930–1939*. Washington, D.C.: Smithsonian Institution Press, 1985.

Oberg, Alcestis R. *Spacefarers of the 80's and 90's: The Next Thousand People in Space*. New York: Columbia University Press, 1985.

O'Connor, Karen. *Sally Ride and the New Astronauts: Scientists in Space*. New York: Franklin Watts, 1983.

Patterson, Elois Coleman. *Memoirs of the Late Bessie Coleman, Aviatrix: Pioneer of the Negro People in Aviation.* N.P.: 1969.

Pellegreno, Ann Holtgren. *World Flight: The Earhart Trail.* Ames: Iowa State University Press, 1971.

Perry, Tony. "Navy Not Biased against Women, Report Finds." *Los Angeles Times,* July 2, 1997.

Pushman, Muriel Gane. *We All Wore Blue.* Miami, Fla.: Pickering Press, 1989.

Rasmussen, Cecelia. "China's Amelia Earhart Got Her Wings Here." *Los Angeles Times,* April 14, 1998.

———. "Policewomen's Battle to Serve and Protect." *Los Angeles Times,* June 11, 1997.

Rawls, Walton. *Disney Dons Dog Tags: The Best of Disney Military Insignia from World War II.* New York: Abbeville Publishing Group, 1992.

Reitsch, Hanna. *Flying Is My Life.* New York: Putnam, 1954.

———. *The Sky My Kingdom.* New York: Putnam, 1955.

Render, Shirley. *No Place for a Lady: The Story of Canadian Women Pilots, 1928–1992.* Winnipeg: Portage and Main Press, 1992.

Rich, Doris L. *Queen Bess, Daredevil Aviator.* Washington, D.C.: Smithsonian Institution Press, 1993.

Richter, Paul, and Steven Gray. "For Women in Uniform, a Place of Honor." *Los Angeles Times,* October 19, 1997.

Ride, Sally, with Susan Okie. *To Space and Back.* New York: Lothrop, Lee, and Shepard Books, 1986.

Ronnie, Art. *Locklear: The Man Who Walked on Wings.* South Brunswick, N.J., and New York: A. S. Barnes and Co., 1973.

Roseberry, C. R. *The Challenging Skies: The Colorful Story of Aviation's Most Exciting Years, 1919–1939.* Garden City, N.Y.: Doubleday and Company, 1966.

Rufus, Maude Squire. *Flying Grandma, or Going Like Sixty.* Ypsilanti, Mich.: University Lithoprinters, 1942.

Russo, Carolyn. *Women and Flight: Portraits of Contemporary Women Pilots.* Boston: Little, Brown and Co., 1997.

Sakurai, Gail. *Mae Jemison: Space Scientist.* Chicago: Children's Press, 1995.

Schultz, Barbara Hunter. *Pancho: The Biography of Florence Lowe Barnes.* Lancaster, Calif.: Little Buttes, 1996.

Scott, Sheila. *Barefoot in the Sky: An Autobiography.* New York: Macmillan, 1973.

Sherrow, Victoria. *The Encyclopedia of Women and Sports.* Santa Barbara, Calif.: ABC-CLIO, 1996.

"Shuttle Returns; Inquiry Due on Errant Satellite." Associated Press, December 12, 1997.

Simbeck, Rob. "Daughter of the Air: The Soaring Life of Cornelia Fort." *Nashville Scene,* May 30, 1996. Also found in back issues on the World Wide Web at www.nashscene.com/cgi.bin/backissue.pl?article=May_30_1996/.

Smith, Elizabeth Simpson. *Breakthrough: Women in Aviation.* New York: Walker and Co., 1981.

———. *Coming Out Right: The Story of Jackie Cochran, the First Woman Aviator to Break the Sound Barrier.* New York: Walker and Co., 1991.

Southern, Neta Snook. *I Taught Amelia to Fly.* New York: Vantage Press, 1974.

Spring, Joyce. *Daring Lady Flyers: Canadian Women in the Early Years of Aviation.* Nova Scotia: Pottersfield Press, 1994.

Stern, Alan. *The U.S. Space Program after Challenger: Where Are We Going?* New York: Franklin Watts, 1987.

Tate, Grover Ted. *The Lady Who Tamed Pegasus: The Story of Pancho Barnes.* Los Angeles: Maverick Press, 1984.

Tereshkova, Valentina. *It Is I, Sea Gull.* New York: Thomas Y. Crowell Co., 1975.

Thaden, Louise. *High, Wide, and Frightened.* New York: Air Facts Press, 1973.

Thruelsen, Richard. *The Grumman Story.* New York: Praeger, 1976.

Tiburzi, Bonnie. *Takeoff! The Story of America's First Woman Pilot for a Major Airline.* New York: Crown Publishers, 1984.

Trento, Joseph J. *Prescription for Disaster.* New York: Crown Publishers, 1987.

Uglow, Jennifer S., comp. and ed. *The Continuum Dictionary of Women's Biography.* New York: Continuum Publishing Co., 1989.

Underwood, John W. *The Stinsons: A Pictorial History.* Glendale, Calif.. Heritage Press, 1986.

Van Meter, Vicki, with Dan Gutman. *Taking Flight: My Story.* New York: Viking Publishing, 1995.

Van Wagenen Keil, Sally. *Those Wonderful Women in Their Flying Machines: The Unknown Heroines of World War II.* New York: Rawson, Wade Publishers, 1979.

Veca, Donna, and Skip Mazzio. *Just Plane Crazy: Biography of Bobbi Trout.* Santa Clara, Calif.: Osborne Publisher, 1987.

Verges, Marianne. *On Silver Wings: The Women Airforce Service Pilots of World War II, 1942–1944.* New York: Ballantine Books, 1991.

Villard, Henry Serrano. *Contact! The Story of the Early Birds.* New York: Thomas Y. Crowell Co., 1968.

Vistica, Gregory L. *Fall from Glory: The Men Who Sank the U.S. Navy.* New York: Simon and Schuster, 1995.

Vogt, Gregory. *Space Library: Space Stations.* New York: Franklin Watts, 1990.

Wagstaff, Patty, with Ann L. Cooper. *Fire and Air: A Life on the Edge.* Chicago: Chicago Review Press, 1997.

Weatherford, Doris. *American Women's History: An A to Z of People, Places, Organizations, Issues, and Events.* New York: Prentice Hall General Reference, 1994.

Welch, Ann. *Happy to Fly: An Autobiography.* London: John Murray Publishers, 1983.

Welch, Ann, and Frank Irving. *New Soaring Pilot.* London: John Murray Publishers, 1968.

Whitehouse, Arch. *The Early Birds: The Wonders and Heroics of the First Decades of Flight.* Garden City, N.Y.: Doubleday and Co., 1965.

Whyte, Edna Gardner, with Ann L. Cooper. *Rising Above It: An Autobiography.* New York: Orion Books, 1991.

Wilson, John R. M. *Turbulence Aloft: The Civil Aeronautics Administration amid Wars and Rumors of Wars, 1938–1953.* Washington, D.C.: Federal Aviation Administration, 1979.

Wride, Nancy. "Right Place, Right Time." *Los Angeles Times*, May 16, 1996.

Yeager, Jeana. *Voyager.* New York: Alfred A. Knopf, 1987.

Yount, Lisa. *American Profiles: Women Aviators.* New York: Facts on File, 1995.

Zimmerman, Jean. *Tailspin: Women at War in the Wake of Tailhook.* New York: Doubleday, 1995.

Illustration Credits

Index

Index

Index